Gloria Gikonyo

Politics and Public Policy

A Christian Response

Politics and Public Policy

A Christian Response

Crucial Considerations for Governing Life

Timothy J. Demy & Gary P. Stewart, editors

Grand Rapids, MI 49501

Politics and Public Policy: A Christian Response

© 2000 by Timothy J. Demy and Gary P. Stewart

Published by Kregel Publications, a division of Kregel, Inc., P.O. Box 2607, Grand Rapids, MI 49501. Kregel Publications provides trusted, biblical publications for Christian growth and service. Your comments and suggestions are valued.

Unless otherwise noted, Scripture quotations are from the *Holy Bible, New International Version*®. © 1973, 1978, 1984 by International Bible Society. Used by permission of Zondervan Publishing House. All rights reserved.

Scripture quotations marked KJV are from the King James version of the Holy Bible.

Scripture quotations marked NASB are from the *New American Standard Bible.* © the Lockman Foundation 1960, 1962, 1963, 1968, 1971, 1972, 1973, 1975, 1977.

Scripture quotations marked NKJV are from *The New King James Version.* © 1979, 1980, 1982, Thomas Nelson, Inc., Publishers.

Scripture quotations marked NLT are from the *Holy Bible,* New Living Translation, © 1996. Used by permission of Tyndale House Publishers, Inc., Wheaton, Illinois 60189. All rights reserved.

Scripture quotations marked NRSV are from the New Revised Standard Version of the Bible, © 1989 by the Division of Christian Education of the National Council of the Churches of Christ in the USA. Used by permission.

Scripture quotations marked RSV are from the *Revised Standard Version.* © 1946, 1952, 1971, 1973 by the Division of Christian Education of the National Council of the Churches of Christ in the United States of America.

For more information about Kregel Publications, visit our web page: http://www.kregel.com

All views expressed in this work are solely those of the authors and do not represent or reflect the position or endorsement of any governmental agency or department, military or otherwise.

Library of Congress Cataloging-in-Publication Data
Demy, Timothy J.
   Politics and public policy: a Christian response: crucial considerations for governing life / by Timothy J. Demy and Gary P. Stewart.
     p.   cm.
   Includes bibliographical references and index.
   1. Christianity and politics. I. Stewart, Gary (Gary P.) II. Title.
BR115.P7 D453   2000   261.7—dc21   00-030946
                                       CIP

ISBN 0-8254-2362-7

Printed in the United States of America

1 2 3 4 5 / 04 03 02 01 00

To those who seek
to "do justice, to love kindness,
and walk humbly with your God"
through service to our
communities, states, and nation

CONTENTS

CONTRIBUTORS

Lawrence Adams, Ph.D., is currently on the faculty of the University of Virginia where he serves as Associate Professor and Director in the Center for University Programs. He is also Adjunct Professor of Political Science at James Madison University. He is the author of works on various policy and theoretical issues in international relations and diplomatic history. He was formerly Associate Professor of Politics at North Park College in Chicago, and worked on Capitol Hill and in policy research organizations in Washington, D.C.

J. Kerby Anderson, M.S., M.A., is President of Probe Ministries and the author of several books, including *Genetic Engineering, Origin Science*, and *Signs of Warning—Signs of Hope*. A lecturer in wide demand, his radio commentaries have been syndicated internationally.

Francis J. Beckwith, Ph.D., is Associate Professor of Philosophy, Culture, and Law and W. Howard Hoffman Scholar, Trinity Graduate School, Trinity International University, where he also holds adjunct appointments in both Trinity Law School, Santa Ana, California, and Trinity Evangelical Divinity School, Deerfield, Illinois. He is also a Fellow at the Center for Bioethics and Human Dignity, The Bannockburn Institute, as well as Senior Research Fellow, Nevada Policy Research Institute. He is the author of numerous journal articles and books, including *Politically Correct Death*.

Darrell L. Bock, Ph.D., is Research Professor of New Testament Studies and Professor of Spiritual Development and Culture at Dallas Theological Seminary. He is the author of *Proclamation from Prophecy and Pattern: Lucan Old Testament Christology* and several commentaries on Luke. He is a corresponding editor for *Christianity Today*, the president-elect of the Evangelical Theological Society, and has lectured widely in universities and seminaries across the country. He also edited and coedited several books and contributed to numerous biblical dictionaries, encyclopedias, and journals.

Harold O. J. Brown, Ph.D., is Professor emeritus of Ethics in Theology at Trinity Evangelical Divinity School and Professor of Philosophy and Theology at Reformed Theological Seminary in Charlotte, North Carolina. He studied at Harvard and at the Universities of Marburg (Germany) and of Vienna (Austria). He has been involved with ethics in medicine since 1975, when together with C. Everett Koop, M.D., and others he founded the Christian Action Council, a leading pro-life ministry. He edits the *Religion and Society Report* and is a contributor to *Christianity Today, Chronicles,* and other journals. He has written extensively on historical theology and contemporary culture.

J. Daryl Charles, Ph.D., is an Affiliate Fellow of the Center for the Study of American Religion, Princeton University, Princeton, New Jersey, and Assistant Professor of Religion and Philosophy, Taylor University, Upland, Indiana. He is the author and coauthor of several books and numerous articles on ethics, social issues, and New Testament studies.

Alberto R. Coll, J.D., Ph.D., is Dean of the Center for Naval Warfare Studies at the U.S. Naval War College, Newport, Rhode Island. He taught previously at Georgetown University and also taught international law and strategy and policy at the Naval War College. From 1990–1993, he served as Principal Deputy Assistant Secretary of Defense for Special Operations and Low-Intensity Conflict. He is the author of *The Wisdom of Statecraft* and *The Western Heritage and American Values* and is the editor of *The Falklands War* and *Legal and Moral Constraints on Low-Intensity Conflict.* His articles have appeared in numerous journals. He has also served as a consultant for the U.S. Institute of Peace, the Center for Strategic and International Studies, the Ethics and Public Policy Center, and the United States Information Agency.

Michael Cromartie, M.A., is vice president of the Ethics and Public Policy Center, Washington, D.C., as well as the director of Evangelical Studies. He is the editor and/or coeditor of numerous books, including *Piety and Politics: Evangelicals and Fundamentalists Confront the World, No Longer Exiles: The Religious New Right in American Politics, Gaining New Ground: New Approaches to Poverty and Dependency,* and *Might and Right After the Cold War: Can Foreign Policy Be Moral?* His articles on issues relating to religion and politics have appeared in many journals, and he has served as a commentator on National Public Radio's "All Things Considered," ABC, and CNN, and has been quoted in newspapers across the country. Mr. Cromartie also serves as an Advisory Editor to *Christianity Today* and is on the Board of Directors for Mars Hill Audio.

Timothy J. Demy, Th.D., Ph.D. (cand.), is a military chaplain and an adjunct instructor at the U.S. Naval War College, Newport, Rhode Island. He has served for nearly twenty years in a variety of assignments with the U.S. Navy,

Coast Guard, and Marine Corps. In addition to his theological training, he holds graduate degrees in European history, human development, and national security and strategic studies. He is a graduate of the U.S. Naval War College and is the author, coauthor, and/or editor of numerous journal articles and books on social issues, ethics, and theology.

Don Eberly, M.A., is the author or editor of six books on topics of culture, including (most recently) *America's Promise: Civil Society and the Renewal of American Culture*. He has founded several nationally recognized public initiatives to promote social renewal, including the Civil Society Project and the National Fatherhood Initiative. His career includes a decade of work in Washington serving in key staff positions in the Congress and the White House. He holds graduate degrees from George Washington University and the Harvard School of Government.

Jean Bethke Elshtain, Ph.D., is the Laura Spelman Rockefeller Professor in the Divinity School at the University of Chicago. She is the author and editor of numerous books and articles, among them *Augustine and the Limits of Politics* and *Just War Theory*.

G. Joseph Gatis, M.A., J.D., is an attorney and graduate student, primarily in First Amendment studies, at Harvard University, Cambridge, Massachusetts.

Carl F. H. Henry, Th.D., Ph.D., is an international lecturer and spokesman for evangelicalism currently serving as a visiting lecturer at Trinity Evangelical Divinity School and The Southern Baptist Theological Seminary. He is the founding editor of *Christianity Today*, the author and editor of more than thirty books—including the six-volume *God, Revelation, and Authority*—and hundreds of articles and essays. He has pursued postgraduate research at Cambridge University, England, and New College, Edinburgh. He has also been awarded honorary degrees by Gordon-Conwell Theological Seminary, Northwestern College, Houghton College, Seattle Pacific University, Wheaton College, and Hillsdale College.

Ed Hindson, Th.M., D.Min., Th.D., D.Phil., is Professor of Religion and Dean of the Institute of Biblical Studies at Liberty University, Lynchburg, Virginia. He has served as a visiting lecturer at Oxford University and Harvard University as well as numerous evangelical seminaries including Dallas, Denver, Grace, Trinity, and Westminster. He is the author and/or editor of many books and articles. He also served as general editor of several study Bibles and was one of the translators for the New King James Version.

Stephen P. Hoffmann, Ph.D., is Professor of Political Science at Taylor University, Upland, Indiana. Before his academic career, he received his

Ph.D. degree in Politics and Russian Studies from Princeton University and worked in the U.S. Department of State as a foreign service officer, serving in Germany and Iraq. He also has taught in Russia at Nizhni Novgorod State University and at the Russian-American Christian University in Moscow. He received a Faculty Open Fellowship from the Eli Lilly Foundation to study civic education and higher education in Russia and America. Among his publications are articles on religion and politics in East Germany, appearing in *The Review of Politics* and *Fides et Historia*. Most recently, he coauthored *Civil Society: A Foundation for Sustainable Economic Development*.

Dennis P. Hollinger, Ph.D., is Dean of College Ministries and Professor of Christian Ethics at Messiah College, Grantham, Pennsylvania. He lectures widely on issues in ethics and society and is the author of numerous articles and essays as well as the editor of an ongoing series of ethics books.

H. Wayne House, M.A., Th.D., J.D., is Distinguished Professor of Biblical Studies and Apologetics at Faith Seminary, Tacoma, Washington; Professor of Law (Trinity Law School) and Professor of Theology and Culture (Trinity Graduate School) at Trinity International University. He was the founding editor of the *Journal of Christian Apologetics* and is the author of more than twenty books and dozens of journal articles on issues of law, theology, contemporary issues, cults, and ethics. He is a former president of the Evangelical Theological Society.

Douglas L. Koopman, Ph.D., teaches political science at Calvin College in Grand Rapids, Michigan, and is Program Director of the Paul B. Henry Institute for the Study of Christianity and Politics. He has been active in practical politics, serving for fifteen years as a personal, committee, and leadership staff person in the U.S. House of Representatives. He is the author of *Hostile Takeover* and many journal articles.

Paul Marshall, Ph.D., is Academic Dean and Senior Fellow in Political Theory at the Institute for Christian Studies, Toronto, and Adjunct Professor of Philosophy at the Free University of Amsterdam. He is the author of three hundred articles and the author and/or editor of more than a dozen books, including *Human Rights Theories in Christian Perspective; Thine Is the Kingdom: A Biblical Perspective on Government and Politics;* and *Their Blood Cries Out*. He also has held visiting professorships at Catholic University, Washington, D.C., and the Faculty of Law of the Free University of Amsterdam and has been Senior Fellow at the Institute on Religion and Democracy.

Eugene H. Merrill, Ph.D., is Distinguished Professor of Old Testament Studies at Dallas Theological Seminary. He is the author of numerous books and articles, including *Kingdom of Priests* and *Deuteronomy* (NAC) and is a contributing editor of the multivolume *New International Dictionary of Old Testament Theology and Exegesis*.

James W. Skillen, Ph.D., is executive director of the Center for Public Justice in Annapolis, Maryland. He is a frequent speaker in the United States and abroad and the author of numerous articles and books on issues in politics, ethics, government, and social concerns, including *Recharging the American Experiment: Principled Pluralism for Genuine Civic Community* and *The Scattered Voice: Christians at Odds in the Public Square*.

Gary P. Stewart, M.A., M.Div., Th.M., D.Min., is a military chaplain in Chicago. In addition to his theological training, he earned an M.A. in bioethics. He is a frequent conference speaker on topics in bioethics, marriage and family, and culture, and is the author, coauthor, and/or editor of numerous books and articles on issues in culture and theology.

Gary L. Visscher, J.D., is a longtime congressional staff person and currently is serving as a commissioner on the Federal Occupational Safety and Health Review Commission.

Frank E. Young, M.D., Ph.D., is the former Commissioner of the U.S. Food and Drug Administration and also served as Deputy Assistant Secretary for Health. He currently serves as Executive Director of Reformed Theological Seminary in Washington, D.C., and Director of Adult Education and Ministries at Fourth Presbyterian Church in Bethesda, Maryland.

ACKNOWLEDGMENTS

THE EDITORS ARE GRATEFUL TO Kregel Publications for the opportunity to present this timely material for dissemination and thought. Publisher Dennis Hillman shared our concern for the topic and enthusiasm for the work. It was, as always, a pleasure to work with the staff at Kregel. We are especially grateful to Rachel Warren, Nick Richardson, Steve Barclift, Janyre Tromp, and David Hill for their efforts behind the scenes. Without them there would be no book. Dennis Peterson has also been an integral part in accurately communicating the message of this volume. As always, Lyn Demy and Kathie Stewart have patiently sacrificed family time for one more project to reach completion. Several chapters were reprinted or expanded from previous publications. We are grateful for permission to use the following chapters:

Chapter 3: "Linking the Bible to Public Policy," in *Biblical Principles and Public Policy*, ed. Richard C. Chewning (Colorado Springs, Colo.: NavPress, 1991), 16–28.

Chapter 6: "The Political Theory of John Calvin," *Bibliotheca Sacra* 153 (October–December 1996): 449–67.

Chapter 7: "Bonhoeffer and the Sovereign State," *First Things*, August–September 1996, 27–30.

Chapter 18: Adapted from *Is the Antichrist Alive and Well?* (Eugene, Ore.: Harvest House, 1998), chaps. 11–12.

Chapter 19: "Keeping the Faith: Religion, Freedom, and International Affairs," *Imprimis* (the monthly journal of Hillsdale College) 28, no. 3 (March 1999): 1–6.

Chapter 20: "Foundations for Post-Cold War International Justice: Creation, Polyarchy, and Realism," *Christian Scholar's Review* 27, no. 1 (1997): 27–45.

Chapter 22: "Some Christian Reminders for the Statesman," *Ethics and International Affairs* 1 (1987): 97–112.

The editors have attempted to bring together many people who share a common concern for issues of church and state and the practice of politics and public policy. This volume is presented in the hope that it will serve as a catalyst for further thought, discussion, and action. It is *a* Christian response, not *the* Christian response. It is our prayer that those who read it and use it will be prompted to action, guided by the Holy Spirit, and continually praying "for kings and all who are in authority, in order that we may lead a tranquil and quiet life in all godliness and dignity" (1 Tim. 2:2 NASB).

INTRODUCTION

JUST LIKE ISRAEL IN BIBLICAL TIMES, the people of all generations long for a great leader, a monarch, or a president who will lead them, give them hope, and make them a great and prosperous people. They want someone who will bring them honor, someone who will make them proud, someone who will protect them. Like the Israelites, they want a person rather than God to lead them. As a result, nations end up with too much of human wisdom and not enough of God's wisdom (see 1 Sam. 8). Until the coming of that great kingdom in which Jesus Christ will reign as the perfect Judge, Lawgiver, and King (Isa. 33:22), we, as believers in Jesus Christ, must accept the reality that our earthly leaders might not rule as we want or live their lives the way we choose to live ours. Until the heart of humanity, which is deceived and desperately wicked (Jer. 17:9), is perfected in the eternal state, a utopia of Christian ideals simply is not possible.

So, what are we to do? Should we separate ourselves from public life altogether and leave politics and public policy in the hands of those who peruse only the pages of secular philosophies? Should we engage in moral assault on the establishments of the secular world to force adoption of policies that honor God when our leaders' hearts are not aligned with His? Or perhaps there is a better way, one that acknowledges both the realities of the human heart and the necessity for active engagement.

In his book *The Children of Light and Children of Darkness*, Reinhold Niebuhr wrote that "man's capacity for justice makes democracy possible, but man's inclination to injustice makes democracy necessary." We in the United States can be grateful that the founding fathers already knew what Niebuhr came to understand. It was not by blind luck that they divided the government into three equal powers (the judicial, legislative, and executive branches). This wise act created a republic that prevents any one person from determining and dictating the policies of the nation. In this nation we have no need or desire for a human king. Checks and balances protect the Constitution and the people of America from the tyranny of the unscrupulous—unless the people choose not to participate in the political process.

In a fallen world, elements of injustice will always exist, but injustice left unchecked by good increases without restraint and ultimately undermines the wisdom of a republic. In a genuine republic, the good and just always have a place in the public square, even if for a time they are unwelcome. The apostle Paul exhorted Christians to recognize the purpose and powers of government and the secular state and encouraged them to coexist peacefully as much as possible under its rule. He also acknowledged the authority of the state but always viewed it as inferior to the authority of Jesus Christ.

In the political campaigns of our time, the behavior of many candidates is unsettling and can tempt us to ignore the whole process altogether. The temptation to follow that impulse and run as far as possible from the wrangling and empty promises is understandable—but to do so is irresponsible (Eccl. 11:9). If we love people—all people—regardless of their personal preferences or idiosyncrasies, and if we desire the best for them; if we love our families; if we believe that Jesus Christ is the antidote for human suffering; if all of these are true, then we must be involved in life in all of its venues: social, scientific, economic, medical, artistic, academic, and political. We must not run from the people we hope to influence positively. We simply cannot forsake our moral responsibility to represent God to the world. The problem, then, is how best to influence and shape America's political landscape. Although we might never fare well, we must certainly try to participate in the political process. To win the world to Christ is not our responsibility; our responsibility is to represent Christ to the world and leave the results of our faithfulness in God's hands (1 Cor. 3:5–8).

It is also important to remember that politics reflects culture, especially in America, where people elect their politicians generally to represent and reflect their own views and desires. Ultimately, if we want to influence politics effectively, we must influence culture. To do so, participants in every aspect of American culture must represent the Christian perspective. We must think and act like Christ in the world to which we are strangers and through which we travel as spiritual pilgrims. Hopefully, God will bless our faithful service and reform our culture, the natural consequence being a population that is more sensitive to moral good and inclined to vote accordingly.

In the early twentieth century, the evangelical church removed itself from involvement in American politics and public policy. Although evangelicals continued to work in the world, the evangelical witness, unfortunately, was removed from the public arena. Consequently, faith became more private and personal in nature. Then, late in the century, evangelicals attempted to force their way back into the fray. Both decisions ended in failure.

Today, as we begin the twenty-first century, the church must devote itself to Scripture and its practical application to the issues of our time, which have both political and social ramifications. We must learn what it means to speak the truth in love, and we must appreciate the fact that unbelievers will not—indeed, cannot—see the world through a divine lens. Therefore, we must graciously reengage our culture, patiently pursue incremental change, and give up the idea that we will succeed simply because we might view this nation as one that has a Christian heritage that it must honor and to which we must return. And do we do this to save the culture? No, we do this for love of God and our neighbors, including unbelievers to whom God gives us the privilege of representing Him and out of whom, by God's mercy and grace, we once came.

This volume brings together contributors from various disciplines and backgrounds whose primary concern is to encourage Christians to deepen their faith in the God of Scripture and to involve themselves in the culture at large and in politics specifically. Christians must learn how to work alongside those of different theological and philosophical views who nevertheless share the Christian's moral concerns about America. We must pursue the hearts of people, for it is from the heart that cultures develop their moral character. If we fail or suffer, let it be because we did what was right and true in a spirit that prefers the interests and well-being of others before our own, and not because we arrogantly assumed a right that God has not given: the right to live in a Christian nation. The kingdom of God is available to all, but it is not yet established, for its King has yet to return.

PART 1

THEOLOGICAL PERSPECTIVES ON POLITICS AND PUBLIC POLICY

An Overview

What is the role of government, and how are Christians to operate within it? In a country as diverse as America, can Christian principles and players (Journalists, lobbyists, and politicians) provide any meaningful dialogue and influence? Explicitly and implicitly, the Scriptures do have something to say about government and its responsibility to and for the people whom it governs. Dennis Hollinger clearly and simply sets forth three basic roles—order, freedom, and justice—that governments must wisely and carefully balance if they are to oversee a generally peaceful, productive, and protected society in "kingdoms" that are not God's.

Chapter One

THE PURPOSE OF GOVERNMENT
A Theological Perspective

Dennis P. Hollinger

MOST DEBATES ABOUT PUBLIC POLICY SOONER or later get around to the issue of one's philosophy of government. What are the primary functions of civil government? Just what is the nature of the state? And what role should government play in a given issue? Unfortunately, when American Christians engage these issues in the service of public policy, they too often forgo in-depth Christian analysis. We are more likely to be informed by a political party or ideology than a Christian perspective on the nature and purpose of government. As a result, we often contribute little that is distinct to civil debates in the public square.

Obviously, we can gain perspective and insights about the nature and purpose of government from history, political philosophy, and experiences of people in the political process. But if we truly desire to bring a Christian perspective to the table, we must connect our Christian worldview to both the philosophy of government and particular issues. A Christian worldview essentially means theological thinking, for in theology we are reflecting on our view of reality as Christians, which is drawn from divine revelation in Scripture and Christ. Indeed, general revelation comes from God's creation, the world. Thus, we can understand some things about society, culture, or human government from reason, history, and human experience. But *the special revelation of Christ and the written Word* are always the final and definitive arbiters for our thinking and actions in all realms of life, including the political. And it is this special revelation that forms the backdrop and anchor for our theological thinking about the state and its purposes, even though it does not offer a textbook approach to politics.

When we engage in theological thinking about matters such as government, we can do so in several ways. First are the direct or explicit teachings of the Bible about government. Using this approach, we think immediately of texts from the Pentateuch that set forth the civil laws of Israel or passages such as Romans 13. Here Paul reminds us that government has been established by God and that its rulers do not bear the sword in vain. When we look to the direct teachings of Scripture, however, we must be careful in our interpretations. For example, the counsel of God to Israel on all matters of life was given to a covenant people who had committed themselves to following God. As a result, Israel bears closer resemblance to the church today than it does to any nations of the world. Hence, many of the so-called civil directives given in the Old Testament can't be simplistically applied to pluralistic civil societies, none of which constitutes a covenant people of God like the church of Jesus Christ.

Similarly, when we examine Romans 13, we see a straightforward, positive description of the state as servant. But Romans 13 must be read alongside Revelation 13, where the state is portrayed as a beast (an enemy of the church) or alongside texts such as Luke 13:32, where Jesus refers to Herod, a government official, derogatively as a fox. Romans 13 and passages such as 1 Peter 2:13–17 ("Submit yourselves for the Lord's sake to every authority") must be understood in light of the rest of Scripture. In other parts of the Bible, we find prophets calling kings to justice (including those outside the covenant community of Israel), and we find the early apostles engaging in civil disobedience by not heeding the government's policy forbidding evangelism, as they proclaim in the court, "We must obey God rather than men" (Acts 5:29). So the *first* approach in doing a theology of government is to draw directly and explicitly from biblical passages, but it is an approach that requires careful hermeneutical processing of the text and context. Moreover, in the final analysis, we must be aware that the Bible doesn't give us a great deal of explicit teaching about government and public policy.

A *second* way in which we do theology is less direct or explicit in terms of specific biblical texts. Using this approach, we draw from the whole of the biblical drama, from broad biblical principles and teachings, or from implied understandings of biblical direction. Much of theology throughout history has been developed in this way. For example, the word *trinity* never occurs in the canonical text and nowhere is there an explicit discussion of the relationship of the Father, the Son, and the Holy Spirit. The church derived a theological understanding of the trinity from varied texts of Scripture that spoke about the three *persona* and their nature, work, and interactions with God's people and the world. In light of these indirect biblical teachings, the Christian church has affirmed the oneness of God in three persons. Much of our theological understanding has emerged similarly. This fact does not mean that our theology is nonbiblical, but rather it is derived from Scripture differently.[1]

When we attempt to understand the nature and functions of human government, we find this approach to be a very rich resource for our theological reflections. It will not tell us exactly how to think about government and public policy for every circumstance, but it will provide a basic frame of reference for engaging the state. This approach will give us parameters for reflecting on public policy issues.

One example of the indirect biblical approach to theological thinking about the state is drawing from the overarching story of the Bible: Creation, the Fall, redemption, and consummation.[2] This biblical paradigm reminds us that God is the author of all things, including culture, government, and human beings who, at the apex of divine creation, are made in God's image. But we also recognize that the world is not what it was intended to be. The fall of humankind into sin means that every sphere of reality (including politics) has been distorted, and the propensity to use God's good gifts for wrong purposes is pervasive in human history. From a Christian standpoint, the fundamental malaise of human beings and of society is located in the distortion of God's good creation—that is, in our fallen, rebellious condition. The Christian answer to the human problem is redemption in Jesus Christ. The ultimate solution is not found in politics or economics but in His redemptive work, which comes to humans not by their own merits but through divine grace and a response of personal faith. Redemption, however, is not a call away from this fallen world but a beckon to live in it to bear witness to the new reality of God's kingdom and to be salt, light, and leaven. But the redeemed community will not restore the world to its original condition by its own good, righteous, and just efforts within society. The ultimate and final restoration will come in the consummation when Christ reigns as King of Kings and Lord of Lords. Our actions and presence within the present world (including the political world) are to be a sign of that coming kingdom.

This portrait of the world and history is the heart of the biblical story and the Christian worldview. No, it is not spelled out explicitly in one or several texts, but it is clearly the overarching framework of the whole Bible, and it is implied in text after text. Indeed, we should interpret the specific texts of God's Word in light of this larger story. Such an approach does not tell us what to do in every social or political situation, but it does provide the starting point and guidelines for political thinking and action. And it clearly reminds us that the state, and even good political action, is not ultimate.

As we think specifically about the purposes of government, we can, I believe, discern from both the *direct biblical teaching* and the *indirect approach* to theological thinking three major purposes of the state: *order, freedom,* and *justice*. Historically, Christian teachings on the state have tended toward an emphasis on one of these purposes to the exclusion of the others. And when we look at secular political thought, we often find the same situation; some opt for a philosophy of order, others for a philosophy of freedom, and still others for a philosophy of justice. Each emphasis represents long-held traditions in political philosophy.

But when we look to a biblically based theology of government, we see that order, freedom, and justice all require affirmation. To isolate one from the others leads to an imbalanced and dangerous form of government and distorts the whole of biblical/theological understanding. Although order, freedom, and justice seem sometimes to be at odds with each other, the genius of this theological affirmation is holding them together in creative tension— a reality we sometimes find in biblical teaching and theology. As we think about public policy issues, Christians should start with this basic philosophy. Although the paradigm will not tell believers what to do on every issue or in each circumstance, it provides perspective, direction, and a clear Christian frame of reference for engaging culture, society, and the political process.

ORDER

Order is perhaps the most obvious purpose of government, if only because historically it has been the dominant expression. The civil state is that institution in society that has power to enforce and limit certain forms of human behavior that are deemed to be threats to others or to society itself. This purpose of government, of course, finds biblical warrant from both explicit biblical teaching and the more implicit form. Romans 13:1–7 is the classical text on order. Because governing authorities are instituted by God, as Paul argues, humans are to submit to their authority. Although Christians have been redeemed through Christ and are now citizens of another kingdom, they are still part of this world and its political domain. Paul then speaks to the order dimension: "Rulers hold no terror for those who do right, but for those who do wrong. . . . For he is God's servant to do you good. But if you do wrong, be afraid, for he does not bear the sword for nothing. He is God's servant, an agent of wrath to bring punishment on the wrongdoer" (vv. 3–4). And 1 Peter 2:13–14 admonishes respect and submission on the grounds that governing authorities "are sent by him to punish those who do wrong and to commend those who do right." Both texts point to the role of the state in preserving order. As was noted earlier, these texts must be read alongside other passages that portray a more pernicious authority, a reality we know all too well throughout history. Neither passage is dealing with that situation; rather, they are stating one particular function of government in the context of guiding Christians' own actions and attitudes within society.

A further theological basis for order is derived more indirectly, namely, the sinfulness of humanity and the social order. The sinful propensities of people everywhere leads to conflicts between people, groups, and nations. The human tendency is to seek power and privilege for one's self or one's own group. Civil government, although itself a sinful institution with the same potential proclivities, has been instituted by God to check those evil tendencies and to preserve peace and order. Therefore, Christians can never accept a view of government or particular public policy proposals that are grounded in a utopian or benign view of human nature. While we must always affirm the dignity, value, and grandeur of humans created in God's image, we must simultaneously affirm their fallenness, which is at the heart of all human and societal problems. Hence, the need for order within and between societies.

The state fulfills the order mandate in two primary ways. *First*, it maintains order through the enactment of laws that seek to guide a society in achieving a harmonious existence. Human law serves as both a positive guide for citizens and a negative restraint upon their self-aggrandizing impulses. Such laws, of course, never do what the Holy Spirit can, namely, bring an internal gyroscope and power to the human soul and behavior. And human law is never as complete or as compelling as divine directives; indeed, they are not identical. But within a fallen world, enacted law does play a significant function in maintaining order through both its positive guidance and its negative restraint.

Second, the state maintains order through physical power or coercion. The state is the institution with ultimate power in a society, and God grants it the power of "the sword." But it is precisely because of its power and its granted privilege to use violence that we face some very thorny ethical issues. We must somehow understand the state's right to use the sword or violence in relation to Jesus' teaching to love the enemy and not to resist the evil person (Matt. 5:38–44) and to Paul's teaching to "not repay anyone evil for evil" (Rom. 12:17, a passage that comes right before the one about submitting to the state). Christians throughout the ages have not always agreed on how to mediate these biblical teachings and, therefore, have not always agreed on when coercive power can be used, how it should be used, and to what extent Christians can be involved in what Martin Luther once called "God's rule with his left hand."

Despite these ethical quandaries—and they are important—the principle of order is clearly one of the primary purposes of human government from a theological perspective. Without order, it is difficult—if not impossible—to achieve the other two purposes, freedom and justice. They can be attained only when some semblance of peace, tranquillity, and order exists within society. At the same time, it is important to recognize that freedom and justice are threatened when order becomes the only—or even the primary—pursuit of government. If order rules the day, freedoms will be significantly curbed for the sake of order, and justice will be limited to ensure conformity to an ordered *civitas*.

Order as a singular pursuit of government has frequently had its defenders down through history. Both Machiavelli and Hobbes so emphasized the brutish side of human nature that power and order were, in their philosophies, the prevailing norms to the exclusion of others. Niccolò Machiavelli, the Italian statesman and political thinker during the Renaissance, argued in *The Prince* that rulers must use coercive and even unscrupulous methods in governing. Looking to the realities of human nature to develop his political philosophy, Machiavelli said, "A prince, therefore, must not mind incurring the charge of cruelty for the purpose of keeping his subjects united and faithful; for, with a very few examples, he will be more merciful than those, who from excess of tenderness, allow disorders to arise, from whence spring bloodshed and rapine." He argued that a ruler "ought to be both feared and loved, but as it is difficult for the two to go together, it is much safer to be feared than loved."[3] Order was clearly his priority.

Similarly, the seventeenth-century British philosopher Thomas Hobbes argued for a political philosophy of order. Developing his politics and ethics from a naturalistic basis of self-interest, Hobbes believed that people are both fearful and predatory by nature; therefore, they must submit to the absolute supremacy of the state. In *Leviathan; or, The Matter, Form, and Power of a Commonwealth Ecclesiastical and Civil*, Hobbes paints human nature as warring and bestial and in need of powerful, external control. He writes, "For the laws of nature, as justice, equity, modesty, mercy, and in sum, doing to others as we would be done to, of themselves, without the terror of some power to cause them to be observed, are contrary to our natural passions, that carry us to partiality, pride, revenge and the like." Because of the brutal nature of individuals and nations, the only way to secure protection is "to confer all their power and strength upon one man, or upon one assembly of men, that may reduce all their wills, by plurality of voices, unto one will."[4]

Societies rooted primarily in order may be safe and secure places to live if you happen to be on the side of the government in power, but they secure order at the expense of human freedom and justice for all. Although governments of order do justice to the sinful, fallen side of human nature, they fail to reckon with the other side—which is not goodness but human dignity, value, and worth. The unique contribution of Christian thinking to politics is its insistence on these two primary facts about human nature: humans embody dignity, value, and worth not by what they do but by their creation in God's image; and, simultaneously, humans are fallen and alienated from God, self, others, and the natural world around them (Gen. 3). Order, therefore, must always be a significant function of human government. But if it is isolated from the other functions, it becomes tyrannical and fails to achieve a society that is commensurate with God's designs for His creatures.

FREEDOM

Since the Enlightenment, the enablement and protection of freedom have been major components of many political philosophies. Government's goal, they contend, is to ensure freedom from tyranny, oppression, and external obstacles to human aspirations and desire. "Life, liberty, and the pursuit of happiness" (or *wealth* in the original version) has become the modern mantra. This Enlightenment conception of freedom has not always rested easy with Christians. As modern democracies developed under the cry of *freedom*, it meant primarily a "freedom from" external restraints—a philosophy built on the assumption of human autonomy. In this formula, self-reliant men and women gathered in communities and societies only to achieve their individual ends by means of a social contract that could facilitate the corporate necessities while preserving their personal rights and desires.

Such notions of freedom were problematic for many Christians at the time. So how do we respond to the Enlightenment story? Is freedom in any way compatible with the Christian story? And what are the crucial differences between the two narratives? I believe that the Enlightenment understanding of freedom missed the boat from the perspective of a Christian worldview. Nonetheless, that version of freedom arose only because of certain Christian notions that were then secularized by Enlightenment thinking. Christians should always bring something new to the table on this subject precisely because redemption is about freedom. But even the Enlightenment understanding, with its secularized and incomplete perceptions of freedom, was onto something; thus, viewed from a theological perspective, a modified view of freedom is indeed a purpose of government.

The Enlightenment version of freedom is rooted in thinkers such as John Locke, Jean-Jacques Rousseau, and John Stuart Mill. Rousseau, the eighteenth-century French *philosophe*, believed that human institutions have corrupted humankind by forcing them from their natural, primitive state of individuality and small natural groupings such as the family. As he observed the world of his own time, he declared, "Man is born free, and yet we see him everywhere in chains."[5] The pursuit of freedom from these chains, he believed, emerges from the natural impulses of human nature, unscarred by modern institutions. "This common liberty is a consequence of the nature of man. His first law is that of self-preservation, his first cares those which he owes to himself."[6] Government, he believed, is legitimate only as an association or social contract of the people's wills to protect the natural liberty and pursuits of individuals. Ironically, some historians believe that Rousseau contributed to modern totalitarianism with his emphasis on the state embodying the abstract will of the people and his arguments for strict enforcement of political and religious conformity.

Similarly, John Stuart Mill, the nineteenth-century British philosopher and advocate of utilitarianism, argued that freedom was the essence of human nature, and it could be thwarted by both political tyranny and social tyranny. Thus, Mill advocated social policies that we usually associate with theories of justice, although he did so under the framework of liberty. Mill believed that "the only freedom which deserves the name, is that of pursuing our own good in our own way, so long as we do not attempt to deprive others of theirs, or impede their efforts to obtain it." He added, "The principle requires liberty of tastes and pursuits; of framing the plan of our life to suit our own character; of doing as we like, subject to such consequences as may follow: without impediment from our fellow creatures, so long as what we do does not harm them, even though they should think our conduct foolish, perverse, or wrong."[7] For Mill, this freedom does not mean a totally unbridled freedom, for we sometimes play roles and carry responsibilities in society that call for a curbing of our own freedom to ensure the freedom and safety of others. Government's role is to ensure this reciprocal relationship of freedoms. But for Mill, liberty is paramount in the world, for "the individual is not accountable to society for his actions, insofar as these concern the interests of no person but himself."[8]

The Christian conception of freedom is a bit different than the ideas of Mills, Rousseau, and their cohorts. The essence of Christian liberty is a *freedom from* sin—its power, consequences, and self-deception—and a *freedom for* obedience to God and love of our neighbor. Jesus gets to the heart of true freedom when He says, "If you hold to my teaching, you are really my disciples. Then you will know the truth, and the truth will set you free" (John 8:31). *Freedom in the Christian story is never a freedom for our own self-pursuits but rather a freedom from such enslavement.* It is always tied to truth, not of our own or society's making, but the ultimate truth of the triune God who frees us in Christ as we become His servants and followers. And such a story of freedom seems a long way from the Enlightenment version of autonomy and self-reliance.

Precisely this contrast between secular, Enlightenment views of freedom and a biblical view has led many people to believe that Christianity is really hostile to civic freedom. After all, until the seventeenth century, most of Christendom took for granted that freedom of religion was to be limited either to protect people from the deadly effects of heresy or to preserve social unity and stability. And today, as some Christians seek to mandate or at least legitimize certain Christian ideas and practices within the *civitas*, the sense that Christianity is inherently antifreedom arises again.

Civil freedom as commonly understood does indeed raise a dilemma for Christian believers. For the freedom espoused by thinkers such as Rousseau, Mill, and some of our contemporaries means a freedom to pursue one's own crass self-indulgence—a freedom to sin and to choose nontruth. Thus, as Glenn Tinder puts it, "When Christians accept liberty they accept the possibility—a possibility that is almost certain to become a reality—of a world unformed and ungoverned by faith." Hence, he adds, "When Christians commit themselves to liberty there follows an enormous complication of Christian morality; they deliberately refrain, in some measure, from resisting evil. They allow the tares to grow with the wheat."[9]

Is there a basis for such a posture? Is there a theological grounding for political freedom—even a freedom to pursue the wrong, the ugly, the immoral? I believe that there is, but only if we hold it in creative tension with the other purposes of government: order and justice. To assert that political freedom of this sort can find theological warrant necessitates a reminder that in the Christian view ultimate freedom is found in the truth of the gospel. This freedom from sin and freedom for God and others is the paramount liberty. Nonetheless, in this fallen world there is a theological basis for the sort of freedom that has informed modern democracies, including a freedom to ignore God and His ways. Indeed, many people have argued that Christianity has done more for the cause of political freedom than any other movement in history, and that even the Enlightenment understanding is ultimately rooted in Christian ideals, even if they were eventually secularized.

Theologically, civic freedom derives from three primary sources, all of which reflect the more indirect way of appealing to divine revelation. The *first* theological source is the church. How? The church marks out a sphere of life that is distinct from and not to be controlled by human government. Thus, the very existence of the Christian church in society is an affirmation that there is to be human freedom within society, including the freedom to say no to the state when Christian conscience dictates. The state, therefore, is limited by the very existence of this body we call the church because it marks out an institution (among others) that is distinct from the state. This situation by it's very nature places limits upon the state and hence points toward a freedom for citizens. The Christian church has been an enigma to governing authorities down through the ages, especially in places where the state is more totalitarian in nature. Persecution of the church has emerged precisely because its very existence and its commitments point to a freedom that places limits on the all-encompassing nature of the state. Thus, conceptually and historically, the church has contributed to political freedom.

The *second* theological foundation for civic freedom is humanity's creation in the image of God. The *imago dei* has yielded various interpretations by biblical scholars and theologians, but one of the central renderings is that we were created as moral beings who have the capacity to choose. Although theologians have long debated how human freedom and divine sovereignty fit together, our creation in God's image means that we stand apart from the created world in being moral creatures. We are responsible for our decisions and commitments in life. We can with Adam and Eve choose evil, self, and sin (our native condition in a fallen world), or we can choose good and righteousness in Christ, who is Himself our righteousness. The very notion of freedom and responsibility is a result of our created nature.

And the *third* foundation for political freedom is the biblical story of the Exodus. The Hebrew people's oppressive enslavement and subsequent liberation by God formed a pattern of divine expectations in their treatment of others. Thus, within their own civil laws, God mandated, "Because the Israelites are my servants, whom I brought out of Egypt, they must not be sold as slaves" (Lev. 25:42). Although slavery of other peoples continued to exist for a time in Israel, it was substantially minimized by the opportunity for release after six years (Exod. 21:2) and with economic provisions in case of unemployment following their release (Deut. 15:13–15). This gradual process of freedom working itself out from God's own pattern with Israel seems to be reiterated in the New Testament. Although slavery was not explicitly forbidden in the early church, the believers were constantly reminded that in Christ "there is neither . . . slave nor free" (Gal. 3:28). And when Paul dealt with the issue of a runaway slave, Onesimus, he admonished Philemon, Onesimus's former master, to accept him back, "No longer as a slave, but better than a slave, as a dear brother" (Philem. 16).[10] The exodus theme seems to be at work in this story.

Thus, one of the purposes of human government is to protect that freedom that is inherent in the very nature of humanity, affirmed by the Exodus, and upheld by the very existence of a body such as the church, an entity distinct from the state. But freedom can never be isolated from the other purposes. A freedom without order and justice is anarchy because it is an undefined autonomy that knows no boundaries. In fact, freedom, when pursued as the central end of life and independent of other purposes and virtues, is the worst sort of bondage. Attempting to discern when freedom should be limited for the sake of order and justice is no easy issue. *Even the freedom of religion and conscience will have some limitations.* For example, if my religion tells me that I must ritually torture my child to achieve salvation, the state will rightfully intervene for the preservation of human life. I can make a martyr of myself for religious beliefs, but I cannot make a martyr of my child.

Although the general principle—and burden of proof—is always ensuring freedom of religion, conscience, and personal choice, matters get complicated in a fallen, secular, pluralistic society. Even our best intentions to protect religious freedom can sometimes come back to haunt us, as occurred from the Religious Freedom and Restoration Act of 1993. Prisons particularly were affected negatively by this act, which went so far in protecting individual liberties that it threatened order and justice. In fact, the upshot in Lorton Prison outside of Washington, D.C., was a drug ring, posing as a church, smuggling cocaine and prostitution into the prison.[11]

Despite the difficult cases that will always emerge in a complex world, we must contend for freedom as an essential purpose of the state. This freedom is not merely a freedom to pursue our own Christian convictions, but also we must contend even for a freedom for people to pursue that which is antithetical to our cherished beliefs and morals. But that freedom can never be isolated from order or from justice; therein are its political limitations.

JUSTICE

Justice is not only the most difficult of the three purposes to define but also the most controversial. When we deal with justice, we are focusing on that which is owed to an individual or a group of people. In the case of political justice, the question is what does the state owe its citizens? Actually, two realms of justice exist, retributive and distributive. Retributive justice refers to what is owed a person in retribution for a wrong done, a wrong that is deemed to be worthy of consequences from the state. From a Christian standpoint, many wrongs and sins do not warrant state-inflicted retributive justice but will await divine judgment. Retributive justice is intimately related to the issue of order in government because much of a state's punishment is to help maintain order within a society.

The second arena of justice is distributive—the positive owing to individuals by virtue of some designated criteria. In this arena, we face our most complex and controversial debates as we ask, "What are the rights, services, goods, and burdens (such as taxes) that the state ought to be in the business of distributing?" It is possible, of course, to mete out justice in various institutions of society and even to some degree in personal encounters, but here our question concerns the role of government in the process.

Much of how we respond to this question hinges on the definition of justice that is espoused. Varying definitions have been offered, leading to very different understandings of the role of government in matters as diverse as economics, religion, health care, sexuality, and civil rights related to race. Essentially, these definitions boil down to three primary theories: merit justice, egalitarian justice, and need justice. The definition that we embrace makes all the difference in the world in our view of government.

Merit justice basically says that we are owed what we deserve by virtue of our actions and efforts. Evident in this version should be impartiality in rewarding human effort but minimal focus on the actual outcomes. The role of government in ensuring merit is as limited as possible. This view is particularly espoused by Robert Nozick, who argues that "past circumstances or actions of people can create differential entitlements or differential deserts to things."[12] Essentially, he espouses the principle that whatever arises from a just situation by just steps is just, regardless of the end state. We are simply owed what we merit.

Egalitarian justice says that we are owed primarily on the basis of a principle of equality. Some people have understood this definition to mean equal outcomes, but most defenders of egalitarian justice stress equality of access with the hope that outcomes will be positively affected. Therefore, government's role is to ensure that all people in particular spheres of life have an equal opportunity to jobs, rights, pay, and housing. This does not mean an actual equality but rather an insurance that no personal or external factors will prevent one from accessing the rights and goods available in a given society. Egalitarian justice will call more for an activistic government than for merit to ensure that what is owed citizens is in principle accessible to all. This approach is particularly evidenced in liberal democratic theory and the likes of John Rawls, who argues, "Each person is to have an equal right to the most extensive total system of equal basic liberties compatible with a similar system of liberty for all."[13]

Need justice argues that justice is owed to individuals primarily on the basis of their needs in a given sphere of life. The defenders of this approach will argue that sometimes equality must be laid aside to respond to particular needs of individuals or specific groups of people. They frequently focus on redressing past injustices or neglect. Justice based on need has traditionally been evidenced in Marxist theory by its classic statement "From each according to his ability, to each according to his need."[14] John Rawls also adds an element of need justice to his deeply egalitarian conception with a strong commitment to acting for the benefit of the least advantaged members of society.[15]

How do we assess these definitions of justice from a biblical and theological perspective? A close examination of biblical and theological material shows that we can actually find support for all three theories. For example, merit justice is supported by passages such as 2 Thessalonians 3:10 (NRSV), "Anyone unwilling to work should not eat," or Jesus' parable of the talents (Matt. 25:14–30), in which one servant is rewarded for faithfulness in managing his resources and another is rebuked for hiding his. Egalitarian justice can be supported by the creation of human beings in God's image, by which each person bears an equal dignity and value before God. It also finds biblical support in Leviticus 19:15, "Do not pervert justice; do not show partiality to the poor or favoritism to the great, but judge your neighbor fairly," and in Jesus' statement, "He causes his sun to rise on the evil and the good, and sends rain on the righteous and the unrighteous" (Matt. 5:45). Also, need justice seems to be supported by God's special care for the oppressed and needy, as in various psalms: "The Lord works righteousness and justice for all the oppressed" (103:6), and "I know that the Lord secures justice for the poor and upholds the cause of the needy" (140:12). God mandates justice toward those with special needs on the grounds that God acted to redeem His people in their need: "Do not deprive the alien or the fatherless of justice, or take the cloak of the widow as a pledge. Remember that you were slaves in Egypt and the LORD your God redeemed you from there. That is why I command you to do this" (Deut. 24:17–18).

If all three theories of justice can be supported biblically and theologically, how do they all fit with the purposes of the state? It might be best to recognize that different definitions of justice apply to different human activities and spheres of reality. For example, merit clearly must apply to economic life in terms of what is owed to people. If a person works sixty hours a week with greater responsibility and output than a person who works forty hours a week with less responsibility and output, justice calls for the merit definition to be operative. However, when a society tries to decide who will get cadaver organs when not enough exist to go around, merit would seem to be an inappropriate definition because one's actions, work, or status within society does not apply to the realm of receiving an organ that will allow some people to live and others not to live. Some egalitarian formula (such as the current procedure in the United States) would seem to be the best definition for this realm. Moreover, when it comes to basic rights—such as job, housing, educational opportunities, or treatment before the law—an egalitarian justice (as equal opportunity, not equal outcome) ought to prevail because such matters seem by their very nature to call forth fairness and equal access in principle. Clearly, however, anyone who takes the biblical teaching seriously will have to agree that justice at some point will respond on the basis of need because certain individuals, given their particular plight or situation beyond their control, can receive justice only by responses to that need.

But what is the government's role in all of this? Some libertarians have argued for only order and freedom, contending that justice (other than mechanisms for merit) ought not to be part of governmental responsibility. It would seem that—on the basis of Scripture, logic, and historic experience—the state must at times be involved in justice. The biblical injunctions to do justice were spoken to individuals as well as those in political authority, including both the covenant community of Israel and pagan nations. Moreover, we know from historical experience that at times government must render justice in an active, distributive sense because it alone has the power to ensure fairness, freedom from harm, or access to certain basic goods without which a person would likely die. *The key in all of this is maintaining creative tensions.* First, tensions must exist between the varying definitions of justice, ensuring that merit, equality, and need operate in the proper spheres of activity—no easy task to be sure. Second, creative tension must exist with the other purposes of government—order and freedom.

There is then, I believe, a biblical and theological mandate for distributive justice by the state. After all, the apostle Paul used his rights as a citizen to appeal to Rome for justice when he declared, "If the charges brought against me by these Jews are not true, no one has the right to hand me over to them. I appeal to Caesar" (Acts 25:11). Although Paul was never granted justice, he believed that he was owed a fair trial and certain rights—a form of justice. And when we look at history, there are clearly times when the government has needed to act in ways that went beyond preserving order, freedom, or merit to ensure a broader justice for its people. For example, in the throes of the Industrial Revolution, the market alone was inadequate to curb significant abuses of workers in unsafe work environments, with unfair pay and extensive hours that were harmful to personal health and the family. In such a case, justice called for a curbing of the freedom of the factory owners by governmental laws for there were no other mechanisms that would or could (at the time) procure justice for the workers. Indeed, justice will always limit someone else's freedom, but it does so that the individual without justice can also come to enjoy the same freedoms and opportunities that others enjoy.

Justice, then, in its various forms and definitions, is a function of the state. However, if justice is isolated from the other purposes of government, it will lead to totalitarianism under the guise of humanitarianism. "From the time of Lenin to the present day, those who hunger and thirst after perfect justice have almost always become, in action if not in principle, enemies of liberty."[16] And such is always the destiny of justice if it does not exist in tension with freedom and order. A commitment to justice need not mean a large, all-encompassing government. After all, many aspects of justice are best done by other social institutions and people within them. But clearly because the state does have the ultimate power within society, at times it alone can procure justice in the midst of a complex world.

A commitment to justice as a function of government is in no way an endorsement of the extreme rights orientation that has come to plague American society. Much of the "rightsism" of our era is not justice at all but pure selfishness or a throwing to the winds constraint, wisdom, and decency. Rights without personal responsibility (which goes beyond mandates by the state) leads to an anarchic society that has lost its way. And the church has a message for such a culture, namely, the gospel. Nonetheless, the state must procure and defend justice, even a justice for groups that are committed to ideals that contradict the Christian faith and its moral framework. But it is a justice that is always in tension with order and freedom.

CONCLUSION

The state is finite and fallen. It is not the most important entity in society, and it is not the cure-all for most of what ails societies and people today. When it is made a savior, it becomes a false god of enslavement. But God did ordain government, and, by virtue of His directives and the worldview that we hold as believers, we can derive its specific purposes: order, freedom, and justice. *The key is to hold them in creative tension.*

Certain ideologues might like to add some things to the list: the production and distribution of goods and services, the enablement of personal righteousness and morality, the protection and control of family life, the delivery of health services, or even education. But when the state begins to take control of these spheres of society, it can become all-encompassing, losing sight of its own fallenness and ruthless potential. It begins to take on activities that our Creator never intended and that are best done by either individuals or other institutions within society. Yes, we may join together under the sphere of government to educate our children to produce an ordered, free, and just society. But the fact that, theologically, education is not a primary responsibility of the state should encourage society to ensure that education is done properly, not over against the family and local communities, the institutions ultimately responsible for education, but in conjunction with them.

Holding order, freedom, and justice together will not necessarily resolve all of our public policy debates, nor will it always lead in one specific political direction. At times, Christian thinking may well baffle the ideologues, as well it should. But holding the three roles of government together in creative tension provides a modest framework for thinking about and acting on issues from a Christian worldview. And that, after all, is one of our primary mandates in this world as we seek not to rule the world by political means but to be salt, light, and leaven within it.

ENDNOTES

1. For an example of this more indirect use of Scripture for political thinking, see Richard Bauckham, *The Bible in Politics: How to Read the Bible Politically* (London: SPCK, 1989). Bauckham, for example, writes, "Without discounting any part of the scriptural witness, judgments will have to be made about what is central and what is peripheral . . . what is provisional and what is enduring. In some cases it will be important not only to report the actual positions reached by particular biblical writings, but to discern the direction in which biblical thinking is moving" (103).
2. For a very helpful overview of the Creation, Fall, redemption, consummation perspective as applied to politics, see Richard Mouw's, *Politics and the Biblical Drama* (Grand Rapids: Eerdmans, 1976).
3. Niccolò Machiavelli, *The Prince*, XII.
4. Thomas Hobbes, *Leviathan; or The Matter, Form.*
5. Jean-Jacques Rousseau, *The Social Contract*, bk. 1, chap. 1.
6. Ibid., bk. 1, chap. 2.
7. John Stuart Mill, *On Liberty* (New York: F. S. Crofts, 1947), 12.
8. Ibid., 95.
9. Glenn Tinder, *The Political Meaning of Christianity: The Prophetic Stance* (New York: Harper Collins, 1991), 102.
10. For a helpful overview of the Exodus and its implications in both the Old and New Testaments, see Bauckham, *Bible in Politics*, 103–17.
11. Charles Hall, "Ring Uses Religion as Cover to Sneak Drugs into Lorton," *Washington Post*, 27 September 1996, A–1.
12. Robert Nozick, *Anarchy, State and Utopia* (New York: Basic Books, 1974), 155.
13. John Rawls, *A Theory of Justice* (Cambridge, Mass.: Harvard University Press, 1971), 302.
14. Karl Marx, *Critique of the Gotha Progamme* (Peking: Foreign Language Press, 1972), 18.
15. Rawls, for example, writes, "Social and economic inequalities . . . are just only if they result in compensating benefits for everyone, and in particular for the least advantaged member of society" (*Theory of Justice*, 15).
16. Tinder, *Political Meaning of Christianity*, 113.

An Overview

If God were to establish a government, what would it look like? Would it be theocratic, monarchial, or even democratic? Would the principles that shaped it be applicable to modern secular governments? What responsibilities do believers, as images of God, have as citizens in secular governments? Eugene H. Merrill surveys the political forms and institutions of Old Testament Israel and then, from this survey, extrapolates five principles that are essential to the welfare of any human government, ancient or modern. Genuine happiness, freedom, and justice are graces given to humanity by the hand of a sovereign God. It is in this hand and no other that governments are upheld and from it can fall.

Chapter Two

GOVERNMENT IN THE OLD TESTAMENT AND ITS RELEVANCE TO MODERN POLITICS

Eugene H. Merrill

THE FIRST COMMAND THE LORD gave to the human race was fundamentally political in nature: "Multiply and fill the earth and subdue it. Be masters over the fish and birds and all the animals" (Gen. 1:28 NLT). In this simple injunction, God, the Creator and Sovereign over all things, delegated to mankind—His very image—the task of exercising government over the universe.[1] Government, then, is not inimical to the purposes of God, but it must be government of the right kind and one that is in line with his kingdom objectives.

Israel eventually became the national expression of this original mandate, albeit in a flawed and incomplete manner because of the Fall and its aftereffects. The Old Testament does, of course, attest sporadically to other political realities in the pre-Israel period (e.g., Gen. 4:17; 9:6; 11:1–9; 14:1–3; 34:1–2; 39:1; 40:37–46), but they are mostly outside the covenant framework and, therefore, without normative theological value. Government—like anything else—that exists apart from a biblically sanctioned paradigm is to that extent inadequate and cannot provide a standard against which to evaluate contemporary political philosophies and structures.

The premise of this chapter is that the only successful political model is one that embraces the principles and mores of government by which God intended Israel to operate. This does not mean, of course, that modern states must emulate ancient Israelite forms. This is not only impossible for practical reasons but also to attempt to impose the theocratic ideal upon modern secular systems is to be oblivious to the unique role of Old Testament Israel and the correspondingly unique framework in which that role was to be implemented.[2] The approach of the chapter, then, is (1) to examine the theological, moral, and political bases of Old Testament Israel's national life in (2) the chronological sequence in which it occurred (3) with the intention of extrapolating principles that can and should be embraced by modern states regardless of their particular forms of government.[3]

THE TRIBAL LEAGUE

Initially, Israel under Joshua's leadership maintained the same seminomadic pattern of life in Canaan as it had in the forty years of migration in the Sinai deserts.[4] Detail is lacking, but apparently Gilgal remained the center of the encampment of tribes throughout the period of conquest (cf. Josh. 5:10; 9:6; 10:6–7, 15, 43; 14:6), perhaps as late as 1375 B.C. or so. Most likely, the organization of the community closely resembled the tribal pattern made clear elsewhere (cf. Num. 2:1–31). Joshua presumably held the same leadership role as Moses (Deut. 31:7–8, 23; cf. Josh. 1:1–9) but, also like Moses, depended on elders and other tribal leaders to assist him in the myriad details of daily life (Josh. 7:6; 8:33).

Gradually at first and then rapidly after the conquest of more and more land, local jurisdictions emerged in the form of tribal territories with their numerous cities, towns, and other local entities. The record is silent after Joshua's death about any central ruler, but the individual tribal areas appear to have been under the rule of a council of elders or the like.[5] They were to hear criminal cases (Josh. 20:4), administer civil law and custom (Judg. 21:16; Ruth 4:1–12), and provide leadership at the local and tribal level (Josh. 23:2; Judg. 11:5–11). Each tribe was more or less independent of the others, a situation that eventually would prove to have negative consequences.

The earliest efforts to create pan-tribal political authority focused on the judges, the earliest of whom, Othniel, was probably contemporary with Joshua's later years. These God-appointed (or sanctioned) leaders had only very limited geographical jurisdiction, however, usually over only a tribe or a tribal district (cf. Judg. 4:5; 10:1–5; 11:1–11; 13:25).[6] They had primarily a military function, leading Yahweh's armies against foreign oppressors (Judg. 2:10; 3:28–29; 4:14–15; 8:28; 11:33; 16:28–31). Little is said about any other responsibility (but cf. Judg. 4:5)—a particularly noteworthy fact given the chaotic times of intertribal warfare noted in Judges 17–21. In fact, the very absence of strong civil leadership led the historian more than once to observe that anarchy reigned because Israel had no king (Judg. 17:6; 18:1; 19:1; 21:25).

PRIMITIVE KINGSHIP

Ideal government throughout the Old Testament is monarchial in form for it posits God as King (Pss. 10:16; 24:7–10; 47:7; 48:2; 95:3; 99:1, 4; 146:10) and views His earthly representatives in that capacity as well (Gen. 1:26–28; 17:6, 16; 1 Sam. 13:14; 2 Sam. 7:11–16; Pss. 2:2, 6–9; 45:6; 89:3–4, 18–29).[7] There is no such thing as a democracy or a republic in the biblical model of governance. In fact, no civilization of the ancient Near Eastern world attests such a model.[8] The tribal league just described might be closest to it, but it proved to be unworkable without strong central authority, as did the concurrent regimes of the judges.

Widespread recognition of the need for national cohesion appears as early as the thirteenth century B.C. in the judgeship of Gideon. After he had put down the Midianite oppressors, he was pressured into assuming kingship over all Israel. In fact, Israel's leaders offered to make him the founder of a dynasty so that his descendants could reign after him. Gideon's response reflected his commitment to the pure theocratic ideal: "I will not rule over you, nor will my son. The Lord will rule over you!" (Judg. 8:22–23 NLT). Taking his cue from this interest in human monarchy, however, Gideon's son Abimelech attempted to seize royal power.[9] This experiment came to an abrupt end and in any case affected only the immediate vicinity of Shechem (Judg. 9:1–57).

Less than two centuries later, the perceived need for kingship had become so intense that the people once more demanded a king, this time of Samuel the prophet. Samuel was also a judge and thus continued in the tradition of local or regional political authority (1 Sam. 7:15–17). His sons were evil, however, so with Samuel's advancing years came a fear that the anarchy typical of the era of the judges would continue and even worsen. Therefore, the populace insisted that Samuel should give them a king like all of the surrounding nations had (1 Sam. 8:4–5). Contrary to much scholarly opinion, Samuel's reluctance to comply was not his resistance to monarchy per se but the circumstances and untimeliness of the request.[10] Yahweh responded that it was He, not Samuel, whom the people were rejecting (1 Sam. 8:7). Later, after King Saul had failed to follow the Lord's direction, God revealed that He had had a candidate for kingship in view all the time, "a man after his own heart" (1 Sam. 13:13–14).

The Lord did allow Israel to have a king after duly warning them about the disappointing results they must expect (1 Sam. 8:10–18). Saul thus became ruler, exercising his regency from the unimposing village of Gibeah in Benjamin (1 Sam. 10:1, 17–27). His "monarchy" was primitive at best with not so much as a standing army. Only when threats to the nation arose did Saul gather voluntary militiamen to put them down. In one humorous example of Saul's less than regal splendor, he emerged from a field where he had been working his oxen in order to attend to a matter involving danger to an area of the kingdom (1 Sam. 11:1–5).

The record discloses very little more about the apparatus of Saul's forty-year kingship.[11] He clearly gained more military strength over time, but even so he was unable to apprehend David with his tiny following. Eventually, Saul fell to the Philistines, whom he should easily have defeated, losing much Israelite territory in the process (1 Sam. 31:6–7). Saul evidently moved the national center of worship to Gibeon (1 Sam. 22:11–19; 1 Kings 3:4–5; 1 Chron. 16:39; 2 Chron. 1:1–6), but nothing else is said about his structures of government or development of bureaucracy. The whole period between Samuel and David should be viewed as a stopgap during the interim, a holding pattern until the long-anticipated legitimate human monarchy appeared on the scene.

THE MAN AFTER GOD'S OWN HEART

A millennium before David's birth, dying Jacob had blessed his sons, saying of Judah:

> The scepter will not depart from Judah,
> nor the ruler's staff from his descendants,

until the coming of the one to whom it belongs,
the one whom all nations will obey.
—Genesis 49:10 (NLT)

From that time forward, the people expected a king to arise from Judah, a connection firmly established in the brief genealogy in Ruth 4:18–22. Most likely, the phrase *a man after his* [God's] *own heart* (1 Sam. 13:14) has nothing to do with human qualification but speaks of God's eternal elective purposes *vis-à-vis* David.[12] He had been in mind a thousand years earlier, and now his time had come. Thus, kingship was not an afterthought or a concession but was integral to God's design from the beginning. Specifically, that design found historical fulfillment in David and his dynasty and awaits eschatological fulfillment in Jesus Christ, the greater son of David (2 Sam. 7:16; 1 Chron. 17:11–15; Matt. 1:1; 21:9, 15; Mark 12:37; Acts 13:22, 34; Rev. 5:5; 22:16).[13]

The purpose of the Davidic monarchy was to model on earth the kingly program of God in heaven. This largely theological deduction finds support in texts devoted to the so-called Davidic covenant. The Lord told David that He would make him famous in his own time and then build him a house, that is, a dynasty that would last forever (2 Sam. 7:9, 13–16; 1 Chron. 17:8–9, 11–15). More than this, David would be considered God's own son who would rule in His place on the throne of Israel (Ps. 2:6–9, 12; cf. Pss. 89:3–4, 27, 34–37; 110:1–2; Acts 13:33; Heb. 1:5–8). This expectation did not die out, as the gospel accounts make clear, for to the multitudes of Jesus' day the coming of David's kingdom was tantamount to the advent of the kingdom of heaven (Matt. 21:4–5, 9: Mark 11:10).

Given this theological foundation, the historical rule of David becomes most instructive in terms of the ideal form and function of human government. At the same time, the ideal was always in jeopardy; in fact, it seldom, if ever, rose to its full potential because of the sin of not only the nation's subjects but also of David himself. One must always try, then, to discover the underlying principles of divine administration through the dark and often distorted lenses of human imperfection.

Immediately following Saul's death, David inquired of the Lord as to where and how he should set in motion his succession to Saul and the establishment of his own long-promised monarchy. It seemed fitting that he should first rule over his own tribal territory of Judah from its principal city, Hebron (2 Sam. 2:1–4a). His subjects were his loyal kinsmen, and his officials were largely the men who had gathered around him in the decade of his desert flight from Saul (1 Chron. 12:1–22). When all realistic claimants to Saul's crown had died, David relocated his capital from Hebron to Jerusalem, a neutral place between his own tribe of Judah and Benjamin, the tribe of Saul (2 Sam. 5:6–7). He then set in place a number of strategic moves to solidify his position as undisputed king of all Israel.

First, he appointed military and political officials to whom he could entrust matters of state (1 Chron. 11:10–47). Then he took measures to protect himself and his people from surrounding enemies, especially the Philistines, who were intent on derailing his fledgling kingdom (2 Sam. 5:17–25). Next, he undertook the construction of a palace and other public buildings to symbolize the integrity of his rule and to communicate to everyone that he was there to stay (2 Sam. 5:9–12). Also, early on David raised a large standing army, waged both offensive and defensive warfare, and began to carve out an empire from surrounding nations (2 Sam. 8:1–14). Finally, and most importantly, he built a tabernacle on Mount Zion as a temporary housing for the ark of the covenant, which he retrieved from its place of exile at Kirjath-jearim (2 Sam. 6:1–17).

Of all David's accomplishments, he clearly viewed this "housing" of the ark of the covenant as the most important—although it fell short of his desire to build a magnificent temple (2 Sam. 7:1–2)—because he recognized his special role as God's adopted son, the one privileged to serve Him as king and priest (Ps. 2; 110; 1 Chron. 15:1–15, 25–28).[14] This fact by no means suggests that divinization of kings was part of Old Testament religious and political ideology, but it does carry the radical idea that heaven and earth met and somehow became coextensive in the rule of David and his dynasty. In theory, at least, Israel was to dramatize for all nations that God is sovereign over all and that He desires to work out that sovereignty in human experience.

The chronicler, in particular, draws out the theological significance of the Davidic monarchy by underscoring at great length David's attention to temple and cult.[15] Of nineteen chapters devoted to his reign, fully ten pertain to these matters. Any assessment of David's view of his responsibilities as head of state that ignores the centrality of proper devotion to and worship of the Lord is bound to be seriously distorted. To David, the very notion of a secular state, or even of a state in which religion was merely peripheral, was unthinkable. His kingdom existed only as an earthly counterpart to the kingdom of heaven, something that he clearly recognized even if others did not.

Evidence of this fact is pervasive in the record (cf. 1 Chron. 17:7–15, 20–24; 22:10–13; 23:25; etc.) but nowhere more apparent than in David's instructions to Solomon about the construction of the temple. It must be built exactly according to the pattern (Heb. *tabĕnît*) that was in his spirit (1 Chron. 28:11–12), a pattern, David says, that "was given to me in writing from the hand of the LORD" (v. 19 NLT). At the very least, David is suggesting that the temple was not the product of his own creative imagination but the earthly expression of a divine and heavenly model.[16] One can only conclude that the temple, the focal point of Israel's religious and political life, represented the entire nation as a microcosm of God's universal dominion.

Israel under David did, of course, take its place among the community of nations. Sometimes it stood apart from them, exhibiting thereby its uniqueness as an elect people. At other times—perhaps more often than not—it compromised its peculiar calling and fell victim to the secular, purely pragmatic way of doing things. David himself as king cannot be wholly exculpated in this, for his own sins and irresponsibility brought God's judgment upon not only himself but also his nation. Nonetheless, at least brief attention to the visible outworkings of Davidic Israel should prove enlightening.

The structure of government during David's tenure was certainly far more highly organized than before, and the sheer size and strength of the kingdom compared to that of Saul required a complex and elaborate bureaucracy.[17] David's principal officials were military commanders, chroniclers and archivists, chief priests, and scribes (2 Sam. 8:15–18). They presided over districts that still conformed to the ancient tribal boundaries, but David's peaceful as well as militaristic international involvements added territories to the kingdom. These areas consisted of either provinces or client states from whom taxation and tribute were demanded (2 Sam. 8:1–2, 6, 14). Such conquests, while enriching the royal coffers, required a network of Israelite officials to oversee the affairs of these territories. In addition, of course, there must be military garrisons built and foreign service personnel stationed throughout the empire in order to guarantee the loyalty and submission of the locals (2 Sam. 8:6, 14; 1 Chron. 29:30). The enormous size and widespread distribution of Israel's armies alone presuppose a chain of command of a highly sophisticated nature (2 Sam. 23:8–39; 24:9).

THE WEIGHT AND COLLAPSE OF THE EMPIRE

Despite David's care to prepare the kingdom for his demise and orderly succession, his intention to seat Solomon on the throne was nearly aborted. He had known that Solomon would rule even before the child's birth (1 Chron. 22:9–10; cf. 2 Sam. 12:24–25), and although Solomon was perhaps only David's tenth son (1 Chron. 3:1–6), David had bypassed all of the others and appointed him as his coregent for his last two years (1 Chron. 23:1; 29:22).[18] Perhaps because Solomon was no more than twenty years old when his father died, his brothers—particularly Adonijah—thought that he would be unable to assert his claim on the throne, so they tried the preemptive strategy of crowning Adonijah even before David died (1 Kings 1:5–10). The plot was uncovered, however, and Solomon was installed before any significant kind of popular movement against him materialized (vv. 32–40).

No one was more keenly aware of his limitations than Solomon himself. He conceded readily not only his chronological immaturity (1 Kings 3:7; cf. 1 Chron. 29:1) but also his lack of experience in matters of governance. What he needed more than anything else was wisdom to lead the large and complex nation that he had inherited from his father (1 Kings 3:9). That Solomon was not entirely bereft of wisdom even then is clear from his recognition that the kind of wisdom that he needed comes from God. Therefore, he made his way to Gibeon, the site of the original Mosaic tabernacle, where he hoped to meet the Lord in a special encounter (2 Chron. 1:3–6). Gibeon was an appropriate place because the shrine there was called the "tent of meeting" (ʾōhel mô ʿēd), that is, the place where God deigned to fellowship with mere human beings.

On the night of the great festivities at Gibeon, Solomon had a dream in which Yahweh offered him whatever be desired. Solomon unhesitatingly requested wisdom to rule his people, a request that God granted along with wealth and honor, unexpected benefits that flowed out of his commitment to proper priorities (1 Kings 3:5–13). Long life would also be his if he walked in his father's footsteps in full covenant obedience (v. 14).

Like David before him, Solomon first stabilized the political situation and attended to matters of a more secular nature before focusing his energies and resources on the religious life of the nation. As to the former, he appointed officials over various departments (1 Kings 4:1–6) and then divided the kingdom into twelve administrative districts the boundaries of which were similar but not identical to the old tribal borders.[19] Each district, under an appointed civil servant, was responsible on a monthly rotating basis to provide support for the central government (1 Kings 4:7–19).[20] In addition, the districts had to provide their fair share of manpower for construction projects, especially the building of the temple (1 Kings 5:13–18). Other labor was conscripted from among the indigenous population, who were consigned, it seems, to virtual slavery (1 Kings 9:15–21). The foremen of these elements were, of course, free Israelite citizens (vv. 22–23). Nothing is said in detail about Solomon's armies except a brief reference to a rather modest cavalry and chariotry (1 Kings 10:26) and the cities built to house them (9:19).

Besides the income of food supplies and other provisions from the districts (1 Kings 4:22–23), Solomon demanded the payment of heavy taxes by his own citizens (1 Kings 10:14–15) and exacted tribute from outlying provinces and client states (4:21). These enormous sources of revenue were augmented by extensive international trade (1 Kings 9:14, 27–28; 10:11–12, 15, 22, 26–29) and by outright gifts from admiring neighbors, even those from afar (9:16; 10:10, 25).[21]

David had laid the foundation for a true empire, and Solomon was able to make it a reality. He inherited the holdings of his father and solidified and expanded them. At the climax of his power, he ruled the entire Levant from the Euphrates River in the northeast to the border of Egypt in the southwest (1 Kings 4:21). Among the peoples and nations under Israel's direct or indirect control were Lebanon (9:19), Aram (4:24), and Edom (9:26). Even mighty Egypt was considered as no more than an equal to Israel, as may be seen in Solomon's marriage to a daughter of the pharaoh (3:1). One may say without exaggeration that Solomon had created a major world power in terms of the criteria by which such judgments are made.

Solomon's predominant preoccupation—at least in his early years—was not in the political, economic, or military spheres, however, but in the spiritual realm. David had desired to build a temple for the glory of God, but, because the time was not right, he could only make preparation for his son to do so. Once the economic and political infrastructures were in place, Solomon set to the task. This activity was early in his reign, his fourth year, and it was an event so singular as to be associated with the Exodus redemption of Israel 480 years earlier (1 Kings 6:1).

Evidently, Solomon commenced the construction of the temple before that of his own palace, the opposite of David's approach (cf. 2 Sam. 7:1–2). This point is clear from the fact that the temple was begun in Solomon's fourth year (966 B.C.) and completed by his eleventh year (959 B.C.; cf. 1 Kings

6:37–38), but the completion time for both projects was twenty years into his reign (951 B.C.; 1 Kings 9:10). Because his palace was thirteen years in the making, it must have gotten under way at 964 B.C. or so, or two years after the temple foundations were laid (7:1). This information is significant because it points to Solomon's intense interest in the things of God, an interest that eclipsed his own selfish concerns.

No expense was spared in the accomplishment of the task of erecting a place of worship suitable to the God of Israel and of the whole world. Solomon employed Phoenician architects and builders—the best in the world at that time—and nothing but the finest and costliest building materials. Even when the magnificent edifice was completed, however, Solomon had to concede that his God was so transcendent that it was absurd to imagine that such a temple, as grand and glorious as it was, could serve as an adequate dwelling place for Him (1 Kings 8:27). Nevertheless, God Himself had designated the temple as the focal point of His relationship with His people and, therefore, had urged them to look to it and to meet Him there in times of personal and national need (8:31–53).

Regrettably, Solomon lost sight of the significance of the temple and, indeed, of the whole spiritual underpinnings of Israel's social and political life. In his latter years, he began to accommodate the religious systems of his many foreign wives, going so far as to build shrines and sanctuaries for their gods (1 Kings 11:1–8). At the same time, he made life miserable for his own people by exacting from them increasingly burdensome tax assessments and forced labor (12:4; cf. 4:7, 22–25; 9:15). The result was a severe rebuke from Yahweh and the tragic announcement that Solomon's kingdom would be divided with only the smaller part remaining to the house of David (1 Kings 11:9–13, 29–38). Thus, a government founded upon covenant principles failed and came to ruin when it transgressed those principles (11:11). *Only Yahweh's commitment to David provided hope for the future* (11:34, 36; cf. 2 Kings 8:19; 19:34; 20:6; 2 Chron. 21:7).

THE TRAIL TO NATIONAL DISINTEGRATION

The seeds of destruction planted by Solomon took root and grew in the twin kingdoms of Israel and Judah, especially in the former. Judah, the house of David and recipient of special promises (cf. Gen. 49:10; 1 Kings 11:32), outlived its northern neighbor by 140 years and, indeed, survived Babylonian exile and returned again to the land as the nucleus of a postexilic community of faith. Even Judah, however, displayed a sorry record of covenant disloyalty, a record interrupted only intermittently by the lives and reigns of certain godly rulers.

The Old Testament contains two accounts—one in Kings and the other in Chronicles—of the divided monarchy era. These two accounts complement each other and at the same time reflect quite different emphases and interests.[22] Kings is more evenhanded in the attention given to each nation; yet, it tends to view Israel as the point of departure to which events in Judah are related. The chronicler, on the other hand, makes Judah central to his account, ignoring much of the material of Kings. To him, Israel is of interest only as that nation comes into contact with Judah from time to time. Both accounts, however, are fundamentally theological renditions. They are "sacred histories" designed to demonstrate that a nation—even Israel (and Judah)—that falls away from God's covenant standards of truth and righteousness has every reason to expect His retributive justice.

The key passage in Kings that makes this point is the reflective résumé of the historian in chapter 17 who observes, "This disaster [the Assyrian deportation] came upon the nation of Israel because the people worshiped other gods, sinning against the LORD their God" (2 Kings 17:7 NLT). This disaster happened despite prophetic warnings for more than two hundred years, until at last the Lord "swept them from his presence" and "only the tribe of Judah remained in the land" (17:18 NLT). To be sure, rulers such as the Judean kings Asa (1 Kings 15:9–24), Jehoshaphat (1 Kings 22:41–50), Joash (2 Kings 12:1–21), and Jotham (2 Kings 15:32–38) brought some measure of spiritual direction, even to the northern kingdom, but their impact was minimal and, in any case, insufficient to arrest the self-destructive path that Israel chose to follow.

One might think that Judah would learn from the disastrous outcome of Israel's behavior, but such was not the case. The historian in Kings, in fact, notes that Judah, too, followed Israel's pernicious ways (2 Kings 17:19), a brief observation attested to later in Kings (2 Kings 21:1–9, 16, 19–26; 23:31–37; 24:8–9, 18–20). Even the chronicler, whose account is generally favorably disposed toward Judah as the house of David, acknowledges that the history of that kingdom following the destruction of the northern kingdom in 722 was pockmarked or scarred by covenant disobedience by rulers and people alike (cf. 2 Chron. 28:1–4, 22–25; 33:1–9, 17, 21–23; 36:5, 9, 11–12). His summation of Judah's history and interpretation of its outcome is no less severe than that of the historian in Kings vis-à-vis Israel. Judah came to its tragic end, he says, despite the fact that "the Lord, the God of their ancestors, repeatedly sent his prophets to warn them. . . ." They gave no heed, however, and, in fact, "mocked these messengers of God and despised their words. They scoffed at the prophets until the LORD's anger could no longer be restrained and there was no remedy" (2 Chron. 36:15–16 NLT).

The history of the divided monarchy, like that of the united monarchy, reveals the timeless principle that as long as God's people are committed to national and personal righteousness, they may expect His continuing blessing. Should they defect from it, however, they invite His inevitable judgment. But there was hope for ancient Israel and Judah just as there is for anyone today who is willing to listen to the message of the chronicler: ". . . if my people who are called by my name will humble themselves and pray and seek my face and turn from their wicked ways, I will hear from heaven and will forgive their sins and heal their land" (2 Chron. 7:14 NLT).

A NEW BEGINNING

For fifty years (586–538 B.C.), no Jewish state in the proper sense of the term existed in Palestine. A Jewish people remained there, but the political and religious leadership by and large had been removed from the land and taken *en masse* to Babylonia. The first semblance of any kind of Jewish autonomy came about following the decree of Cyrus in 538, when he permitted the Jews to return home and authorized a semi-independent state to be established under Jewish leadership. This government was not a monarchy, as had been the case in pre-exilic times, but a provincial entity administered by a governor who was answerable to the Persian satrapy governing the vast area of which Judea was a part.[23]

The first of these governors was, however, of royal blood. He was Zerubbabel, a grandson of Jehoiachin, Judah's last Old Testament monarch (1 Chron. 3:17–19; Ezra 3:2, 8; Hag. 1:1). His important role gave the postexilic community great hope that the Davidic dynasty would continue and that the Davidic covenant would remain in force. No evidence exists that a descendant of Zerubbabel succeeded him as governor, but the fact is clear that the messianic promise continued through and beyond him to Jesus Christ Himself (Matt. 1:12–16; cf. Hag. 2:23; Zech. 4:6–10).[24]

Information is skimpy about the form that the Jewish commonwealth took under its succession of governors. Some scholars use the term "dyarchy" to describe it, suggesting that power was shared between the governor and the chief priest.[25] Although this situation seems to be attested in Zechariah for the late sixth century (Zech. 3:1–5; 4:1–14; 6:9–15), little or no other support for this notion exists in the other postexilic biblical literature. Both Ezra and Nehemiah recognize the supreme authority of the governor (Ezra 2:63; 6:7; Neh. 5:14–19), although both also (especially Ezra) acknowledge a major role for the priest as well (Ezra 7:1–10, 21; 10:1–17; Neh. 8:1–18; 12:26). Besides the offices of governor and priest, Ezra refers to elders who, especially in the premonarchic period of history, provided leadership at a local level. In the postexilic state, they seem to have composed a legislative-like body under the overall direction of the governor (Ezra 5:5, 9; 6:7, 8, 14; 10:8, 14).

The record indicates that things did not always go smoothly in the last 140 years or so of the Old Testament period. Nehemiah suggests that governors who preceded him might have been somewhat greedy (Neh. 5:14–15), and, of course, he had his hands full of controversy with chief priests who abused their authority (13:4–9, 28). Even he as governor and Ezra as priest seem to have differed greatly on certain policies. For example, Ezra commanded all Jews who had married foreign women to divorce them (Ezra 10:3) whereas Nehemiah, who faced the same issue a few years later, merely chastised those who had entered such relationships and made them swear never to do such a thing again (Neh. 13:23–27).

Government in postexilic Judea appears to have been an interim arrangement forced upon the Jews by a powerful and coercive Persian imperialism. Monarchy was still the ideal, and the people looked longingly for the day when a Davidic king would once more occupy the throne of Israel (Hag. 2:20–23; Zech. 9:9–10; 12:1–14).

OLD TESTAMENT GOVERNMENT: DERIVATIVE PRINCIPLES

The preceding survey of political forms and institutions in the Old Testament has brought to the fore certain historical and theological phenomena that are instructive in their own right because they reflect the affairs of God's people Israel as they lived before Him in either obedience or disobedience. More important to the modern citizen of the kingdom, however, is the question of whether the history of that ancient people in that social, economic, and political context has any relevance to the beginning of the Third Millennium. To what extent can and should the political ideologies and structures of biblical Israel inform contemporary models of human government?

Before that question can be answered, it is essential once more to underscore the fact of the uniqueness of Old Testament Israel as a theocratic community, one never replicated subsequently, even in the church. That said, it is still possible for one to extrapolate principles integral to that community and to apply them to the modern world no matter how steeped in sin and alienated from God its various national entities might be. These principles can be listed and elaborated only briefly.

1. *All human government is of divine origin.* A fundamental and overriding biblical truth is that the God of the Bible is absolutely self-sufficient, independent, and sovereign. That is, He existed before time and Creation, has no need of anything outside of Himself, and is responsible for and in control of everything else that exists. It follows, then, that not only humankind but also all human institutions, including government, fall within His purview (Gen. 1:26–28; 2:15; 9:5–6; 11:1–9; Exod. 9:29; 19:5–6; Deut. 2:9–12, 19; 4:32–35; 26:18–19). Even the Fall—with all of its attendant evils, such as human rebellion and self-sufficiency—has not robbed God of His ultimate dominion, a fact confessed by no less than Satan (Job 1:6–12; 2:3–6; cf. Deut. 32:8; Acts 17:26–28).

2. *Earthly government should be a counterpart of heavenly government.* Inasmuch as God has not surrendered His sovereignty, human government, no matter how corrupt, continues to function on His behalf (Rom. 13:1–7). He raises up and deposes earthly rulers according to His own pleasure. One cannot, of course, blame God for the oppression, exploitation, and brutality inflicted by autocratic, dictatorial regimes against their own people. He may allow such harsh measures for reasons known only to Him, but He is not their immediate cause. On the other hand, political structures that operate according to at least some modicum of biblical principle convey by such behavior something of God's beneficence. That is, they become to some extent at least the model of a heavenly archetype.

3. *Government exists for the glory of God and for the good of humankind.* The arrogance of human leaders easily obscures the fact that even what they do in willful ignorance of God somehow redounds to His glory (1 Peter 2:13–17). This fact usually can be seen only through the retrospective lens of history, for those who are caught up in the vortex of contemporary events, which

seem to be disproportionately tragic and meaningless, have difficulty indeed detecting the hand of God. The people of Israel during the awful days of the judges are a case in point. As they looked about them and saw nothing but chaotic lawlessness, they could not sense the Lord's presence in any way—"everyone did what was right in his own eyes." The delightful episode of Ruth, however, dismisses the notion that God was absent for it displays most beautifully His providential control and care. It clearly portrays His glory in the process; the narrative shows how otherwise random events coalesced into a mosaic depicting the redemptive character of the accession of David and eventually that of His greater Son.

   4. *Government exists in spheres of responsibility.* The pattern of Old Testament government is most akin to a pyramid in which God forms the apex and mankind, in general, the base. Because the only clear example is the theocracy of Israel, one may best understand the concept as a whole by use of Figure 1.

Figure 1

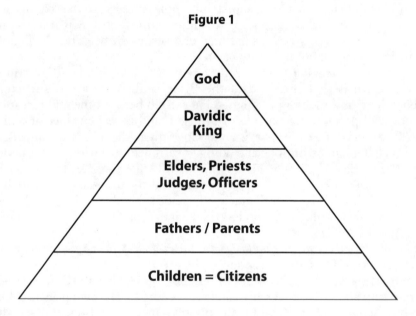

Israel, of course, was the ideal and as such may be considered the model upon which the Lord intended all human government to be based. Study of political and social patterns of contemporary ancient Near Eastern nations also suggest at least rough analogies to this biblical ideal. Obviously, sin distorted the shape of both Israelite and pagan structures, however, so that, for example, a pantheon of deities stood in the place of the one true God.

   A modern ideal—one seldom, if ever, attested to in the millennia of human history—might conform somewhat to Figure 2.

   Although some people would try to create this pattern by imposing an Old Testament theonomy (law or rule of God) on a modern secular world—a misguided effort doomed to failure—others urge at least that government

Figure 2

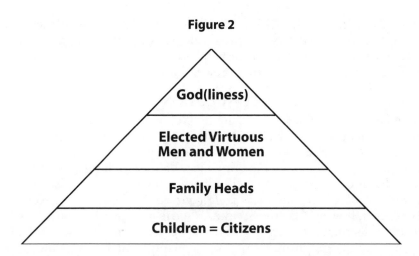

be in line with biblical principles of morality and righteousness. Even this worthy objective seems impossible to attain in a postmodern culture, as has been demonstrated, it seems, by the inability of evangelicals in America to bring about lasting change rooted in a Bible-based political and social ideology. The idea, however, is too worthwhile to be abandoned without continuing struggle, for the "model prayer" still implores that God's "will be done on earth as it is in heaven" (Matt. 6:10).[26]

5. *The ideal is monarchy, but, because of the Fall, the reality is something short of that.* One of the most powerful epithets of the Lord in the Old Testament is that of King (1 Sam. 12:12; Pss. 5:2; 10:16; 24:7–10; 29:10; 44:4; 47:2, 6–7; 48:2; 68:24; 84:3; 95:3; 98:6; 145:1; 149:2; Isa. 43:15; 44:6; Jer. 10:7, 10; Zeph. 3:15; Zech. 14:16–17; Mal. 1:14). This fact, of course, follows from the theological proposition that God is sovereign, a proposition that allows for no sharing of power and, hence, for no political form but monarchy. This form of authority was, however, delegated to humankind in general as the ideal (Gen. 1:26–28) and then promised to Abraham and his descendants. God was to sire kings (Gen. 17:6), human counterparts to his own regal office. These would arise in Judah (Gen. 49:10), specifically in David (1 Sam. 13:14), and would be confined to his lineage (2 Sam. 7:11–16), culminating at last in Jesus Christ, the King of kings and Lord of lords (Zech. 9:9; Matt. 21:1–11; Rev. 19:16). Thus, divine kingship envelopes human history, *begun in the Father and continuing forever in the Son.*

God's intention clearly was for mankind, as His image, to reign over all things as vice-regents. But this grand design was subverted almost before it could commence because the very beneficiaries of its privileges rebelled against the Lord who granted them (Gen. 3:1–8). The result was a crippling of human capacity to reign (vv. 9–24). The promise of an unfettered dominion in which all of God's people were kings must be deferred until a day when God's kingdom in its pristine and perfect form comes to pass on the earth. Then, once more they will live and reign as God intended from the beginning

(2 Tim. 2:12; Rev. 5:10; 11:15; 20:6; 22:5). In the interim, any government that hopes to provide for its citizens any degree of happiness, prosperity, and justice must at least embrace the principles of righteousness embodied in the model provided by Old Testament revelation.

CONCLUSION

The God of the Bible, an unchanging God with unchanging principles to regulate human behavior, has created all things according to a perfect design. This design includes the administration of government, a form intended from the beginning to be monarchic but which, because of human rebellion, has taken other forms that, despite their imperfections, *can be successful to the extent to which they adhere to divine standards of righteousness.* These interim expressions are only that, however, for the Scriptures speak of a day when earthly politics and political structures will give way to the heavenly model in which the Lord of glory, the sovereign of history and eternity, will sit enthroned over a kingdom that knows no end. The task of the believer is to employ whatever moral and spiritual means he or she can to work righteousness into existing human systems and to seek to reach and prepare men and women for the kingdom yet to come. We believers dare not isolate ourselves from the cultural and political systems in which God has placed us; rather, we, with humility and wisdom, must engage even if the only result is a voice for genuine goodness, justice, and moral decency.

ENDNOTES

1. William J. Dumbrell, *Covenant and Creation* (Nashville: Nelson, 1984), 34.
2. The fundamental fallacy of so-called "theonomy" or "dominion" theology is that it assumes that the principles and standards of Old Testament covenant law are normative, even binding on contemporary political regimes. This view takes no account of the suspension of the theocratic model and erroneously equates the church with Old Testament Israel. See Kenneth L. Gentry, *God's Law in the Modern World* (Phillipsburg, N.J.: Presbyterian & Reformed, 1993); Gary North, *Theonomy: An Informed Response* (Tyler, Tex.: Institute for Christian Economics, 1991); Greg L. Bahnsen, *No Other Standard: Theonomy and Its Critics* (Tyler, Tex.: Institute for Christian Economics, 1991); and William S. Barker and W. Robert Godfrey, eds. *Theonomy: A Reformed Critique* (Grand Rapids: Zondervan, 1990).
3. The position taken here is that the life and history of ancient Israel can be known definitively only from the Old Testament text. At the risk of a perceived reductionism, the data of the canonical text alone will provide the foundation upon which any description of ancient Israel's political forms and functions can be possible.
4. The literature on the question of Israel as a nomadic culture is enormous. See F. S. Frick, *The Formation of the State in Ancient Israel* (Sheffield: Almond, 1985); C. H. J. deGeus, *The Tribes of Israel* (Amsterdam: Van Gorcum, 1976); N. K. Gottwald, *The Tribes of Yahweh* (Maryknoll, N.Y.: Orbis, 1979); Baruch Halpern, *The Emergence of Israel in Canaan* (Chico, Calif.: Scholars, 1983); N. P. Lemche,

Early Israel: Anthropological and Historical Studies on the Israelite Society Before the Monarchy (Leiden: Brill, 1985); id., *Ancient Israel* (Sheffield: JSOT, 1988); and id., *Prelude to Israel's Past* (Peabody, Mass.: Hendrickson, 1998). Most of these studies refuse to consider the Old Testament to be a source of authentic historical information, but they do shed light on the vexing matters of nomadism, seminomadism, and sedentarism and the possibility of movement among the three.

5. Roland deVaux, *Ancient Israel: Social Institutions* (New York: McGraw-Hill, 1965), 4–13.

6. Harry Orlinsky, "The Tribal System of Israel and Related Groups in the Period of the Judges," *Essays in Biblical Culture and Bible Translation* (New York: KTAV, 1974), 66–77; Hanoch Reviv, "The Pattern of the Pan-Tribal Assembly in the Old Testament," *Journal of Northwest Semitic Languages* 8 (1980): 85–94; and S. M. Warner, "The Period of the Judges Within the Structure of Early Israel," *Hebrew Union College Annual* 47 (1976): 57–79.

7. Dumbrell, *Covenant and Creation*, 139; and Keith W. Whitelam, "Israelite Kingship: The Royal Ideology and Its Opponents," *The World of Ancient Israel*, ed. R. E. Clements (Cambridge: Cambridge University Press, 1989), 134–36.

8. Wolfram von Soden, *The Ancient Orient* (Grand Rapids: Eerdmans, 1994), 63–67. For the suggestion that a kind of "primitive democracy" existed earlier than monarchy in Mesopotamia, see Thorkild Jacobsen, "Mesopotamia," in *Before Philosophy*, ed. Henri Frankfort et al. (New York: Penguin, 1974), 141.

9. Baruch Halpern, "The Rise of Abimelek ben-Jerubbaal," *Hebrew Annual Review* 2 (1978): 79–100.

10. J. Robert Vannoy, *Covenant Renewal at Gilgal* (Cherry Hill, N.J.: Mack Publishing, 1978), 228–30.

11. J. M. Miller, "Saul's Rise to Power: Some Observations Concerning 1 Sam. 9:1–10:16; 10:26–11:15; and 13:2–14:46," *Catholic Biblical Quarterly* 36 (1974): 157–74; and K. Vander Toorn, "Saul and the Rise of Israelite State Religion," *Vetus Testamentum* 43 (1993): 519–42.

12. P. Kyle McCarter Jr., *I Samuel*, Anchor Bible, vol. 8 (Garden City, N.Y.: Doubleday, 1980), 229.

13. Dumbrell, *Covenant and Creation*, 150–52.

14. Eugene H. Merrill, "Royal Priesthood: An Old Testament Messianic Motif," *Bibliotheca Sacra* 150 (1993): 50–61.

15. H. G. M. Williamson, *1 and 2 Chronicles*, New Century Bible Commentary (Grand Rapids: Eerdmans, 1982), 28–31.

16. For various translation and interpretive options for verse 19, cf. Sara Japhet, *I and II Chronicles* (Louisville: Westminster/John Knox, 1993), 497–98.

17. Herbert Donner, "The Interdependence of Internal Affairs and Foreign Policy during the Davidic-Solomonic Period (with Special Regard to the Phoenician Coast)," *Studies in the Period of David and Solomon and Other Essays*, ed. Tomoo Ishida (Winona Lake, Ind.: Eisenbrauns, 1982), 205–14; and Hayim Tadmor, "Traditional Institutions and the Monarchy: Social and Political Tensions in the Time of David and Solomon," *Studies in the Period of David and Solomon and Other Essays*, ed. Tomoo Ishida (Winona Lake, Ind.: Eisenbrauns, 1982), 239–57.

18. Eugene H. Merrill, "The 'Accession Year' and Davidic Chronology," *The Journal of the Ancient Near Eastern Society* 19 (1989): 112.

19. John Bright, "The Organization and Administration of the Israelite Empire," *Magnalia Dei, the Mighty Acts of God: Essays on the Bible and Archaeology in Memory*

of G. Ernest Wright, ed. Frank M. Cross et al. (Garden City, N.Y.: Doubleday, 1976), 193–208.

20. J. Alberto Soggin, "Compulsory Labor Under David and Solomon," *Studies in the Period of David and Solomon and Other Essays*, ed. Tomoo Ishida (Winona Lake, Ind.: Eisenbrauns, 1982), 259–67.

21. Yutaka Ikeda, "Solomon's Trade in Horses and Chariots in Its International Setting," *Studies in the Period of David and Solomon and Other Essays*, ed. Tomoo Ishida (Winona Lake, Ind.: Eisenbrauns, 1982), 215–38; A. R. Millard, "King Solomon's Gold: Biblical Records in the Light of Antiquity," *Bulletin of the Society of Mesopotamian Studies* 15 (1988): 5–11.

22. See, for example, P. R. Ackroyd, "History and Theology in the Writings of the Chronicler," *Concordia Theological Monthly* 38 (1967): 501–15; and James D. Newsome Jr., "Toward a New Understanding of the Chronicler and His Purposes," *Journal of Biblical Literature* 94 (1975): 201–17.

23. Sean McEvenue, "The Political Structure in Judah from Cyrus to Nehemiah," *The Catholic Biblical Quarterly* 43 (1981): 353–64; and Peter R. Ackroyd, *Exile and Restoration* (Philadelphia: Westminster, 1968), 1–38, 138–52.

24. Eugene H. Merrill, *Haggai, Zechariah, Malachi* (Chicago: Moody, 1994), 55–58.

25. Carol L. Myers and Eric M. Myers, *Haggai, Zechariah 1–8*, Anchor Bible, vol. 25B (Garden City, N.Y.: Doubleday, 1987), 350–51.

26. For a recent appeal for evangelicals to disengage themselves from efforts to reform American life by overtly political means, see Cal Thomas and Ed Dobson, *Blinded by Might: Can the Religious Right Save America?* (Grand Rapids: Zondervan, 1999).

An Overview

For more than half a century, Carl F. H. Henry has been a leading voice in American evangelicalism. In this essay, he reviews the hopes and the failures of twentieth-century evangelicals in applying biblical principles in the arena of public policy. He argues that evangelical timidity and confusion in matters of public policy is the result of the lack of a comprehensive Christian social ethics rooted in the creation mandate. Because evangelicals have not always thought in a broad, comprehensive theological and philosophical framework, they have been unable to engage successfully in matters of public policy. As a result, their efforts have been marginalized or relegated to special interests. However, biblical principles do have an important role for public policy. It is possible to use biblical principles for direction of priorities and goals in politics and public policy. But when doing so, one must use wisdom in delineating that which is derived from biblical interpretation and that which is derived from political ideology.

Chapter Three

LINKING THE BIBLE
TO PUBLIC POLICY

Carl F. H. Henry

MANY DEVOUT AMERICAN ECONOMISTS take quite for granted that public policy and social action ideally involve some clear linkage to biblical values. Even radical academicians enamored of recent theologies of revolution and/or of liberation present Marxist theory, justifiably or not, in the context of the Hebrew Exodus from Egyptian oppression and of Jesus' promise of final deliverance from injustice.

During the forepart of the twentieth century, ecumenical churchmen addicted to the so-called Social Gospel politicized their expectation of the coming kingdom of God and professed to derive from Jesus of Nazareth and from the Old Testament prophets their confidence that history moves inescapably toward a socialist utopia. They displaced the evangelical insistence on humanity's need of personal spiritual regeneration by speculative evolutionary notions that mankind is essentially good and that earthly history edges inexorably toward a flawless future.

At the same time, most fundamentalist Protestants withdrew from cultural involvement and abandoned public affairs to theological modernists. They did so for several reasons. Dispensational premillennialists viewed religious liberalism's disavowal of basic New Testament beliefs as telling evidence that history had declined into end-time apostasy. Because modernism had defaulted from the Christian church's redemptive task, fundamentalists made personal evangelism and foreign missions their primary burden. Modernist efforts to reform culture and society while neglecting the salvific role of Jesus Christ, religious conservatives complained, were a betrayal of the mission of the church.

By the mid-twentieth century, a rectification of fundamentalist/evangelical withdrawal from social concerns was already getting under way. An awakened interest in public involvement was encouraged in part by my lamentation *The Uneasy Conscience of Modern Fundamentalism* (1948) and by a social action commission subsequently sponsored by the National Association of Evangelicals (NAE). NAE did not, however, go much beyond adopting resolutions at annual conventions and sporadically conferring with sympathetic public officials.

Gradually, however, evangelical colleges enlarged course offerings in political science and economics. Graduates pursued doctorates in law and related fields, and some evangelicals ventured political campaigns for public office. The emergence of the Moral Majority—in response to federal intrusion into the arena of religious values such as prayer in public schools and public funding of abortions—activated large masses of fundamentalists and other religious conservatives. They engaged in public demonstrations and wrote officeholders, expressing their views on specific legislative proposals.

In contrast to modernism's Social Gospel program, the religious right concentrated on an agenda of specifics more than on a comprehensive social vision. To be sure, modernist churchmen had their own agenda of specifics. But local church constituencies more and more repudiated ecumenical hierarchies that professed to speak for them. The religious right demonstrated massive numerical strength, even when allowance was made for promotional exaggeration. The religious right did not, to be sure, speak for all evangelicals any more than Pat Robertson's presidential candidacy was a "panevangelical" effort. Many evangelical college students were turned off by the confrontational tactics of Jerry Falwell's followers, and some of those students were less "radically right." Evangelical college professors, especially sociologists, moreover, tended to be less conservative than their students.

What was clear, however, was that evangelicals had ended their public silence and civic nonparticipation. Insofar as they specified public objectives and opposed social evils, they recovered continuity with the eighteenth- and nineteenth-century Evangelical Awakening in England and with American abolitionist evangelicalism of the post-Civil War era.

Emphasis on the regenerate church as a new society over which Christ rules by the Holy Spirit through the inspired Scriptures was correlated afresh with two convictions. First, the church as light to the world is called to model in society at large what happens when God's people live by the precepts and power of the risen Lord. Creative pilot projects could mirror the community of faith's endeavor to live by both neighbor love and social justice. The church need not survive only as a subsociety of Amish believers or of Hasidic Jews withdrawn from the world and confined to their own institutions. The separatist option had made evangelism difficult and had deprived the Christian community of some values of modernity. But, no less important, it deprived the church of its divinely intended role of public light, salt, and leaven. The Creator's moral creation mandate no less than Christ's evangelistic mandate presupposes universally valid ethical imperatives and divinely established social institutions such as the monogamous family and governmental authority.

Second, the church is to proclaim to the world the criteria or standards by which Christ, at His end-time return in power and glory, will finally judge all humanity and the nations, and by which He is anticipatively judging them even now. As redeemed sinners once identified with the world's rebellion but now by divine grace on privileged speaking terms with the coming King, the people of God are to share with secular society the best of all good news: God offers forgiveness of sins and new spiritual life to all who trust in Christ's saving work.

Yet, this return to social involvement lacked a dimension that evangelical scholars are now beginning to address more earnestly, the arena of public policy. Reasons for their recent neglect of this area are not difficult to identify. To speak compellingly about public philosophy and policy concerns requires both cognitive competence and vocational expertise. Forfeiture of social concern by an earlier generation had left evangelicals with few qualified spokesmen in many areas of government and economics. Few things served the evangelical movement more poorly than mere aphorisms and verbal blips on the thin surface of worthy debate. A secular press readily probed evangelists and televangelists rather than evangelical educators and editors for a clue to the direction of Christian social thought.

But a still deeper reason accounts for evangelical timidity and confusion in matters of public policy. Religiously conservative scholars have not developed a comprehensive Christian social ethic that connects the universal divine creation mandate with the Decalogue as a divine covenant-republication of creation ethics. To neglect God's creation ethics mandated before the Edenic Fall and its relationship to the Decalogue tends to leave nebulously in midair the significance of the Mosaic Law and the ethics of the Old Testament prophets for contemporary Christian social engagement.

Some of this confusion is evident when, for example, extreme dispensationalists wholly dismiss Mosaic legislation as belonging to a now superseded dispensation (and then divert the Sermon on the Mount away from the church age to a future kingdom age or millennium). Theonomists, on the other hand, insist on the universal and permanent validity of the entire corpus of Mosaic legislation for civil government in all times and places. The confusion that here concerns us exists among avowed evangelicals, not simply among nonevangelical interpreters who deny the propositional validity of biblical morality and who substitute for objectively revealed principles and precepts an internal disposition identified as a vague sentiment of love.

The failure of evangelical ethicists to engage in public policy formulation has had costly consequences. It cast evangelicals in a pluralistic society in a role of concern for only their own special interests and not for justice and equity as a public cause that embraces an evangelical agenda along with that of all other citizens.

Evangelicals in earlier centuries shared a concern for the public good. At our country's founding, Americans embraced a sense of the nation's universal mission and manifest destiny. Some people regarded the United States as "the new Israel" standing in a covenant relationship to God and divinely assigned a mission of Christianizing the world. They particularized a universal conviction that divine providence underlies the origin of all nations and stressed that America's destiny as an intentionally pluralistic republic was nonetheless contingent upon faithfulness to the Judeo-Christian heritage.

Only public policy involvement that transcends a partisan agenda and envisions social justice as a universal due—reflecting God's universal demand for righteousness—can invalidate the complaint that evangelical orthodoxy is concerned for justice only when and as its own interests are violated. Although humanity's fall into sin precipitated a catastrophic culture shock, the tragedy of Eden did not strip rebellious humans of all moral illumination. God holds humans responsible for their rebellion in Adam and also on their own account.

The Old Testament leaves no doubt that the Gentiles, although unenlightened by special revelation and nonparticipants in covenant ethics, nonetheless have light that they deliberately spurn. Cain is held accountable for his murder of Abel; Israel's pagan neighbor-nations—Syria, Edom, Ammon, Moab, and others—are condemned for crimes of treaty breaking, enslavement of captives, violence, and savage conduct.

Any society that does not deal ethically with sex and marriage, with labor and economics, and with divinely willed structures of authority will accommodate the sinful warping of social components that need to be reclaimed for their divinely created intention. So, too, attention is required to civil government as a divinely intended context for human preservation and order in a fallen society.

If one neglects God's creation ethic, which the redemptive scriptural ethic restates and aims to reinforce, the risk multiplies of propounding only partisan policy preferences, and of doing so on extrabiblical grounds. When evangelicals seek to distill a program of contemporary moral policy and action solely from Israel's specially revealed covenant ethics, they are prone to compensate for their neglect of the significance of general or universal revelation by speculative theories of natural law or to rely on unacknowledged ecclesiastical tradition to strengthen their positions. Or they are prone to imply a revelatory basis for their own social judgments.

What is espoused as "Christian public policy" inferred from biblical principles is readily promoted as normative Christian commitment and regarded as a necessary expression of a well-formed faith. But the authenticity of such inferences depends on their biblical legitimacy and the logical rigor of an intellectual process. Whenever God's will is precariously identified with acceptance of certain political or social preferences, what begins as a worthy effort to preserve the relevance of biblical revelation to the pressing social problems of modernity may through misjudgment or overstatement unwittingly invite doubts over what is declared to be biblical. When relativities are changed into absolutes, absolutes are more easily perceived as relativities. In view of this absolutizing of the relative in the name of God, other professedly Christian sociologists and political scientists, moving from sociology to theology with unclear theological priorities, may in turn even question whether divine revelation actually takes the form of rational propositions and objective principles.

For all of that, biblical principles are indeed a verbal particularization of God's will. Beyond their significance for personal obedience in the world lies their equally important significance for public life and policy. Scripture is interested in comprehensive righteousness—personal and social. The self-revealing Creator and Governor of the universe commands universal justice. Scripture concerns itself with human thought and action in government and in business and economics no less than in education and culture and in marriage and the family.

Does that concern embrace the nature and purpose of economic systems and legislation touching the marketplace? Do scriptural references to labor and economics hold priority—in part or in whole—over the sphere of civil government, or does the state have the final say? Does "doing the truth"—a basic Christian requirement—involve a definitive view of the state's role in the foundation and practice of business? Ancient Hebrew society operated within certain divinely stipulated structures. Is their significance limited wholly to the ancient faith community? Are those structures relevant to secular society today?

The Bible is not, of course, a guidebook on policy; however, to ignore it in public policy formulation is to neglect the brightest moral and spiritual illumination available. Yet, it is an easy—and also a risky—leap from the conviction that the Bible is a divinely inspired book whose moral imperatives illumine every sphere of human behavior to the emphasis that it offers ready-made solutions—if only we trouble ourselves to find them—for any and every social dilemma. As true as it is that Scripture constitutes a transcendent ethic that surpasses even "the wisdom of the ages," it is nonetheless the case that the Bible gives no direct answers to numerous contemporary problems. We are left to make inferences from revealed principles. To have revealed social and political principles is, to be sure, an immense asset. But our inferences from such foundation truths are not necessarily infallible. Attention to logic and hermeneutics will no doubt go a long way toward keeping us on the proper track. If we fall into error, the fault is not with guiding principles but with unsound exegesis.

The need for caution is illustrated by proposals for political action that some well-intentioned religious spokesmen promote. In the area of foreign policy, both the right and the left have claimed Christian legitimacy for very diverse positions on such matters as nuclear defense, troop reductions, military actions, international treaties, and much else. Nobody need be surprised, therefore, that what some interpreters view as "an evangelical recovery of political responsibility" is regarded by others as "a politicizing of evangelical piety."

Some political scientists warn that both the religious left and the religious right have promoted public policy positions and taken specific legislative positions presumably on Christian grounds when their positions in fact arise less (if at all) from an expressly scriptural basis than from a subjectively preferred political stance. For example, whether one thinks the minimum wage in the United States should presently be raised, and, if so, by how much, might well turn more upon one's political outlook than upon direct biblical sanction. Some radical Christians have even revered Marxian economic analysis as an extension of general divine revelation. If religious conservatives often were unwitting apologists for the status quo, religious liberals have tended to view themselves as successors of the biblical prophets.

Historically, fervent appeals have been ventured—on supposedly biblical grounds—in behalf of the so-called Social Gospel (usually a form of socialism), liberation theology, theology of revolution, and fundamentalism's withdrawal from politics and the world at large. In such cases, not only have wrong inferences been drawn from biblical principles but also philosophical prejudices extraneous to the Bible were antecedently imposed upon it.

The governing hermeneutical approach to biblical ethics, all too much ignored in the effort to shape Christian policy decisions, is therefore critically important. Confusion is unavoidable if one begins by merely transferring to present-day secular society those ethical elements from the Old or New Testament that seem to have burning moral relevance while skipping over those that have fallen by the cultural wayside. On what basis does one avoid transferring to our times all—and not only part—of the biblical ethic? Are we to resort to natural law? Or should one function like a closet theonomist? Or do a divine creation mandate and general revelation contribute factors that we dare not ignore? Does it make a vital difference that the Old Testament prophetic vision of a universal era of justice and peace is correlated with the return of Messiah?

Some interpreters hold that the Sermon on the Mount provides all of the revealed principles and divine guidance we need for any and every role in public affairs today. But the Sermon deals essentially with interpersonal relationships, not with official and international relationships. The Sermon is intended basically, moreover, for the new community of Christ's followers; it is not to be coercively imposed on unbelievers. To transfer the Sermon to official public life would disadvantage public agencies as well as misunderstand its intention.

Most contributors to this volume support the sanctity and perpetuity of the Old Testament moral law but find no reason to perpetuate the institutional forms of theonomic rule in which it was first expressed. In legal affairs, we are not now legislating for a future millennium or for a contemporary theocracy.

Biblical principles nonetheless have a decisive importance for public policy matters in our fallen society in which God mandates the state to restrain injustice and to preserve order. God in His providence restrains human inordinacy and faces His people with the continuing task of reaffirmation and reformation in legislative and policy specifics. Because human unregeneracy will not automatically lead to justice and the public good, will not legislative regulation have some necessary role in a fallen world? Or are the principles of a market economy laws of nature? Are the checks and balances of a free market system adequate to contain entrepreneurial greed and inordinate self-interest? So-called Christian Reconstructionists would superimpose upon all of the nation-states Old Testament law, which was the basis of ancient Israel's theocratic rule. That law remains permanently valid, theonomists insist, not simply as an expression of God's moral will for humanity but as a legal corpus that civil government should universally enforce even in the present era.

But are the 613 divine laws in the Torah to be received and promoted as obligations of all modern states? Are Christians, as a test of their submission to the lordship of Christ, to champion an "all or nothing" restoration of theonomic rule?

Most evangelicals hold the view that since New Testament times the regenerate church has been universally and intentionally scattered under diverse forms of government to witness to the lordship of Jesus Christ as final judge of the nations. By proclamation and by example they are to promote universally the justice that God seeks and the justification that He offers to penitent believers in Christ. Although evangelicals do not equate democratic or republican political structures with the kingdom of God, most of them nonetheless consider democratic government preferable in present fallen history because of its promotion of political self-determination and the safeguards that it offers against secular totalitarianism.

Much Mosaic teaching is doubtless ongoingly significant for politics and economics, not least of all its support for private property, free enterprise, and concern for human welfare. Yet, the modern state of Israel, although Jewish to the core, has not revived Jewish religious law but deliberately pursues a secular economic program.

Meir Taman, chief economist of the Bank of Israel, holds that the ideal would be an entrepreneurial religious Jewish state. It would preclude Jews from charging other Jews interest on loans, he declares, avoid inflation, balance employment levels with preservation of the work ethic with social morality, rely on a tax to provide survival funds until the unemployed find work, and shut down failing companies rather than bail them out.

These proposals face us with specific interpretations that some exegetes of the Torah might well question and disavow as reading into the Torah some social proposals not self-evidently inherent. No less important is the question of selectivity. Is all Mosaic legislation to be carried forward as an obligation of a modern Jewish religious state? Orthodox Jews seek literally to follow the Torah's more than six hundred commandments. Should the Israeli state then revive death by stoning for all crimes so designated by the ancient theocracy, in which capital punishment was stipulated for adultery, homosexuality, and juvenile delinquency, among other offenses?

Christian Reconstructionists would extend theocratic legislation to all modern nation-states on the ground that all of the Mosaic teaching has permanent and universal validity for civil government. Some dissension is occasioned within the movement's ranks by Reconstructionists who would make certain exceptions—for example, retention of the menstrual laws—whereas others insist that every "jot and tittle" of the Mosaic teaching remains applicable.

The alternative view shared by most evangelicals was reflected by then British Prime Minister Margaret Thatcher's address to the General Assembly of the Church of Scotland in May 1988. Thatcher granted that democracy as a form of government is "not in itself especially Christian, for nowhere in the Bible is the word *democracy* mentioned. Ideally, when Christians meet, as Christians do, to take counsel together, their purpose is not (or should not be) to ascertain what is the mind of the majority but what is the mind of the Holy Spirit—something which may be quite different. Nevertheless," Thatcher continued, "I am an enthusiast for democracy. And I take that position not because I believe majority opinion is inevitably right or true—indeed, no majority can take away God-given human rights. But because I believe it most effectively safeguards the value of the individual, and, more than any other system, restrains the abuse of power by the few. And that is a Christian concept."

We should go on to echo Prime Minister Thatcher's further comment because few Christian leaders have served as effectively as Thatcher in leading a powerful modern nation in public policy affairs. She added, "There is little hope for democracy if the hearts of men and women in democratic societies cannot be touched by a call to something greater than themselves. Political structures, state institutions, and collective ideals are not enough. We parliamentarians can legislate for the rule of law. You, the church, can teach the life of faith." Then she recited from a cherished hymn about "another country" whose King cannot be seen and whose armies cannot be counted, yet "soul by soul and silently her shining bounds increase."

The difficulties attending the formulation of "evangelical public policy" are helpfully indicated in *Evangelicals and Foreign Policy: Four Perspectives*, which is concerned with international more than economic policy.[1] After assessing conflicting attempts to derive an evangelical public philosophy based on biblical revelation, political scientist Dean Curry concludes that "no distinctively biblical approach to foreign policy" seems possible. Alberto Coll, professor of international law, thinks that we are locked up to prudential decision making that presupposes broad Christian principles. Richard John Neuhaus more fully emphasizes the democratic process in which evangelicals and others seek to shape a public philosophy. Sociologist James Davison Hunter cautions that lack of consensus might deprive evangelicals of the public policy influence they might otherwise have.

In a doctoral dissertation completed in the late 1980s at Boston University under sociologist Peter Berger and titled "Recent Evangelical Appraisals of Capitalism and American Class Culture," Craig M. Gay notes that the evangelical debate over social and economic policy has arisen within a specifiable social context that pulls the "right" and the "left" quite predictably in contrary directions and that the debate itself, moreover, has become one of the more important frameworks through which contemporary culture is unsuspectedly "modernizing" or secularizing Protestant orthodoxy. He gives an overview of the divergent evangelical appraisals of capitalism, from those on the right who, like Carl McIntyre, defend capitalism as a natural outgrowth of biblical Christianity, to those on the left who, like Jim Wallis, have declared capitalism to be an unjust system and have blamed it for many of the world's ills.[2]

Gay then charts less extreme and more centrist views. He protests that many views succumb to ideological abuse of Scripture and to the de facto confession of the ultimacy of economic life and of material existence. The resulting confusion, he thinks, was reflected even by the 1974 International Congress on World Evangelization in Lausanne, where leading evangelical activists put social engagement on a par with evangelism in direct contradiction of Billy Graham's keynote emphases.

More recently, Christian Reconstructionism has essentially equated capitalism with the emerging kingdom of God, he protests, while evangelical radicals like Ronald Sider and a growing circle of Christian Reformed spokesmen champion government interventionism, and World Evangelical Fellowship increasingly provides a sounding board for related emphases. The left identifies capitalism as an economic system essentially incompatible with Christian theology and ethics and promotes "an evangelical theology of liberation," taking its lead from radical secular analysis charging that a capitalist political economic elite manipulates society for its own advantage.

Meanwhile, the defenders of capitalism, Gay suggests, fall into several groups. Some people anchor capitalism in the laws of nature; others hold that only Christian values make it work; still others ground it in Mosaic legislation assumed to be perpetually and universally valid. Gay notes the influence of socialist sources even on the evangelical center, through its interaction with the intellectual "new class" as a knowledge elite, an influence that not even neofundamentalists wholly escape. Gay does not express final judgment on the conflicting views but emphasizes the urgency of further evangelical discussion of the relation of evangelical theology to rival contemporary social, economic, and political approaches. Significantly, he comments that not "'separatism' but . . . socio-political activism" comprises the most pressing temptation facing evangelical intellectuals.

Amid the ideological conflicts of our times, the first temptation might be to identify capitalism as Christian or biblical, all the more so now that socialism almost everywhere is emptying into disillusionment. To escape economic despair and to share in the capitalist creation of wealth, erstwhile socialist leaders are returning in stages to the market system they have long despised. But do the striking loss of confidence in socialism and the equally striking resurgence of the free market system justify us in dignifying capitalism as Christian economics? Socialism seems to have been an artificially contrived collectivist theory whereas free enterprise is compatible with the deepest human instincts. Yet, to claim that capitalism is essentially Christian is to assimilate to Christianity an economic system capable of ethical indifference and injury.

Is it more factual, then, simply to hold that free market economics was superimposed on a religious outlook stressing voluntarism, hard work, and prudent management and that the providential result was an unprecedented expansion in material production and wealth and in a remarkable improvement in the living standards of much of the citizenry? Shall we regard free enterprise as an ethically neutral system, or is it not rather the case that

Christianity requires us to forgo the notion of value-free mechanisms? Given humanity's present fallen condition, capitalism is readily placed in the service of human inordinacy. While it is true that competition and the law restrict such inordinacy, does not mass media advertising create for shysters an unprecedented opportunity to disadvantage the consumer?

In a speech at the American Enterprise Institute's annual policy conference, Paul Johnson remarked that capitalism must address the exclusion of perhaps a fifth of society from a life of modest decency.[3] Capitalism offers hope that "this minority problem of failure . . . the biggest single task our societies [face] today . . . can and will be overcome." The socialist systems cannot produce wealth; capitalist society knows that "a solution can be found" for permanent mass poverty, "and we have an inescapable moral obligation to find it." Yet, Johnson granted the compatibility of the capitalist market system with Christianity, and he exhorted all who are rooted within the Judeo-Christian system of ethics "who value freedom, who strive for the just society, and who recognize the enormous productive potential of market capitalism" to engage in the entrepreneurial tasks of linking the free market system to the principles and practices that will promote regenerate moral ends. "It is a mistake," Johnson affirmed, to consider capitalism inherently moral rather than to recognize it as an incomparable system for producing wealth. But, he held, "it is possible to run it in tandem with public policies which make use of its energies while steering it in a moral direction." This task, Johnson averred, calls for a considerable agenda: absolute equality before the law; equality of opportunity, in which he included giving the poor access to education and to capitalism itself (as by stock ownership and small businesses); free trade; and by instructing the poorer nations in the skills of market capitalism. Capitalism is not the economics of the kingdom of God, but neither is it a grotesque ideology; it has openly exhibited its efficiency as a wealth-producing system, and biblical principles can prod it toward the ethical purposes that protect it from inordinate misuse.

Evangelical economists are unanimous that the current distribution of wealth is not morally ideal. This is evident from the biblical exhortation that we respond to the poor and to cases of hardship. Yet, they are equally unanimous in declaring that complete equality of income distribution is not a biblical standard. Indeed, as Marvin Kosters comments, such redistribution would offend other principles of fairness in relation to rewards and needs.[4]

We are often told nowadays that the ideal state will be marked by justice and by compassion or love. This emphasis gets a ready hearing in the once-Christian West, in which all of the humanitarian movements arose in the past from the theology of the Cross and evangelical affirmation of the *imago Dei* in all humanity. But love, or compassion, is a relationship between persons, not between institutions or between institutions and persons. No improvement can be made on an entirely just government; in community relationships, justice is the course that neighbor love takes. The continual modification of government policy in the name of compassion contributes to a misunderstanding of both compassion and justice. Love is always preferential; it gives itself voluntarily, not because the giving is legally due another. These confusions, which have important bearing on Christian social ethics, lead also to a speculatively compromised view of God because they tend to elevate compassion as the essence of divinity and subordinate to it all other divine perfections, including righteousness or justice. One consequence is that God is depicted as not seriously offended by sin and iniquity; another is that the concept of justice itself is weakened whereas that of compassion is distorted. The unhappy end product of compassionate government is the hoax of the welfare state.

The contributors to this volume discuss the bearing of the biblical tenets of Creation, Fall, and redemption on the legal aspects of economic structures, on the regulation and control of business, and on political discourse and public policy. Their concern not to ignore the fact that the public political route is great gain unless one confuses such involvement with "bringing in the kingdom of God." The relationship of particular political and economic proposals to theological orthodoxy is quite tenuous. If one thinks that a particular position on a nuclear weapons freeze is more sure and more important than the doctrine of a final resurrection of the dead to divine judgment, one seriously confuses his or her priorities. How, then, we may and must ask, are public policy commitments to be legitimated as Christian or biblical? Or is any and every such claim that is made on their behalf misleading?

In respect to the governing biblical sources, Christian economists differ over both the nature and meaning of the supposedly relevant scriptural data and precisely what illuminating inferences to public policy we are to derive from Scripture. Are these differences more a matter of semantics than of substance?

When writers speak of "broad implications of a biblically based vision," of Bible-engendered "nuances" and "insights" and "perspectives," and of Scripture as a major "source of ethical discernment," we are far removed from objective principles from which valid inferences can assuredly be drawn. The greater the gulf between express biblical doctrine and an agenda of precise legislative specifics, the harder it becomes to invoke express biblical authority for policy.

To be sure, each Testament is addressed primarily to a single faith community. In what way does the biblical ethic "apply to" and "illumine" public policy problems in a secular society?

Must a policy that is "compatible with" biblical principles rule out the possibility that another policy might also be compatible? "The spirit" of biblical teaching is sometimes invoked—in distinction from the teaching itself—in a manner that implies a devout mysticism. Some writers rely so much on parables for the content of social ethics that one wonders whether they are inclined to channel all biblical principles into subjective relational concerns. When economists speak quite generally only of knowing "God's desires" or of nurturing human desires that are truly scriptural, our task becomes more demanding. How does one compare desires if the validity of propositional revelation is unsure?

The Bible deals with human nature and with personal relationships more than with specific problems. But much of its teaching nonetheless expressly bears on concerns of public policy. All humans are finite creatures, yet all humans are made in God's image. We are fallen sinners, yet we are responsible for our choices and the stewardship of our possessions. We must not confuse the abundant life with materialism, and we must be compassionate toward the poor. The biblical work ethic implies that in a fallen world labor is not to be shunned because it is sometimes an exasperating experience.

Even if Scripture includes general governing principles—for example, about the dignity of and the need to work—can we confidently infer that government is obliged to enforce one's right to work as an absolute right or merely insist that society must create a climate disposed to provide more jobs? Can one get assuredly from scriptural principles to cooperatives and to profit sharing?

The confusion over the Bible and public policy is in some respects due to the questions we address to Scripture. The Bible does not contain an answer to all twenty-first-century public policy concerns; in respect to some other issues, it says very little. If we ask specifically whether the development of nuclear energy is the best option to cope with the fuel shortage in the future, the biblical writers are silent. Devout Christians know no more than do secular humanists about some of these concerns; indeed, all of our calculations might be upset if cold fusion turns out to be more than a hoax. So intricate are public policy issues, moreover, that an economist may well distinguish positions that rest obviously on governing principles from those that depend on fallible inferences and from still other positions that seem simply to be prudent.

Biblical principles can provide direction for rational priorities and inherent goals. Economics can define a decision-framework and specific approaches, but Scripture must remain the norm if we are to avoid reducing Christian concern to mere world concern. As responsible carriers of light and leaven, Christians are to be identified with the world, speaking to the soul of the nation, pointing to a higher way, and modeling and exhorting the masses to obey the coming King.

A scholar is to be commended rather than criticized if caution requires him to avoid claiming direct biblical authority for a view that seems compatible with Scripture and yet is not expressly demanded by it. To claim biblical justification for certain aspects of public policy is both unnecessary and ill-advised when all that is clear is consistency within a concern for justice. Sincere Christians might differ over particular guidelines for national policy, but they should not blame the Bible for differences that arise from contrasting political platforms. Policy decisions are a response to God's call to justice, but we should be cautious about unqualifiedly calling them "God's will." Yet, in a pluralistic society, Christians must strive as individuals and as a new community to approximate as fully as possible the Creator-Redeemer's moral imperatives. But the difficulties of transforming scriptural general principles into specific policy prescriptions must not discourage us. In a fallen world, utopia must wait for the Lord's return.

ENDNOTES

1. Michael Cromartie, ed., *Evangelicals and Foreign Policy: Four Perspectives* (Washington, D.C.: Ethics and Public Policy Center, 1989).
2. See Craig M. Gay, *With Liberty and Justice for Whom?* (Grand Rapids: Eerdmans, 1991).
3. Paul Johnson, *Washington Times*, 21 February 1989, 5.
4. Marvin H. Kosters, "Biblical Principles Applied to a National Policy on Income Distribution," in *Biblical Principles and Public Policy: The Practice*, ed. Richard C. Chewning (Colorado Springs: NavPress, 1991), 35–51.

An Overview

In politics—as in family life, agriculture, music, and every other sphere of life—Christians should exercise their daily responsibilities in ways that acknowledge Christ's kingship and authority. But what does it mean politically for individuals and nations to live under the supremacy of Jesus Christ? In this essay, James Skillen argues that Jesus Christ reigns supreme over governments and political life and that this truth bears directly on the kind of political societies that Christians should help shape in obedience to Christ.

In seeking to establish a framework for Christian political responsibility, two principles of pluralism—structural pluralism confessional pluralism—are especially important for Christians to acknowledge and to try to implement to show our obedience to Christ. Although these principles do not exhaust the criteria by which governments should act, and although various matters of distributive justice and retributive justice must be dealt with in ways that extend beyond them, they are basic. They call Christians to pay serious attention to both the creation order and God's timing of judgment and redemption in history. As long as God withholds final judgement, Christians must seek to uphold governments that act with the same nondiscrimination among citizens that God exercises. Christians should work for societal justice for all people regardless of their religious perspective. The functional outworking of these principles requires that we ask whether democracy can be consistent with Christ's supremacy. In turn, we must try to answer three questions: How should Christians act politically in obedience to Christ in a democratic society where other, perhaps most, citizens do not acknowledge His authority over politics? How does Christ exercise His authority in the face of sin and injustice? How do the principles of justice—particularly the principles of pluralism—express themselves in specific public policies?

Chapter Four

LIVING IN TUNE WITH CHRIST'S SUPREMACY

James W. Skillen

NEAR THE BEGINNING OF HIS LETTER to the Colossians, the apostle Paul writes that the incarnate Son of God is both before and above all powers and authorities, "so that in everything he might have the supremacy" (1:18). Jesus Himself told His disciples after His resurrection, "All authority in heaven and on earth has been given to me" (Matt. 28:18). Jesus Christ is supreme; He holds supremacy.

Evangelical Christians do not hesitate to affirm that Christ is head of the church and supreme over individual lives. We also have little difficulty affirming that when Christ returns in glory, He will defeat every enemy and reign supreme. Where we have difficulty, however, is in understanding how Christ reigns, politically speaking, supreme right now, especially over those who do not acknowledge His authority. Some Christians believe that Satan now rules the earth. Others believe that although Christ rules the church, God the Father oversees politics and allows those who are not subject to Christ to govern; God the Father is somehow supreme, but not Christ.

These ideas, however, simply do not square with biblical revelation, including the preceding two passages from Colossians and Matthew. Jesus did not claim that all authority in heaven and on earth would be given to Him after He returns. Paul did not say that only in the future would Christ have supremacy.

FROM THE BEGINNING

If Christ reigns supreme even now, then one of the most important questions we have to answer is how we should live our political lives in submission to the supreme Christ. Let's approach this question by starting where Paul, John, and the author of Hebrews begin. They proclaim that the supreme Savior and Lord—the incarnate son of God—is the one in and through whom all things were created in the first place and that in Him all things hold together (John 1:1–3; Col. 1:16–17; Heb. 1:2–3). The entire creation, from the beginning, reveals and holds together in the Son of God, who is from now on, forever, also fully human—Jesus Christ. To be disciples of Christ, therefore, we must know who we are following. If we are to learn

71

to obey Him in everything, then we must learn what it means to be created in the image of God with responsibility as stewards of creation and caretakers of one another. Being a Christian means more than being a worshipper, an evangelist, and a patient anticipator of Christ's return. It means learning how to honor the One in and for whom family life, education, agriculture, science, art, and politics were made. All of these dimensions of life belong to human beings who are created in the image of God to serve Him. Or, to say it another way, Christ the Redeemer has come to restore and fulfill God's original purposes. God in Christ does not take souls to heaven; He redeems whole persons—body and all—for full human life in this world and for resurrected life in the new earth. In Him all things hold together.

When we ask the question of how we should obey the supreme Christ in political life and government, therefore, we have to ask how and why God wants us to do justice, to love mercy, and to care for our neighbors politically for the common good of all citizens. We must pay strict attention to the reality before us and to the created world in which we live and take seriously the political dimension of human life.

By analogy, think of Paul's command to Christian spouses to love one another. He intends that married partners should practice daily a way of life— in pain and weakness, in joy and strength, in sickness or in health—that seeks the good of the other in everything. Married couples have to do more than go to church and pray together to obey Christ. They have to make a home together; balance their finances; do the dishes; love their parents, friends, and in-laws and, in most cases, raise children. There is no blueprint for how to do all of this. Although each couple creates a unique marriage, the Scriptures say very little about how they should conduct their marriage. The Scriptures tell spouses to love one another; the spouses must work out that love and all concrete details of their lives. Marriage, in other words, is part of God's creation that is intended to reveal Him in its actual practice. God's redeeming love in Christ, at work in spouses, gives us a beautiful picture of Christ's love for His bride, the church. Yet, this purpose of marriage has been part of God's revelatory purpose from the beginning. Thus, to experience Christ as our Bridegroom, we must practice obedience in our marriages, for our marriages themselves, when lived obediently, reveal something of God in Christ.

The same could be said for politics and government. The Scriptures tell us very little about how a modern town, state, or nation should design streets or highways, dispose of sewage, encourage the education of citizens, protect the innocent from thieves and violence, or uphold basic civil rights. Humans must figure out how to do these things in response to God's command to do justice, under the supreme kingship of Jesus Christ. In politics, we are not left alone in a so-called "secular" world without any revelatory light from God. To the contrary, the whole creation breathes God's presence and testifies to his will and purposes because the whole creation, including all dimensions of human life, holds together in Jesus Christ, for whom and through whom all things were created. To follow Christ the King, the true Judge, the just

Governor, we must practice obedience in our own civic practice, for political life also falls under Christ's supremacy.

To understand the framework of Christian political responsibility, therefore, we must emphasize both creation and redemption. For one thing, we should act as citizens with the recognition that our redemption in Christ belong together because all of life is bound together in the one who is both the originator and the redeemer of creation. In our basic creatureliness, we recognize that all human beings have the same identity—the image of God—and that all people live under the same commandments from God. Only one world and one Creator exist. Moreover, all human beings are also sinners, alienated from God in their disobedience. We all have participated in and continue to participate in those actions that darken human understanding and distort life with our neighbors, God, and all creation. With the first coming of the Son of God in Jesus, the thing that changes is not the creation order but the way God deals with creation and sin to fulfill His purposes.

HISTORY AND THE POLITICS OF THE KINGDOM

From Abraham to the coming of Jesus, God encouraged anticipation of the time when Israel would be fulfilled, when the creation would be restored, when sin would be judged and overcome, precisely so that God's purposes for creation could be fulfilled and God would be glorified. When Jesus dwelt among us, suffered death on the cross, rose from the dead, and ascended into heaven, God revealed that Jesus Christ is God's ultimate illuminator of life's mysteries—the one whom Israel was properly anticipating all along. At the same time, God did not complete everything during Christ's early life before His death and resurrection. In other words, as we now realize, the revelation of Christ's supremacy is taking centuries and generations (as we measure time) to be revealed in its fullness, and it will not be completed until Christ returns in glory. The fact tells us a great deal about the meaning of history, about the way we should look back to Christ's coming and ahead to His coming again. Although the creation order of God's commandments have not changed, history has now entered a final phase in which human discipleship and anticipation take on a new character because the Messiah has already dwelt among us and has been identified. He is Jesus, the Christ.

The political implications of the revelation of Jesus Christ are immense. God did not send Jesus simply to liberate Jews from Roman rule. He did not come to occupy one piece of land among others as His Christian kingdom. Christ's kingship did not originate within this world; it will be fulfilled only through His dominion over the whole earth. Jesus and the apostles also made clear that Christ's followers should not try to build that kingdom by force, as if they could bring it in by typical conquering means. In obedience to Christ's supremacy, Christians must do as Christ did. Until Christ returns, God is sending rain and sunshine on the just and the unjust alike and calls Christ's followers to be like Him. We are to do justice to every human being with the knowledge that only God will separate the sheep from the goats in final judgement. Consequently, human exercise of public governance that is tuned to Christ's supremacy—politics of the kingdom—requires at least two things: structural pluralism and confessional pluralism. Let me explain these two terms briefly.

By *structural pluralism* I mean that a constituted government—by judicial, legislative, and executive means—must do justice within a wide variety of responsibilities that God has given to human beings. Most responsibilities do not belong to government but rather to people by God's direct creational assignment. In other words, a *structural diversity* is built into created life that must be given its due: agriculture, art, business, family life, intellectual life, and much, much more. Government does not create any of these areas. Only God through Christ governs all life, and He has called political authorities to fulfill a particular responsibility of doing justice to people in both their civic and their noncivic capacities. This truth is the basis, for example, of the distinction of institutions—such as church, family, and state—from one another. The "separation" of church from state, for example, is not simply a way to limit government, keep people from religious warfare, or honor individual freedom. It is, first of all, the way to acknowledge that God has given church institutions and political institutions different responsibilities. The way for government to do public justice to churches and other nongovernmental institutions is to begin by recognizing the full structural complexity of reality as God created it. Public justice requires structural pluralism in contrast to totalitarianism.

By *confessional pluralism* I mean that government should act in accord with God's patience, the patience exhibited by Christ's current governance of the world. God in Christ, by the power of the Holy Spirit, gives the same blessings of creaturely life to believers and unbelievers alike. Although a big difference exists between faith in God through Christ and faith in other gods or no gods, God has not called Christians to act politically to try to separate citizens according to those different faiths. Governments that hold the power of the sword govern communities of citizens, not comminutes of faith, and they should not grant political privileges to people of one faith over people of other faiths. Political societies are civic communities that bind people together as citizens. Therefore, government should uphold the same civil rights and the same penalties of retribution for all people of all faiths, including those who say that they have no faith. God's grace and patience are being exercised right now through the supreme authority of Jesus Christ over all political authorities on earth. Human governance should be in tune with God's governance in Christ, who sends rain and sunshine on the just and the unjust alike. As long as God withholds final judgment, Christians must seek to uphold governments that act with the same nondiscrimination among citizens that God exercises.

God's gracious patience in Christ is the true basis of religious freedom, the only firm ground of confessional pluralism. To support equal civil rights for people of all faiths does not imply that Christians thereby affirm the equal validity of all faiths. That is not what God implies by sustaining the life of believers and unbelievers alike in this age. If Jesus Christ alone is supreme, then, in submission to Christ's authority, Christians should work for governments that act in accord with Christ's patience between his first and second comings and give the same justice to all people within the territory of each state. It is proper and God-honoring for Christians to bear testimony to Christ by standing up for the civil rights of our atheistic neighbors. As Christians, we should be confessional monists; as Christian citizens, grounded in that monistic confession, we should affirm that *government's* responsibility, under Christ, is to act as a humble confessional pluralist. Confessional pluralism under government is a true consequence, a principle outcome of the Christian confession that Jesus Christ *alone* is Lord.

These two elements—structural and confessional pluralism—establish part of the framework for Christian political responsibility. They do not exhaust the criteria by which governments should act. Various matters of distributive justice and retributive justice must be dealt with in ways that extend beyond these two principles of pluralism. Nevertheless, these two principles are basic, calling us to pay serious attention to both the creation order and God's timing of judgment and redemption in history. They call us to admit both the structure of society and the historical unfolding of God's gracious revelation in Jesus Christ.

My argument to this point has been that Christ reigns supreme over governments and political life and that this truth bears directly on the kind of political societies that Christians should help shape in obedience to Christ. The two principles of pluralism are especially important for Christians to acknowledge and try to implement to show our obedience to the supreme Christ. To extend and illustrate the argument, we must now do three more things. First, we must try to answer the question of how Christians should act politically in obedience to Christ in a democratic society where other, perhaps most, citizens do not acknowledge His authority over politics. Second, we must address the question of how Christ exercises His authority in the face of sin and injustice. Doesn't politics simply go on by itself under human control? If Christ is supreme right now, isn't He, in fact, a rather ineffective King? Finally, we must try to illustrate how the principles of justice—particularly the principles of pluralism—can express themselves in specific public policies.

CAN DEMOCRACY BE CONSISTENT WITH CHRIST'S SUPREMACY?

How should Christians act politically in obedience to Christ in a democratic society where perhaps most citizens do not intend to act in obedience to Him? Isn't it necessary in a democratic system to appeal to the majority to make things happen? Because Christians share political life with those who are not Christians, don't they have to put aside any distinctively Christian view of politics to help shape the common good? Christians should not try to impose Christianity on others, should they?

Part of what it means to live in an open society, where government does not force all citizens to conform to the same faith, is to experience God's patient grace in Christ. God does not compel all people to believe in Him.

The very meaning of faith is that a person believes from the heart, with intentional commitment, without compulsion. Of course, if most people in a society do not give themselves in faith to the true God, that society might be very dark and discouraging indeed. Yet, Christians' response to this condition should be to live righteous lives, bearing testimony to God before their neighbors. We ought to live thus as we raise our children, as we work and worship, and yes, as we do politics. Politically, we should work to ensure that our civic neighbors suffer no civic disadvantage simply because they are not Christians. By all of these acts, we will help demonstrate to our neighbors that they also live in this world only because of God's grace in Christ.

Nevertheless, a political society that upholds religious freedom and a limited government does *impose* a particular kind of political order. Such a system makes it impossible, for example, for those who want an established church to achieve that desire. It frustrates the aims of those who would like to establish a totalitarian government. In other words, those who believe that an open, pluralistic society is just should work politically to uphold this kind of imposition because they believe that it does justice to all. By its very nature, every political system represents some kind of imposition that excludes other kinds of political systems. The question we have to answer, then, is why a limited form of government, which protects a diversity of nongovernment institutions and a diversity of faiths, is more just than other systems. We must show why a political constitution *should* impose religious pluralism in a place of religious monopoly, why it should prohibit totalitarianism rather than prohibit an open society. In this respect, Christians should have a strong political agenda that they are working to implement. Christians are not relativists or mere majoritarians who say that anything goes, that no rules should apply. Such an approach is not principled pluralism but rather unprincipled confusion.

Recognizing that governments do impose and enforce law also means that Christians can simultaneously respect the responsibilities of the majority while never accepting that the majority makes right. Respect for majority rule in an open democratic society means respect for elections and debates that allow citizens to try to convince one another of the best road to take and the best laws to make. New elections and new legislation can always lead to change. To uphold the majority's governing authority within a constitutional system is one way of making it possible for citizens to try to convince one another of what they believe a government should do. The very purpose of a representative political system is to call citizens to the responsibility of articulating and voting for what they believe is best—to make their best cases for justice. Therefore, the aim for Christians should never be simply to win the majority or to stand on the side of every majority regardless of what the majority believes. Rather, our aim as citizens ought to be to argue and work for what is just to all citizens. Sometimes, the majority will do what is right and just; at other times, it will not. Justice for all, not majoritarianism, is our first principle.

IS CHRIST'S RULE EFFECTIVE?

The second question to which we now turn concerns the effectiveness of Christ's governance in a sinful world where many, if not most, governments do not acknowledge Christ's supremacy. What sense does it make to say that Christ rules supreme if, in fact, governments are perpetuating injustice and even getting away with murder? This question can be answered only by taking seriously what God has thus far revealed in Jesus Christ.

Human sinfulness has continued ever since Adam and Eve first disobeyed God in the Garden of Eden. Most of Israel's kings were unfaithful in the performance of their duties. The question of how God puts up with unjust governments did not arise with the advent of democracy. Read the biblical prophets. When Jesus was born and was finally recognized by His disciples as the Messiah, many people expected that the rule of God would finally eliminate all enemies and do away with oppressive governments. Yet, at His first coming Jesus did not enact the final judgment. He gave up His life to suffer God's judgment for us. He went to the grave bearing the sins of the world. Jesus Christ came to redeem the world, which means, among other things, to make it possible for humans to fulfill their God-given responsibilities—the responsibilities given them as God's stewards and governors of this world.

In other words, the point of Christ's death, resurrection, and ascension is to call humanity to repentance so that He might lead a people to the praise of God with all that they are and have. When Jesus ascended into heaven, God released the Holy Spirit to come to convict the world of sin and to draw repentant sinners to faith in Christ. This is the God who is governing the world now, and in doing so the supreme Christ upholds God's creation ordinances. The fact that parents often do not love their children properly does not represent God's intention for parenting and does not carry Christ's approval. But the responsibility and the opportunity that parents have to love their children—and to fail to love their children—is sustained by God's grace in Christ. God sticks to His purposes for creation, showing His fidelity to the creatures to whom He gave dominion over the earth. He does not dispense with them or do away with their humanness; rather, He comes in Jesus Christ to identify fully with them and to redeem creation. To put it another way, we can say that God has not allowed human sinfulness to destroy all parental love or to obliterate the parents' obligation to love their children. The possibility of parenting with love remains, by God's grace. Many parents who do not know or love God nevertheless give their children bread rather than stones to eat. And many parents who once did not show proper love to their children become loving parents when they turn to God in repentance through Jesus Christ. God's grace remains steadfast, even in a fallen world.

Despite the fact that Christ has not yet returned in final judgment, He continues to rule by restraining sin, by upholding the creation, and by calling sinners to repentance. This fact holds for politics as well as for family life, for governing as well as for parenting. We should not expect government to be sinless or for all governments to acknowledge Christ's supremacy any more than we should expect any parent to be sinless or all parents to acknowledge Christ's supremacy. Christ is ruling now through the power of the Holy Spirit to fulfill God's purposes and to allow all human generations to exercise their responsibilities. Because all humans are sinners, Christ's governance also means giving time and making space for all to come to repentance. Earthly government is part of the way Christ rules, by making it possible for governments to do their duty—to protect the innocent, to enhance the common good, to establish justice. Any government that achieves even a minimum of these purposes reflects the gracious goodness of Christ's rule and in that sense is showing obedience to Christ even if those who govern do not acknowledge Christ's supremacy. Likewise, to the extent that any government fails to uphold justice and protect the innocent, it manifests human sinfulness and thus deserves God's judgment.

Our tendency as sinful humans is to blame God when we suffer injustice and to give credit to human goodness and ingenuity when we enjoy well-being and good government. We praise humanity for democracy and blame God for the Holocaust. But we should do just the opposite. Good government is due to God's grace in Christ, and the Holocaust was due to human depravity. The fact that not all Jews were destroyed by the Holocaust and that millions more people were not destroyed by the communists, fascists, and nationalists is due to God's grace. The fact that much injustice exists under democracy around the world is due to human depravity. By God's grace, a government that is not accountable to an electorate might be as able to uphold justice as a democratically elected government. At the same time, both majorities and minorities can exercise unjust governance.

Our responsibility as Christians—wherever we live and under whatever form of government we find ourselves—is to seek justice for all and to live at peace with all of our neighbors insofar as it depends on us. Our political way of life, as every other dimension of our existence, should be to acknowledge Christ's supremacy and to live in accord with His own grace and patience until His return.

SOME POLICY CONSEQUENCES

Finally, let me try to illustrate the implications of this point of view in a few matters of public policy. We have already mentioned the most familiar American example of structural and confessional pluralism: the separation of church and state. The two institutions are recognized as different and with different responsibilities. Government recognizes the independence of churches and neither establishes one of them nor assumes responsibility for their internal governance. This principle leads, consequently, to the equal treatment of all faiths. If government is neither responsible for nor identical with these institutional religious bodies, then it also has no authority to give privilege to one or another of them. Public justice demands equal treatment of them all, with the same provision of police and fire protection, legal protection, and so forth. Debates and arguments over which is the true faith must be left in the noncoercive realm of public discourse.

The mistaken conclusion often drawn from this pattern of American religious freedom, however, is that "religion" can and should be confined entirely to church life and that everything else, including politics, is nonreligious or secular. This view is neither implied in the U.S. Constitution nor required by structural and confessional pluralism. This mistaken notion can be exposed in several ways, which will also help us illustrate additional policy conclusions.

First, take the family. Are families "religious" or "secular" entities? They are neither churches nor states. They are a different kind of institution. Many families do, of course, consider themselves to be deeply religious, not only because they worship but also because they understand the family itself to be a creation of God, and they acknowledge that the responsibilities of spouses to one another and of parents to children are responsibilities given by and accountable to God. Nothing in the law requires that families must be religious or nonreligious. Thus, when government's tax policies grant a deduction for dependents, the tax break goes to families without regard to whether they are religious. Government simply recognizes the independence of families and their freedom to be as religious as they please. Parents even have authority to take their children to church with them or to keep them away from any worshipping community. Religious freedom is something that belongs to families and not only to churches. Churches and states should be distinguished and not confounded, but religious faith directs the whole of life. It cannot be confined to churches or to private life.

Likewise, in federal law is now a Charitable Choice provision that governs welfare policy. The provision recognizes that many organizations that provide services to the needy are self-declared religious organizations. When state governments cooperate with nonprofit service organizations, the federal law now states explicitly that religious nonprofits must be treated the same as organizations that call themselves secular agencies. The fact is that religious convictions and commitments extend beyond church walls and outside families to shape the way people serve their neighbors and function in public life. Government must not only keep from hindering such action but also should treat it with equal protection and provision.

Unfortunately, many of government's laws that control housing, employment, and education, to name just a few affected areas, still presume that public life is nonreligious. Charitable Choice, which requires equal treatment of both religiously explicit and self-identified secular organizations in welfare policy, is new and unusual. More and more public policies ought to be redrafted to acknowledge both structural and confessional pluralism.

The next most important area of American life in which these principles ought to be implemented is elementary and secondary education. Again, I would emphasize the structural difference between school and state, parallel to the structural difference between family and state, and church and state. The government does own and operate schools, but not all schools are government-run, and no necessary reason exists for government to own and operate schools. Regardless of whether government-owned and -operated schools exist, the principle of structural pluralism should hold: government should recognize the unique responsibility of schools and of those who administer them. In the United States, generally speaking, states do recognize independent schools and homeschooling alongside government-run schools, and in that regard they recognize that schooling is a responsibility distinct from government.

However, we do not yet have equal treatment of all schools without regard to their religious confession. Movements for more diversity in education are growing, with the consequence that charter schools and even voucher schools are now arising. But even where limited voucher experiments exist (as they do in Milwaukee, Cleveland, and across Florida), government funding does not go equally to all students and all schools. Many organizations that oppose government funding of independent schools still argue that religion is a private matter and that government should not fund religious schools, and certainly not fund them equally.

The principle of confessional pluralism, however, argues that citizens should not be discriminated against in public life because of their faith, whether that faith is in God or in something else—even atheism. If, for some parents, the education of their children is as religious a matter as the family and the church, then it is unjust for government to require all children to attend school but then withhold tax support from the children who do not attend secular, government-run schools. The only way to do justice to the diverse faiths in American society is to allow parents to choose freely from among all schools—both independent and government-run, both religious and secular—and to receive equal public funding for their children's education regardless of which faith controls that education.

CONCLUSION

Whether in education or in welfare services, in family policy or in the treatment of churches and other religious bodies, public law ought to build on the principles of structural and confessional pluralism. These principles are matters of public justice and ought to reflect the supremacy of Christ, who is governing with patience and grace toward all. In politics as in family life, agriculture, music, and every other sphere of life, Christians should exercise their daily responsibilities in ways that acknowledge Christ's kingship and authority. We have a long way to go to work out in political life the implications of the truth that all things were created in and for the Son of God, in whom all things hold together. Not until we understand fully the supremacy of the incarnate Son of God, Jesus Christ, will we understand the true meaning of politics and civic responsibility.

An Overview

The "Clinton Confession" and "Religious Leader's Prayer Breakfast" in August and September of 1998, respectively, forced an immediate response from various Christian ethicists, philosophers, and columnists. The reaction to Clinton's view of repentance and forgiveness was published in a book titled *Judgment Day at the White House*, which J. Daryl Charles here critically reviews. The review is included in this volume to provide a general overview of the reaction of the religious community to Clinton's private and public behavior and because it raises timely questions with which believers must grapple if Christianity is to become a viable player on the political landscape of American life during the twenty-first century. Isolation is certainly not the answer, but neither are threats and certainly not anxiety—for the Lord still reigns. The Clinton affair has awakened the nation, perhaps as no other event in recent years, to the possibility that character and morality do matter. May our lives and the love of Christ that we portray to our nation depict a character that understands and sympathizes with the human condition—but never at the expense of truth and honor.

Chapter Five

Judgment Day at the White House[1]
A Critical Review

J. Daryl Charles

> I pray Heaven to bestow the best of blessings on this house and on all that shall here-after inhabit it. May none but honest and wise men ever rule under this roof.
>
> —John Adams,
> Second President of the United States,
> in a letter to Abigail, November 2, 1800

INTRODUCTION

THE TITLE OF THIS VOLUME suggests hell-fire and brimstone and a type of apocalyptic foreboding that would make any fighting fundamentalist proud. The rather cumbersome subtitle—"A Critical Declaration Exploring Moral Issues and the Political Use and Abuse of Religion"—by contrast suggests an authorship that is more concerned with things on this side of the eschaton. Indeed, the subtitle tells the more accurate story.

Judgment Day at the White House begins with a declaration—specifically, a "Declaration Concerning Religion, Ethics, and the Crisis in the Clinton Presidency." Originally drafted by biblical scholars, the Declaration was revised in response to feedback and signed by more than 140 teachers and writers. Most of the contributors are teachers of religion, ethics, and public policy. It was precisely one year ago that these individuals assembled at the national meeting of the American Academy of Religion/Society of Biblical Literature in Orlando to express their corporate commitment to not only personal virtue but to social justice and public morality. Two events in particular triggered this response through declaration. The first event was President Clinton's televised statement on August 17, 1998, concerning his grand jury testimony the same day. The second event was the White House-orchestrated "Religious Leaders' Prayer Breakfast,"[2] which took place on September 11, 1998. To their credit, a significant number of Evangelical Theological Society (ETS) members were among the Declaration's signatories, who, one should note, represent a diversity of political views. (In fact, a number of the contributors who are most critical of the current administration either expressly state or imply Democratic Party allegiance;

83

thus, it is baseless to view *Judgment Day at the White House* as some sort of partisan outcry.)

Following prefatory remarks by editor Gabriel Fackre, the volume begins with the formal Declaration, which consists of six points that protest the manipulation of religion and the debasement of moral language as it relates to recent presidential behavior. Condensed, these six points are as follows.

1. We worry about the political misuse of religion, and we fear that the religious community is in danger of blessing politically motivated and incomplete repentance that seeks to avert serious consequences for wrongful acts.
2. We challenge the widespread assumption that forgiveness relieves a person of further responsibility and serious consequences. When the President continues to deny any liability for the sins he has confessed, it suggests that his public display of repentance was intended to avoid political disfavor.
3. Certain moral qualities are central to the survival of our political system, among these truthfulness, integrity, respect for the law, respect for the dignity of others, adherence to the constitutional process, and a willingness to avoid the abuse of power.
4. We are concerned about the impact of this crisis on our children and on our students. We maintain that there is a reasonable threshold of behavior beneath which public leaders should not fall.
5. We urge the society as a whole to take account of the ethical commitments necessary for a civil society and to seek the integrity of both public and private morality.
6. While some of us believe presidential resignation or impeachment to be appropriate and others of us do not, we are all convinced that extended discussion of ethical and religious issues raised by the current Presidency are necessary for the long-term health of our body politic.[3]

Part One of *Judgment Day* consists of eleven essays of varying length that take up two overarching themes—"The Ethics and Politics of Repentance and Forgiveness" and "Biblical, Pastoral, and Theological Perspectives on Public Morality." Part Two is devoted to how critics of the Declaration responded. This section was as disappointing and instructive as Part One was thoughtful and exhilarating. Part Three includes several penetrating essays by columnists and were not written at all from a religious viewpoint, while Part Four consists of two transcripts—one of President Clinton's televised statement of contrition to the nation the same day of his grand jury testimony (August 17, 1998) and the other a transcript of Mr. Clinton's "Religious Leaders' Payer Breakfast" speech.

Why is such a volume necessary? And why do we present a review of this volume? This reviewer—as a teacher of ethics, a father, a citizen of two kingdoms, and one who has done public-policy work—shares the burden of the signers that after the dust has settled (i.e., when people simply want to forget the bad dream of the last twelve months and "move on"), we had better awaken from our bad dream and realize what is at stake. Perhaps we are not simply to "move on," as most people would have it. Do these events constitute something of a watershed in our cultural life? Do they matter? What is to be learned? What would God have us do? Given our times, what does responsible citizenship entail?

The deeper issues raised by contributors to this volume demand that we continue the conversation started by the signatories. We now turn to these critical issues.

SOULCRAFT AND STATECRAFT: WHAT DOES THE LORD REQUIRE?

Time does not allow an in-depth examination of each of the eleven essays included in Part One. This constraint is unfortunate because each essay is deserving of consideration. Following, therefore, is a brief summary of each.

1. "Politics and Forgiveness: The Clinton Case." Jean Bethke Elshtain, professor of social and political ethics at the University of Chicago, laments the fact that we are awash in confession these days—in its low form, such as on day-time television talk shows, and in its slightly higher form, such as in bookstores. Public integrity has given way to what Prof. Elshtain calls "contrition chic,"[4] meaning a "bargain-basement way to gain publicity, sympathy and even absolution by trafficking in one's status as victim or victimizer."[5] What Prof. Elshtain calls for (and rightly so) is that we distinguish between instances of "contrition chic" and serious acts of public or political forgiveness.[6] This is a necessary first step. The second step is that we examine with clearheadedness and justice the relationship between contrition/forgiveness and the rule of law.[7] That is, when the person seeking forgiveness is not simply a "private" person but the holder of an office, what rules should pertain in evaluating when forgiveness wipes the slate clean?[8] Public repentance—and forgiveness—of a political figure cannot be simply a matter of words because "forgiveness" leaves unresolved a whole series of complex political and legal questions that relate to the person's ability to carry out the duties of his or her office.[9] As Prof. Elshtain reminds us, nothing is "private" about the President's recent bizarre behavior. A secretary, friends, cabinet members, loyal supporters, a team of lawyers, public resources, and even the President's wife were all brought into the orbit of deceit and cover-up. Because the President went before ministers of God and sought absolution, the religious community must scrutinize—and adjudicate—his political use of religion.

2. "Broken Covenants: A Threat to Society." Max Stackhouse, professor of Christian ethics at Princeton Theological Seminary, is concerned about the President's violations of public covenants, particularly since Mr. Clinton freely used the notion of "covenant" in his first campaign to become President and then, unaccountably, abandoned it once in office. Because of the public nature of covenants, Stackhouse believes it to be a tragic error to view social relationships, ethics, and political life in terms of a public-versus-private

dichotomy. The idea of covenant not only portrays God's relationship to his people but also is the model for responsible participation in all spheres of public life.[10] It is legitimate to ask publicly if the President—who has violated the marriage covenant—violated his pledge before God and the American people to uphold the Constitution when he lied in a legal deposition in a civil court, not to mention his orchestration of a grand web of deceit that entailed lawyers, members of his cabinet, advisors, and close friends with whom he violated personal covenant.[11]

3. "Why Clinton Is Incapable of Lying: A Christian Analysis." Duke University ethicist Stanley Hauerwas posits that to be a liar is something of a "moral achievement" insofar as a lie "at least must pay homage to some notion of the truth."[12] But because American politics no longer presumes to be about truth in any shape or form, we therefore get the politicians we deserve. For Hauerwas, the fact that President Clinton has no sense that a public sin requires public penance should not be all that surprising because "American Protestantism has no sense of it either."[13] Alas, confession, repentance, and reconciliation would entail that the church be a disciplined community, which it is not; thus, for Hauerwas, the question is not whether Bill Clinton should be impeached but why he is not excommunicated.[14]

4. "President Clinton and the Privatization of Morality." Matthew L. Lamb, professor of theology at Boston College, observes that the privatizing of morality follows on the privatizing of religion; thus, we are reaping what we have sown in the public domain. The result is what Michael Sandel has called procedural liberalism. The American version of privatized morality, for Lamb, is rooted in a twofold abandonment. Gone is the classical insistence on moral and intellectual virtues among citizens and politicians. Gone, as well, is the Judeo-Christian affirmation of theological virtues—faith, hope, and charity—that buttress the other virtues in the face of evil and widespread injustice.[15] One of the strengths of Catholic moral theology, as Father Lamb reminds us, is that it prevents the divorce of public and private morality.

5. "Missing the Point on Clinton." In a letter to the editor reprinted from *The Christian Century*, Don Browning, professor of religious ethics at the University of Chicago and frequent contributor to *The Christian Century*, is under obligation to state even as a professing "liberal Democrat" that the publication's editorials "are not providing the churches with the leadership" on moral issues that they need.[16] For Browning, editor James Wall's plea to call off the impeachment process avoids the deeper issues that are stake and is extremely disheartening.

6. "Dawdling toward Judgment: The Impeachment Issue and the Perennial Problems of Casuistry." John Lawrence, professor emeritus of philosophy at Morningside College, examines the moral schizophrenia of the American public as exemplified by Mr. Clinton's consistently high ratings despite the embarrassing nature of revelations about his personal behavior. Lawrence sees this schizophrenia as rooted in conflicting religious agendas—one "prophetic" and the other "pastoral," one condemning while the other tending to be sympathetic.

7. "Confession and Forgiveness in the Public Sphere: A Biblical Evaluation." In perhaps the most penetrating essay in this volume, Robert Jewett, professor of New Testament Interpretation at Garrett Evangelical Theological Seminary, asks whether President Clinton's confessional speeches on television and at the "Prayer Breakfast" have any place in the political arena. Ready answers to this question, of course, have been provided by people such as Jesse Jackson, Philip Wogaman[17] (Mr. Clinton's pastor), and James Wall of *The Christian Century*, who cite King David as a model for forgiveness. For Jewett, a biblical scholar, comparisons to King David are illegitimate and thus require more careful exegesis. Nowhere do the Scriptures suggest that sincerity of confession relieves persons of consequences or legal liability; much to the contrary.[18] In noting the symbiotic relationship between forgiveness and honor, Jewett wonders whether the public should continue to honor someone whose political tenure is marred by repeated lying—and wholesale dishonor.[19] Without honor, "there is no possibility of maintaining a democratic system of government, which requires a relationship of 'trust and trustworthiness'[20] between leaders and the public."[21] The sincerity and depth of Mr. Clinton's contrition, as reflected in the President's "Prayer Breakfast" speech, are telling for Jewett. In delineating his priorities, the President announced, "First, I will instruct my lawyers to mount a vigorous defense using all available, appropriate arguments."[22] At the same time, denials issuing from White House lawyers were positively Orwellian. Consider, for example, the statement issued on September 12, the day after the President's "Prayer Breakfast": "It is, however, the President's good faith and reasonable interpretation that oral sex was outside the special definition of sexual relations provided to him."[23] Thus, in reality, the President dispatches his lawyers to deny what in fact the confession seems to admit. Religion, in the end, would appear to be no more than propaganda, with its own cadre of "useful idiots" to serve as priests.[24]

8. "How Shall We Respond to Wrongdoing? Is Moral Indignation Permissible for Christians?" The essays by Elshtain and Jewett notwithstanding, perhaps the best piece of clear thinking in this volume comes from Klyne Snodgrass, professor of New Testament Studies at North Park Theological Seminary. Concerned over the ease with which we dispense forgiveness in therapeutic culture, Snodgrass poses a disturbing question. Had Mr. Clinton, the chief executive, sexually wronged one of our own daughters, we would not treat his violation of public office lightly. But for those who care about how society functions, is moral condemnation, with its attendant consequences, allowed only when we are personally violated? If not, what then distinguishes the President from Slobodan Milosevic, aside from technicalities, legal posturing, and a photogenic face?[25] In the end, to fail to respond to Mr. Clinton's moral failure is to lower the standards for all of society.[26]

9. "A Biblical Perspective on the Forgiveness Debate." Troy Martin, associate professor of religious studies at St. Xavier University, examines the scriptural basis for forgiveness. Three inescapable elements are to be detected.

First, confronting and holding the offender accountable must precede forgiveness. Second, thoroughgoing repentance is requisite. And third, responsibility for an unrepentant offender must be committed to God. Martin finds the forgive-and-forget mentality that characterizes national discussions of forgiveness to be utterly bankrupt.

10. "African-American Pastoral Theology as Public Theology: The Crisis of Private and Public in the White House." The reader is unsure what to do with this essay, contributed by Edward Wimberly, a professor of pastoral care and counseling at the Interdenominational Theological Center. Wimberly attempts, somewhat unsuccessfully, to add the element of race to the discussion. This argument might be in part because of Mr. Clinton's concerted attempts to draw support from the African-American community, which in the end might be tempted to feel betrayed by the President.

11. "Christian Doctrine and Presidential Decisions." Editor Gabriel Fackre, professor emeritus of Christian theology at Andover Newton Theological School, is struck by the diversity of doctrinal positions represented among the Declaration's signatories. The unity of this diverse lot is nevertheless rooted in the classical Christian understanding of the church's relationship to the powers, and it is the wisdom of this historic understanding that should serve as a present guide.

DISSENTING FROM THE DECLARATION:
WHAT SOME DO NOT REQUIRE

Augmenting this volume are six essays by people who purposely did not sign the Declaration: Nicholas Wolterstorff of Yale, John Burgess of Pittsburgh Theological Seminary, Lewis Smedes of Fuller Seminary, William Buckley of the *National Review*, Glen Stassen of Fuller Seminary, and Donald and Peggy Shriver of Union Seminary in New York City.

To the credit of the editor, allowance was made in the volume for these expressions of dissent. Unfortunately, these contributions, despite the authors' good intentions, are riddled with muddled ethical thinking and sloppy sentimentalism. Tragically, the line of thinking adopted in this group of essays proves disastrous when translated into public policy. Even more tragically, the worst of the essays are written by people who should know better; three of them are Christian ethicists and a fourth is a professing evangelical who teaches philosophy at an elite institution and who has maintained an extremely high visibility in the academy.

Four of the six dissenters express outrage over Special Prosecutor Kenneth Starr[27] and other people such as William Bennett[28] or Henry Hyde,[29] in addition to groups such as the Christian Coalition[30] and the National Rifle Association.[31] The dissenters think that such individuals and groups, not the President, constitute the real problem. Glen Stassen resurrects racism as the real national problem being obscured by our obsession with Mr. Clinton.[32] Donald and Peggy Shriver are put off that people are so sanctimonious as to question the President's sincerity of contrition; meanwhile, Kenneth Starr is the real "abuser of power."[33] Lewis Smedes would remind us of Teddy

Roosevelt's "obscenely obsessive love of war, any war," which surely was "a character defect most unwanted in a national leader."[34] Moreover, the difference between Mr. Clinton's sins and those of other presidents, according to Smedes, is "not that his are qualitatively worse but that we all know about his, and the public did not know about the sins of the others."[35]

Perhaps the most disappointing of the six dissenting responses is that of Nicholas Wolterstorff, who teaches philosophical theology at Yale. Wolterstorff writes,

> Clinton's self-recognition of doing wrong implies that, in this case, we are not confronted with a person with low moral standards. We are confronted instead with a quite extraordinary case of weakness of will, at least when it comes to sexual temptation . . . But rather than finding the President unusually corrupt on this point . . . , I must say that I find him all too human—no different from most of us in his attempt to conceal what he knew was wrong and shameful.[36]

To ensure that he is not misunderstood, Wolterstorff reiterates:

> To say it once more: who of us, having done something shameful that we recognize to be wrong, would want it to come to light? My view, then, is that we should be gratified by Clinton's recognition that what he did was morally wrong, and [we] should accept with gratitude his repentance and expression of repentance rather than reacting with sour grumpiness. . . .[37]

Remarkably, Wolterstorff goes so far as to make the following rather breathtaking statement: "I submit that one cannot determine a person's moral standards just from observing what he or she does."[38] In the end, Wolterstorff is optimistic about the future: "My own prediction is that Clinton's immoral sexual behavior will have no abiding effects whatsoever on our civil life—nor will his perjury, if perjury it proves to be."[39]

SOULCRAFT AND STATECRAFT:
WHAT DO COLUMNISTS REQUIRE?

With the final group of essays, the reader is pulled out of a depression that has set in as a result of the previous six readings. Theologically speaking, it is a sad state of affairs when op-ed writers seem to have a better grasp of religion, ethics, and politics than do Christian ethicists and philosophers. Stephen Carter[40] challenges the "moral sloppiness" of Mr. Clinton's defenders, who have reminded us *ad nauseum* that this is a privacy issue. Carter goes so far as to say that adultery itself "is ultimately a public wrong."[41] Additionally, Carter directly challenges Mr. Clinton to abandon his bad habit of resorting to legalism, obfuscation, and blaming others for his humiliation.[42]

Andrew Sullivan, former editor of *The New Republic*, is troubled by a President who exhibits little personal integrity and yet orders cruise missile strikes against terrorist countries (Sudan and Afghanistan).[43] Should a

President who lies to the nation be trusted with acts of war? Sullivan, a Brit, frames the issue rather bluntly:

> If the most accomplished British prime minister in history were shown to have lied directly and knowingly to the House of Commons, he would still have no choice but to resign. But in many respects Clinton has done far worse than this. He has lied baldly to his own party, to his own staff, to members of Congress, to the representatives of the legal system, and, in the most direct and unmistakable terms, to the American people. He has lied under oath, and he has lied when he has had no need to whatsoever. He even lied when he semi-apologized last Monday, in saying his testimony in the Jones suit was legally accurate.[44]

No saint himself,[45] Sullivan is forced to ask, "At what point does one begin to balk at this kind of cynicism and to regard it not simply as contemptible in itself but as a corrosive force in the culture as a whole?"[46]

The final contribution to the volume is by Shelby Steele, a fellow at Stanford's Hoover Institution. His brief but brilliant piece, "Baby Boom Virtue," is a reprint of an earlier column published in *The New York Times*.[47] Steele believes that the retention of Mr. Clinton's unusually high approval ratings is due to the inherent bifurcation of baby boomer morality, whereby identifying with political and social causes, not personal morality, is the defining feature of a person's character. Thus, Mr. Clinton consistently scores high points regarding women's issues, race and affirmative action, sexual freedom, and health care. The virtue-by-identification formula is able to work wonders; it produces ideas that resonate while creating a virtual "good" in which private moral responsibility is of secondary importance. But, as Steele notes, the current state of politics could not have been made possible without a generational corruption that allowed virtue to be achieved by mere identification.

CONCLUSION: WHAT DOES THE LORD REQUIRE?

This volume was both a delight and an outrage to read. Between the front and the back covers one learns both how to do and how not to do ethics responsibly. Happily, the former far outweighs the latter. Yet, both aspects make the volume an excellent starting-place from which to think about issues of soulcraft and statecraft. Issues raised by the contributors demand our thoughtful and ongoing reflection. Do we hold public officials accountable— at all? On what basis? By what standard? What about public covenants? Should public office-holders be held to a higher standard (or a lower standard) of accountability? What about the public-private dichotomy? Who will address this issue and on what grounds? How does the Christian community handle the social effects of sinful acts in the political sphere? And what about the manipulation of religion and religious categories for political purposes? How should the religious community respond when such instances occur, especially when they are thrust in our cultural face?

Judgment Day at the White House can be highly recommended for the classroom, for discussion groups, and for private reading. Several of the volume's contributors believe that the events of the last eighteen months constitute no less than a watershed for this nation. Such might not be the case, but then again, if it is, a considerable burden rests on the shoulders of those of us who are called to teach and to train others—whether in our families, our classrooms, or our churches. Dissecting the relationship between statecraft and soulcraft has always been sticky business, and Protestant evangelicals, in recent history, have not been particularly adept at this task (as exemplified by the fact that relatively few evangelicals end up doing social and public policy work). Nevertheless, we must wrestle with what, in fact, the Lord does require of us at this cultural moment. What does faith require of the Christian in the public square? And in the present context, what does statecraft require of soulcraft?

Contributors to this volume have rendered a supreme service. Their burden is that after the dust of the current administration settles, the fundamental issues themselves will not fade away. May the questions they set before the wider Christian community be much on our minds, so that with prophetic wisdom, knowing and understanding the times like the sons of Issachar, we might respond accordingly.

ENDNOTES

1. G. Fackre, ed., *Judgment Day at the White House: A Critical Declaration Exploring Moral Issues and the Political Use and Abuse of Religion* (Grand Rapids: Eerdmans, 1999).
2. According to Maureen Shea in the White House's Office of Public Liaison, the White House chose participating clergy to attend this event.
3. Emphasis mine.
4. Fackre, *Judgment Day*, 11.
5. Ibid.
6. Ibid.
7. Ibid.
8. For John Paul II, who barely survived an assassin's bullet, to "forgive" the assassin is extraordinary when compared to the therapeutic nonsense that masquerades as "forgiveness" in America these days. Yet, this instance, as remarkable as it is, falls outside of the rule of law.
9. Fackre, *Judgment Day*.
10. Ibid., 23.
11. Ibid., 24–25.
12. Ibid., 28.
13. Ibid., 30.
14. Ibid., 31.
15. Ibid., 33.
16. Ibid., 39.
17. Wogaman made impassioned public statements to the effect that he "does not think the President should resign or be impeached. To demand either would

be judgmental because we are all sinners" (K. L. Woodward, "The Road to Repentance," *Newsweek*, 28 September 1998, 44).
18. Ibid., 65–67.
19. Ibid., 54–60.
20. Jewett is here drawing from the theme of Stanley Renshon's recent work, *High Hopes: The Clinton Presidency and the Politics of Ambition*, 2d ed. (New York/London: Routledge, 1998).
21. Fackre, *Judgment Day*, 58–60.
22. According to the transcript of the "Religious Leaders' Prayer Breakfast," reproduced in *Judgment Day*, 185–87.
23. "Response of President's Lawyers to Independent Counsel's Report," *The New York Times*, 14 September 1998, A14.
24. According to Philip Wogaman, the "Religious Leaders' Prayer Breakfast" was "almost uniformly positive and supportive" (cited by J. Purdue in "Forgiving a President: Religious Leaders Tell of Giving Clinton Absolution After Prayer Breakfast Confession," *Northern Illinois Conference United Methodist Reporter*, 25 September 1998). United Methodist Bishop James K. Matthews told reporters, "There seemed to be a mood there that morning to offer him absolution; and, indeed, when I spoke to him personally, I did speak words of absolution to him," while James Forbes, pastor of Riverside Church in New York City, could gush that this was "a holy moment . . . I have never seen anything like this in public life" (cited by Jewett in Fackre, 64 n. 31).
25. Fackre, *Judgment Day*, 81–82.
26. Ibid., 74–75.
27. Ibid., 117 (Wolterstorff); 145 (Beckley); 154, 157 (Stassen); 163 (Shrivers).
28. Ibid., 116 (Wolterstorff).
29. Ibid., 113 (Wolterstorff).
30. Ibid., 133 (Smedes).
31. Ibid., 133.
32. Ibid., 158–59.
33. Ibid., 163.
34. Ibid., 132.
35. Ibid.
36. Ibid., 112 (emphasis mine).
37. Ibid., 114 (emphasis mine).
38. Ibid.
39. Ibid., 116.
40. Carter's contribution, "Lies That Matter" (169–72), originally appeared in the Sunday edition of *The New York Times*, 23 August 1998. Carter teaches law at Yale University and is the author of *Civility: Manners, Morals, and the Etiquette of Democracy* (New York: Basic Books, 1998).
41. Fackre, *Judgment Day*, 170.
42. Ibid.
43. It was not by accident that commentators drew parallels with *Wag the Dog*, a film in which war is invented by spinmeisters to counter a presidential sex scandal.
44. Fackre, *Judgment Day*, 174.
45. As the former managing editor of *The New Republic*, Sullivan was not averse to using his bully pulpit to agitate for normalizing homosexual relations.
46. Fackre, *Judgment Day*, 175.
47. Shelby Steele, "Baby Boom Virtue," *The New York Times*, 25 September 1998.

PART 2

HISTORICAL PERSPECTIVES ON POLITICS AND PUBLIC POLICY

An Overview

It would probably be difficult to overestimate the influence of the French reformer John Calvin upon the Protestant Reformation and its heritage of the last 450 years. Regardless of whether one agrees with his thought, either as a whole or in particulars, it is very hard to ignore it. In this essay, G. Joseph Gatis explores Calvin's political theory and the effects of it on Geneva and upon subsequent thinkers. He argues that, contrary to the belief of many, Calvin supported a doctrine of separation of church and state, not separation of religion and state. Calvin had a well-thought-out political theory that advanced a distinction between church and state, upheld checks and balances, supported submission of citizens to the state, and proclaimed the state's responsibility to God. Calvin opposed the propagation of Christianity by means of the sword, and he upheld the right of Christians to protest. Because Calvin took politics and public policy seriously, attempting to integrate it into the Christian worldview, he serves as a model for contemporary Christians to study in both his actions and his thoughts.

Chapter Six

THE POLITICAL THEORY OF JOHN CALVIN

G. Joseph Gatis

THE WELL-KNOWN FRENCH REFORMER John Calvin advanced a doctrine of separation of church and state, not separation of religion and state. Because God is sovereign, Calvin postulated that He should rule both church and state because both of them are religious entities predicated on God's authority, even though the two structures are distinct organizations. The state rules the church's environs, maintaining domestic tranquillity so that the church can execute its mission to evangelize and make disciples of all citizens. By fostering the maturity of its Christian flock, the church nurtures the state by producing model citizens; thus, church and state are mutually inclined. The state is to have jurisdiction over temporal matters, and the church is to have jurisdiction over doctrinal and spiritual matters, although both entities are to be religious. Theocracy and religiosity were fundamental to Calvin's Reformed society because be believed that the entire state should be ruled by God, draw its laws from God, and be devoted entirely to Him.[1] Calvin's political theory includes a distinction of church and state, checks and balances on power, the citizen's submission to the state, and the state's responsibility to God.

CALVIN'S THEORY OF CHURCH AND STATE

Although church and state are to be distinct, Calvin said that their spheres overlap. The church of Geneva was ruled by a representative body, the consistory. Nine pastors, elected by their several congregations, deliberated as men of the cloth; twelve elders and four syndics (executives), elected democratically by all church members, represented the church. To hold any office, of course, a person had to be a church member in good standing. Voting was a right accorded on the basis of good standing within the church.

Ecclesiastical and political dimensions of the Genevan community interacted. Ecclesiastically, in the exercise of church discipline, the consistory—nominated and elected by the church—could punish only by keeping people from the sacraments. If individuals were not sufficiently penitent, they were excommunicated, that is, kept from the sacraments (but still allowed to attend services) until they mended their ways.[2] Politically, the impenitent were then remitted to the care of the small council. Three democratically elected bodies ruled the Genevan city-state: the two hundred-member lower council, the council of sixty, and the council of twenty, also called the small council. The lower council, elected by the populace, elected the council of sixty, and the council of sixty elected the council of twenty, which possessed executive power to punish impenitents. The small council sentenced people to fines, the stocks, imprisonment, banishment, or, as a last resort, execution.

When the Genevan consistory asked Calvin to contribute to the city's codification efforts regarding new laws and edicts, he turned to the Roman *Corpus Juris Civilis* for a model of contract law, property law, and judicial procedure.[3] In the humanist tradition of the day and at the suggestion of his friend Guillaume Bude, Calvin expanded his legal studies to include other literature. Bude showed Calvin that a study of law and *bonare litterae* (a humanist slogan for good literature) could complement each other.[4] Calvin's theory of law, then, grew with his exposure to legal sources, good literature, and the Bible, but ultimately, the Bible was his final legal sourcebook.

In Calvin's view, the civil magistrate has the authority to enforce both tables of the Ten Commandments—that is *pietas* and *aequitas*.[5] The authority of fathers over their wives and children,[6] monogamy,[7] duty of paternal care for families,[8] breastfeeding,[9] obligation of promises,[10] the need for more than one witness in the case of murder,[11] the prohibition of incest,[12] adultery,[13] slavery,[14] and respect for the old[15]— in Calvin's thinking, all of these obligations derive from natural law as well as biblical law.[16]

According to Calvin, a symbiosis of purpose exists between church and state, but they also have distinction of purpose. The state sets the stage for the church, and the church does not obstruct the state.[17] Calvin held that state and church were mutually religious because the state adjudicated temporal matters under God opposing evil. Evil—spiritual, social, doctrinal, moral, and temporal—is the common enemy that unifies the two divinely instituted bodies. In Calvin's vision, a society that was composed of a Reformed church comprised of Reformed citizens was a fist that beats back the world and all of its evil manifestations spiritually, morally, culturally, legally, and politically.[18]

Calvin, therefore, envisioned church and state as a united force that protects the people. Van Ruler contends that according to Calvin, the state's vision and *raison d'être* derives from the church: "The state must have some vision, some insight into the truth, into the essence of things."[19] Van Ruler says that Calvin saw the church's influence on the state in terms of the First Commandment, the imperative of which encompasses both church and state: "Yahweh . . . tolerates no other gods beside him. He demands an exclusive obedience of the whole man and his whole life. This has an immediate impact on all aspects of political life."[20] God demands an obedience that circumscribes every facet of human existence-sociology, law, government, and politics as well as religious belief and ritual.

Calvin's view of the relationship uniting church and state is neither Erastian nor "ecelesiocratic" because both schemes deny reciprocity. Erastus advanced the notion that the church is an arm of the state, such as in Henry VIII's Supremacy Act. In an ecclesiocracy, however, the state is an arm of the church.

Church officials, using state institutions, run society—that is, they raise and spend state revenue, settle disputes, provide for the common defense, and regulate the economy and social relations. Calvin envisioned neither. Rather, he envisioned a religious republic, both theocratic and theonomic. In a theocracy, God rules both the state and the church. In a theonomy, all law derives from God's law. Calvin viewed a Christian state as God's rule by God's law.

Calvin did not insist, however, that all Mosaic judicial law should be enacted and enforced.[21] Instead, he denounced totalitarian theonomists of his day who insisted that the "political system of Moses" was mandatory for civil government.[22] If those who represented Geneva's citizenry voted to enact the entire "political system of Moses," Calvin would not have opposed them because he saw the "political system of Moses" as an ideal but not mandatory requirement for a Reformed state. Calvin viewed the Mosaic political system as ideal because it was inspired by God.

Calvin said that the state is a religious entity and, hence, is a stabilizing force in society. This view is recorded in book four of his *Institutes:* "The External Means or Aids by Which God Invites Us into the Society of Christ and Holds Us Therein." In McNeill's edition, however, only thirty-five pages deal with the state, a meager seven percent of the work, with the remaining part of book four discussing the role of the church.[23]

Calvin wrote of the need for constancy in applying law: "When laws are variable, many are necessarily injured, and no private interest is stable unless the law be without variation; besides, when there is liberty of changing laws, license succeeds in place of justice."[24] Rewards and punishments are "part of a well-ordered administration of a commonwealth." He interpreted the term *praise* (Rom. 13:1–7) according to its Semitic biblical origins, noting that its meaning is varied.[25] Calvin saw the term "praise" as general benefit, including protection and prosperity.

In sum, Calvin viewed both church and state as unified by the overarching purpose of arresting evil but separated by a porous membranes—a membrane dividing their respective functions into spheres, one sphere focusing on the spiritual, the other on the temporal. To Calvin, church and state were to be two hands washing each other under God.

CALVIN'S THEORY OF CHECKS AND BALANCES ON POLITICAL POWER

Calvin said that tyranny is the demon that stalks the state, seeking to possess it. Tyranny threatens whenever power is in the hands of the few. To him, power unchecked is power unjustified because he believed that too often power, especially absolute power, has corrupted those who hold it. According to Calvin, absolute power can become so corrupting that those in power cannot call themselves ministers or servants of God (Rom. 13:4, 6). In such a case, the powerful sink to a level where there is "no trace of that minister of God, who had been appointed to praise the good, and to punish the evil." Calvin said state officers are good, though evil might eclipse the good to such an extent that the officers are no longer a moral force.[26]

Calvin noted the danger of entrusting power to one or a few; therefore, he argued for a "system compounded of aristocracy and democracy."[27] McNeill believes that Calvin's reference to the "rule of principal persons" does not refer to blood aristocracy but rather to those chosen by their fellows.[28] To Calvin, the presence of any hereditary ruling caste is an infringement of liberty.[29] Even judges do not escape unscathed.

> It is much more endurable to have rulers who are chosen and elected . . . and who acknowledge themselves subject to the laws, than to have a prince who gives utterance without reason. Let those to whom God has given liberty and freedom (franchise) use it . . . as singular benefit and a treasure that cannot be prized enough.[30]

Calvin saw as the highest good a state that is governed by elected representatives. "I readily acknowledge that no kind of government is more happy than this, where liberty is regulated with becoming moderation and properly established on a durable foundation (ad diuturnitatem)."[31] In February 1560, on the eve of an election, Calvin pleaded with the General Assembly "to choose [their magistrates] with a pure conscience, without regard to anything but the honor and glory of God, for the safety and defense of the republic."[32] Because he believed that the republic was the highest form of government, the highest form of loyalty to a nation was that given to a Christian republic.

In Calvin's thinking, theocracy and democracy are "easily and naturally associated."[33] The civil government has the God-given burden of maintaining peace and tranquillity so that the church can flourish: "Yet civil government has as its appointed end, so long is we live among men, to cherish and protect the outward worship of God, to defend sound doctrine of piety and the position of the church, to adjust our life to the society of men, to form our social behavior to civil righteousness, to reconcile us with one another, and to promote general peace of tranquillity."[34]

Calvin, however, included within the state's ambit the defense of "sound doctrine," an arrangement that might seem strange today but that was the norm in Calvin's time.

> Let no man be disturbed that I now commit to civil government the duty of rightly establishing religion, which I seem above to have put outside of human decision. For, when I approve of a civil administration that aims to prevent the true religion which is contained in God's law from being openly and with public sacrilege violated and defiled with impunity, I do not here, any more than before, allow men to make laws according to their own decision concerning religion and the worship of God.[35]

Neither did the reformer advocate that governments necessarily enact all of the Old Testament judicial laws.[36] In fact, as was already noted, he denounced the radical theonomists of his day who insisted that the "political system of

Moses" was mandatory for civil government.[37] Mosaic judicial law was the ideal but not an immediate requirement.

For Calvin, the highest form of political development is representative democracy modeled on the biblical example. "In this consists the best condition of the people, when they can choose, by common consent, their own shepherds; for when any one by force usurps the supreme power, it is tyranny, and when men become kings by hereditary right, it seems not consistent with liberty."[38] In his lectures on Amos 7, Calvin rebuked civil authorities in England and Germany,[39] saying that Henry VIII, as the self-appointed head of the church, was a "blasphemy." Neither should princes in Germany "become chief judges as in doctrine as in all spiritual government," but rather, they should support the church, using their temporal power to "render free the worship of God."[40] When a city-state comes under the influence of God's Word, then that body is held to a higher function. "When a city becomes renowned for having received the Word of God, the world will reckon that the city ought to be, as a result, so much better governed, that such order will there prevail as to accord right and justice to one and all."[41]

The Reformation did not originate the political theories that dominated the seventeenth and eighteenth centuries, but it did accelerate and intensify the growth of theories already in existence.[42] Early in the Reformation, the monarchs of Spain, France, Scotland, the Netherlands, and, to some extent, England were polemic Roman Catholics ready to stamp out Protestantism. The Reformation began at the local level, among estates, cities, provinces, and the nobility; as it expanded, it enveloped those who opposed all absolutist practices. The thought of absolutism was present in the writings of both the Renaissance and the Reformation.[43] The Reformation had to contend with proponents of absolutism, who rejected its pluralism,[44] preferring instead to believe in one God, one king, one creed, and one law.[45]

A variety of theorists argued for the sovereignty of the people in contradistinction to the sovereignty of a monarch, including Marsilius of Padua, Occam, Ptolemaeus of Lucca, Bartolus, Gerson, d'Ailly, and Cusanus.[46] Each of these men taught that under natural law the people's sovereignty is protected by a political contract that binds both ruler and subjects.[47] Italian humanists saw the self-governing city-state as a breeding ground for antimonarchist tendencies. Machiavelli, for instance, argued that "where there are many states, there arise many efficient men; where the states are few, the efficient men are rare."[48] The Italian humanists wanted to restore the Republica Romana, a state where people were free. Martin Bucer, a contemporary of Machiavelli, desired a restoration of the early Israelite confederacy before the kingdom of Saul, the state of a free people.[49] The reformation at Strasbourg mirrored the paradigm shift of the Italian city-states, Nuremberg and Strasbourg being economically self-sufficient as well as self-governing German city-states.[50]

According to Bucer, the existence of *magistratus inferiores* (i.e., of self-governing city-state authorities) is a product of a historical political development directed by God. Any overlord attempting to limit the authority of minor powers is acting against the will of God. All minor authorities must protect and beautify the Sparta entrusted to them by God against encroachments of a higher power that threatens true religion.[51]

Bucer wrote that "wherever absolute power is given to a prince, there the glory and the dominion of God is injured. The absolute power, which is God's alone, would be given to a man liable to sin."[52] He recognized the benefits of husbanding one's resources in times of need, reminding his readers that the Roman republic allowed for dictatorial emergency powers when that was necessary.[53] Calvin agreed with Bucer.

Because the absolute power of princes diminishes the sovereignty of God, grounds for limiting the princes are religious.[54] If the power over others is hereditary, then the prince's capacity to judge according to God's judgment is limited.[55]

> There ought to be room for divine selection of those whom God will place at the helm of the state, and whom He benefits with the spirit of His wisdom. Elective monarchy, and not a hereditary kingdom, is the constitution favored by religion. This, stated Bucer, would be the ideal order of a state: either one or a few men would have the power; but these men ought to be designated by God. They would govern on the basis of a legal order. Absolute power would not be conferred on any ruler.[56]

Israel's offer of a throne to Gideon, who had rescued the nation, was justified, but conferring royal power by hereditary right to Gideon's family was impious.[57] Calvin later argued for the *magistratis populares*, the leaders elected by the people for the people.[58]

Calvin urged moderation on a sovereign, remarking that "no virtue is so rare in kings as moderation, and yet none is more necessary; for the more they have in the power, the more it becomes them to be cautious lest they indulge their lusts, while they think it lawful to desire whatever pleases them."[59]

Moreover, he warned them not to be ruled by their subjects. "Thus princes also who are not free agents through being under the tyranny of others, if they permit themselves to be overcome contrary to their conscience, lay aside all their authority and are drawn aside in all directions by the will of their subjects."[60] Calvin voiced his approval of classical republican traditions.

> Inasmuch as God had given them the use of the franchise, the best way to preserve their liberty for ever was by maintaining a condition of rough equality, lest a few persons of immense wealth should oppress the general body. Since, therefore, the rich, if they had been permitted constantly to increase their wealth, would have tyrannized over the rest, God put a restraint on immoderate power by means of this law.[61]

Calvin did not identify an ideal way to govern, nor did he denounce the monarch, recognizing that good government was a prerogative of kings (as he exhorted Francis I). However, Calvin's frequent disparagement of ungodly kings, as in his sermons on Job (in 1554) and Deuteronomy (in 1554–55) and his lectures on Daniel (in 1561), do comprise convincing denunciations of "kings" in general.[62] He cannot be regarded as a monarchist, for ample evidence indicates that he was not.

People's vices and inadequacies make it safer and better that the many (plures) hold sway (gubernacula). Thus may rulers help each other, teach and admonish one another, and, if one asserts himself unfairly, act in concert to censure, repressing his willfulness (libidinem).[63] Calvin differed from Aquinas, who in the second chapter of The Governance of Princes argues for a monarchy for the sake of national unity, and to remove the danger of the many tyrannizing the few.[64]

Calvin viewed 2 Thessalonians 3:15 as evidence of the virtue of "fraternal correction." In his thinking, mutual admonition provides checks and balances against arrogance. He believed in it so thoroughly that he had "fraternal correction" incorporated into the constitution of the church at Geneva. In 1557, Calvin influenced the small council, the chief deliberative body for civil government, to admonish the recalcitrant in secret quarterly "fraternal charity" sessions.[65]

> For the condition of the people most to be desired is that in which they create their shepherds by general vote. . . . When anyone usurps the supreme power by force, that is tyranny. In addition, where men are born to kingship, this does not accord with liberty. Hence, the prophet says [Mic. 5:5], we shall set up princes for ourselves; that is, the Lord will not only give the church freedom to breathe, but also institute a definite and well-ordered government, and establish this upon the common suffrages of all.[66]

Calvin might have agreed with Knox's statement: "To bridle the fury and rage of princes in free kingdoms and realms . . . it pertains to the nobility, sworn and born to be councilors of the same, and also to the barons and people, whose votes and consent are to be required in all great and weighty matters of the commonwealth."[67]

Samuel warned Israel that an absolute monarch with judicial, legislative, and executive powers would oppress the people. In his first proposition, Samuel contended "and this will be the manner [mispat] of the king that shall reign over you" (1 Sam. 8:11 KJV; Calvin translated mispat with the French "puissance," implying that he saw the word in terms of a legal right).[68]

CALVIN'S THEORY OF THE CITIZEN'S RELATIONSHIP TO GOVERNMENT

Regardless of the particular form of government, in Calvin's view all subjects of that state are responsible for their own obedience. "Subjects should be led not by fear alone of princes and rulers to remain in subjection under them (as they commonly yield to an armed enemy who sees that vengeance is promptly taken if they resist), but because they are showing obedience to

God himself when they give it to them; since the rulers' power is from God."[69] Because a ruler's authority is from God, his citizens are obliged to obey the ruler, no matter what his character might be. "I am not discussing the men themselves . . . , but I say that the order itself is worthy of such honor and reverence and that those who are rulers are esteemed among us, and receive reverence out of respect for their lordship."[70] "We are not only subject to the authority of princes who perform their office toward us uprightly and faithfully as they ought, but also to the authority of all who, by whatever means, have got control of affairs, even though they perform not a whit of the princes' office."[71]

Calvin viewed the higher authorities as having been "placed there by the Lord's hand" and rebellion against these authorities as rebellion against God Himself. "He who attempts to invert the order of God, and thus to resist God himself, despises his power; since to despise the providence of him who is the founder of civil power, is to carry on without him." The purpose of these acts of providence is the "preservation of legitimate order."[72]

Magistrates have a duty to resist tyranny, but, in general, unjust rulers were to he viewed as a judgment from God. Drawing on Romans 13:3, Calvin exhorted his readers to accept that a wicked prince is the result of divine judgment visited on the governed as punishment for their sins. "For since the wicked prince is the Lord's scourge to punish the sins of the people, let us remember that it happens through our fault that this excellent blessing of God is turned into a curse."[73]

> There are indeed always some tumultuous spirits who believe that the kingdom of Christ cannot be sufficiently elevated unless all earthly powers be abolished, and that they cannot enjoy liberty given by him except they shake off every yoke of human subjection, This error, however, possessed the minds of the Jews above all others; for it seemed to them disgraceful that the offspring of Abraham, whose kingdom flourished before the Redeemer's coming, should now, after his appearance continue in submission to another power.[74]

Because rulers, whether good or evil, are appointed by the providence of God, Calvin did not promote revolution.[75] If benevolent, the ruler is a blessing; if not, the ruler is a curse. Nebuchadnezzar was still God's servant, even though he was an instrument of divine chastisement, one whom Calvin called a "pestilent and cruel tyrant."[76] When ruled by wicked persons, believers must not resist, but instead should consider their sins, repent, and implore divine help. Providence will lay proud tyrants low; moreover, God will raise up leaders who are His appointed instruments.[77]

In his commentary on Romans, written in 1539, Calvin forbade any "private man" from seizing government from a ruler who is appointed by God[78] as the "higher" power (Rom. 13:1–7); but people must obey the "highest" power, God, above any other (Acts 5:29).[79] Calvin's last edition of the *Institutes* gives biblical support for the contention that citizens' highest allegiance is to God, if God and government conflict (Dan. 6:22–23). Here, in Daniel 6, the king abrogated his right to reign by raising his hand against God. Hosea 5:11 points out that people who submit to the religious decrees of an idolatrous king have merited God's condemnation.

The duty and responsibility of popular magistrates is to protect people from the license of kings. Calvin applauded the ephors of Sparta, the demarchs of Athens, and the tribunes of Rome for their observance of this principle. To Calvin, elected leaders have not only the right but also the obligation to oppose an idolatrous king's violence and cruelty. For a king to "betray the liberty of the people" is a "nefarious perfidy."[80] Calvin believed that lower magistrates, when confronted with a choice between obeying God or obeying a higher magistrate, should obey God.

Calvin believed that the lower magistrates of England, Scotland, Sweden, Denmark, Norway, Poland, Bohemia, Hungary, and Spain; the diets of the Swiss confederation; and the imperial diets of Germany should assume the role of the Spartan ephors, thus limiting the tyranny of idolatrous kings.[81] Although citizens must submit to government, Calvin said that these magistrates should not "wink at kings who violently fall upon and assault the lowly common folk."[82] McNeill remarks that in "all these European organs of quasi-representative government [Calvin] saw at least the possibility of some guarantee of liberty and security for the people."[83] This rationale for political resistance inspired John Knox, John Ponet, Christopher Goodman, and Samuel Rutherford in their moves against the state and its spiritual profligacy.

John Knox, Christopher Goodman, and John Ponet, three adherents of the Reformation in Scotland, contended that God's people, like the Israelites of the Old Testament, are in covenant with God to defend true worship both by doctrinal persuasion and political/military power.[84] This Scottish triumvirate argued that the magistracy, nobility, and estates are commanded by God to execute all idolaters, including kings.[85] Goodman wrote, "First we may hereof justly conclude, that to obey man in any thing contrary to God, or his precepts though he be in highest authority, or never so orderly called there unto . . . is not obedience at all, but disobedience . . . there is no obedience against God which is not plain disobedience."[86]

For what is King, Queen, or Emperor compared to God? Of the which we may justly conclude, that by the ordinance of God, no other kings or Rulers ought to be chosen to rule over us, but such as will seek his honor and glory, and will command and do nothing contrary to his Law. . . . But if they will abuse his power, lifting themselves above God and above their brethren, to draw them to idoatrie, and to opresse them, and their contrie: then are they no more to be obeyed in any commandments tending to that end. . . . For the same God commanded Moyses to hange up all the capitaynes and heads of the people, for that by their example they made the people idolaters also: he had no respect to their authorities because they were Rulers, but so muche the rather woulde he have them so sharplie punished, that is, hanged agaynst the sunne without mercy.[87]

Both Goodman and Knox contend that negatively the ruler's duties prevent harm to God's people; positively, the rulers root out evil and repudiate "all forms of idolatry and tyranny." Therefore, the duty of rulers is to become Christians and actively, by force if necessary, to enforce the law of God in their domains. Because each nation is in covenant with God, each citizen is obliged by a sacred duty not only to disobey passively but also to resist actively and to remove all idolatrous or tyrannical magistrates.[88] Therefore, failure to resist idolatrous rulers was covenantal disobedience, and all covenantal disobedience merits divine punishment. As Ponet warned, if subjects submit to "idolaters and wicked livers, as the papists," then God will punish them with famine, pestilence, seditions, and wars.[89]

In the same vein, Goodman warned that failure to remove all idolatrous and tyrannical rulers would bring "the great wrath of God's indignation."[90] According to Knox, failure to resist and remove is to conspire with princes, nobility, and evil people. God's vengeance will punish the whole nation, the governors and the governed, for "conspiring together against Him and His holy ordinances."[91] Therefore, in the opinion of Knox, Goodman, and Ponet, anything less than open rebellion constitutes submission. Submission is conspiracy, conspiracy is sin, and sin guarantees divine punishment.[92]

According to Woodhouse, Samuel Rutherford's *Lex Rex* was a Puritan response to John Maxwell's *Sacrosancta regum majestas*. Rutherford declaimed, "The Presbyterians hold (I believe with warrant of God's Word): if the king refuse to reform religion, the inferior judges and assembly of godly pastors and other church officers may refer; if the king will not do his duty in purging the House of the Lord, may not Elijah and the people do their duty and cast out Baal's priests?"[93] Later, he added, "And wherever God appointed a king, he never appointed him absolute and a sole independent agent, but joined always with him judges, who were no less to judge according to the Law of God (2 Chron. 19:6) than the king (Deut. 17:15)."[94]

The substance of Calvin's thinking about submitting to and resisting oppressive regimes is evident in the following statements.

> The reason why we ought to be subject to magistrates is, because they are subject to God's ordination. For since it pleases God thus to govern the world, he who attempts to invert the order of God, and thus to resist God himself, despises his power; since to despise the providence of him who is founder of civil power, is to carry on war with him.[95]

> For though the exploiting administration of earthly or civil rule be confused or perverse, yet the Lord will hive men to continue still in subjection. But when the spiritual government doth degenerate, the consciences of the godly are at liberty, and set free from obeying unjust authority; especially if the wicked and profane enemies of holiness do falsely pretend the title of priesthood to overthrow the doctrine of salvation.[96]

Therefore all dignity, which is appointed for maintenance of civil government, ought to be reverenced and had in honour. For whosoever he be that rebelleth against or resisteth the magistrate, or those who are appointed to rule, and are promoted unto honour, he would have no government. And such a desire tendeth to the disturbing of order. Yea, it shaketh and overthroweth all humanity.[97]

Christians are free to protest. However,

they may not boil over in anger, and match injury with injury . . . but strive to overcome evil with goodness. This does not prevent them from complaining of the injuries done to them, or from convicting the ungodly of their guilt, by summoning them before the judgment of God, provided that they do so with a calm mind and without ill-will or hatred.[98]

CALVIN'S THEORY OF THE RELATIONSHIP OF GOVERNMENT TO GOD

Calvin opposed the idea of forwarding Christianity by the sword.

Though godly kings defend the kingdom of Christ by the sword, this is done in a different manner from that in which worldly kingdoms are wont to be defended; for the kingdom of Christ, being spiritual, must be founded on the doctrine and power of the Spirit. In the same manner, too, its edification is promoted; for neither the laws and edicts of men, nor the punishments inflicted by them, enter into the consciences. Yet this does not hinder princes from accidentally defending the kingdom of Christ; partly, by appointing external discipline, and partly, by lending their protection to the Church against wicked men. It results, however, from the depravity the world, that the kingdom of Christ is strengthened more by the blood of martyrs than by the aid of arms.[99]

Magistrates, too, are subject to God's glory. "We know how earthly empires are constituted by God, only on the condition that he deprives himself of nothing, but shines forth alone, and all magistrates must be set in regular order, and every authority in existence must be subject to his glory."[100]

Lewis Mumford, cited by Graham, argues that one reason the Greek city-states failed was their lack of "moralized trade."[101] By contrast, Calvin's political theory includes a doctrine of moral trade, that is, economic transactions should be governed by God. Regarding usury, for instance, in Calvin's *Ecclesiastical Ordinances* of May 17, 1547, he wrote, "Let no one lend at usury or for profit higher than five percent, under penalty of confiscation of the principal, and of being assessed an arbitrary fine according to the requirements of the case."[102]

Sunday, the day of resurrection, was a day of rest by Genevan law. City ordinances prohibited work on Sunday and also prohibited celebrating festivals on Sunday, declaring that "this should be commanded district by district under penalty."[103]

Labor unions were forbidden. "Item: that no laborer nor other workers may plot together in order to divert the course of the above proclamations and ordinances, under penalty of being chastised according to the exigency of the case."[104] R. H. Tawney claims that the Venerable Company of Pastors in the Consistory freed the "cannon balls of Christian Socialism." Actually, none of the Consistory's policies were socialist. Unlike the Hutterites, who applied the principle of love to the common ownership of property, under Calvin's political theory, private property and business were regulated according to the Consistory's interpretation of Scripture.[105]

Government, endowed by God with the power of coercion (Rom. 13:1–7), is responsible to God. The phrase *minister of God* means, in Calvin's exegesis, one who is responsible, accountable, and answering to God.[106] Therefore, political authorities, regardless of how they are installed, must obey God. Their function is to be regulated by God, who communicates His manifold will to them by His Word.[107]

CONCLUSION

John Calvin, a man of his day, approached the matters of law, public policy, and political science from presuppositions different from those in present-day democracies. He did not distinguish religion from life. Religion is all of life, and all life is religion. Therefore, all life, law, and politics are pervaded by religion; they are not separate from it. Furthermore, Calvin did not approach politics from the perspective of Kantian dualism—the "noumenal" and "phenomenal" realms were both subject to God's law, a holy monism. The reformer said that law, whether moral, civil, or religious, derives from God, and God pervades all things. Calvin's view of the institutions of church and state, checks and balances on power, the citizen's relationship to government, and the government's relationship to God stem from his theological convictions.

Modern secularists will find Calvin's political views distant, almost otherworldly. He did not labor under the sacred/secular dualism that characterizes current prevailing cultural values. Although Calvin's premises might be considered outmoded today, his hatred of tyranny, love of limited government, and passion for justice are values not to be ignored.

ENDNOTES

1. John Calvin, *Institutes of the Christian Religion*, ed. John T. McNeill, trans. Ford Lewis Battles, 2 vols. (Philadelphia: Westminster, 1960), 4.20.9.
2. Ibid., 4.12.
3. Harro Hopfl, *The Christian Polity of John Calvin* (Cambridge: Cambridge University Press, 1982), 6–7.
4. Ibid., 7.
5. Ibid., 172.

6. John Calvin, *Commentaries* (Edingurgh: Calvin Translation Society, 1843–1859), 1 Corinthians 7:37; Ephesians 5:31; 1 Timothy 2:11–15; 5:8.
7. Ibid., Genesis 26:10; 38:24.
8. Ibid., 1 Timothy 5:8.
9. Ibid., Genesis 21:8 (primogeniture with some qualifications); Genesis 27:11.
10. Ibid., 1 Corinthians 9:1.
11. John Calvin, *Harmony of Moses*, 4 vols. (Edinburgh: Calvin Translation Society, 1843–1859), 3:45.
12. Calvin, *Commentaries*, Genesis 29:27; Calvin, *Harmony of Moses*, 3:20.
13. Calvin, *Commentaries*, Genesis 26:10; Calvin, *Harmony of Moses*, 3:77.
14. Calvin, *Harmony of Moses*, 3:18, 98.
15. Calvin, *Commentaries*, Genesis 12:15; Ephesians 6:1.
16. Hopfl, *The Christian Polity of John Calvin*, 180.
17. E. William Monter, "The Consistory of Geneva," *Enforcing Morality in Early Modern Europe* (London: Ashgate Publishing, 1987), 467–84.
18. Calvin, *Institutes of the Christian Religion*, 4.20.9.
19. Arnold A. van Ruler, *Calvinist Trinitarianism and Theocentric Politics—Essays Toward a Public Theology*, trans. John Bolt (Lewiston, N.Y.: Mellen, 1989), 157.
20. Ibid., 153.
21. Calvin, *Institutes of the Christian Religion*, 4.20.14, n. 36.
22. Ibid.
23. W. Fred Graham, "Calvin and the Political Order: An Analysis of the Three Explanatory Studies," in *Calviana: Ideas and Influence of Jean Calvin* (Kirksville, Miss.: *Sixteenth Century Journal* Publishers, 1988), 55.
24. John Calvin, "Commentaries on Daniel," in *On God and Political Duty*, ed. John T. McNeill (Indianapolis: Bobbs-Merrill, 1956), 92 (Lecture 28, Dan. 6:8–9).
25. Calvin, "Commentaries on the Epistle to the Romans," in *On God and Political Duty*, 86 (Rom. 13:3).
26. Calvin, *Institutes of the Christian Religion*, 4.20.25.27
27. Ibid., 4.20.7.
28. John T. McNeill, "Calvin and Civil Government," in *Readings in Calvin's Theology*, ed. Donald McKim (Grand Rapids: Baker, 1984), 273.
29. Ibid.
30. Jean Calvin, *Ioannis Calvini Opera Quae Supersunt Omnia. Ad Fidem*, ed. Guilielmus Baum, Eduardus Cunitz, and Eduardus Reuss (Brunsvigae: Appelhans & Pfenningstorff, 1890), 43:374.
31. Calvin, *Institutes of the Christian Religion*, 4.20.3.
32. McNeill, "Calvin and Civil Government," 274.
33. Ibid.
34. Ibid.
35. Calvin, *Institutes of the Christian Religion*, 4.20.3.
36. Ibid., 4.20.26, n.36.
37. Ibid., 4.20.26.
38. John Calvin, *Commentaries on the Twelve Minor Prophets*, 5 vols. (1846–1849; reprint, Grand Rapids: Eerdmans, 1948), 3:306–10.
39. Ibid., 2:349.
40. Ibid., 2:349–50.
41. Alastair Duke, "Calvin the Preacher-Extracts from 'Calvin's Sermons on Micah,'" in *Calvinism in Europe 1540–1610–A Collection of Documents* (Manchester: Manchester Univ. Press, 1992).

42. Hans Baron, "Calvinist Republicanism and Its Historical Roots," *Church History* 8 (1939): 32.
43. Ibid., 33.
44. Ibid., 34.
45. Ibid., 32.
46. Ibid.
47. Ibid.
48. Ibid., 33–34, and Machiavelli, *Arte della Guerra, in Opere* (Italy: 1813), 4:271.
49. Baron, "Calvinist Republicanism and Its Historical Roots," 36–37.
50. Ibid., 35.
51. Ibid., 36.
52. Ibid., 30–42; Martin Bucer, *In Librum Judicum Enarrationes* (Geneva: 1554), 448; cf. Martin Bucer, *Acta colloquij in comitjs Imerij Ratisponae habiti, hoc est articuil de religione conciliati, & non conciliati omnes, ut ab Imperatore Ordinibus Imperij ad iudicandum, & deliberandum propositi sunt (Argentorati [Per Vuendelinum Ribeliu]*, 1542.
53. Bucer, *In Librum Judicum Enarrationes*, 473.
54. Hans Baron, "Calvinist Republicanism and Its Historical Roots," 37.
55. Ibid., 37–38.
56. Ibid., 38.
57. Ibid., 30–42.
58. Ibid., 38.
59. Calvin, *Commentaries on Daniel*, 94 (Lecture 29, Dan. 6:8–9).
60. Ibid., 100–101 (Lecture 30, Dan. 6:16).
61. John Calvin, *Harmony of Moses*, 3:154.
62. McNeill, "Calvin and Civil Government," 270.
63. Calvin, *Institutes of the Christian Religion*, 4.20.8.
64. McNeill, "Calvin and Civil Government," 272.
65. Ibid.
66. Calvin, *Ioannis Calvini Opera Quae Supersunt Omnia. Ad fidem*, 43:374.
67. McNeill, "Calvin and Civil Government," 273.
68. Graham, "Calvin and the Political Order: An Analysis of the Three Explanatory Studies," 53; Keith W. Whitelam, *The Just King: Monarchical Judicial Authority in Ancient Israel* (Sheffield: JSOT, 1970). Whitelam traces the legal and political ideal through ancient Near Eastern cultures and concludes that "it was the kings' primary duty to guarantee the true administration of justice throughout the land. By so doing, this governed not only right social relationships, as expressed in the king's concern for the underprivileged, but also guaranteed prosperity and fertility for the nation as a whole." Whitelam derives his conclusion from the Mesopotamian sources of Ur-Nammu, Lipit-Ishtar, Eshnunna, the Syro-Palestinian sources of Alalakh, Ras Shamra, and the Yehimilk inscription, the Egyptian sources of the Kuban Stele of Rameses 11, the tale of Merneptah, the inscriptions of Mentuhotep, and, most importantly, those of the Babylonian king Hammurabi.

    According to Whitelam, sources of law in premonarchical Israel include family law, clan law, and sacral law. Adjudication occurred first with the *paterfamilias* in the patriarchally structured family. Aggrieved parties in family-level adjudication could appeal to the clan in rural settings or to the town in urban settings. Both clans and towns were ruled by regional councils of elders. Furthermore, aggrieved parties could appeal from clan- and town-level adjudication to the local Levitical priests.

On the one hand, Whitelam observed limitations on the authority of the *paterfamilias* based on Numbers 5:11–31; Deuteronomy 21:18–21; and 22:13–21. In the latter passage, the *paterfamilias* no longer has the authority to impose the death penalty (unlike Judah's authority to impose capital punishment on Tamar in Genesis 38). On the other hand, Whitelam underscores the apparent breakdown of family solidarity and prophetic rebuke in Isaiah 1:17; Jeremiah 7:6; and 22:13–21.

Extrapolating from the priest's judicial function in the case of undetected adultery (Num. 5:11–31) and the Urim and Thummim, Whitelam concludes that priests were a higher tier of judicial review.

69. Calvin, *Institutes of the Christian Religion*, 4.20.22.
70. Ibid.
71. Ibid., 4.20.25.
72. Calvin, *Commentaries on the Epistle to the Romans*, 84 (Rom. 13:1–2).
73. Ibid., 85 (Rom. 13:3–4).
74. Ibid., 83 (Rom. 13:1). Thomism requires submission to secular authorities. Aquinas argued that "our flesh was still in subjection; we can but await a freedom both of spirit and body, 'when Christ shall have delivered all the kingdoms to God the Father, when he shall have brought to nought all principality and power'" (Thomas Gilbey, *The Political Thought of Thomas Aquinas* [Chicago: University of Chicago Press, 1958], 157).
75. McNeill, "Calvinism and Civil Government," 268.
76. Ibid.
77. Ibid.
78. Ibid.
79. Ibid., 269.
80. Calvin, *Institutes of the Christian Religion*, 4.20.31; and McNeill, "Calvin and Civil Government," 270.
81. McNeill, "Calvin and Civil Government," 270.
82. Calvin, *Institutes of the Christian Religion*, 4.20.31.
83. McNeill, "Calvin and Civil Government," 270.
84. John Knox, *The First Blast of the Trumpet against the Monstrous Regiment of Women* (Geneva, 1558); idem, *Appellation to the Nobility, and Estates of Scotland* (Geneva, 1558); Christopher Goodman, *How Superior Powers Ought to Be Obeyed of Their Subjects, and Wherein They May Lawfully by God's Word Be Disobeyed and Resisted* (Geneva, 1558); and John Ponet, *A Short Treatise of Politick* (Strasbourg, 1556).
85. Carlos M. N. Eire, *War Against the Idols: The Reformation of Worship from Erasmus to Calvin* (Cambridge: Cambridge University Press, 1986), 301; Richard L. Greaves, "John Knox, the Reformed Tradition, and the Development of Resistance Theory," *Journal of Modern History* 48 (September 1976): supplement; "Calvinism, Democracy, and the Political Thought of John Knox," Occasional Papers of the American Society for Reformation Research 1 (December 1977): 81–91; Robert Linder, "Pierre Viret and the Sixteenth-Century English Protestants," *Archiv für Reformationgeschichte* 58 (1976): 149–70; Dan G. Danner, "Christopher Goodman and the English Protestant Tradition of Civil Disobedience," *Sixteenth Century Journal* 8 (1977): 61–70; Leo F. Solt, "Revolutionary Calvinist Parties in England Under Elizabeth I and Charles I," *Church History* 28 (1958): 234–39; and Marvin Anderson, "Royal Idolatry: Peter Martyr and the Reformed Tradition," *Archiv für Reformationgeschichte* 69 (1978):157–70.

86. Goodman, *How Superior Powers Ought to Be Obeyed, cited in Edmund S. Morgan,* ed., *Puritan Political Ideas, 1558–1794* (Indianapolis: Bobbs-Merrill, 1965), 2; cf. Eire, *War Against the Idols—The Reformation of Worship from Erasmus to Calvin,* 302.
87. Goodman, *How Superior Powers Ought to Be Obeyed,* cited in Morgan, *Puritan Political Ideas, 1558–1794,* 4–5, 11; and Eire, *War Against the Idols,* 302.
88. Goodman, *How Superior Powers Ought to Be Obeyed,* 180; John Knox, "The Appellation from the Sentence Pronounced by the Bishops and Clergy," in *The Works of John Knox,* ed. David Laing, 6 vols. (New York: AMS, 1966), 4:505; and Eire, *War against the Idols,* 302–3.
89. John Ponet, "A Short Treatise of Politicke Power," reprinted in W. S. Hudson, *John Ponet, Advocate of Limited Monarchy* (Chicago: 1942), 176, 178.
90. Goodman, *How Superior Powers Ought to Be Obeyed,* 11, 93.
91. Knox, *Application to the Nobility and Estates of Scotland,* 4:498.
92. Eire, *War Against the Idols,* 303.
93. A. S. P. Woodhouse, ed., *Puritanism and Liberty—Being the Army Debates (1647–1649)* (reprint, London: Dent, 1938), 199–200.
94. Ibid., 202.
95. John Calvin, *Commentaries on the Book of Romans* (Grand Rapids: Baker, 1981), 19:478 (Rom. 13:1).
96. John Calvin, *Commentaries on the Book of Acts* (Grand Rapids: Baker, 1981), 19:318 (Rom. 13:1).
97. Ibid., 18:318 (Acts 32:5).
98. Ibid.
99. Ibid., 19:318 (John 18:36).
100. Calvin, *Commentaries on the Book of Daniel,* 101 (Dan. 6:16).
101. W. Fred Graham, *The Constructive Revolutionary: John Calvin and His Socio-Economic Impact* (Atlanta: Knox, 1971), 116.
102. Ibid., 119.
103. Ibid., 128.
104. Ibid., 142.
105. Ibid., 144.
106. John Calvin, *Commentaries on the Book of Romans,* 19:481 (Rom. 13:1).
107. Ibid.

An Overview

Dietrich Bonhoeffer was a patriotic German and a Lutheran pastor and theologian who became deeply disturbed over the activities of Hitler's Nazi regime. He was so disturbed that he participated in the resistance activities against Hitler and knew of the conspiracy to assassinate him; therefore, the Nazis imprisoned and executed him. Bonhoeffer's story is a significant historical and theological case study on the ethics, limits, reasons, and boundaries of political action. He acted not because he believed it was his choice, but because he believed it would be immoral for him *not* to act. In this essay, Jean Bethke Elshtain explores the religious and philosophical environment that led to Bonhoeffer's actions. When political claims of nation-state sovereignty collide with theological claims of God's sovereignty, Christians must seriously consider the ramifications and application of Christianity. Whether we agree or disagree with the perspective and actions of Bonhoeffer, his life and death are solemn reminders that the cost of following Jesus Christ is very high and that the truths of Christianity have serious ramifications.

Chapter Seven

BONHOEFFER AND THE SOVEREIGN STATE

Jean Bethke Elshtain

THE DECISION TO ATTEMPT THE ASSASSINATION of Hitler, to "cut off the head of the snake," was difficult for many of the conspirators involved in the 1944 "July 20th Plot." But it was particularly tormenting for the Lutheran pastor Dietrich Bonhoeffer, who had long felt the attraction of pacifism and who had planned a sojourn in India with Gandhi. Some of Bonhoeffer's later readers have looked to his writings for a general rationale for opposing tyrannical power even to the point of violence. But they have been disappointed because Bonhoeffer never penned a full-fledged justification of his determination to resist.

In part, I think, Bonhoeffer refrained from writing such a justification because he feared that it might be taken as grounds for resistance in situations less dire than his own: if hard cases make bad law, extreme political situations set bad precedents for everyday situations. And in part, of course, he could not write it because his Nazi executioners did not give him time. But we may gain an understanding of just how desperate Bonhoeffer saw his situation to be if we examine certain key themes in his writings: his tantalizing and underdeveloped notion of responsibility, his concept of deputyship, and, especially, his historical analysis of the growth of modern adoration for sovereignty—of the entwining in the Enlightenment of sovereignty over the nation and the sovereignty of the self. We may even gain from such an examination a general understanding of what, for Bonhoeffer, we must—or must not—render unto Caesar.

Bonhoeffer saw himself as a faithful follower of Luther in his refusal of what Germans were asked to render to their terrible Caesar. Any reduction of Luther's doctrine of the "Two Kingdoms" to a notion that there are two spheres—"the one divine, holy, supernatural, and Christian, and the other worldly, profane, natural, and unchristian"—Bonhoeffer held to be a vulgarization. The modern reading of the Two Kingdoms—a reading shaped (Bonhoeffer would say deformed) by the Enlightenment—unwittingly finalized the separation of Christian concerns from the secular and profane. "On the Protestant side," he wrote, "Luther's doctrine of the Two Kingdoms was misinterpreted as implying the emancipation and sanctification of the world and of the natural. Government, reason, economics, and culture arrogate to themselves a right of autonomy, but do not in any way understand this autonomy as bringing them into opposition to Christianity." Over time, the Lutheran misunderstanding of Luther contributed to the Enlightenment cult of reason and the emergence of the self-mastering self.

With that triumph came an idolatrous faith in progress that could result only in nationalism—the "Western godlessness" that became in modern times its own religion. In the "apostasy of the Western world from Jesus Christ," a massive defection from our collective recognition of finitude, we abandoned the knowledge that we are creatures as well as creators. This, for Bonhoeffer, is the backdrop to twentieth-century totalitarianism, a terrible story of what happens when we presume to stand alone as Sovereign Selves within Sovereign States, a terrible story of what happens when individual hubris meets nationalism.

Bonhoeffer was no simplistic basher of modernity. He understood the impossibility of undoing the Enlightenment and recovering the premodern world. But he believed that we could tame and chasten modern profanations—including the notion that human beings are sovereign masters, unencumbered in their sway. The key seems to be a recognition of the ironic reversal that follows the enthronement of reason. The Enlightenment proclamation of man as the rational master and unlimited sovereign of his own fate contrasts oddly with Nazi invocations of "the irrational, of blood and instinct, of the beast of prey in man," but the Nazi invocations succeeded, in part, primarily because appeals to reason, human rights, culture, and humanity—appeals that "until very recently had served as battle slogans against the Church"—could not succeed in Nazi Germany. Such appeals depended for their success upon a culture upheld by the very church that had been weakened and compromised. The uninhibited "Will to Power" that constitutes totalitarianism is born from sovereign and unlimited reason, but reason itself gets battered and bloodied when sovereignty goes too far, when it refuses to acknowledge a limit.

It is in the ironies of the French Revolution, especially, that Bonhoeffer saw the first joinings of freedom and terror, a terrible godlessness in human presumption of godlikeness. Man begins to adore himself. He denies the Cross, denies the Mediator and Reconciler. He is avid in his regicide, idolatrous in his deicide. The radical, Bonhoeffer declared, has fallen out with the created world and cannot forgive God His creation.

Thus it is that those who deify man actually despise him. God, who does not deify man, loves human beings and the world: "man as he is; not an ideal world, but the real world. . . . He does not permit us to classify men and the world according to our own standards and to set ourselves up as judges over them." But this is precisely what the deifiers of human sovereignty do: they become their own standard, with the result that human beings devour themselves. Western godlessness underwrites the triumph of modern totalizing ideologies that recognize no limits.

The confluent forces of post-Enlightenment politics—the self-sovereignty of both the self and the state—deepened the overall quotient of "folly" in the human race. Demagogues found it all too easy to play to human weakness. Weak human beings are ripe for mobilization, ever susceptible to becoming tools in the hands of tyrants. "Any violent display of power, whether political or religious, produces an outburst of folly in a large part of mankind," wrote Bonhoeffer. Exploiters and charlatans arise. Often, they do only limited damage, but when they triumph, as they had in Bonhoeffer's time and place, traditional ethical responses seem inadequate to oppose them.

A review of the history of modern sovereignty and the nationalism to which it gave rise might help us understand the virulent political idolatry that Bonhoeffer faced. The answer to the question of what makes a nation-state a state at all is a sovereignty that is self-proclaimed and duly recognized. The proclamation alone won't do; recognition must follow. Hegel's bloody-mindedness about war as the definitive test of a state's existence is a culmination of the state system that triumphed with the 1648 Treaty of Westphalia. As every first-year student of political history learns, Westphalia marks the codification of the nation-state precisely because it constitutes the *recognition* of such states. With sovereignty, rulers and states take unto themselves powers previously reserved to the Sovereign God. Too often, no longer seeing nations under God's judgment, they proclaim the state the final judge of its own affairs. Indeed, claims to state power as dominion, a notion essential to early modern theories of state sovereignty, were parasitic upon older proclamations of God's sovereign power.

That God is Sovereign, the Progenitor and Creator, is central to Hebrew and Christian metaphysics. From God's sovereignty comes the "right of dominion over his creatures, to dispose and determine them as seemeth him good," writes Elisha Coles in his 1835 *Practical Discourse of God's Sovereignty.* "There can be but one infinite; but one omnipotent; but one supreme; but one first cause; and He is the author of all."

John Murray, speaking at the First American Calvinistic Conference in 1939, noted that "the moment we posit the existence of anything independent of God in its derivation of factual being, in that moment we have denied the divine sovereignty. . . . The moment we allow the existence of anything outside of His fiat as its principle or origination and outside of His government as the principle of its continued existence, then we have eviscerated the *absoluteness* of the divine authority and rule."

God's right is coterminous with His power; it is a right of dominion, rule, and possession in which human beings are subject to the sovereignty of the God who misses nothing and attends to everything. And yet, although this vision dominated "sovereignty talk" for centuries, it ironically helped establish the modern nation-state. Sovereignty migrated, so to speak, from God's domain—or a particular version of it—to a domain devised by man and arrogated unto himself. When modern man forgot that he was not God, as Václav Havel recently put it, "sovereign mastery" was the name he gave this forgetfulness.

Consider Jean Bodin's claim: "Sovereignty is that absolute and perpetual power vested in a commonwealth which in Latin is termed *majestas*." Or consider the claim of Thomas Hobbes, one of the most canny and most inventive of all sovereign-discoursers:

> [T]he only way to erect such a Common Power . . . is to conferre all their power and Strength upon one Man, or upon one Assembly of men, that they may reduce all their Wills . . . unto one Will . . . as if every man should say to every man, "I Authorize and give up my Right of Governing my selfe, to this Man, or to this Assembly of men, on this condition, that thou give the Right to him, and Authorise all his Actions in like manner." . . . This is the Generation of that great Leviathan, or rather (to speak more reverently) of that Mortall God, to which we owe under the Immortal God, our peace and defence. . . . And he that carryeth this Person, is called Soveraigne, and said to have Soveraigne Power; and ever one besides, his Subject.

Hobbes enumerates the sovereign's rights and powers: to judge all opinions, to name all names, to defend all as "a thing necessary, to Peace, thereby, to prevent Discord and Civill Warre." Hobbes, Bodin, and a small army of legalists helped to give the emerging centralized monarchies a basis in legal and political theory. But to do so, they also relied upon (and appropriated to their own purposes) a whole body of prestatist sovereign theory, some of it indebted to elaborate defenses of the power of the papacy (under the Sovereign God, I must add). As historian Antony Black puts it:

> It now seems clear . . . that much of this was already created for them by papal theory. Certainly long before this period, Roman imperial doctrine had been used by national kings and territorial princes to justify the overriding of positive laws and a centralized system of legislation and appointment. Papal doctrine both endorsed this . . . and also supplied something of the more abstract and more generally applicable notion of sovereignty which was to be fully developed in the works of Bodin.

The difference between earthly powers and God is that the earthly sovereign, although untrammeled in his power in the temporal space that is history, is subject to God's grace or punishment. But having taken unto himself all of the features of the Deity—including, in some sense, the creating of a perpetual earthly domain—the sovereign finds precious little constraint on his sovereignty. "Absolute sovereignty," the twentieth-century political theorist Raymond Aron writes, "corresponded to the ambition of kings eager to free themselves from the restriction Church and Empire imposed upon them, medieval residues. At the same time it permitted condemning the privileges of intermediate bodies: feudal lords, regions, cities, guilds— privileges which no longer had any basis if the sovereign's will was the unique source of rights and duties."

In sum, then, is that the Sovereign God gets displaced in the early modern theory of sovereignty, taking up residence at a much greater remove than He had for medieval Europeans, who incessantly enjoined God's sovereignty as a brake on the king's designs. (The medieval history of the authority of the church is another story. To say that the church was unhappy with the presuppositions codified at Westphalia is an understatement.)

But a second displacement occurs when, after the Treaty of Westphalia, even kings begin to find their sovereignty usurped by the political body over which they rule. Sovereignty shifts from king to state, and the state "can no more alienate its sovereignty than a man can alienate his will and remain a man," as Charles Merriam, a rather sober proponent of the classical theory, puts it. Jean-Jacques Rousseau protected sovereignty thus through his postulation of the inalienability of the general will: the state and sovereignty are one. Popular sovereignty is, if anything, even more absolute and terrifying than that of the king, if the French Revolution and its aftermath is any indication.

After Westphalia, then, sovereignty signifies the freedom of a sovereign entity to regulate its own affairs without interference. In the words of Supreme Court Justice George Sutherland, in the 1936 *U.S. v. Curtiss-Wright Export* decision, "Rulers come and go; governments end and forms of government change; but sovereignty survives. A political society cannot endure without a supreme will somewhere. Sovereignty is never held in suspense." All who speak of sovereignty seem to share a deep preoccupation with the notion of a unified will. As God's will is singular, so must be the will of the sovereign states, whether as Hobbes' Leviathan or Russeau's General Will.

This preoccupation with willing "the final say" is but one point in the discourse of sovereignty, but it helps us understand Bonhoeffer's principled, theologically grounded refusal to obey an idolatrous state and its utter abandon to the singular will of the leader. Bonhoeffer joined a violent revolt to defeat idolaters who travestied Christian values and authentic German patriotism. The Nazi Caesar asked Bonhoeffer and others to render too much.

For Bonhoeffer, what constitutes legitimate state authority is a concept of *deputyship*. Parents act in behalf of the children, but what they can and should do occurs within the bounded order of the family. Similarly, what the state can and should do occurs within the bounded order of political government. Responsible action flowing from legitimate authority is always limited. Bonhoeffer reminds us that "the term *state* means an ordered community; government is the power which creates and maintains order. . . . Government is divinely ordained authority to exercise worldly dominion by divine right. Government is deputyship for God on earth."

But modern Lutheranism—at least in Bonhoeffer's Germany—had acquired a notion of the "natural state through Hegel and romanticism" that makes of the state not so much the fulfillment of "the universally human and rational character of man, but of the creative will of God in the people. The state is essentially a nation-state." Thereby, the state becomes, as it was for Hegel, its own ground of being, "the actual subject or originator of . . . the people, the culture, the economy, or the religion. It is 'the real god'"—which makes it very difficult for the average citizen to see the state's coercive power directed against man.

The original Lutheran Reformation, however, in its return to Augustine, was a turn against such concepts of sovereignty, claims Bonhoeffer. Sin and the Fall are what make government necessary. As such, government is not that which helps the human person to flourish, and Luther insists on the restraints and limits of government. Government is indeed, Bonhoeffer declares, "independent of the manner of its coming into being." It is "of God," and an "ethical failure" on the part of government does not automatically deprive it of "its divine dignity." Thus, to say "my country, right or wrong," need not be an expression of political chauvinism so much as a tragic recognition that it is *my* country, right or wrong, and I am in some way responsible even as I am in some way beholden. Government's tasks are legitimate in certain limited ways, in Bonhoeffer's characterization. We owe obedience under normal circumstances.

We do not owe government our very selves, however, for it does not create us. It may curb, compel, and chastise us. Indeed, the individual's "duty of obedience is binding . . . until government directly compels him to offend against the divine commandment, that is to say, until government openly denies its divine commission and thereby forfeits its claims. In cases of doubt, obedience is required because the Christian does not bear the responsibility of government. But if government violates or exceeds its commission at any point—for example, by making itself master over the belief of the congregation—then at this point, indeed, obedience is to be refused, for conscience's sake, for the Lord's sake."

But we must not generalize from this dire circumstance a *duty to disobey*. Disobedience is always concrete and particular whereas "generalizations lead to an apocalyptic diabolization of government. Even an anti-Christian government is still in a certain sense government. . . . An apocalyptic view of particular concrete government would necessarily have total disobedience as its consequence; for in that case every single act of obedience obviously involves a denial of Christ."

This argument is very austere. Many people will argue that Bonhoeffer unacceptably downplays the good possibilities of states and that he sets up a too strenuous requirement once the threshold of disobedience is crossed. But it is very much in tune with Bonhoeffer's determination to explore the "in between" (in this instance, in between state idolatry and state diabolization). Action against an evil government is part of the realm of concrete responsibility, always undertaken in the "midst of the needs, the conflicts, the decisions of the immediate world around us from which there is no escape into general ideals and principles."

Bonhoeffer could never have made his peace with any regime that promoted rabid nationalism or that eclipsed the space for the free exercise of human responsibility—for in a "world come of age" human beings are called to account, and any system that demands the surrender of our identity to what Havel has called the "social-autotality" is an order whose claims on us are suspect. Neither could he support a regime that served cynicism; collusion in evil deeds; human isolation, desolation, and terror; or that worshipped history and power and accepted no brake by definition on its sovereign designs—for such a regime repudiates the Sovereign God who holds the nations under judgment.

For Bonhoeffer, I need not "wear myself out in impotent zeal against all wrong, all misery that is in the world." But neither am I "entitled self-satisfied security to let the wicked world run its course so long as I cannot myself do anything to change it and so long as I have done my own work. What is the place and what are the limits of my responsibility?"

Bonhoeffer leaves us with this question. We have no easy answers about what we must render, to whom, and under what circumstances. But we can at least banish the false pride that demands that we be "sovereign" in all things, even as we accept our real but limited responsibility.

In our tormented time, he wrote from prison, the church is an area of freedom, a repository of culture and quality and human decency. It can and should recover its links with the Middle Ages, Bonhoeffer told us, but he left tantalizingly under-developed (in the short time that he had left) what that recovery might entail. "Liberal theology" cannot help us here: "The weakness of liberal theology was that it conceded to the world the right to determine Christ's place in the world; in the conflict between the Church and the world it accepted the comparatively easy terms of peace that the world dictated. Its strength was that it did not try to put the clock back, and that it genuinely accepted the battle, even though this ended with its defeat."

There is ground left for the church, of course, but only in the light of the Christ who called human beings away from their weakness and to strength. To restore a rightful balance in the order of things, Bonhoeffer insisted that we participate in the powerlessness of God in the world as a from of life even as we acknowledge God's sovereignty over all of life. I suppose that this is what might be called Lutheran irony and it goes—as they say today—all the way down. Our adoration of sovereignty makes us weak; we have rendered altogether too much and we have gotten the Caesars we deserve. That is the solemn lesson that Dietrich Bonhoeffer left us.

An Overview

Twentieth century evangelical engagement in politics and public policy was sporadic and achieved mixed results. At times, the efforts were intentional; at other times, the absence of an evangelical presence was equally intentional. In this essay, originally delivered at a conference on evangelicals and politics at Union University, Michael Cromartie surveys the history of evangelical political activism in the twentieth century. The spectrum of apathy to activism is broad and the presuppositions are many. He describes the various social forces, cultural trends, and theological beliefs that shaped evangelical responses and reminds readers that responsibility in the arena of politics and public policy is an enduring challenge for Christians as they seek to follow Jesus Christ and apply Scripture to every area of life.

Chapter Eight

THE EVANGELICAL KALEIDOSCOPE
A Survey of Recent Evangelical Political Engagement

Michael Cromartie

IN A COVER STORY IN THE INFLUENTIAL literary magazine *The Atlantic Monthly*, liberal theologian Harvey Cox shares his observations on having been a visiting lecturer at Pat Robertson's Regent University in Virginia. Professor Cox was surprised to find that the conservative Christians at Regent University were not monolithic in their political views. He found that although fundamentalists, evangelicals, and charismatics are often lumped together in the press, they in fact "represent distinct tendencies that are frequently at odds with one another."[1]

Harvey Cox is not unlike many observers outside of the evangelical movement who are often surprised when they discover just how diverse evangelical intellectual opinions are on political and social issues. The late historian Timothy Smith described evangelicalism as being like a large "kaleidoscope"[2] that includes not only a diversity of denominations but also Christians from the political right, left, and center. Evangelicals are by no means monolithic in their political views. Although they have largely maintained an alliance with political conservatism, they do have a moderate, liberal, and left-wing contingent that has had an important influence.

Many political pundits and observers still believe that Christian conservatives represent a mass movement of cultural dinosaurs with religious views akin to what journalist H. L. Mencken called a "childish theology" for "half wits," "yokels," the "anthropoid rabble," or the "gaping primates of the upland valleys."[3] The Washington Post, although not as colorful as Mencken, more recently said that Christian conservatives were "poor, uneducated, and easy to command."[4]

Well, to the bewilderment of many people, the poor, uneducated, easy to command gaping primates from the upland valleys are still very much with us, and they have become a very large voting bloc.[5] Mencken said in 1924, "Heave an egg out a Pullman train window and you will hit a Fundamentalist almost anywhere in the United States today."[6] And if Mencken were living today he might put a different spin on it: "Heave an egg out a window anywhere on Capitol Hill today and you will likely hit an evangelical political activist." And although that activist is most likely to be a conservative politically, he or she might be just as mad at the Republican party as at the Democratic party.[7]

Political involvement by evangelicals once was seen as a worldly, or even sinful, activity. Now, political celibacy, if you will, is considered a dereliction of Christian responsibility. The change has resulted in American evangelicals creating a lively debate among themselves about social justice and the nature and extent of political involvement. My task is to present an overview of how these issues have developed and to highlight the diversity that resides within the conservative Protestant community on political and social questions. I will conclude with a few personal concerns about the public rhetoric of conservative Christians involved in the public arena.

For several decades in this century, from roughly 1925 until the end of World War II, a large sector of conservative Protestant social thought was influenced by a pessimistic form of dispensational eschatology and a pietistic individualism that looked with disdain on efforts to improve social conditions and political structures. Conservative Christians had originally believed that the process of secularization was simply irreversible, and this pessimism was reinforced by their premillennial theology.[8] But this had not always been the case.

Historian Winthrop Hudson wrote that as late as 1900 "few would have disputed the contention that the United States was a Protestant nation, so self-evident was the fact that its life and its culture had been shaped by three centuries of Protestant witness and influence."[9] Up until the Scopes Trial in Dayton, Tennessee, in 1925 (where a biology teacher, John Scopes, challenged a Tennessee law that banned the teaching of Darwinism), conservative Protestants had aggressively addressed almost every major social and political question in American public life. At the Scopes trial, William Jennings Bryan defended the Tennessee law and won, but his performance against American Civil Liberties Union (ACLU) lawyer Clarence Darrow was so embarrassing that it was ridiculed in the press, and he and fundamentalism lost in the court of public opinion. As George Marsden has pointed out, this result made it increasingly difficult to take conservative Protestantism seriously and caused evangelical and fundamentalist Christians to retreat from society and politics. Marsden points out that "within the span of one generation, between the 1890s and the 1930s, the extraordinary influence of evangelicalism in the public sphere of American culture collapsed. Not only did the cultural opinion makers desert evangelicalism, even many leaders of major Protestant denominations attempted to tone down the offenses to modern sensibilities of a Bible filled with miracles and a gospel that proclaimed human salvation from eternal damnation only through Christ's atoning work on the cross."[10]

The preeminence of conservative Protestant Christianity was challenged from all sides. Theological liberalism was growing in influence as it attempted to accommodate modern scientific thought with its theology. The fundamentalist-modernist controversy led to radically different understandings of salvation, evangelism, and the authority of Scripture. These disputes led to opposing views concerning the proper Christian response to social action and political activity. As theological modernists began to interpret the entire

Christian message in terms of its social implications, evangelicals and fundamentalists began to grow suspicious of social activism. Fundamentalist leader William Bell Riley labeled liberal understandings of the gospel a form of "social service Christianity."[11]

In theological circles was a controversial debate surrounding the redefinition of the Christian message led by leading liberal Protestant thinker Walter Rauschenbusch. His influential book *A Theology for the Social Gospel* (1917) challenged conservative Protestants for having an individualistic approach to personal salvation that neglected social reform. His concept of the social gospel was an attempt to enlarge and intensify the older message of salvation. He said, "The individualistic gospel has taught us to see the sinfulness of every human heart and has inspired us with faith in the willingness and power of God to save every human soul that comes to him. But it has not given us an adequate understanding of the sinfulness of the social order and its share in the sins of all individuals within it."[12] Rauschenbusch redefined sin to mean that it was selfish in its essence,[13] and he argued that the essential concerns of the gospel "lie on earth, within the social relations of the life that now is."[14] His strong critique of capitalism led him to believe that to renounce it in favor of socialism was to "step out of the Kingdom of Evil into the Kingdom of God."[15] His influence was far reaching, and his redefinition of the Christian meaning of salvation can still be seen in many of our mainline Protestant churches today.

The reaction of conservative Protestants to the influence of Rauschenbusch might be summarized by looking at two very different responses to the challenges of the social gospel. In an essay in the book *The Fundamentals* (1914), Princeton theologian Charles Erdman expressed his deep concern about the social gospel movement. He emphatically stated that it was dangerous to identify the Christian message with any political or economic system. He was especially concerned with the attempts by many people to identify socialism with Christianity. He cautioned that socialism could become a substitute religion that was hostile to Christianity and warned that although "the strength of socialism consists largely in its protest against existing social wrongs to which the Church is likewise opposed," these wrongs can be "finally righted only by the universal rule of Christ."[16] Erdman was critical of socialism, but he was emphatic that the Christian gospel should never be ultimately linked to any political or economic system.

But another outspoken fundamentalist critic was less nuanced. Presbyterian fundamentalist Carl McIntire constructed in his book *The Rise of the Tyrant: Controlled Economy vs. Private Enterprise* (1945) a more strident response to the growing social gospel movement. McIntire argued that capitalism, free enterprise, and individual liberty were "grounded in the moral nature of God. "The Bible, he said, "teaches private enterprise and the capitalistic system, not as a by-product or as some sideline, but as the very foundation of society itself in which men are to live and render an account of themselves to God."[17] McIntire even insisted that many, if not most, of the major figures of biblical history, including Abraham and Moses, had been capitalists.

We should note here, then, the diversity of evangelical and fundamentalist opinions concerning politics and economics, their varied responses to the challenge of the social gospel movement. It is clear, says Craig Gay of Regent College (in Canada), that "somewhere in between Charles Erdman and Carl McIntire a theological line had been crossed. Although Erdman had maintained the impossibility of identifying Christ with any particular political-economic system, McIntire had all but equated modern industrial capitalism with the will of God in the world."[18] This form of theological reductionism is ironic because it collapses economic and political concerns to a "this-worldly" level in an attempt to make the Christian faith relevant to the economic debate—the very charge leveled at leaders of the social gospel movement in its promotion of socialism.

In the early 1940s, a number of more moderate fundamentalists began to question the militant and confrontational style of fundamentalists such as McIntire. In 1947, Carl Henry published *The Uneasy Conscience of Modern Fundamentalism*. Its impact was significant. It was a clarion call for evangelicals to confront the modern world with a Christian apologetic that was intellectually respectable and socially responsible. According to Henry, the theological separatism of fundamentalism had led to a separation from cultural and social responsibilities and to a mistaken disengagement from the important issues of the day. This backlash reaction to the social gospel movement had created an almost complete avoidance of social programs and politics for fear of resembling the social gospel. This divorce between Christian proclamation and Christian compassion, Henry argued, was an abandonment of the clear mandates given by Scripture and church history. Henry condemned this tragic development in the strongest terms. He argued that "against Protestant fundamentalism the non-evangelicals level the charge that it has no social program calling for a practical attack on acknowledged world evils . . . on this evaluation, fundamentalism is the modern priest and Levite, by-passing suffering humanity."[19] He agreed that although capitalism was a superior economic system, that fact was no excuse for neglecting the clear biblical teachings regarding the duty and obligations of evangelicals toward social and political problems. He pointed out that "fundamentalism in revolting against the Social Gospel seemed also to revolt against the Christian social imperative."[20] Furthermore, he complained that fundamentalism "is a stranger, in its predominant spirit, to the vigorous social interest of its ideological forbears. Modern Fundamentalism does not explicitly sketch the social implications of its message for the non-Christian world; it does not challenge the injustices of the totalitarianisms, the evils of racial hatred, the secularisms of modern education, the wrongs of current labor-management relations, the inadequate bases of international dealings. It has ceased to challenge Caesar and Rome . . . The apostolic Gospel stands divorced from a passion to right the world. The Christian social imperative is today in the hands of those who understand it in sub-Christian terms."[21]

Parenthetically, on the fortieth anniversary of the founding of Fuller Seminary and the fortieth anniversary of the publication of his *Uneasy*

Conscience, Henry gave a lecture at Fuller where he remarked that looking back on his book two things surprised him: how little he had said and how boldly he had said it! But in that same lecture he admitted that one of the weaknesses of his book was that he "failed to focus sharply on the indispensable role of government in preserving justice in a fallen society. Essential as regenerative forces are to transform the human will, civil government remains nonetheless a necessary instrument to constrain human beings—whatever their religious predilections—to act justly, whether they desire to do so or not."[22]

Making connections between faith and politics was quite novel and, at the time, controversial among evangelicals. Neo-evangelical leaders such as Henry, E. J. Carnell, and Harold Ockenga had their persistent critics among separatist fundamentalists on their right. But critics began to form on their left as well. The many issues and questions raised by the political activism and social turbulence of the 1960s caused a further reexamination of evangelicalism's often cozy link to the establishment status quo.

A new younger generation of "radical evangelicals" felt that Henry and the neo-evangelicals had not gone far enough in their critique of capitalism and social injustices in American society. They accused the mainstream evangelical establishment of being "ideologically captive" to a "decadent American capitalist culture."[23]

The founding of the magazines *The Other Side* in 1965 and *Post American* in 1971 (renamed *Sojourners* in 1974) created forums for an ongoing critique of what the editors saw as a "truncated gospel" that neglected to attend to the abundance of biblical passages exhorting believers to seek justice for the oppressed and care for the poor. Jim Wallis, the editor of the radical evangelical magazine *Post American*, said in the first issue of that publication, "We have become disillusioned, alienated, and angered by an American system that we regard as oppressive; a society whose values corrupt and destructive. We have unmasked the American Dream by exposing the American Nightmare. . . our ethical revolt against systemic injustice, militarism, and the imperialism of a 'power elite, is accompanied by our protest of a technocratic society and a materialistic profit-culture where human values are out of place. . . Money is a measure of status and worth in a society of created needs and garbage heaps of wasted abundance in the midst of want; a society in which things are valued more than people. . . the ulcerating drive for air-conditioned affluence has not given satisfaction or fulfillment, but has instead, produced lives that are hollow, plastic, and superficial; characterized by economic surplus and spiritual starvation."[24]

Such pleas for compassion to the poor and the oppressed corrected a prior imbalance in evangelicalism's history. However, some of these calls for social justice on behalf of the poor and the oppressed almost always looked for statist solutions to these intractable problems without any consideration that the state might make matters worse. I want to emphasize that within the evangelical academic community (and the larger religious community as well there are some very strong differences exist regarding just what "social justice" is and to what extent and degree the state is ultimately responsible for maintaining it.

The early impact of the radical evangelicals was significant, as these magazines further pricked evangelicals' "uneasy conscience" on issues such as racism, sexism, and poverty. And their writers and editors played a vital role in the drafting of a landmark statement in 1973.

"Some day," wrote a reporter for the *Chicago Sun-Times* in December 1973, "American church historians may write that the most significant church-related event of 1973 took place last week at the YMCA Hotel on South Wabash."[25] There, some fifty evangelical leaders gathered for a two-day workshop that culminated in what became known as the "Chicago Declaration of Evangelical Social Concern." This significant statement on evangelical social responsibility was drafted and signed by evangelicals as diverse as Carl Henry, Frank Gaebelein, Vernon Grounds, Bernard Ramm, and younger self-styled "radical evangelicals" such as Ronald Sider (who had convened the meeting) and Jim Wallis, editor of *Sojourners*. "We affirm," the statement said, "that God lays total claim upon the lives of his people. We cannot, therefore, separate our lives in Christ from the situation in which God has placed us in the United States and the world. We confess that we have not acknowledged the complete claims of God on our lives."[26] The statement further emphasized that God requires His people to be loving, just, and abounding in mercy, but "we have not demonstrated the love of God to those suffering social abuses" and "have not proclaimed or demonstrated his justice to an unjust American society."[27] The declaration acknowledged the need for repentance from the racism, sexism, materialism, and militarism that afflicted the attitudes of the church and the nation.

The "Chicago Declaration" set the tone and themes for much that was to be written about evangelical social concern. It (along with the important publication of *Rich Christians in an Age of Hunger* by Ronald Sider[28]) put on the table for vigorous discussion the need for evangelicals to take just as seriously the admonitions in the books of Amos and Jeremiah as they do concerns for fulfilling the Great Commission. It also helped initiate a lively interaction of different Christian approaches to social ethics and sparked a healthy debate among, for instance, Anabaptist social ethicists and Reformed political philosophers.[29] And with the growth of the "health and wealth" gospel preached by many televangelists, radical evangelical writers sharpened dull consciences by calling their fellow Christians to simpler lifestyles, wiser stewardship, and compassion for the victims of poverty, racism, and other foes of social and political injustice. While statistically small in numbers, the influence of the radical evangelicals has been far greater than the credit they are often given. Their books and magazines provided an invaluable service in keeping evangelical leaders aware of the need to be compassionate toward the poor and the hungry.

This new interest in finding the proper balance between evangelism and social responsibility also had effects in the larger worldwide evangelical movement. The International Congress on World Evangelization in

Lausanne, Switzerland (July 1974), produced the significant document *The Lausanne Covenant*. *Time* magazine called the Lausanne Congress "possibly the widest ranging meeting of Christians ever held."[30] More than 2,700 participants attended from 150 nations and covered the whole spectrum of evangelical Protestant denominations. It was an international forum on world evangelization but the issue of Christian social and political involvement was debated vigorously. The drafting of Section 5 on "Christian Social Responsibility" sparked vigorous discussion among the international leaders at the Congress. The debate continued all day and night and was not settled until the early morning hours. The final version affirmed that "although reconciliation with man is not reconciliation with God, nor is social action evangelism, nor is political liberation salvation, nevertheless we affirm that evangelism and socio-political involvement are both part of our Christian duty. For both are necessary expressions of our doctrines of God and man, our love of neighbor and our obedience to Jesus Christ."[31]

But the biggest growth of evangelical political activity did not come as a result of reading passionate proclamations from statements drawn up at international congresses or declarations from Chicago. Edward Dobson, a former assistant to the Reverend Jerry Falwell, has said that Reverend Falwell realized how much potential there was to influence the political process in 1976, when, on his national television program, he criticized presidential candidate Jimmy Carter for giving an interview to *Playboy* magazine. Much to his surprise, Falwell soon received a call from the President's special assistant, Jody Powell, asking that he refrain from making such comments. "Back off," Powell said to him. Falwell was startled to find that what he said had caused such concern in the White House. He came to perceive this incident as his "initial baptism" into the world of politics.[32]

Many members of the evangelical Right had similar triggering experiences on a personal level, which left them obliged to become politically involved, something they had not been inclined to do previously, largely for theological reasons. Their emergence on the political scene in the late 1970s caught many journalists and public policy experts by surprise.

A standard sociological theory used to explain new social movements is what has been called the "status defense" theory. Theorists such as Daniel Bell, Seymour Martin Lipset, and Richard Hofstadter developed this view in the 1950s to explain the rise of McCarthysim and radical right groups such as the John Birch Society. It argues that the loss of economic and social status causes many people on the right to become involved in social and political movements. Daniel Bell observed in 1962, "What the right as a whole fears is the erosion of its own social position, the collapse of its power, the increasing incomprehensibility of a world—now overwhelmingly technical and complex—that has changed so drastically within a lifetime."[33] Similarly, social scientist Joseph Gusfield has argued in his study of the American temperance movement that moral reform campaigns were the result of a cultural group engaging in political action as a clear form of "status defense." He argued that a moral reform movement can acquire public affirmation of its own status if it can persuade the state to affirm and endorse its values."[34] Against status defense theories for the origins of social movements, I want to argue that it was a concern for their conservative Protestant subculture, rather than their social and economic status, that many people in the new Christian Right thought was in danger and that caused them to organize politically.

The original priority of religiously conservative leaders was not so much to persuade others of their views as it was to sensitize other evangelicals, fundamentalists, and charismatics to become involved in public issues that concerned them. It was not an easy task because many of them had been taught for decades that such activity was irrelevant and, in fact, unbiblical. But increasing pressures from a number of factors caused these evangelical leaders to feel, as sociologist Steve Bruce says in *The Rise and Fall of the New Christian Right*, that "they were not getting their due and their due could be got[ten] if they organized to claim it."[35]

And organize they did. Their effective use of television and direct mail, the declining membership of liberal denominations, and the increasing numbers within evangelical churches and denominations gave them confidence and combined to make political involvement appear to be a promising and worthwhile endeavor.

What stirred them most was a sense that various Supreme Court decisions were giving increasing power to the opponents of traditional Christian values. They became engaged in what Harvard professor Nathan Glazer has called a "defensive offensive"[36] against what they saw as an aggressive imposition of secular views on American society, including their own private communities of faith. They felt pushed into action against what they perceived as an aggressive imposition by secular forces bent on disrupting their enclaves of traditionally conservative Protestant faith.

In due course, religious conservatives began to be accused of "imposing their views" and "forcing their beliefs" on the community. But was this really the case? Gary Bauer, director of the Family Research Council, observed, "Our opponents will often picture us attempting to exert our values on the rest of society. I think the people we work with see what has happened in the last ten years as being more of a reaction of self-*defense* than as an effort to violate American pluralism."[37] Nathan Glazer made a similar observation more than fifteen years ago:

> Abortion was not a national issue until the Supreme Court, in 1973, set national standards for state laws. It did not become an issue because evangelicals and fundamentalists wanted to strengthen prohibitions against abortion, but because liberals wanted to abolish them . . . Pornography in the 1980's did not become an issue because evangelicals and fundamentalists wanted to ban D. H. Lawrence, James Joyce, or even Henry Miller, but because in the 1960's and 1970's under-the-table pornography moved to the top of the newsstands. Prayer in the schools did not become an issue because evangelicals and fundamentalists wanted to introduce new prayers or sectarian prayers—but because the Supreme Court ruled against all prayers.

Freedom for religious schools became an issue not because of any legal effort to expand their scope—but because the IRS and various state authorities tried to impose restrictions on them that private schools had not faced before.[38]

This imposition of a liberal ethos by what many social scientists have called the "new class elites" (made up of newspaper journalists, television producers and commentators, and the "knowledge class" from the universities) is what aroused many previously apolitical and socially indifferent evangelicals to action. Although many evangelicals have always found plenty about which to complain in the wider culture, the rapid changes in American society during the sixties and seventies sent shock waves through their community. Sociologist Steve Bruce has pointed out that "Conservative Protestants of the 1950s were offended by girls smoking in public." But by the late 1960s, "girls were to be seen on newsfilm dancing naked at open-air rock concerts."[39] In short, the era of Eisenhower's America was far different than the America of the 1960s and 1970s.[40]

Moreover, Bruce points out that "by the 1950s and the 1960s . . . the Supreme Court and the Congress were imposing cosmopolitan values on the South . . . in 1976, there were 77 federal regulatory bodies and 50 of them had been created since 1960 . . . at the same time the distinctiveness of regional culture had been threatened by the growth of national corporations, population movements caused by four wars, gradual concentration of the media. Putting it simply, the 'Bible Belt' was penetrated by cosmopolitan culture."[41] Or, as political analyst Kevin Phillips has put it, "the world of Manhattan, Harvard, and Beverly Hills was being exported to Calhoun County, Alabama, and Calhoun County did not like it."[42]

This concern about the secularized views of reality being promoted by cosmopolitan and elite culture was not the sole concern of only religious conservatives. The late social democrat Christopher Lasch made the following observation in the last book he wrote, *The Revolt of the Elites and the Betrayal of Democracy:*

> Our public life is thoroughly secularized. The separation of church and state, nowadays interpreted as prohibiting any public recognition of religion at all, is more deeply entrenched in America than anywhere else. Among elites it [religion] is held in low esteem—something useful for weddings and funerals but otherwise dispensable. A skeptic, iconoclastic state of mind is one of the distinguishing characteristics of the knowledge classes. Their commitment to the culture of criticism is understood to rule out religious commitments. The elites' attitude to religion ranges from indifference to active hostility.[43]

If Lasch's description is correct, then it would help explain why so many conservative Christians believe that they live in an environment totally devoid of and actively hostile toward their most fundamental Christian beliefs. As a result, they have formed and developed what William Kristol calls a "parallel culture"[44] that has been totally foreign to those who attend cocktail parties in New York and Washington. But that foreign parallel culture has become an avid curiosity for our national media as evidenced by frequent cover stories in our major news magazines.[45] In a cover story in a recent issue of *The New Republic*, Peter Beinart argues that those who are involved in the politics of the Christian Right believe that they are living in an alien environment that is radically different than the world in which they grew up. They believe that the "cultural liberalization" and the "cultural pluralism" of American society are undermining their schools and their homes.[46] "Time and again," writes Beinart, "Christian conservatives . . . described the same epiphany: the day they realized that the schools were not teaching with them but against them. Sometimes the epiphany was not about schools but about some other arm of the government . . . but the epiphany always involved an undermining of the home."[47]

It is hard to predict what the future holds for Christian conservatives who are involved in politics. It is clear that at some point, barring a revival and a reformation of the culture, they will have to face the fact that America will not soon become, as Irving Kristol has observed, "a twenty-first-century version of 'Our Town.'"[48] Meanwhile, they must develop what sociologist John Murray Cuddihy calls an "esthetic for interim" that encourages patience and "puts a band on all ostentation and triumphalism *for the time being*"[49] while working for what are often very lofty and seemingly insurmountable goals. As I have suggested, Christian conservatives who are involved in politics have been reactive and not proactive. They see themselves as defendants, not the aggressors, in the culture war. As a result, they became involved in politics for cultural reasons without seeking theological justification for that involvement until after the fact. One gets the impression that the underlying public philosophy for such activism is constantly evolving and is still being framed from election to election and issue by issue.

Arguably, this situation might explain why the political rhetoric of some religious conservatives reminds one of the careless and reactive language of fundamentalists from earlier in this century. Unfortunately, some evangelical leaders have at times been divisive and have used unnecessarily strident language toward their opponents—and even toward some of their natural allies.

Taking positions for righteousness in the public arena without being seen as self-righteous requires spiritual discipline and enormous effort. But it is an effort that must be made. Richard Mouw reminds us why: "The antithesis between godliness and ungodliness is very real; but it is discernible not only in the larger patterns of culture, but also in the inner battlegrounds of our own souls. How we speak and act faithfully in the larger public realm while working out our own salvation with the requisite fear and trembling—this challenge is of supreme importance for evangelicals as we think about the proper rhythms of the life of discipleship."[50]

Some leaders have expressed similar concerns about the public witness of

Christian activists. Ralph Reed, in his book *Active Faith*, dwells at length on the need for Christian activists to remember that they will be judged by God "not according to political victories . . . but by whether our words and our deeds reflect His love."[51] Whether Reed's advice will be heeded remains to be seen, but clearly, all Christian activists should display more epistemological humility, public modesty, and charity toward even their strongest opponents. Mark Noll challenges evangelical activists that they should never forget "that they are not God."[52]

He further warns, "A Christian politics that forgets the cross, a Christian politics that neglects the realities of redemption, a Christian politics that assumes a godlike stance toward the world, is a Christian politics that has abandoned Christ."[53]

It is strange that twentieth-century evangelical Christians would have ever needed to be convinced that they have a duty to be concerned about social problems. Their spiritual forebears always had been. The compassion and fervor of William Wilberforce and Lord Shaftesbury animated the campaigns against the slave trade and child labor in England. Such faith in action was the basis of many reform initiatives of the early nineteenth century.[54] According to American religious historian Grant Wacker, "evangelicals, seeking to be the moral custodians of the culture, have always known how to play political hardball when the prayer meeting let out."[55]

The intermingling of Christian faith with social and political concerns was always a part of our country's history. In his classic book *Democracy in America*, Alexis de Tocqueville wrote, "In the Middle Ages the clergy spoke of nothing but a future state. . . . But the American preachers are constantly referring to the earth, and it is only with great difficulty that they can divert their attention from it."[56] The claim that the faith of American Christians should always be only an intensely private affair between the individual and God would have been surprising news to such diverse persons as John Winthrop, Jonathan Edwards, Abraham Lincoln, the abolitionists, fifteen generations of the black church, civil rights leaders, and antiwar activists.

Therefore, religious values have always been a part of the American public debate. The argument should never have been whether evangelicals ought to be involved in social and political issues. Rather, the issue should be about what matters we should be most concerned and what are the most prudent ways to express such convictions. Our duty is to be concerned citizens, indeed, to strive, as Richard John Neuhaus has said, "to build a world in which the strong are just, and power is tempered by mercy, embraced, in which the weak are nurtured and the marginal and those at the entrance gates and those at the exit gates of life are protected both by law and love."[57]

Working for social and political change often requires the patience of Job because politics is, as Max Weber once said, "a strong and slow boring of hard boards."[58] Many evangelicals have learned that politics frequently requires prudent and principled compromise and that it is the art of the possible and not the reign of the saints. Some of them have come to realize that in the political realm even the most prudent Christian sometimes has to make choices between "relative goods" and "lesser evils." And some of them have even learned through the hard knocks of battles fought, victories won, and disappointments beyond measure that politics is, because of the effects of the Fall, "the method of finding proximate solutions to insoluble problems,"[59] as Reinhold Niebuhr put it.

Evangelicals of every perspective no longer need to be convinced that political and social concern is an important part of Christian discipleship. It is a settled issue that "the least of these" among us must be treated with both charity and justice. Now the debates focus on prudential questions regarding which policies are in fact the most effective in meeting the normative standards of justice. Many times, these questions are empirical and require honest and rigorous exploration.

Although the problems of the modern world will not soon disappear, the existence of those very problems will keep evangelicals engaged in social and political activism. But noteworthy is the fact that, just as conservative Christians have gathered momentum to have influence in the political arena, many of the seemingly intractable problems facing American society are cultural in nature and not easily affected by political solutions.

Evangelicals and fundamentalists are quick to remind us that this age, like all ages, is "standing in the need of prayer." The ravages brought on our culture by social and political injustice, by the corroding effects of secularization, and by the debilitating ethos of rampant moral relativism are sobering. But, as evangelicals have always insisted, miracles still happen and grace has always been amazing. And for the love of Christ and the duties of charity entailed by following Him, they will continue to be engaged with not only the world but also, because of their own diversity, each other.

ENDNOTES

1. Harvey Cox, "The Warring Visions of the Religious Right," *The Atlantic Monthly*, November 1995, 62.
2. Timothy Smith, "The Evangelical Kaleidoscope and the Call to Christian Unity," *Christian Scholar's Review* 15 (1986): 125–40.
3. Quoted in James D. Hunter, *Evangelicalism: The Coming Generation* (Chicago: University of Chicago Press, 1987), ix. The very impressive work of, for instance, evangelical historians, philosophers, and political scientists has since demolished the stereotypes Mencken so enjoyed promoting.
4. Michael Weisskopf, "Energized by Pulpit or Passion, the Public Is Calling," *The Washington Post*, 1 February 1993, 1.
5. The most comprehensive recent studies are John C. Green, James L. Guth, Corwin E. Smidt, and Lyman A. Kellstedt, *Religion and the Culture Wars: Dispatches from the Front* (Lanham: Rowman & Littlefield, 1996); Mark J. Rozell and Clyde Wilcox, eds., *God at the Grass Roots: The Christian Right in the 1994 Elections* (Lanham: Rowman & Littlefield, 1995); and Duane M. Oldfield, *The Right and the Righteous: The Christian Right Confronts the Republican Party* (Lanham: Rowman & Littlefield, 1996).
6. Quoted in George M. Marsden, *Fundamentalism and American Culture: The*

Shaping of Twentieth-Century Evangelicalism 1870–1925 (New York: Oxford University Press, 1980), 188.

7. See *U.S. News & World Report*, 4 May 1998, cover story on the influential ministry of Dr. James Dobson to see just how disappointed and displeased he and many of his followers are with current Republican party leadership.

8. See Joel A. Carpenter, *Revive Us Again: The Reawakening of American Fundamentalism* (New York: Oxford University Press, 1997), esp. chap. 5, "A Window on the World," for an illuminating description of how their eschatology lead to a pessimistic view of human progress. According to fundamentalists, "terrible times were descending upon the world, and the progression of evil was quickening. Only Christ's second coming could redeem and restore humanity and the creation" (90).

9. Winthrop Hudson, *American Protestantism* (Chicago: University of Chicago Press, 1961), 128.

10. George M. Marsden, *Reforming Fundamentalism: Fuller Seminary and the New Evangelicalism* (Grand Rapids: Eerdmans, 1987), 4.

11. Quoted in Robert D. Linder, "The Resurgence of Evangelical Social Concern," in *The Evangelicals: What They Believe, Who They Are, Where They Are Changing*, ed. David Wells and John Woodbridge (New York: Abingdon, 1975), 198.

12. Walter Rauschenbusch, *A Theology for the Social Gospel* (1917; reprint, New York: Abingdon, n.d.), 5.

13. Ibid., 50. "Sin is essentially selfishness. That definition is more in harmony with the social gospel than with any individualistic type of religion."

14. Ibid., 31.

15. Ibid., 117.

16. Quoted in "When Evangelicals Take Capitalism Seriously," by Craig M. Gay, *Christian Scholars Review* 21, no. 4 (June 1992): 348.

17. Ibid., 349.

18. Ibid., 350.

19. Carl F. H. Henry, *The Uneasy Conscience of Modern Fundamentalism* (Grand Rapids: Eerdmans, 1947), 17.

20. Ibid., 32.

21. Ibid., 45.

22. Carl F. H. Henry, "The Uneasy Conscience Revisited" (unpublished lecture delivered on November 3, 1987, at the fortieth anniversary of the founding of Fuller Theological Seminary in Pasadena, California), 5. For an interesting critique of Carl Henry's view of the State, see Nicholas Wolterstorff, "Contemporary Christian Views of the State: Some Major Issues," in *Christian Scholar's Review*, 1974, 319–22.

23. Jim Wallis, "Revolt on Evangelical Frontiers: A Response," *Christianity Today*, 21 June 1974, 20–21.

24. Jim Wallis, "Post American Christianity," *Post American* 1 (fall 1971): 2.

25. *Chicago Sun-Times*, 1 December 1973.

26. Ronald J. Sider, ed., *The Chicago Declaration* (Carol Stream, Ill.: Creation House, 1974), 1.

27. Ibid.

28. Ronald J. Sider, *Rich Christians in an Age of Hunger* (Downers Grove: InterVarsity, 1977). A twentieth-anniversary revision was published by Word in 1997.

29. See especially Richard J. Mouw, *Politics and the Biblical Drama* (Grand Rapids: Eerdmans, 1976); Robert K. Johnston, *Evangelicals at an Impasse* (Atlanta: John

Knox, 1979), particularly chap. 4; and John Howard Yoder, *The Politics of Jesus* (Grand Rapids: Eerdmans, 1972).

30. *Time*, 5 August 1974.

31. John R. W. Stott, ed., *Making Christ Known: Historic Mission Documents from the Lausanne Movement, 1974–1989* (Grand Rapids: Eerdmans, 1997), 24.

32. Edward Dobson recounted this story at a conference sponsored by the Ethics and Public Policy Center in Washington on "The New Religious Right: Assessing the Past, Scouting the Future" in November 1990. He further observed, "The Religious New Right was a disenfranchised movement, a countercultural movement not accepted by any of the cultural elites or the mainstream. When President Reagan embraced the evangelicals, leaders like Jerry Falwell assumed that this legitimized a movement that had been demeaned, ignored, and branded as 'double-knit, Appalachian, pew-jumping, holy-roller, anachronistic, white-socks,' and all that. Once we got into the White House, we thought 'we are now legitimate because we are now equal partners.' But we never were. Many put on 100 per cent wool suits and became politicized by the activist process but, as a consequence, lost some of their impact." See Michael Cromartie, ed., *No Longer Exiles: The Religious New Right in American Politics* (Washington: Ethics and Public Policy Center, 1993), 53.

33. Daniel Bell, ed., "The Dispossessed," in *The Radical Right* (Garden City, N.Y.: Anchor Books, 1964), 2.

34. Joseph Gusfield, *Symbolic Crusade: Status Politics and the American Temperance Movement* (Urbana: University of Illinois Press, 1963).

35. Steve Bruce, *The Rise and Fall of the New Christian Right* (Oxford, England: Clarendon, 1988), 49.

36. Nathan Glazer, "Toward a New Concordat?" *This World* 2 (summer 1982): 113.

37. Bauer, quoted by Duane M. Oldfield in *The Right and the Righteous*, (Lanham: Rowman & Littlefield, 1996), 55.

38. Glazer, "Toward a New Concordat?" 112.

39. Bruce, *Rise and Fall of the New Christian Right*, 22.

40. Of course, the liberalization of our cultural mores did not begin in the 1960s. For a brilliant analysis of this point see Rochelle Gurstein, *The Repeal of Reticence: A History of Americans' Cultural and Legal Struggles over Free Speech, Obscenity, Sexual Liberation, and Modern Art* (New York: Hill and Wang, 1996). She offers a fascinating history of the arguments for and against the forces that altered public discourse between the late nineteenth century, when they first appeared, and the 1960s, when new controversies erupted about mass culture, avant-garde art, and sexual liberation. She shows how the "party of exposure" successfully opened American public life to matters that had once been hidden away in private and looks at the unexpected consequences of their victory over the "party of reticence."

41. Bruce, *Rise and Fall of the New Christian Right*, 31.

42. Ibid., 68.

43. Christopher Lasch, *The Revolt of the Elites and the Betrayal of Democracy* (New York: W. W. Norton, 1995), 215.

44. William Kristol, quoted in *U.S. News & World Report*, 24 April 1995, 39.

45. See, for instance, "The Power of James Dobson," *U.S. News & World Report*, 4 May 1998; "For God's Sake," *U.S. News & World Report*, 24 April 1995; "The Right Hand of God," *Time*, 15 May 1995; "Pat Robertson's God, Inc.," *Esquire*, November 1994; and "Life Beyond God," *The New York Times Magazine*, 16 October 1994.

46. Peter Beinart, "Battle for the 'Burbs,'" *The New Republic*, 19 October 1998, 25–29.
47. Ibid., 27.
48. Irving Kristol, "Conservative Christians: Into the Fray," *The Wall Street Journal*, 22 December 1995.
49. John Murray Cuddihy, *No Offense: Civil Religion and Protestant Taste* (New York: Seabury, 1978), 201.
50. Richard J. Mouw, "Evangelical Ethics in the Time of God's Patience: Recovering Some Neglected Themes" (unpublished remarks at the inaugural conference for the Alonzo McDonald Professorship in Evangelical Theological Studies, Harvard Divinity School, February 13–14, 1998), 8–9.
51. Ralph Reed, *Active Faith: How Christians Are Changing the Soul of American Politics* (New York: Free Press, 1996), 262–263. Reed expressed the hope that when future historians look back at the Christian Coalition they will reflect on a movement that "had an uncommon commitment to caring for those in need, loving those who attacked us, and displaying the love, dignity, and decency that are the hallmarks of an active faith" (281).
52. Mark A. Noll, *Adding Cross to Crown: The Political Significance of Christ's Passion* (Grand Rapids: Baker and Center for Public Justice, 1996), 18.
53. Ibid., 32.
54. See especially Timothy Smith, *Revivalism and Social Reform: American Protestantism on the Eve of the Civil War* (Baltimore: Johns Hopkins University Press, 1980; first edition 1957); Donald Dayton, *Discovering an Evangelical Heritage* (New York: Harper & Row, 1976); Garth Lean, *God's Politician: William Wilberforce's Struggle* (London: Darton, Longman, and Todd, 1980); Ernest Marshall Howse, *Saints in Politics: The Clapham Sect* (London: Allen and Unwin, 1974); and J. Wesley Bready, *England: Before and After Wesley* (London: Hodder and Stoughton, 1939).
55. Grant Wacker, "Uneasy in Zion: Evangelicals in Postmodern Society," in *Evangelicalism and Modern America*, ed. George Marsden (Grand Rapids: Eerdmans, 1984), 26.
56. Alexis de Tocqueville, *Democracy in America* (New York: Vintage, 1945), 2:135.
57. Richard John Neuhaus, "The Christian and the Church," in *Transforming the World*, ed. James M. Boice (Portland: Multnomah, 1988), 120.
58. Max Weber, "Politics as Vocation," in *From Max Weber: Essays in Sociology*, ed. H. H. Gerth and C. Wright Mills (New York: Oxford University Press), 128.
59. Reinhold Niebuhr, *The Children of Light and the Children of Darkness* (New York: Charles Scribner's Sons, 1944), 118.

An Overview

Over its relatively short history, the church has followed no less than four tenuous tracks in its relationship with politics and government: (1) it assumed the power of the state with horrible social and political consequences; (2) it assimilated the state's social and political agenda, making the church socially and theologically secular; (3) it isolated itself from politics and the state, making the church socially and theologically irrelevant; and (4) more recently, it attempted to force itself on the state, making the church appear socially and theologically tyrannical. Stephen Hoffman looks at the history of the church from Constantine to the present, suggests reasons why the church often fails socially and politically and discloses the consequences that fall on society as a result, shows the impact that the church can have when it maintains theological integrity in the midst of political turmoil, and, ultimately, proposes a fifth track the church can follow that outlines the relationship of good and influential citizenship to well-rounded civic education conducted by Christian colleges and churches. To impact politics effectively, the church must develop in its youth a love for the world and a passion for understanding thoroughly its diverse and often controversial agendas. The church must remember that *this is a world in which believers are sojourners with citizenship responsibilities.* With humility, adequate academic skills, and a genuine reliance on God, the church can more effectively influence the values of a democratic political system while simultaneously creating a better environment that is more tolerant of faith and the sharing of it.

Chapter Nine

DISCIPLESHIP, CITIZENSHIP, AND CHRISTIAN CIVIC EDUCATION

Stephen P. Hoffmann

CHRISTIANS WHO ARE CONCERNED ABOUT the integrity of the church are likely to regard Constantine's vision of Christ's cross in the sky in A.D. 312 as more ominous than inspirational.[1] For at least some of Constantine's critics, the message "Conquer by this sign" might as well have read "Conquer this sign." Henceforth, as its history unfolded, the church, in contrast to its Lord (as recorded in Matt. 4:8–10) would too often succumb to the temptation of power. The apostle Paul seemed to regard his Roman citizenship not as a source of identity but as a personal attribute useful for spreading the gospel. His education afforded him the opportunity to speak to philosophers in Athens. His citizenship gained him access to the politicians in Rome. "Our citizenship," he told the young church (Phil. 3:20), "is in heaven." Constantine's conversion meant that Christians no longer had to be alienated from the state. From an anti-Constantinian perspective, being a good citizen of Rome was problematical.

Augustine, though steeped in Greco-Roman culture, was acutely aware of the danger of identifying the kingdom of God with the world or even the institutional church. "What are earthly kingdoms," he wrote, "but great robberies?" As members of the spiritual "City of God," believers must sooner regard themselves as "sojourners" than as citizens. Nevertheless, Augustine's great work *The City of God* was motivated by a desire to refute the pagan argument that Christianity undermined civic-mindedness and was therefore responsible for undermining a great civilization. Although it was not written as a work of political philosophy, *The City of God* demonstrates a sophisticated understanding of the dilemmas of power. He refutes the charge against Christianity in part by criticizing the Roman state's misuse of its God-given power. However, he is equally concerned to argue that Christians were in fact model citizens of Rome. Even admirers of Augustine must acknowledge, however, that his conception of good citizenship required a degree of moral compromise that many citizens of modern democracies would find unacceptable.

Augustine cleverly points out the shortcomings of human justice. Similarly, he exposes the discrepancy between the practice of slavery and the divine value of every human being. But he does not entertain the possibility of institutional

139

change to remedy injustice. Christians must be merciful, but they must accept the system as an inevitable feature of a sinful world. Augustine himself justified the state's persecution of the Donatists, religious dissenters, for the sake of maintaining law and order. Whatever one thinks of Augustine's accommodation of the political realities of his time, the Bishop of Hippo was acutely sensitive to the ethical dilemmas that Christian citizens faced. Ultimately, the Christian finds himself throwing up his hands and entreating God to "deliver me from my necessities." We must look to Aristotle, however, for the classic statement of the conflict between citizenship and morality.

Unlike Augustine, Aristotle was a student of politics. On the one hand, Aristotle shared Plato's assumption that virtue and citizenship can and even must be compatible. In Plato's vision of the ideal state, as articulated in *The Republic*, the wisest and most virtuous people, the philosophers, are the model citizens and hence deserved to rule. But Aristotle argues that this ideal is incompatible with social reality. One could assume neither a succession of such perfectly wise rulers nor willing acceptance of rule by an intellectual elite. Accordingly, for Aristotle, human perfection is something to be achieved above and beyond politics by those few who could apprehend the depths of philosophical wisdom. But essential to wisdom is an understanding of ethics, the application of morality. For Aristotle, the essence of citizenship was ethical deliberation. Therefore, even in an imperfect world, citizenship ought to be an ennobling experience, even though philosophers could not rule and most citizens could not be philosophers.

Aristotle's systematic study of many ancient political systems led him to conclude that constitutions are as various as the historical and social context in which they exist. Political values differ from one system to another. A tyranny is likely to measure loyalty according to behavior that would be unacceptable in a republic. Therefore, it is easier in some systems than in others to be considered a good citizen and also to be virtuous. We can readily translate this into a Christian frame of reference if we understand a "good man" (using Aristotle's terminology) to be a believer who openly professes the faith and who seeks to embody Christian moral teachings in all areas of life. In the former Soviet Union, members of the Communist Party were considered the best citizens. By definition, Christians could not be good citizens. In liberal democracies, it was easier to be both.

The relationship between morality—especially religion—and citizenship is a perennial issue of politics. My contention is that because many Christians do not have a sophisticated understanding of this complex relationship, they are prone either to regard active citizenship as irrelevant or even harmful to their faith or to have unrealistic expectations about what religiously motivated citizens can accomplish. A greater commitment to adequate civic education within Christian institutions is desirable as a means of overcoming this weakness in relating one's faith to this important sphere of social life. Christian civic education can also promote interaction between Christians and the broader community through dialogue about the relationship between values and citizenship.

I define *civic education* here as "the acquisition of values and skills necessary for meaningful participation in civic life." Such skills may include knowledge of intellectual traditions and historical experiences addressing the relationship between Christianity and politics. Accordingly, I have chosen to make the case for Christian civic education first by suggesting how an awareness of efforts to relate Christianity and politics in theory and practice can enrich an understanding of the good man-good citizen dilemma. In Christian terminology, we can refer to this as the discipleship-citizenship dilemma. Then I will suggest how one kind of Christian institution, the evangelical college, can promote civic education within the Christian community and beyond.

PERSPECTIVES ON CHRISTIANITY AND CITIZENSHIP

By allowing individual rulers to determine which religion would prevail in their respective territories, the Peace of Augsburg (1555) established a measure of religious plurality in Europe. The difference between this and modern notions of toleration is about as great as that between the principle of an eye-for-an-eye (a means of limiting vengeance) and the Sermon on the Mount's law of love. Catholics and Protestants alike—even Anabaptists—assumed that a society should not be merely a framework for economic exchange and government but a community held together by a common religion. However, several distinctly different perspectives on the proper relationship between church and society, including the state, are associated with major traditions. The massive religious and social revolution that Luther unwittingly set in motion brought these differences to the fore.

From a Catholic perspective, Europe was "Christendom," a spiritual realm presupposing harmony under the guidance of a religious hierarchy governed from Rome. The elaborate philosophical system of Thomas Aquinas, in which everything had its proper place within a unified whole, is an appropriate symbol of this point of view. For Thomas Aquinas, the state is junior partner to the church in the moral development of individuals, even as faith is the fulfillment of reason. Accordingly, no contradiction should exist between one's political obligations and one's religious obligations. Despite important differences in theology and ecclesiology, an assumption of harmony between the roles of parishioner and subject is as characteristic of Eastern Orthodoxy as it is of medieval Catholicism. Traditionally, to be Polish was to be Catholic, and to be Russian was to be Orthodox. This Catholic perspective lives on even among Christians in pluralistic democracies such as the United States, including conservative Protestants. Let there be varieties of worship, but let the constitution be rooted in principles of natural law ultimately derived from Christian teachings. There need be no contradiction between God and country, between being a good Christian (or Jew) and being a good citizen.

Perhaps it should not be surprising that for Luther tension, rather than harmony, characterized the relationship between discipleship and citizenship. He was, after all, an Augustinian monk. He was also appalled at the way power had corrupted the Roman church. No Christian should be under the illusion that government could be a Christian enterprise. It is nothing more than an expedient to contain the disorder that is an ever-present danger in a sinful world. Politics is not a means of moral improvement. Because government is necessary, Christians should willingly assume the obligations of citizenship, as long as they can do so without risk to their primary task of worship. Their Christian influence is primarily on a personal level; it does not emphasize reform of social structures. In one memorable passage in *On Secular Authority*, Luther advises any Christian who is asked to serve the state as an executioner to be "the best hangman there is."

It may seem that a Lutheran perspective precludes criticism of the state, but Luther himself did not hesitate to do so, especially earlier in his career. He condemned revolutionaries for undermining authority, but he also admonished the authorities for provoking revolution with oppressive policies. Even as Augustine justified the state's persecution of the Donatists, Luther called for repression of the radical Anabaptists, who declared themselves unbound by the laws of sinful governments. "Stab, smite and slay all you can," said Luther. "You can't meet a rebel with reason. Your best answer is to punch him in the face until he has a bloody nose." Ironically, however, Anabaptists and Lutherans both imply that Christians should be highly skeptical of politics. Luther's suspicion of political authority is evident in his remark that "most rulers are either knaves or fools." From this perspective, *being a good Christian ought to avoid linking citizenship with discipleship*. American evangelicals who are disappointed by their failure to change society through politics have expressed such a disconnection between discipleship and citizenship.

A Calvinist viewpoint represents a third approach. Like Catholics, Calvinists have traditionally been relatively optimistic about the possibilities for Christian influence in all areas of life. Whereas Lutherans and Anabaptists have tended to associate government with the restraint of sin, Calvinists and Catholics have been more likely to connect it with creation and redemption. As children of the Reformation, however, Calvinists have had less faith in the institutional church as being a source of authority for the society as a whole. Social entities such as the state, the family, and the business corporation are also God-ordained. Church-related vocations are no more holy than secular vocations for Christians who seek to glorify God in whatever sphere He places them. A Reformational sensitivity to human sinfulness and the ability to overcome it through God's grace has led Calvinists to emphasize the need for active engagement more than Catholics were traditionally inclined to do. Christians must honor God by discerning the implications of biblical principles for all areas of life. Then they must make efforts to reform those areas so that they might more closely resemble what God intended them to be. *Active citizenship is therefore an expression of discipleship*. This high expectation for relating virtue to politics owes more to Aristotle than to Augustine. The European Christian Democratic movement (and the reformed Catholic doctrine that spawned much of it) reflects the influence of Calvinist ideas.

Even those who value the Reformation's contributions to Christianity and to civilization in general must acknowledge the social upheaval that grew out of it. Religion became the primary source of political ideology. The wars that devastated large parts of Europe in the sixteenth and seventeenth centuries were, to a large extent, religious wars. The Enlightenment's emphasis on reason rather than revelation sought to domesticate religion by controlling its impact on politics. Liberalism is a political philosophy with strong roots in eighteenth-century rationalism. By separating church and state, liberals sought to prevent governments from claiming divine approval for whatever they chose to do. They also sought to give individuals freedom to worship according to the dictates of their conscience and churches freedom from state control. Individual liberty and limited government, along with rationalism, are essential characteristics of historical liberalism. Another important means of limiting government was to promote representation and, eventually, democracy. Insofar as liberals believed that moral virtue and citizenship were related, religion was no longer assumed to be the source of that virtue.

The most radical modern thinkers rejected any role for religion in public life. Unlike many of his contemporaries, Jean-Jacques Rousseau believed that religion was essential for a healthy polity. However, the religion he advocated in *Social Contract* was a distinctly nondoctrinal "civil religion." He condemned orthodox Christianity as divisive for two reasons. First, "[i]n giving men . . . two homelands, it subjects them to contradictory duties and prevents them from being simultaneously devout men and citizens." Second, Rousseau asserted that whereas a good, "civil religion" is characterized by "sentiments of sociability," Christianity contains "dogmas . . . contrary to the duties of a citizen." Christianity is unacceptable because "[i]t is impossible to live in peace with those one believes to be damned."

John Stuart Mill's eloquent defense of free speech in *On Liberty* makes frequent reference to the social intolerance of Christians, who dominated English society. The German sociologist Max Weber warned that a failure to rise above religious values would cloud political judgment and lead to bad public policy. John Dewey tended to regard religious belief as a hindrance to progress and democracy. Referring indirectly to the Christian doctrine of original sin, Dewey asserted that "the whole tendency of this view has been to put a heavy discount upon resources that are potentially available for betterment of human life." Clearly, *for many liberals being a good Christian and a good citizen is at best problematical.*

However, some other people would not make this judgment. Although strong advocates of separation of church and state and of religious tolerance, they regarded religion as an important source of social stability and civic virtue. Alexis de Tocqueville emphasized the importance of religion to stable democracy even more. All religions in America, even Catholicism, were tolerant. Religion was crucial to the vigorous associational life that prevented the disintegration of democracy into isolated individuals who could be easily manipulated. It was also an important source of the enlightened self-interest necessary for social trust. Glenn Tinder, a contemporary Christian political philosopher, agrees that liberalism and the democracy that it implies are the most desirable alternatives. However, he points out that liberalism depends on Christian assumptions, especially the idea that each individual has a divine worth. Furthermore, he argues that secular liberals such as Dewey put an inordinate amount of faith in the possibility of true community based on rationality and tolerance. In effect, he reverses their argument that religion's insistence on moral rectitude undermines good citizenship. Their broad interpretation of liberalism and tolerance imperils moral responsibility. *Liberalism devoid of its religious roots means that good citizens are less likely to be good people.*[2]

RELATING CHRISTIANITY AND CITIZENSHIP IN PRACTICE

Let us turn now from theories about discipleship and citizenship to a dramatic two-dimensional case study from twentieth-century German history about the relationship between religious integrity and political influence. *In the first half of that century,* active Lutherans made up the most influential segment of the population, but on the whole they saw little conflict between Christian principles and cooperation with a regime that came to epitomize disorder and injustice. Here, a failure to attempt political influence compromised the integrity of the church. *In the second half of the century,* practicing Lutherans in communist East Germany attempted the difficult task of coexisting with a hostile state, in which they were a distinct minority, without losing their ability to criticize it. To some degree, the church in East Germany seems to have repeated the error of its counterpart during the Hitler period in its effort to coexist with the state. However, its effort to accommodate itself to the state was motivated to some extent by a desire to influence the state's policies, however modestly, in some areas. Therefore, one could argue that in this case the church endangered its integrity more through attempts to increase its influence than through inaction.

In Hitler's Third Reich and in the Communist German Democratic Republic (GDR), the Lutheran Church's integrity was compromised by its desire to find ideological common ground with the state. Under Hitler, the common ground was *nationalism;* under Erich Honecker, the Communist leader of the GDR, it was *socialism.* In both cases, the seemingly admirable concept of the church as *Volkskirche* (church of the people)—the idea that the Church should rise above its sectarian interests and concern itself with the good of society as a whole—helps to explain this ideological affinity.

Not long after Adolf Hitler assumed power, the National Socialist regime attempted to gain control of the Evangelical Church through the *Deutsche Christen* (German Christians), a faction of the church seeking to incorporate elements of Nazism into Christianity. For example, one German Christian pastor declared that "God speaks in blood and *Volk* a more powerful language than He does in the idea of humanity." A synod under their control passed a law prohibiting pastors or their wives to be of "Jewish blood."[3] Eventually, most Lutherans resented this attempt to redefine Christianity and politicize the church. The German Christians' influence declined rapidly, and, as a result, the Nazi Party no longer aspired to inject its ideology into the church.

Failing to Nazify the church, the Hitler regime changed its strategy. It would tolerate religious autonomy as long as the church did not become a source of political opposition. Like most conservative Germans, Lutherans were quite susceptible to patriotic, antisocialist and anti-Semitic appeals. They distrusted liberal democracy and were inclined to defer to those in power for the sake of law and order. During the Weimar Republic, Lutherans preferred the traditionally conservative German National Peoples Party to the Nazis.[4] Once Hitler won, however, no conservative alternative existed. Therefore, the National Socialist state could count on most Lutherans to be "good Germans" and avoid active opposition when they did not indeed become active supporters. Even the most radical opponents of cooperation with the state were concerned primarily with protecting church autonomy and found their way to political opposition only after considerable soul-searching. Most of them did not want to be perceived as unpatriotic.

Similarly, when the communist state could not convert Lutherans into active supporters of the Marxist-Leninist Socialist Unity Party of Germany (*Sozialistische Einheitspartei Deutschland*, or SED), it focused on getting them to associate socialist ideals with antifascism, as interpreted by the Communist authorities. Moritz Mitzenheim, bishop of Thuringia, coined the phrase "church within socialism" *(Kirche im Sozialismus)*. This formula held that as long as the state allowed Christians to relate the gospel to political or social matters, they should fully accept the authority of the East German state and not engage in political opposition.[5]

What *socialism* meant was never clear. As did other Communist Parties, the ruling SED used the word as shorthand for the Soviet-style system it ruled. To say that the church was "for" socialism would suggest that the church and the state were partners. To say that it was "against" socialism would associate the church with a Cold War mentality that labeled West Germany as good and East Germany as bad. To say instead that the church was simply "within" socialism acknowledged that the church needed to accept its environment and commit itself to ministry there. However, in practice the formula implied a common ground between the church and the state on the basis of "socialist-humanist" ideals. Claiming to represent these ideals, the SED hoped that all Lutherans would affirm that "this state has become for us in the past thirty-five years not only a natural homeland, but also a political and spiritual home."[6]

For Manfred Stolpe, one of the top leaders of the East German Church, "church within socialism" meant that the church should actively contribute to making the socialist German state more stable and just. After intensive discussions among top clergy about the church's proper role in "a closed socialist society," Stolpe remembers, "we decided it was our task to try to improve the society in the interests of human beings. We understood church within socialism as a mandate for action." Stolpe was still promoting this view in the very last days of GDR communism. Lecturing at the University of Greifswald in November 1989, he described Marx's ideal society as one in which production would be oriented to human needs, goods would be justly distributed, and free persons would maintain a sense of responsibility to their society. This goal, he contended, resembles the values that Christians today consider to be the mandate of the gospel. Earlier the same year, at the East German Lutheran Church's conference in Leipzig, Stolpe emphasized that a better GDR did not mean a capitalist GDR because capitalism furthered "egoism, wasteful consumerism, frivolity, and ruthlessness."[7]

The essence of the concept of *Volkskirche* is that the Church belongs neither to its hierarchy nor to the state, but to all people identified as members, regardless of the degree to which they are active participants. The Evangelical Church had a favored position in Wilhelmian Germany. The conservative Protestant state assumed that the proper relationship between church and state was an "alliance of throne and altar." Bismarck's brand of conservatism included an alliance with liberals for the purpose of promoting modernization. Although some traditional conservatives who opposed Bismarck's reforms were Protestant, on the whole it was Catholics, not Protestants, who were accused of standing in the way of the German unity and power. The Catholic Center Party and the working-class Social Democratic Party emerged as the two main sources of political opposition by the turn of the century. The alliance of throne and altar ended with the defeat in World War I and the abolition of the monarchy.

Amid the political and economic instability that followed the war, evangelical leaders reexamined the place of the church in public life. It could no longer prosper as chaplain to the state and bulwark against socialism. Germany had become a republic encumbered by economic depression and political division. The church had no more faith in the republic than did most Germans. The patriotism that had united socialist and monarchist, Catholic and Protestant upon the outbreak of war in 1914 seemed a more promising basis for renewal than Weimar's liberal ideals. As *Volkskirche*, the church sought to promote a degree of dialogue and social reform for the sake of national unity, both within the church and between Lutherans and others. As the Weimar Republic fell victim to increasing political instability, this relatively liberal nationalism was eventually seduced by a fear of socialism and by the chauvinistic appeals of extreme nationalists. In the Third Reich, the German Christians reinterpreted *Volkskirche* in terms of National Socialist ideology. Antifascist Lutherans, who called themselves the Confessing Church, rejected *Volkskirche* in favor of the idea of the church as *Freikirche* (free church). A "free church" would be able to preserve its spiritual integrity by relying neither on state support nor on public approval.[8]

In the aftermath of World War II, most Lutherans in the West again looked to the *Volkskirche* ideal to define the church's role in postwar Germany. This time they were joined by German Catholics, who became a mainstay of the Christian Democratic movement, a powerful force in postwar Western European politics. The church established "Evangelical Academies," conference centers designed—in the spirit of liberal democracy—to bring together people of different religious and political persuasions for an open and honest discussion of public issues. West Germany's two major parties, the Christian Democrats (CDU) and the Social Democrats (SPD) counted active laymen from both churches among their leaders. The overwhelming majority of West Germans belonged to the Catholic Church or the Evangelical Church. Each of these church organizations received substantial sums from a head tax that the state collected on their behalf from their members, active or not. Each conducted religious education within the public schools. National church organizations were among those major social entities that the government consulted regularly. The churches felt responsible to make the new Federal Republic succeed, and they were quite at home in it. Some members of the Confessing Church remained opposed to the church as *Volkskirche*. Their experience under Hitler and the Cold War politics that quickly enveloped Germany convinced them that the church was again being co-opted by an antisocialist nationalism.

In East Germany, by contrast, circumstances were not favorable to the reestablishment of the church as *Volkskirche*. The church in East Germany enjoyed none of the resources or status granted to churches in West Germany. Church involvement declined steadily in both parts of Germany as postwar European society became increasingly secular. Because of its privileges, the West German church continued to be a prominent social institution despite this trend. Erosion from secularization only exacerbated the even greater pressure of an antireligious public policy. In the early years of the GDR, the harshness of the antireligious campaign was reminiscent of the persecution that dissenting Christians experienced under National Socialism. In coming to terms with life under communism, the East German Lutheran church had reconciled itself to a marginal role in society. Some people described it as a *Nischkirche* (church in a niche), which, like many ordinary East Germans, passively conformed while cultivating a private world.[9]

However, other people characterized the situation more positively. Veterans of the Confessing Church were a stronger presence in the East than in the West. In keeping with their suspicion of the *Volkskirche*, they regarded powerlessness as an asset. It was desirable not because it allowed the church a niche in which to preserve its assets but because it freed the church to conform to Christ's example of service to "others." This commitment to selfless service, regardless of ideology, represented the "church in socialism" idea at its best. From this perspective, separation from the West German Lutheran Church, which the East German regime demanded, was not entirely negative. It was consistent with repeated appeals from the church in both the East and the West that East German Christians abandon the GDR for greener pastures in the West. In signifying its acceptance of the GDR as a legitimate state, it put the church in a stronger position to appeal for an end to discrimination against individual Christians and for recognition of the legitimacy of the church's ministry. An historic meeting on March 6, 1978, between delegations led by Bishop Albrecht Schönherr, head of the *Bund der Evangelischen Kirchen* (BEK, i.e., Federation of Evangelical Churches), and Ulbricht, chief of the SED, seemed to represent a normalization of church-state relations that would make such concessions possible.

For Richard Steinlein, a high administrator in the Berlin-Brandenburg church, this "summit meeting" and the creation of the BEK represented a clear victory in the state's effort to control the Lutheran Church. In establishing its own Federation of Churches, the hierarchy was in effect adding bricks to the Berlin Wall. The 1978 meeting succeeded in giving the public the impression that the church had become part of the system. He argues that most clergy and laity approved neither the separation nor the "church in socialism" idea as a basis for a modus vivendi with the state.[10]

Supporters of the meeting could point out that Bishop Schönherr had been one of Bonhoeffer's students at the Confessing Church's underground seminary at Finkenwald. Like his mentor, he believed strongly that Christianity should be "emancipated" from captivity to any particular culture or political doctrine. Schönherr was not interested in perpetuating the tendency of German Lutheranism to emphasize order in public life and to suppress social criticism.[11] "Church in socialism," properly understood, did not require deference to the regime. Heino Falcke, an important leader of the church in Erfurt, stated that "biblical humanity means service to humanity[12] . . . [which is] the strongest bond between Christians and socialists." But Falcke did not equate socialism with the policies of the SED. Instead, socialism was a standard by which to judge those policies. A paper reflecting Falcke's philosophy identified "social deficits" in the GDR and suggested what a real socialist society should look like. Nervous East German officials, interpreting the paper as a virtual opposition party program, warned the authors that they could be accused of "slandering the state," a criminal offense in the GDR. Falcke himself was denied permission to travel, even to communist Eastern Europe.[13] Were the leaders who met with the SED in 1978 co-opted, or were they able to maintain a critical distance? In neither case could they pretend to represent a *Volkskirche* in the GDR.

Falcke's was not the only critical voice. In the 1970s, clergy increasingly questioned government policy. Individual churches began to provide sanctuary for conscientious objectors and political dissidents. Meditations on Bible passages during youth-oriented "blues masses" at the Church of the Redeemer in East Berlin often spotlighted problems the government preferred to sweep under the rug. In 1982, the Nikolai Church in Leipzig began regular Monday evening prayer services for peace. These eventually spread throughout the country. State-sponsored peace campaigns linked militarism exclusively to NATO. Peace services held in churches, in contrast, sent a message that the state did not welcome: "all have sinned," including—and even especially—the socialist German state. Nonreligious people joined church members to set up, on church premises, task forces on such issues as political prisoners, emigration, and pollution. In the spring of 1988, a church-based group in Wittenberg issued twenty theses protesting censorship, militarism, and violation of human rights. It advocated a "third way" between American-style capitalism and Soviet-style socialism.[14]

Respect for the church's role as a place for genuine discourse and as the conscience of society peaked during the mass demonstrations of 1989. The Lutheran Church hierarchy publicly accused the state of fraud in connection with the May 1989 municipal elections. This was a courageous act. No one at this time had any reason to believe the system had only six months to live. In June, a group of Christians marched silently from the church offices to the State Council building with a petition demanding an explanation of the discrepancy between the official election results and the actual returns. Police and security personnel stopped the march and broke up a sit-down demonstration held later in front of one of the churches. The regime signaled its intolerance of dissent when it alluded to Beijing's justification of the brutal crackdown that same month on pro-democracy demonstrators in Tienanminh Square. Two East Berlin churches displayed the Chinese character for democracy and beat timpani around the clock in protest. Unrest among the East German population began to escalate during the summer, and more and more people fled when they learned that it was now possible to pass through Czechoslovakia and Hungary to the West. Pastors organized prayer services and public meetings to discuss the political crisis. Street demonstrations after the meetings were powerful but peaceful. Church leaders constantly admonished people to renounce the use of force. In September, the Kirchenbund synod at Eisenach called for freedom of speech and political pluralism.[15] Within two months, the Communist regime came to an end after more than forty years.

By 1933, Germany had been exhausted by years of violent civil conflict and economic depression. The Hitler regime was relentless and effective in crushing political opposition from the very beginning. No assurance exists that a church-based campaign against the government would have shaken it. However, a distinguished German historian of National Socialism suggests that the churches had greater potential for opposition than other sectors of society, for 95 percent of Germans were at least nominal Protestants or Catholics. What might have happened if courageous leaders had taken advantage of the successful resistance to the Nazi attempt to take over the churches and organized massive protests against repression in general? *When churchmen became involved in resistance activities later in the 1930s, it was too late.*[16]

In 1946, Lutheran leaders issued a statement acknowledging the church's guilt for not trying hard enough to oppose the Hitler regime. It was analogous to the collective prayer of confession found in many Protestant worship services. Properly understood, it is neither a perfunctory apology nor a verbal self-flagellation. It is a recognition of the seriousness of sin and of the human inability to escape its pervasive influence. It is a heart-felt cry to God for deliverance. The sheer malevolence of National Socialism and the scale of destruction it unleashed continues to astonish. The Lutheran Church was a major force in German society in the 1930s. Their politically conservative instincts made most Lutherans receptive to the nationalism to which the Nazis appealed in strengthening their grip on Germany. The confession of 1946 was an appropriate way of acknowledging the disastrous consequences of their blindness.

The Lutheran Church's presence in East German society and its opportunity for influence was more limited. However serious, the SED's crimes were not at all comparable to the Third Reich's. Church leaders did hold the regime accountable for its actions, if not as publicly as they should have. The "free space" that the church provided was crucial for developing elements of a civil society in the midst of totalitarianism. The concerted effort of many pastors to deflect violence, by teaching and by example, contributed significantly to the surprisingly peaceful end of a repressive political system. But the story of the German Lutheran Church in the GDR shows that falling under the control of the state is not a problem unique to conservative Christians under a right-wing repressive regime. A former Nazi and wife of a pastor in the Confessing Church has the right perspective:

> . . . Some acquaintances from earlier times ask me today how it is possible for me to be a Christian and not in the SPD [Social Democrat Party]. But you know, back then the Confessing Church fought the *Zeitgeist* of the 1930s [the spirit of the times]. Today, the *Zeitgeist* in our city is red—in the church as well—and I ask myself, are they really concerned about the independence of the church . . . or are they going along now with this *Zeitgeist*? . . .[17]

The *Evangelische Kirche in Deutschland* (i.e., the Evangelical Church of Germany, or EKD) authorities seemed reluctant to acknowledge the extent to which church leaders cooperated with the communist state. They have been slow to open church archives to those seeking more information on the extent and nature of that cooperation, citing the need to protect individuals from witch hunts. A public commitment to finding the truth about church-state relations in the GDR, however painful or embarrassing, seemed more appropriate than a declaration of guilt. In the words of Falcke, "a church of whitewashers is worse still than a guilty church."[18]

It is tempting to fault German Lutherans for having failed the test of standing up to dictatorship not once but twice. Are they uniquely lacking in political courage? Bishop Leich urges West Germans not to be so quick to condemn the behavior of church leaders in the East. His words also apply to non-Germans who are assessing either of these two historical situations:

> In painfully small steps we tried to breach the iron front against the people. Whoever did not experience this little war together with us can today easily criticize the Church for not promoting a grand confrontation and open political opposition. I know I was no hero in this little war, was often anxious, and reacted in a cowardly manner. When someone who sat in a GDR prison because of his brave conduct holds that over me, I say: "You are right, I concede." But when I encounter a didactic and judgmental person who, living in economic prosperity and political freedom, has experienced the hard life of the GDR citizen only from afar, I ask him: "How would you have behaved in my place? Would you have been more courageous? Who gives you the right, to set yourself above us?"[19]

"Let the church be the church," the Confessing Church demanded in resisting the Nazis' efforts to politicize it. The primary business of the church is not political engagement. However, the price of remaining "above party" in a highly conflictive situation can be irrelevance or even complicity.[20] Whatever a church's relationship to its political environment in any given case, it can take two measures to avoid becoming politically acculturated. The *first measure is to ensure that theology determines politics, and not politics theology.* In Richard Steinlein's view, the East German Lutheran Church too often failed to do so: "This is how it's done in the Church: one bows under the pressure of external realities, and the theological justification always comes later."[21] The *second measure is to retain a strong sense of mission.* The concept of the church as *Volkskirche* is attractive for its emphasis on service to all who are within its parish, whatever their degree of religious commitment, and on promoting dialogue. But thinking of the church as *Volkskirche* is likely to understate the inevitable tension between its Christian mission and its constituency's culture or subculture. This was the burden of the Confessing Church. Thinking of the church as *Missionskirche* is more likely to encourage the "distance" needed to resist acculturation without sacrificing commitment to those on the outside. In conducting a meaningful mission, it is far more important to illuminate blind spots than to preach to the converted. Bishop Krusche's suggestion of how to approach the issue of human rights exemplifies sensitivity to the danger of acculturation. Because the GDR's systemic bias was to concentrate on social rights at the expense of individual rights, the church's obligation was to emphasize the protection of individual rights. In capitalist societies, the church's emphasis should be on social rights.[22]

It is more comfortable, but less responsible in terms of mission, to tell people or their governments what they want to hear. The church is called instead to tell them what they need to hear.

CHRISTIAN EDUCATION AND CIVIC EDUCATION

Different Christian institutions should have different, but complementary, roles with respect to civic education. Three major Christian institutions significantly involved in public policy are local church congregations, Christian colleges, and parachurch organizations. (The latter, of course, are more likely to be found in liberal democracies.) Obviously, education is the primary concern of the colleges. I would argue that worship is more essential to congregations than education whereas political action (including efforts to mobilize the Christian public) is the primary concern of the public policy-oriented parachurch organization. Of course, worship can and should be an important part of community life at a Christian college. Local congregations are the main source of grass-roots Christian education. Pastors, for example, should intentionally address the implications of God's Word for all of the roles that members of the body of Christ play. The role of citizen is only one of these roles. Parachurch organizations are an important source of information and applied knowledge.

I have chosen to focus here on the question of civic education within the Christian college. Historically, a *strong relationship has existed between liberal arts education and civic leadership*, especially in the United States. A well-known fact is that most of the most venerable institutions of higher education in America began as Christian institutions. Evangelical colleges, especially, should undertake to continue this tradition in a consciously Christian context, a context that has long since ceased to exist in most American postsecondary institutions.

People generally agree that "community" requires some degree of common experience, values, and emotional commitment, although the many conceptions of the basis and extent of community have made defining it difficult. Ferdinand Toennies, a pioneering German sociologist, understood community, or *Gemeinschaft*, to be a family-like association characterized by intensive, long-term relationships, a common tradition, and loyalty. Society, or *Gesellschaft*, in contrast, is a contractual relationship rather than a way of life. Its members are motivated more by the desire to accomplish a particular end than by duty. For Toennies, society means the rationalism, commercialism, and individual freedom characteristic of modernity. It threatens to undermine the local and personal relationships that are the root of community. In practice, the line between community and society is not as easy to draw as Toennies suggested. Groups with a strong element of *Gemeinschaft* can become more pragmatic and open to a broader segment of society as they pursue a particular goal.[23] This fact is evident, for example, in the transition of an ideologically focused political movement such as the German social democrats from a workers' opposition movement to a governing party. Exemplars of *Gesellschaft*, such as business corporations, have sought to imbue in their constituencies a sense of collective identity transcending mere interest. Credit unions claim to distinguish themselves from ordinary banks on this basis. Most communities are some combination of *Gemeinschaft* and *Gesellschaft*.

Christian colleges sometimes refer to themselves as a "family." This signifies a degree of shared values and interpersonal concern more characteristic of kinship than of organization. The image of family should not obscure the fact that they define themselves primarily as institutions of higher education. This admonition should be heeded especially by those who think the primary role of the Christian college as "family" is to be a "haven in a godless world."[24] Taylor University, for example, defines its mission as the education of believers for "ministering the redemptive love of Jesus Christ *to a world* in need."

"Mediating institution" is a concept that more accurately reflects this mission than "family." A mediating institution is a social structure that bridges the gap between private and public life. Entities such as families, churches, and schools can teach individuals to rise above personal interest while preventing the state from dominating public life.[25] In totalitarian societies, social units function, in Lenin's phrase, as "transmission belts" to bring all spheres of life into conformity with an established orthodoxy. *Private life is not encouraged.* In fragmented societies, social units are preoccupied with protecting turf and serving constituent interests. *There is little sense of social obligation.* A civil society is one that exhibits tolerance of deeply-rooted differences as well as a strong sense of responsibility for the public good. The problem of how to maintain such an equilibrium has preoccupied theorists of American democracy in recent years.[26] A mediating institution promotes a balance between liberty and unity, both within its own body and in relation to other institutions. Even Christians do not realize their life within just one community.[27] The Christian college can be thought of as a mediator between private communities in the form of churches or families and public communities in the form of not only professional bodies related to higher education but also of the citizenry as a whole.

The thesis of Mark Noll's *The Scandal of the Evangelical Mind* is that American evangelicals have failed to appreciate how important intellectual engagement is to the mission of the church. Interestingly, he traces the problem to some of the same cultural tendencies by which Marsden explains the vitiation or weakening of liberal Christianity. He argues that dispensationalism emphasized the supernatural at the expense of a respect for tradition and reason, a respect that is deeply embedded in the history of the church. Its assumption that spiritual truths were to be apprehended and applied intuitively encouraged "Christian thinking about the world . . . marked by naivete and an absence of rigorous criticism."[28] This anti-intellectual tendency might seem quite different from the belief that there is no conflict between science and faith. However, both views suggest that theological inquiry is unnecessary. Truth is self-evident. Noll also links this weak intellectual tradition to American evangelicalism's historically activist mentality. Organizing for the conversion of the masses is not readily compatible with reflection on the relationship between Christian ideas and complex problems. While liberals pursued cultural influence by trying to maintain their position in the intellectual establishment, fundamentalists sought to win America from below. They expected evangelism, not the social gospel, to create the best citizens and thereby a more godly nation.[29] The problem is that they left those whom they evangelized isolated from and ill-prepared to interact with civil society.

Marsden regrets that liberals acquiesced as academia banished theology to a ghetto-like existence in churches or seminaries. Noll laments that evangelicals "have nourished millions of believers in the simple verities of the gospel but have largely abandoned the universities, the arts and other realms of 'high culture.'"[30] Both men plead for greater evidence of truly Christian scholarship. Thinking of Christian colleges as mediating institutions can help us to understand their role in getting the culture to pay serious attention to biblical ideas. The lack of a functioning religious commitment reflected in theology and behavior means that whatever impact an institution has, it is unlikely to be a distinctively Christian impact. Academic life will be focused on the pursuit of excellence for its own sake, personal development, public service, or the protection of disciplinary or other special interests. We should expect a genuinely Christian college to have a strong sense of community in the sense of *Gemeinschaft*. However, if *Gemeinschaft* promotes a degree of unity beyond that which is necessary for a college properly to be called Christian, then it hinders engagement with other communities. This interpretation of community is unduly influenced by cultural considerations rather than by theological and academic considerations.

A Christian community of higher learning should also be understood as a *Gesellschaft* in the sense that it serves a very specific purpose for the church and the world. In carrying out its task of education and training, it offers opportunities for Christians and non-Christians alike to think deeply and freely about the relationship between theology and any other area of study. Let me suggest three ways in which a Christian institution of higher education, as a mediating institution, might affect how we carry out our primary mission of educating people to interact effectively in both the private realm and the public square.

First, viewing a Christian college as a mediating institution can encourage a greater tolerance of diversity, ambiguity, and controversy associated with a vigorous intellectual life without fear of losing its integrity as an evangelical Christian community. A concern to avoid offending culturally based sensibilities of others in the name of community limits the diversity possible within the context of Christian commitment. Similarly, a fear of being "divisive" exacerbates the lack of appreciation among many students for the importance of intellectual experience beyond course responsibilities. It is therefore important to provide regular opportunities outside the context of chapel for engagement with speakers likely to stimulate discussion of significant issues of culture or public policy, regardless of the religious or political perspective they represent.

Second, a Christian college, working as a mediating institution, promotes a better understanding of and relationship between Christian commitment and public life, including the quasi public life of academia. A few years ago, a subcommittee of the American Association of University Professors asserted that institutions that define academic freedom within the context of commitment to a religious community have no "moral right to proclaim themselves as authentic seats of higher learning." Postmodernism might preach the importance of hermeneutics in establishing truth claims, but accrediting agencies and other elements of the academic establishment can be remarkably ignorant of the fact that a religious perspective need not constrain intellectual inquiry but can further it. However, anti-intellectual elements in their heritage can tempt American evangelicals to behave as if their mission exempts them from respecting the conventions of evidence and argument necessary for credible intellectual inquiry. Those who succumb to this temptation are no better than purveyors of political correctness, whom they are often eager to condemn.[31] In the broader sphere of civic life, evangelicals have similarly been encumbered by both establishment prejudice and by their own tendency to avoid hard questions for the sake of confident assertions. They have vacillated between insulating religious life from social concerns and embracing politics as a weapon for winning a culture war. Insofar as a Christian college is able to realize the goal of integrating faith and learning, it challenges the assumption of many in the academic and civic communities that religion outside private life has no constructive role to play.[32] A Christian college should be able to demonstrate that values-based education need not suppress religious doctrine in the name of tolerance.

Third, a high correlation exists between education and political participation and a significant heritage of evangelical involvement in social reform. Conservative Protestants emerged as a political phenomenon during the 1980s. However, students at evangelical colleges do not seem to be distinguished by an interest in public affairs. There is even less appreciation of how important social science is to an understanding of public issues. An ability to analyze different points of view and to argue effectively are highly desirable citizenship skills. However, a particular knowledge of institutions and behavior is also necessary if one is to be able to relate fact and value.[33] Christian college faculty should help students, alumni, and interested congregations understand how believers can apply biblical principles to such salient issues as welfare reform, criminal justice, affirmative action, environmental protection, and world order. In so doing, they can contribute to the development of a Christian public that is more than just another special interest group.

CONCLUSION

Evangelical Christian churches, colleges, and parachurch organizations should make more of an effort to cooperate in nurturing among their constituency a strong "attentive public." An attentive public is distinguished from the general public by a level of knowledge and concern about public affairs that allows its members to be meaningfully involved in activities that are important to citizenship in a democracy. Those who are part of the attentive public are in a position to vote more intelligently than many do. They are more resistant to image manipulation and more likely to judge leaders and policies on substantive grounds. They are more likely to try to influence public policy by becoming interested in particular issues and contributing to certain organizations. The attentive public is also a source of "opinion leaders"—commentators, scholars, and community leaders—who are crucial to the promotion of public discourse in a democracy. It is also a source of the decision-makers, who formulate or implement public policy.

The degree to which it is possible to be a Christian disciple and an active citizen will, of course, vary according to interest, ability, and opportunity. My contention, however, is that Christians—especially Christians in a functioning democracy—should be as committed to being good citizens in the name of Christ as they are to loving their families, participating faithfully in a church, and offering an honest day's work. They need not discount the importance of power and interest to be motivated by service.

In the Soviet Union was once a statue to Pavel Morozov, a youth who was considered to be an ideal communist because he turned in his family for hiding grain that the state was trying to force farmers to surrender. At Princeton University in the nineteenth century, during the heyday of "muscular Christianity" (which equated "Christian" with "gentleman"), was a statue of the "ideal Christian youth." Both statues were torn off their pedestals by those who rightly rejected the sort of "goodness" that each statue represented. Were a monument to the "ideal Christian citizen" to be erected, perhaps it could depict the theologian Karl Barth's image of *a person holding a Bible in one hand and a newspaper in the other*. Glenn Tinder suggests a balanced perspective for those who would be faithful Christians and good citizens. They must not only be obedient to authority and attentive to public life but also be willing to criticize governments and political ideologies whenever necessary. The late Christian social philosopher Jacques Ellul reminds us that our engagement must be in a spirit of humility. Perhaps his words would be an appropriate inscription for our monument:

> It is after doing what is commanded, when everything has been done in the sphere of human decisions and means, when . . . every effort has been made to know the will of God and to obey it, when in the arena of life there has been full acceptance of all responsibilities . . . and conflicts, it is then and only then that [we may say]: . . . all this we cast from us to put it in thy hands, O Lord.[34]

ENDNOTES

1. See, for example, Rodney Clapp, *A Peculiar People* (Downers Grove, Ill.: 1996), 23ff.
2. Glenn Tinder, *The Political Meaning of Christianity: The Prophetic Stance* (New York: Harper Collins, 1991).
3. Victoria Barnett, *For the Soul of the People: Protestant Protest Against Hitler* (New York: Oxford University Press, 1992), 27, 34.
4. George L Mosse, *The Crisis of German Ideology* (New York: Grosset and Dunlap, 1964), 24–45.
5. Udo Hahn, *"Vverminten Land"*; Gottfried Müller, *"Wo Luthers Vorfahren ihre Heimat hatten,"* *Rheinischer Merkur/Christ und Welt*, 20 January 1989.
6. *Neues Deutschland*, 4 April 1984.
7. Hahn, *"Verminten Land,"* 5; Hahn, *"Gemeinsame Werte betont,"* *Rheinischer Merkur/Christ und Welt*, 21 August 1992; Jürgen Engert, *"Kommt Zeit, kommt Stolpe,"* *Rheinischer Merkur/Christ und Welt*, 4 October 1991; *Rheinischer Merkur/Christ und Welt*, 15 September 1989; Hahn, *"Geheimdiplomat mit Sympathie für Sozialismus,"* *Rheinischer Merkur/Christ und Welt*, 24 January 1992; and Heinrich Stubbe, *"Am Bischof scheiden sich die Geister,"* *Rheinischer Merkur/Christ und Welt*, 4 August 1989.
8. Diephouse, *Pastors and Pluralism* (Princeton, N.J.: Princeton University Press, 1987), 19–20, 363; and Barnett, *For the Soul of the People*, 246–47.
9. See Mary Fulbrook's discussion of the "niche society" notion in *Anatomy of a Dictatorship: Inside the GDR, 1949–1989* (New York: Oxford University Press, 1995), chap. 5.
10. Thomas Berke interview of Reinhard Steinlein, *Rheinischer Merkur/Christ und Welt*, 14 August 1992, 22. Acceptance of the church within socialism and the creation of the Kirchenbund varied. The Lutheran Church in Thuringia, where Mitzenheim was bishop, was most accepting. Steinlein's Berlin-Brandenburg

Church was one of the least supportive, but there was at least as much opposition in Görlitz; see Robert F. Goeckel, *The Lutheran Church and the East German State: Political Conflict and Change Under Ulbricht and Honecker* (Ithaca, N.Y.: Cornell University Press, 1990), 78–85.

11. Udo Hahn, *"Zwei Zimmer mit einer Schiebetür,"* Rheinischer Merkur/Christ und Welt, 16 June 1989.

12. In German, *"Biblisches Menschsein ist Mitmenschsein."*

13. Marlies Menge, *"Hoffen auf einen besseren Sozialismus,"* Die Zeit, 19 May 1989

14. Wallace Bratt, *Reformed Journal*, September 1989, 2–3.

15. William Echikson, "A Pastor with a Political Mission," *The Christian Science Monitor*, 28 December 1989.

16. Karl Dietrich Bracher, *The German Dictatorship: The Origins, Structure, and Effects of National Socialism* (New York: Praega, 1970), 384–89.

17. Interview cited in Barnett, *For the Soul of the People*, 279.

18. Interview with Werner Leich, *Rheinischer Merkur/Christ und Welt*, 22 May 1992; Hahn, "Kirche im Sozialismus: Aus den Stasi Akten wächst ein Alptraum," *Rheinischer Merkur/Christ und Welt*, 17 January 1992.

19. Werner Leich, *"Ein Hirte, umringt von Wölfen,"* Rheinischer Merkur/Christ und Welt, 18 September 1992.

20. Diephouse, *Pastors and Pluralism*, 258–60, 359.

21. Scholder, *Churches*, vol. 1 (1918–34); *Fortress*, 1988, 425; Steinlein interview.

22. Goeckel, *The Lutheran Church*, 216.

23. Robert Booth Fowler, *The Dance with Community: The Continuing Debate in American Political Thought* (Lawrence: Univ. of Kansas Press, 1991), 3–4; Robert V. Hine, *Community on the American Frontier: Separate but Not Alone* (Norman, Okla.: University of Oklahoma Press, 1980), 19–20.

24. I am paraphrasing the title of Christopher Lasch's book, *Haven in a Heartless World: The Family Besieged* (New York: Norton, 1977).

25. James Luther Adams, "Mediating Structures and the Separation of Powers," in *Democracy and Mediating Structures*, ed. Michael Novak (Washington: American Enterprise Institute, 1980), 2–4.

26. Among the most significant recent works that have discussed the degree to which unity is possible in a liberal society are Robert Bellah et al., *Habits of the Heart: Individualism and Commitment in American Life* (New York: Harper & Row, 1986); Arthur Schlesinger Jr., *The Disuniting of America: Reflections on a Multicultural Society* (New York: Whittle Direct, 1991); and Michael Sandel, *Democracy's Discontent* (Cambridge: Cambridge University Press, 1996).

27. Hine, 4, citing R. M. MacIver.

28. Mark Noll, *The Scandal of the Evangelical Mind* (Grand Rapids: Eerdmans, 1994), 130.

29. Ibid., chap. 6.

30. Ibid., 3.

31. George M. Marsden, *The Soul of the American University* (New York: Oxford University Press, 1994), 431, 437; and Robert Wuthnow, *The Struggle for America's Soul* (Grand Rapids: Eerdmans, 1989), 162–63; the anti-intellectual heritage of American evangelicalism is a major theme in Noll's *The Scandal of the Evangelical Mind*.

32. Two good discussions of the relationship between religious commitment and public life from an evangelical Christian perspective are Os Guiness, *The American Hour* (New York: Free Press, 1993); and James Skillen, *Recharging the*

American Experiment: Principled Pluralism for Genuine Civic Community (Grand
Rapids: Baker, 1994).
33. An inner-city pastor recently contrasted evangelicals' lack of sophistication in
    social science with their expertise in biblical scholarship. He regarded this as a
    serious impediment to relating the gospel to issues of social justice. Eugene
    Rivers, "Separate and Equal," *Christianity Today*, 5 February 1996, 14–24.
34. Jacques Ellul, *The Politics of God and the Politics of Man* (Grand Rapids: Eerdmans,
    1972), 195–96.

An Overview

The current "all or nothing" posture by many Christians who engage in politics has done little to alter America's sliding moral landscape. In fact, it has probably done more harm than good. Douglas L. Koopman and Gary L. Visscher lay out for us the career and convictions of a man who, as a Christian politician, understood that politics is a process that brings together conflicting ideas for the purpose of discovering mutually acceptable solutions. Although he was faithful and committed to Christian principles, Paul Henry also understood that meaningful progress politically, in the best interest of true justice, is incremental in nature and often involves collaboration and compromise. His public service exemplified Christlike humility, deep concern for the interests of all of the people he represented, and love for those with whom he differed philosophically. A Christian's role is not to *threaten* those who differ with him or her but rather to *influence* with compassion, humility, reasoning, and sound judgment in the hope that true justice will ultimately be served.

Chapter Ten

PAUL HENRY
*A Model for Integrating
Christian Faith and Politics*

Douglas L. Koopman and Gary L. Visscher

ONE THURSDAY MORNING MORE THAN ten years ago, one of the authors[1] was riding the elevator up from the basement of a Washington, D.C., congressional office building with our boss, U.S. Representative Paul B. Henry of Michigan. As the elevator climbed to the first floor, its doors opened and in stepped two other members of Congress, each from a different southern state. They both were acquaintances of Paul because they were all Republicans first elected to the U.S. House in 1984. All three had just attended the weekly members-only prayer breakfast held that morning and every Thursday morning in a small meeting room in the U.S. Capitol building. As the two southerners entered the elevator, one of them said to Paul, "Wasn't that an inspiring story that 'Bill' (a representative who had given his Christian testimony at the prayer breakfast that morning) shared with us? I really admire his ability to tell his story." Paul allowed that, yes, "Bill" did provide a moving personal testimony and that he seemed to be a very vocal Christian. The other southern representative chimed in, "Yes, and the great thing about 'Bill' is that he never lets his faith get in the way of how he votes." Paul smiled weakly. At that point, the elevator reached the fourth floor, and the two southerners hurried out to their offices. As the two of us continued the ride up, Paul joked, "Well, you can sure tell that they're not Reformed."

Paul Henry's firm conviction was that politics and Christian faith were intimately intertwined, that politics uninformed by faith was without purpose and that faith without political action was incomplete. Faith influenced how Paul voted, as well as how he thought, spoke, and worked. He concluded his 1974 book *Politics for Evangelicals* with the words from Matthew 5:14–16.

> You are the light of the world. A city set on a hill cannot be hid. Nor do men light a lamp and put it under a bushel, but on a stand, and it gives light to all in the house. Let your light so shine before men, that they may see your good works and give glory to your Father who is in heaven (RSV).

This chapter looks at the life and work of one person who certainly let his light shine in the darkness of the political world—former U.S. Representative Paul B. Henry. Paul would probably be cautious about an article that uses his own political career as the model for Christians in politics. He was a frequent and popular speaker, whether to adult Sunday school classes or academic conferences, on the relationship between Christianity and politics. But he was always cautious about explaining his own votes or political positions in that context, concerned that doing so could not avoid being, or appearing to be, self-serving. And he would be quick to point out that there are many thoughtful and sincere Christians with whom he shared his vocation but who had different views from his own on many issues.

This chapter is not impartial. We are two of literally hundreds of persons uplifted by Paul Henry's personal character, educated by his political skills, and inspired by his example of how a serious Christian should understand and act in the political arena. We were both privileged to work on Paul's congressional staff and to know him as a mentor and friend. We also grew up in the same Reformed Christian tradition that influenced Paul, a tradition that has an especially positive attitude toward Christian political engagement.[2]

The first portion of this chapter is a narrative of Paul Henry's career, ending with a brief review of how he viewed some of the key issues of the day. The second portion of the chapter recites some of Paul's own reflections on the mixture of politics and Christian faith and puts those reflections in a slightly larger philosophical context, both politically and religiously. We do so in the hope that readers of various faith traditions can better grasp Paul's personal journey in faith and politics and also interpret that journey in new situations.

CAREER

Paul Henry was a respected politician, recognized by secular commentators in his home state of Michigan and at the national level as both a skillful politician and a model public servant.[3] Paul viewed politics as an honorable profession. He liked to remind his students that the Greek philosopher Aristotle had written that politics—the proper exercise of the political art— is the highest of all human endeavors, the "master science."

Paul was also a Christian who took seriously the implications of his faith for his vocation. He was well known in the evangelical community not only for his own record of accomplishment in politics and his leadership in helping fellow evangelicals understand their political responsibilities but also as the son of Dr. Carl F. H. Henry, one of the leaders of evangelical Christianity in this century.[4] He was recognized not only in the Christian community but also in the wider political community, as "a deeply religious man who did not hide his evangelical beliefs."[5]

Paul began his political career shortly after graduating from Wheaton College in Illinois and serving two years in the Peace Corps in Liberia and Ethiopia. During his graduate school studies in political science at Duke University in the 1960s, Paul spent two periods of time as a congressional staff person, working for Rep. John Anderson, then a Republican from Illinois.

Years later, as a congressman himself, Paul advised many young people who were seeking to work for Congress to "be willing to start at the bottom." He told them about his own first job as a congressional staff person—feeding a mimeograph machine for most of each day, copying Anderson's press releases and constituent newsletters. Paul's second time working as congressional staff, in 1968–69, was higher up. By then, Rep. Anderson had been elected Chair of the House Republican Conference, the third-ranking leadership position for House Republicans. Paul served as Acting Staff Director for the Conference, having been named by Anderson to that post.[6]

In 1970, having obtained his Ph.D. degree in Political Science at Duke University, Paul and his family moved to Grand Rapids, Michigan, and Paul became professor of political science at Calvin College. He also became involved in local political and community activities, including the Republican Party and serving as an advisor and sometimes campaign manager for numerous political candidates. In 1974, the local Republican Party as well as the national political scene, received a shock when, in the midst of Watergate, a Democrat was elected to take the local congressional seat long held by Gerald Ford, who had resigned to become vice president of the United States. In the aftermath of that shock, Paul was asked and became chair of the Kent County Republican Party, and later served as chair of the 5th Congressional District Republican Party, which is centered in Kent County.

By then, Paul's political skills and ambitions were publicly known. He was refreshingly candid about his ambitions for office, believing that his God-given gifts and abilities would lead him in such a direction. In 1975, Michigan's Republican governor, William Milliken, appointed Paul to a seat on the Michigan State Board of Education. In 1978, Paul entered politics full time when he ran for and won an open seat in the Michigan State House of Representatives. In his first term, he was elected by his colleagues as Assistant Republican Floor Leader and served four years in that leadership position, trying to push a Republican governor's agenda in a legislature controlled by a Democratic majority. While in the Michigan House of Representatives, Paul was appointed to a statewide commission on prison reform, sparking an interest in criminal justice issues that continued throughout his career.

In 1982, Paul ran for and won a seat in the Michigan State Senate. Due to the recall a year later of two Democrat state senators and the subsequent election of Republican replacements, in 1984, for one year (and for the only time in his legislative career at the state or national level), Paul was able to serve in the majority party.

In the majority, Paul chaired the Senate Committee on Education and Health. The position allowed him to push education reform in Michigan, including a proposal to improve the quality of science and math teaching in Michigan schools by making it easier for individuals with experience and training in those areas to move into teaching. He also took on a number of controversial health issues, such as giving the families of persons with emotional and mental illness greater authority and responsibility over their treatment. Although he had a reputation as a pragmatic politician, he often tackled issues that, while serious, seemed to have considerable political risk and little political benefit. Paul liked to see such issues raised and discussed, even if he knew that consensus was not possible. His style of leadership—his openness to listening to others, his candor in expressing his reasons for disagreeing, and his evident thoughtfulness—often gained him people's support for putting such issues on the legislative agenda despite their lack of political payoff.

In 1984, Paul also sponsored an amendment to the Michigan constitution to protect the Michigan Land Trust Fund. The Fund had been set up by the state legislature in the mid-1970s to take revenues that the state received from oil and gas drilling on state-owned lands to hold "in trust" for the sole purpose of purchasing additional public lands. Successive governors and legislatures, however, had frequently used Fund money for current spending programs. Paul had opposed such "raids." Consequently, when a number of environmental and sportsmen's organizations began exploring the possibility of protecting the Fund by proposing its protection as an amendment to the state constitution, Paul was an eager sponsor and legislative champion. The state legislature passed a proposed constitutional amendment, and Michigan voters overwhelmingly approved it in November 1984.

The Land Trust Fund was one of Paul's favorite legislative accomplishments. It brought together two strands of Paul's conservatism: fiscal and environmental. In a *Christianity Today* interview in 1990, Paul put the connection thus:

> I have fairly consistently taken the posture that as a conservative, I have something to say about environmental conservation. There is also an analogy with fiscal issues. When you exploit the environment you are simply building up "debt" that is passed on to the next generation. . . . We ought to apply the same standards of stewardship to the environment and not waste it in such a way that it is denied to others in the next generation. In the modern economic order, we've become highly productive, but we have in some cases become equally wasteful. From a purely secular point of view, it is our wastefulness that will ultimately catch up with us. . . . From a Christian perspective, in the beginning in the order of creation, man, as the pinnacle of God's creation, was charged with stewardship of the garden. One of the effects of the Fall was that all aspects of the created order came under the Curse. But in the redemptive order, as early as the Mosaic code, there were injunctions to use and care for the land under the biblical concepts of stewardship.[7]

In the spring of 1984, the incumbent congressman from Michigan's Fifth District announced he would not seek reelection. Paul won the race to replace him, obtaining a majority in a multicandidate Republican primary and receiving 62 percent of the vote in the fall general election. He won reelection in 1986, 1988, and 1990, each time receiving more than 70 percent of the vote in his district, usually a higher percentage than any other area candidate for any office. He was also strongly reelected in 1992, two weeks after he was diagnosed with a brain tumor. It was hoped that the surgery that took place before the election—which successfully removed most of the tumor— would lead to recovery. Indeed, for a while Paul did regain his strength, enough so that he was able to attend his swearing in at the beginning of the 103d Congress in January 1993. However, he gradually became weaker and died while still holding office on July 31, 1993.

Paul Henry was a Republican who was most often placed within its moderate wing, as is common in the Midwest and Northeast. But the "moderate" label did not capture Paul's own set of convictions. In the 1993 edition of the *Almanac of American Politics*, the authors said of Paul, "[O]ver the years Henry developed a reputation as one who defies labels—neither a rigid conservative, nor a moderate. He generally votes with his party (70 to 80 percent of the time) and he most often takes the party line in Education and Labor Committee sessions. Despite all of this, Henry has remained independent-minded, and he has broken ranks on some key issues when his principles dictated."[8]

One such issue early in his congressional career was a vote in March 1985 that he cast against authorizing additional spending for the MX missile system, a major strategic weapons system sought by the Reagan Administration. The MX vote came amidst very heavy lobbying by both sides—the President and those who were opposed to the continued arms buildup he had begun. While the public debate focused largely on the MX as a referendum on the arms race, Paul's principal concern was budgetary. He came to Congress deeply concerned about and opposed to continued deficit spending by the federal government, and he believed that the only way to reach political agreement to bring such deficit spending under control would be through spending restraint across the board, in both defense and in nondefense spending.

Later that year, on another very controversial issue, Paul voted for the Reagan Administration's request for funding for the Nicaraguan "Contras." Even while supporting the Reagan Administration's goals in Nicaragua of countering and containing its communist government, Paul became increasingly critical of the Administration's policy, which he viewed as focusing almost entirely on supporting the contras. In 1987, he announced that he would no longer support aid to the Contras, unless it was accompanied by a "multidimensional" and "multilateral" policy that included serious diplomatic efforts by the United States and the involvement of the governments of the other Central American countries. In the aftermath of diplomatic efforts initiated in 1988 by the Reagan Administration that eventually ended the fighting and led to scheduled elections that replaced the communist government of Nicaragua, Paul received some credit from colleagues in Congress for having helped redirect Administration policy.

Paul had the academician's instinct for reevaluating rather than repeating prevailing arguments. His reputation as a policy moderate often came more out of disagreement with both sides of a debate than with an intention to simply "split the difference" between two previously staked-out positions.

One such issue was funding for the National Endowment for the Arts (NEA). In 1989, a number of conservative organizations brought to light that the NEA had been the source of funding for several projects that were graphic in sexual content or irreverent with regard to Christian teaching or tradition. Paul shared the outrage that such projects had received government funding. But he disagreed with both sides of the ensuing political debate—NEA supporters who argued that Congress could not or should not impose any additional accountability on the NEA, and NEA opponents, who sought to eliminate funding for the agency. In the end, language that he proposed was adopted into law. It required that the NEA "take into consideration general standards of decency and respect for the diverse beliefs and values" when deciding whether a project has "artistic excellence and artistic merit" and is, therefore, eligible for funding.

For the most part, though, Paul's legislative career was spent less in the limelight, but, insofar as a minority party member is able, being a constructive participant in shaping legislation and in addressing issues on behalf of his constituents and the country. Political writer and journalist David Broder wrote about Paul's years in Congress:

> Henry represents the other side—the unpublicized side—of politics and Congress. When people express their scorn for politicians and legislators, it tells me that we in the press have not done our jobs in depicting what the honorable men and women in those fields contribute through their service. . . . Similar to every other Republican in the House, he chafed under the frustrations of seemingly permanent minority status, but he never became cynical. He has been a valuable, contributing member of the Education and Labor and Science, Space, and Technology Committees, and a voice of sanity and conscience in party councils at home and in Washington.[9]

Among the issues and proposals on which Paul worked and achieved success was the first set of education accountability provisions in a federal education program. Before that, the federal government had distributed funds with extensive bookkeeping requirements to show that funds were not siphoned off into unapproved programs. But the federal government did *not* require schools receiving funds to show any educational gains by the students being served. Paul also introduced legislation to make it easier to use savings bonds for college education after a constituent wrote to him with that suggestion. The idea was later supported by the Bush Administration and successfully enacted into law. And Paul introduced and had enacted the first disclosure requirements to assure greater accountability for college and university athletic programs.

Because of his background and interests in religion, issues involving church and state and the role of religious institutions in society seemed to gravitate to him. He worked to protect the distinctiveness of religious higher education and was instrumental in shaping child care legislation that allowed parents to receive vouchers that could be used at religious day care centers of the parents' choosing.

In the environmental area, he helped gain passage of the Michigan Wilderness bill, national legislation that had been stalled by lack of bipartisan support. He also pushed for several years to enact a national "bottle bill" similar to one in place in Michigan and several other states, requiring a return deposit on soft drink and similar containers. In his work on the Science Committee, he pushed for additional federal support for applied (as opposed to "pure") science, particularly to assist the country's manufacturers who were undergoing immense change and challenge from international competition. He was also among the first in Congress to raise concerns about the extent to which federal funding for science research directed to America's colleges and universities was ignoring American students and supporting foreign students.

On budget issues, Paul was consistently conservative. In several years, he opposed every appropriations bill because of the government's continued deficit spending in the 1980s and early 1990s. His belief in the sanctity of life was unshakable, and he consistently voted against abortion. In 1992, he did vote, however, to allow fetal tissue research to go forward, a measure that some right-to-life organizations opposed on the grounds that it would encourage abortion. Paul argued that the potential for restoring the wholeness and fullness of life, which such research promised, could not be so easily dismissed by those who were fully pro-life. He did not oppose the death penalty on principle but was concerned about its uneven application and sometimes voted against it on those grounds. He voted for some gun control measures, including the "Brady bill" waiting period for handgun purchases.

Paul had a deep sense of the importance of personal and public integrity and honesty, and he did not think that one could be separated from the other. At the same time, he was, as the *Grand Rapids Press* observed, "unpretentious, far more taken with the seriousness of his work than of his own importance in doing it. And his professionalism enabled him to separate policy differences with other people from his personal feelings toward them."[10]

His personal conduct and character were apparent to those with whom he worked. Someone who lobbied Paul on environmental issues wrote, "Mr. Henry was a truly decent, honorable man. He was the kind of person you really looked forward to seeing. He was friendly and warm, and never seemed to forget a face. He was truly one of the 'good guys' one meets less often than we would like in government, the kind of person whose career is an example to young people."[11] His colleague, fellow Wheaton College graduate and now Speaker of the House Dennis Hastert, observed that Paul was "a stickler for what was right, for what was good, for what was decent, for what was fair . . . His example and all of the examples of how Paul lived his life, I think, certainly is the marker that any man, certainly any legislator, can lay out as a measure, as a measure that others following behind him can live up to, can follow, can try to emulate."[12]

At the close of Paul's life, among the many who spoke or wrote of the "light" that Paul had shone was a former chairman of the Democrat Party in Paul's congressional district:

> Being of different political parties, we naturally did not always agree. But we laughed a lot, shared interests, and agreed that public service was an honorable calling.
>   Paul died too young. He had decency and character, a wonderful sense of humor, and faith in reason which compelled respect. His loss is not so much of a particular point of view; it is of a person who had the power to lead by example.[13]

CONVICTIONS

Paul amplified on his view of politics and on the relationship between Christian faith and politics in his book *Politics for Evangelicals* and in a number of later speeches and articles. In his book, Paul encouraged evangelical Christians to get involved in politics at a time when evangelical Christian involvement in American politics and government was sorely lacking.

> The Christian community must learn to recognize that civic involvement is in itself a legitimate form of Christian service. To deny this is to suggest a truncated Christianity which arbitrarily separates the sacred from the secular. Such a viewpoint refuses to acknowledge that Christian calling and commitment pertain to all of one's life, not just what goes on inside the church walls.[14]

The political life was a legitimate calling for a Christian and one that Paul himself felt strongly and acknowledged openly. The sense of calling and vocation, a hallmark of Reformed theology, argues that God is actively involved in all activities in this world and that Christians need to be "salt and light" in a wide range of professions far outside traditional religious occupations.[15]

Most of Paul's life in politics was as an elected U.S. representative, trying to represent in Washington, D.C., the more than 600,000 residents in his western Michigan congressional district. A legislator has an especially difficult job, for he or she represents a specific geographical location with a range of interests. This geographic representation is balanced in a representative's job with reasonable loyalty to a political party label, a necessity in running for office and in attaining influence in the legislature, where most rewards and punishments are meted out by partisan considerations. Finally, the constituency and party loyalties must combine with a representative's personal convictions and his or her set of gifts and limitations.

Paul told constituents looking for a shorthand explanation of how he determined his position on issues, "[W]hen I vote on a piece of legislation, I am guided by more than what is 'politically correct.' I take into consideration the following criteria as the basis for my voting patterns: my conscience, my country, my district, and my party. There are times those criteria have been at odds—and it is especially in those occasions I need and covet your prayers. I ask that you pray not only that I have the wisdom to know what is right, but also the courage to do it!"[16]

Paul believed that while Christians brought a unique perspective to political issues, they did not bring "the one right answer." He expressed at least part of that perspective in a letter to a constituent who was critical of a vote that he had cast, writing, "I may not always be right—but I do try not to deliberately mislead my constituents, and to remain open to correction, knowing that ultimately I am subject to higher judgment and accountability than that of the electorate."[17]

Paul was aware of the common opinion that politics was unusually corrupt. But Paul worked hard to make a distinction between true and intentional corruption—which needs to be rooted out—and natural corruption (the inherent problems that accompany human sin in a fallen world, e.g., limited knowledge and trust, especially in conjunction with the nature of government and politics)—which needs to be dealt with wisely and humbly. He wrote on the nature of politics and moral ambiguity of political issues:

> [I] have suggested that all political activity is involved in the struggle between good and evil. But at the same time, in the world of politics, it is always extremely difficult to say with certainty what is good and what is bad. Politics is surrounded by problems of moral ambiguity.[18]

He viewed both partisan conflict and provisional compromise as essential elements of politics, including in that of his own involvement in politics.

> Conflict stemming from self-interest must therefore be seen to lie at the heart of politics. Were there no conflict, there would be no need for politics. . . . Because politics is a never-ending cycle of conflict seeking consensus, moralists of all stripes become quickly frustrated. They seek absolute answers of eternal significance as opposed to the calculated compromises of politics . . . But the ability to accept compromise is the mark of political maturity. It is the very stuff out of which politics is made.[19]

With the increased political activism of evangelicals in the late 1970s and 1980s, Paul became more concerned about *how* some Christians were getting involved than that they be involved. In a 1985 interview, Paul cautioned that "[t]he real danger at this point in the evangelical community is not the mistaken notion that Christians ought not be involved—we're coming through that. Now the danger lies in how we're being involved and whether we're listening and following, as it were, the promptings of the Spirit, or simply manipulating religious symbols."[20]

Paul's view of politics as a noble profession together with his sincere acknowledgment of a "higher judgment and accountability" led to a distinct and, we think, admirable style of politics. Indeed, it was in his style of politics more than in his work on any particular issue or issues that Paul's "light" was most evident. Paul tried to hold constantly in tension the need for involvement and the need for humility. An excerpt from an article written for the Just Life Educational Fund may be his best statement in this regard:

> We are called to seek justice, to let our lights shine, to be the salt of the earth. Involvement in the political process is one of many ways in which the Christian community can be faithful to the redemptive power of the gospel. . . . Our democratic institutions afford us the opportunity to effect change and promote wholeness within our society and between the nations. To forsake this opportunity is to bear responsibility for the consequences of our inaction, as well as to leave the public sector solely in the hands of those who may not be sensitive to Christian values . . .
>
> At the same time, we must remember the prophetic injunction to walk humbly with our God. Just as surely as the Scriptures make plain that we are to seek justice, we cannot simply reduce the Christian message to some sort of religious party platform from which incontrovertible political specifics can be drawn. The Bible and the teachings of the Christian community point to broad principles which we dare not neglect in our Christian witness to society. But we must guard against the temptation to exploit those principles on behalf of particular applications when other equally plausible affirmations of the Christian conscience can be drawn from them. We must avoid the temptation to manipulate or exploit Christian conscience on behalf of hidden agendas, thereby using God's name rather than being used by God . . .
>
> Above all, Christian conduct in the public order ought to be marked by sensitivity toward those outside the Christian community who may disagree with us at the most fundamental level, as well as sensitivity to those within the Christian community who may disagree with us at the practical level. Remember the words of St. Paul: "The fruit of the Spirit is love, joy, peace, patience, kindness, goodness, faithfulness, gentleness, and self-control." We must never forget that Christian virtue does not stop at the water's edge of the political process.[21]

Along with reminding evangelical Christians of their responsibilities to act as Christians in the political process, Paul also advised them to understand and appreciate the role of politics in human society. It was a subject that he addressed in a 1989 speech entitled "Morality vs. Moralism: In Defense of Politics" delivered at Pepperdine University.

> The question of politics is not the elimination of the reality of evil in the human condition which reflects itself in politics, but in seeking practical means whereby to contain it. The problem is not new. The struggle to address it is not new. And the officials who wield power are qualitatively neither better nor worse than previous generations. A bit of humility in the face of history and the human condition will do much to inject realism into the current political debate—a humility which moves us closer to genuine moral critique of the political process and away from political moralism.

The Judeo-Christian worldview has consistently fought the modernist heresy that men are essentially shaped by their environment, and that better laws *ipso facto* make better men. But at the behavioral level, I have found things quite different. Preachers in the pulpit decry the heresy that mankind is inherently good and perfectible. But when they enter the political arena they are tempted to pitch the battle in terms of men versus angels, and refuse to admit that all political actors—including themselves—are still affected by the human condition . . .

The ancient prophet exhorts us to seek justice, love mercy, and walk humbly with our God. Somehow we have all been tempted to lose sight of the last of those injunctions—that of humility. The religious community is not particularly different from the secular community in the temptations to speak in political absolutes and certitude. But anyone who claims to speak in the name of God runs the risk of using God's name in vain as opposed to speaking in humility, admitting the fallenness and limitations of human nature to which our own religious teachings attest. When the religious community does this, it becomes secularized and loses the very salt whereby it can savor the political arena to which it seeks to speak.

Second, we must not lose sight of the legitimacy of politics. The religious community, as well as the secular community, has tended to romanticize and optimize its assessment as the nature of man. It has also tended to romanticize and optimize its assessment as to what the political process itself involves.

Politics involves resolving conflicts between competing demands within society. Not just competing demands in the abstract, but the competing demands as to how society's goods are going to be allocated—allocated in such a way that there are always winners and losers. Altogether too often, religious communities fall into the trap of endorsing one set of values and demands without recognizing the legitimacy of competing sets of values and demands. Political justice involves allocations on behalf of both rich and poor, black and white, producer and consumer. Politics involves mediating the differences between competing demands—and such mediation seldom involves situations where political virtue is exclusively on just one side of the equation.

Christianity does not condemn the advocacy of interest, per se. Rather it tells us to elevate our neighbor's interest to a degree of intensity with which we are prone to defend our own. Disdain for interest group politics or special interests reflects a lack of understanding pertaining to the inherent nature of the political process itself. . . . Too often religious groups enter the political arena with inherent disdain not only for the political process but in opposition to the concept of politics itself. And once again, it reflects a yielding to temptation to secularize the eschaton in the name of the Kingdom of God.[22]

CONCLUSION

We have little to add to the testimony of Paul's life in politics and his reflections upon the critical issues involved. We would only make a few points that we believe have some broader application to Christians who are contemplating the intersection of their faith with active involvement in or reflection about political life.

The first point is the legitimacy of a Christian calling into politics. Paul Henry's life showed that a Christian could be deeply involved in politics at the most intense levels and still maintain integrity and perspective. Christians are persons of principle, and holding fast to principle is an essential characteristic of integrity in life and politics. Yet in politics, as in the rest of life, our reason and logic are clouded by sin. We must be careful not to be too confident in the ultimate truth of our conclusions. *The nature of politics is incremental change:* we move forward, at best, one step at a time. The essential character of a Christian in politics is the willingness to work constantly for progress toward the truths and policies in which he or she believes while simultaneously acknowledging that even the most firmly held beliefs can be subject to correction and modification.

A second, though related, principle is the uniqueness of a Christian calling into politics for each particular person in each particular office. Pursuing a God-given calling fulfills and deepens one's gifts and personality; it does not create a "cookie-cutter" Christian politician who votes and acts in a particular way. Paul was a Republican, mostly because the party's more limited view of government's role fit better with his view about limiting government because of human sin. But it was also important to Paul that Michigan's Republican Party had respectable records on the environment and civil rights, issues of prime concern. Paul had a gregarious nature, a brilliant mind, an informal grace, and a creative and self-deprecating humor. Paul's outgoing nature and superior intellectual capacity made him a particular type of politician who conducted himself in a particular way in his western Michigan district and in Washington, D.C. Paul carried out a highly visible and energetic district schedule, and an intellectually sophisticated legislative program focused on the details of issues naturally within his committees' jurisdictions and personal expertise.

Paul Henry was a natural "representative," thriving in the role of listening to and balancing the varied interests of the persons he represented and articulating those interests in the legislature. He might have acted quite differently had he been a governor or a judge; but as a representative, he was wise enough to ensure that his personality converged with the requirements of the representational offices that he held. Other Christians, with other gifts and in other positions, might define their jobs quite differently and still carry it out in a faithful Christian manner.

A third principle that we find is the need for Christian humility in the face of the moral ambiguity that often surrounds politics. Politics is both complex and intense. Combining these facts with the fallenness of human motivations and the frailties of the intellect should make any Christian reluctant to claim complete understanding and authority over a particular issue or position. Rather, political and spiritual realities demand great humility by all who participate in the political arena, but especially by Christians whose theology so clearly identifies and points out the consequences of overestimating human ability.

A fourth principle of Christian action is the balance between conviction and cooperation. One must be willing to go against the grain of the dominant set of issues and positions on them. Christians are born to a new life in Christ and should more easily discard the values and answers of the dominant secular culture, including the political culture. As such, Christians are freer than others to examine critically the needs of society and the limits and possibilities of politics to meet those needs more effectively. At the same time, democratic politics is a "team sport." *It requires working with others to achieve specific, limited, and incremental goals,* both immediately and over the longer term. It is built on relationships with those in power, and with those who seek power because such power is necessary to bring about the public changes that Christians in politics seek.

Fifth, we believe that Christians operating in politics should be the exemplars of civility. Too much of politics is overheated rhetoric and *ad hominem* attack. Christians with a full understanding of the limits and possibilities of politics, and of the precarious state of their own souls should be the last to engage in such tactics despite the obvious temptations to do so. At Paul's 1993 memorial service, Bob Michel, then the Republican Leader in the House, said,

> One word comes to mind when I think of Paul's contribution to our public life, and the word is "civility." We Americans, unfortunately, have developed a rich political vocabulary for the ugly side of public life. How often we hear it is not enough to get mad, we have to get even, play hard ball. But civility seems to have no similar public vocabulary. So we might ask, what is this quiet but vital public virtue that was at the heart of Paul Henry's life? I define it this way, and I think Paul would have agreed:
>
> Civility means knowing that raising the level of your voice doesn't raise the level of discussion. It means recognizing that listening is a very good way of communicating.
> Civility means realizing that peaks of uncommon progress can be reached by paths of common courtesy.
> Civility means being tough without being mean, and being principled without being fanatic.
> Civility means believing in the power of reason to influence public debate, and the power of the spirit to transform private lives.
> Civility is the public embodiment of the golden rule: Do unto others as you would have them do unto you.
>
> By those standards, Paul Henry was the embodiment of civility.[23]

Paul Henry's call for us to understand the role and nature of politics and to reflect Christian character in our political action is pretty basic, perhaps quite "plain vanilla" to some. Get involved in politics; understand, respect, and play by the rules of politics; and act as a Christian while doing so. As Paul's own life and career reflected, it is possible to be a faithful witness both to a transcendent God and to the task of politics. At a time when some leaders of Christian groups urge withdrawal from politics, his guidelines for action seem as necessary as ever.

The task of integrating faith and politics is difficult but not impossible. Václav Havel, the Czech playwright and political leader, wrote:

> To sum up: if your heart is in the right place and you have good taste, not only will you pass muster in politics, you are destined for it. If you are modest and do not lust after power, not only are you suited to politics, you absolutely belong there. The *sine qua non* of a politician is not the ability to lie; he need only be sensitive and know when, what, to whom, and how to say what he has to say. It is not true that a person of principle does not belong in politics; it is enough for his principles to be leavened with patience, deliberation, a sense of proportion, and an understanding of others. It is not true that only the unfeeling cynic, the vain, the brash, and the vulgar can succeed in politics; such people, it is true, are drawn to politics, but, in the end, decorum and good taste will always count for more. My experience and observations confirm that politics as the practice of morality is possible. I do not deny, however, that it is not always easy to go that route, nor have I ever claimed that it was.[24]

Paul may have been thinking of this special difficulty when he penned the following advice:

> The Christian who enters politics must do so with the aim of achieving public justice. He does this by subjecting his own personal ambitions and desires to the scrutiny of God's revelation in the Scriptures. And as God gives the grace to do so, he learns to make the needs of his neighbor his own. In so doing, his search for justice becomes an act of sacrificial love.[25]

This statement surely describes Paul Henry. He literally spent his adult life pursuing the faithful integration of Christianity and politics in practice and in theory. We know that others like him exist, and we pray that the future brings many more.

ENDNOTES

1. The authors would like to thank the Paul B. Henry Archives at Calvin College for its assistance.
2. For a very readable explication of Reformed and other Christian views on politics, see James W. Skillen, *The Scattered Voice: Christians at Odds in the Public Square* (Grand Rapids: Zondervan, 1990).
3. David Broder, "Voters Demand Facts This Time," *Grand Rapids Press*, 4

November 1992, sec. A; and Richard E. Cohen, "Henry: Winning Respect," *National Journal*, 27 January 1990.

4. Paul was sometimes asked why he didn't follow in the footsteps of his father, to which Paul would, jokingly, recall the remark that has been attributed to Martin Luther, "Send your good men to the ministry, send your best men to politics."

5. David Kaplan, "Michigan Rep. Henry Dies: Republicans Mull Race," *Congressional Quarterly Weekly Report*, 7 August 1993.

6. In 1980, when John Anderson ran for president, Paul served on his campaign and directed his campaign in Michigan. Paul resigned from the campaign when Anderson announced that he would drop out of the Republican race and run as an independent.

7. Paul B. Henry, "Stewardship in the Garden," *Christianity Today*, 23 April 1990.

8. Michael Barone and Grant Ujifusa, *Almanac of American Politics 1994* (Washington, D.C.: National Journal, 1993).

9. Broder, "Voters Demand Facts This Time," sec. A.

10. "Paul Henry: Citizen, Friend—Grand Rapids and the Country Well-Served by This Uncommon Man," *Grand Rapids Press*, 2 August 1993, sec. A.

11. Ann Woiwode and Carl A. Zichella, "Paul Henry Earned Respect from All," *Grand Rapids Press*, 13 August 1993, sec. A.

12. U.S. Congress, *Memorial Tributes Delivered in Congress, Paul B. Henry 1942–1993, Late A Representative from Michigan*, 103d Congress, 2d Session, 1994.

13. Rhett H. Pinsky, "A Few Words About Congressman Paul B. Henry," *Grand Rapids Bar Association Newsletter*, September 1993.

14. Paul B. Henry, *Politics for Evangelicals* (Valley Forge, Pa.: Judson, 1974), 122.

15. The concept of "call" runs counter to currently popular ideas such as term limits and part-time citizen legislatures. If political service can be seen as a calling, it is inconsistent to argue that those holding it should be forcibly removed after attaining a certain number of years in service.

16. Personal correspondence file 1992, Paul Henry Archives.

17. Ibid.

18. Henry, *Politics for Evangelicals*, 72.

19. Ibid., 67, 70.

20. Paul B. Henry, "A First-Term Congressman Looks at Faith and Politics," *Christianity Today*, 15 March 1985.

21. Paul B. Henry, "Getting Involved in Politics," *Just Life Education Fund. A 1988 Election Study Guide for Justice, Life, and Peace*, October 1988, 13.

22. Paul B. Henry, "Morality vs. Moralism: In Defense of Politics," delivered at Pepperdine University, Malibu, California, 26 January 1989.

23. U.S. Congress, *Memorial Tributes*, 73–74.

24. Václav Havel, *Summer Meditations* (New York: Knoph, 1992), 11–12.

25. Henry, *Politics for Evangelicals*, 123.

An Overview

This chapter discusses the recent debate over the manner in which human stem cells are obtained for research. Should stem cells be taken from aborted fetuses, spare cryopreserved embryos that remain after *in vitro* fertilization, or from adults? This chapter is included to show that professional and academically qualified Christians can have an influential voice in ethical discussions at the national political level. Frank E. Young is a medical doctor, philosopher, educator, and Christian whom God has allowed to participate in many critical contemporary discussions. This chapter details the stem-cell issue and discloses numerous ways in which Christians can participate in the political arena. An appendix contains the testimony of Dr. Young before the Senate Appropriations Committee on Labor, Health, and Human Services.

Chapter Eleven

CHRISTIANS IN THE VORTEX OF NATIONAL CONTROVERSY

Effectively Debating Stem-Cell Research in the Political Arena

Frank E. Young

THE TWENTIETH CENTURY HAS WITNESSED an explosive revolution in molecular and cellular biology. Health care has progressed from nonspecific homeopathic remedies at the dawn of the twentieth century to highly specific molecular medicine at its close. Remarkable advances have been made in understanding the function and structure of the molecules, of cells, and in the pathophysiology of animals and plants. These discoveries have ushered in major advances in medicine such as antibiotic therapy, cancer chemotherapy, the unraveling of the genetic code, procedures for the management of cardiovascular disease, and new medicines produced through biotechnology. The complete genome of the common fruit fly, *Drosophila*, was sequenced recently.[1] The Human Genome Project promises to elucidate the genetic code of human beings by the year 2003. This monumental scientific achievement, coupled with the unraveling of the genetic sequences in a wide range of organisms, will probably result in the identification of common sequences, the identification of compounds that regulate cell function, and the ability to design new medicines. Human gene therapy likely will become a reality and cellular regeneration likely will introduce new ways to extend life. The recent medical breakthroughs that might be possible by using embryonic stem cells have been a source of excitement for scientists and patients alike. The pace of scientific discovery is extraordinary.

These technological advances, however, have raised major ethical questions concerning the manipulation, extension and termination of life. In particular, the need to disintegrate human embryos to harvest embryonic stem cells has collided with long-standing prohibitions against using human embryos for research. Before we sweep away such restrictions for the sake of scientific progress, we should consider the implications. As Frankel noted, the promise of stem-cell research offers significant potential benefits for scientific progress as well as engendering considerable consternation. He maintained that "it seems sensible to consider how to best balance the promise of such research with the genuine concerns about proceeding with it that are held by some segments of society."[2] More than four hundred years ago, Rabelais prophetically stated, "Science without conscience is but death of the soul." Thus, the influence of science on society should be considered as part of the decision to fund particular fields of investigation. As Robertson points out, "Science is not an unmitigated blessing. It is expensive, and its discoveries, like the tree of knowledge in Eden, expands man's capacity for evil as well as good. More knowledge is not a good in itself, nor is it necessarily productive of net good. Society, as the provider of resources, the bearer of costs and the reaper of the benefits, has an overriding interest in the consequences of science, and hence the direction and routes that research takes."[3]

Let us look at the route by which we arrived at this crisis of conscience—that is, the discoveries, the societal concerns, the ethical impact, and the scientific contributions of the debates surrounding the recombinant deoxyribonucleic acid (DNA) revolution—and extend this analysis to the current scientific and ethical issues surrounding the manipulation of embryos. Then we will look at these technologies from a theological perspective and explore the machinery of our government so that God-fearing people will be *empowered to participate more broadly in public debates.* The discussion of technological breakthroughs requires the participation of faith communities, as both science and religion have equal and different contributions to make toward arriving at the ethical decisions that face mankind.

RECOMBINANT DNA TECHNOLOGY AND DEBATE: THE PAST A PROLOGUE TO THE FUTURE

Mendel's 1865 discovery of inherited traits in peas began a search for the basis of heredity. These observations documented, for the first time, the sorting of traits from one generation to another. In 1910, Morgan noted a spontaneous mutation in the eye color of a fruit fly, *Drosophila*, and observed that the mutation rate could be increased by radiation. This finding provided evidence that genetic changes could be induced. Bacteria were the ideal model systems to study genes because they multiplied every twenty minutes. Therefore, genetic changes could be studied rapidly and relatively inexpensively. In 1928, Griffith observed that if he injected mice with heat-killed pathogenic (disease causing) bacteria together with nonpathogenic (harmless) bacteria, the harmless bacteria were transformed into pathogenic bacteria.[5] Later, Avery and coworkers identified the transforming principal as DNA. This discovery was astounding because DNA was thought to be only a structural scaffold in the nucleus of the cell.[6] In the Fifties, Watson and Crick set the stage for the molecular genetic revolution by identifying the three-dimensional physical chemical structure of DNA. This achievement established the chemical basis of heredity. Subsequent essential basic science discoveries led to the advent of Recombinant DNA (rDNA) technology, a procedure for manipulating and specifically transferring genes among widely divergent species. With the use of these new methodologies, it was now possible to take a piece of DNA from one organism and introduce it into another. A whole new field of molecular genetics emerged.

In the Seventies, a team of scientists led by Berg used these fundamental discoveries to introduce self-replicating elements containing the genome of a tumor virus into *Escherichia coli*, a common bacterium that lives in the intestinal track of humans. The scientific community emitted an outcry, expressing a fear that this organism could escape and produce cancers in people.[7] Accordingly, scientists called for a moratorium on this research to determine whether it was scientifically and ethically appropriate. Within approximately eight months, in 1975, 140 scientists from 18 countries assembled in Asilomar, California, to determine whether—and if so, how— to use this new technology. While some representatives of the press and of the legal profession were at this government-sponsored conference, the recommendations were made primarily by scientists. Scientist after scientist urged caution to ensure that there would be no inappropriate release of harmful genetic elements producing new diseases. Interim guidelines were developed. Then, in 1976, the federal government promulgated more elaborate guidelines.[8] During this process, great debate occurred within the scientific community and in the press. Numerous congressional hearings also were held. Concerns were expressed about not only public safety but also the appropriateness of mixing genomes that had been separated from the dawn of creation. Even the potential for cloning human beings was discussed.

The Department of Health and Human Services (DHHS) established a twenty-five-member Recombinant DNA Advisory Committee (RAC) to monitor the safety of the experiments under the guidelines. Particularly relevant was the makeup of the committee. Individuals of many persuasions— some people in support of and some people in opposition to rDNA research— were included. Some participants thought that the guidelines were too stringent and claimed that this research was no different than any other type of molecular genetic experimentation. Others contended that this technology introduced a new eugenics. Still others concluded that it was a feasible process in view of the uncertainties. *A number of public meetings, conferences, and opportunities for regulatory input were afforded the public.* The key societal concerns were identified, and, after much debate, most of them were resolved. (See Figure 1.)

Two areas of controversy still remain unresolved over the possibilities opened through genetic engineering. First, although the regulations for pharmaceuticals harvested from genetically engineered microorganisms and diagnostic medical devices derived from biotechnology were widely accepted, the regulatory guidelines and public acceptance of genetically engineered foods have been more contentious. Although the Organization for Economic Cooperation and Development proposed concepts and principles for resolving this dilemma, the consensus was subsequently abandoned.[9] Substantial protest to using these products now exists, especially in Europe. This objection is related primarily to lower perceived benefits and unknown or imagined risks of consuming biogenetically engineered food.

Second, the use of rDNA for gene therapy in human beings remains controversial. In this kind of therapy (somatic cell gene therapy), viruses

Figure 1

CONCERN	RESOLUTION
Fear of release of organisms by local communities	Establishment of local biosafety committees to review research protocols
Hazards attending the mixing of genomes from different organisms	Restriction of permissible experiments in accordance with levels of biological and physical containment of the experiments
Ethics of mixing genomes from various species	Discovery of extensive movement of genes among different organisms in nature
Confusion and ambiguity in regulatory guidelines the for evaluation of biotechnology	Establishment of a coordinated regulatory policy for product review thereby harmonizing regulations of government agencies
Conflict in guidelines used by developed nations for rDNA research	Harmonization of guidelines through the Organization for Economic Cooperation and Development

containing genes are used to infect children or adults on the theory that a single injection of a gene could provide a permanent cure for certain conditions. For example, if one could inject into a diabetic a gene for production of insulin, it could correct the genetic defect. However, the promises made by scientists for successful gene therapy have yet to be realized. As noted by Rosenberg and Schechter, "despite repeated claims of benefit or even cure, no single unequivocal instance of clinical efficacy exists in the hundreds of gene therapy trials."[10] Furthermore, significant safety problems have been involved in these experiments. In September 1999, a patient, Jess Gelsinger, died following an injection of a virus carrying genetic material. This news was accompanied by disclosures of irregularities in following the U. S. Food and Drug Administration (FDA) regulations. These infractions led to a reprimand of medical scientists at the University of Pennsylvania by the FDA. Beyond the concerns of safety are the ethical problems that arise when healthy people are infected with viruses containing new genetic information and in the inherent conflict of interest between the patients' desire for access to a new medical discovery and the scientists' interest in clinical research.

A more disputatious debate is the use of gene therapy to correct genetic defects in fetuses before birth.[11] Unlike somatic cell gene therapy, these therapies could pass on genetic alterations to the next generation. Because of the risks, the government built in safeguards in these and other clinical experiments. The safeguards include informed consent by the patient, review by the local Investigational Review Board (IRB) for evaluation of safety of clinical experimentation, deliberation by the RAC of the scientific merits at the national level, approval of the clinical protocols by FDA, and full public disclosure. Yet, some ethical and legal problems remain unresolved. Because the therapy is likely to be given early in gestation (around the eleventh week of pregnancy), before the maturation of the immune system, is the fetus to be considered a living person with legal rights or a part of the mother? The answer to this question will determine who gives informed consent (the mother or both parents) and who can sue for an adverse outcome (the father, the mother, or the child). This research likely will force a reevaluation of when life begins, the adequacy of the regulations on human experimentation, and the regulations on informed consent.

Because of the continued fears expressed by the public, a President's Commission was established in 1980 to investigate the ethics of genetic engineering.[12] One of the particular concerns was the possibility of cloning people. The specter of human cloning is now nearer to reality than ever and remains a focus of debate with both the secular and the religious communities.

CLONING OF MAMMALS AND HUMANS: THE VORTEX OF CONTROVERSY

The recent successful cloning of a sheep through somatic cell nuclear transplantation (SCNT) raised the level of concerns about ethics. Cloning produced by SCNT involves the introduction of an adult nucleus into an enucleated egg, leading to the birth of a live infant that is genetically identical to the adult from which the nucleus was taken.[13] Cloning challenges our understanding of the very nature of humanness that was first addressed in the report of the Presidential Commission in 1982 and awakened the fear of Frankenstein-like experimentation. The announcement of this discovery resulted in a call by President Clinton for a moratorium on further cloning research in the United States and a rapid review by the National Bioethics Advisory Commission (NBAC).

Subsequently, cloning by SCNT has successfully produced cattle, mice, goats, and pigs. A public outcry against cloning human children by SCNT occurred, and religious groups by and large opposed this research. A number of bills were introduced in Congress, although no legislation has yet been passed, and the NBAC published its findings and recommendations, which are summarized in Figure 2.[14]

Although the presidential moratorium still precludes the use of public funds for cloning, there is little to impede the use of private dollars for this end, as exemplified by the public outrage when Dr. Seed declared his intention to clone humans.

Figure 2

1. The current moratorium on the use of federal funding in support of any attempt to create a child by SCNT should be continued.
2. An immediate request should be issued to all firms, clinicians, investigators, and professional societies in the private and non-federally funded sectors to comply voluntarily with the intent of the federal moratorium. Professional and scientific societies should make clear that any attempt to create a child by SCNT . . . would at this time be an irresponsible, unethical, and unprofessional act.
3. Federal legislation should be enacted to prohibit anyone from attempting, whether in a research or a clinical setting, to create a child through SCNT cloning.
4. The federal government and all interested and concerned parties should be encouraged to deliberate these issues widely and continually to further our understanding of the ethical and social implications of this technology and to enable society to produce appropriate long-term policies.

EMBRYO DISINTEGRATION TO OBTAIN STEM CELLS

Shortly after the successful cloning of mammals raised major ethical and theological issues, a new and even more controversial discovery arose. Pluripotent stem cells were isolated and grown in a tissue culture through privately funded research from a spare embryo donated by a couple following *in vitro* fertilization (IVF).[15] To put this discovery into perspective, it is necessary to explain in general terms the initial stages of development of an embryo and the potential for this research.

When a sperm fertilizes an egg, the cell that results is termed a *zygote*. As cell division occurs, the zygote divides first into two cells (if the cells separate, twins occur) and then into four and then eight cells called *blastomeres*. Each of these blastomeres retains the capacity to develop into a whole individual when it is separated and implanted into a prepared uterus. Such a cell is termed *totipotent*, that is, it can develop into an embryo. As the cells in the embryo continue to divide, the mass of cells form a cavity (or blastocyst) and a central mass that will develop into the individual. As growth and differentiation occurs, the cells are less capable of producing all of the tissues in the body. At an early stage of growth, the embryo can be disintegrated and the stem cells can be isolated. Although these cells cannot produce an embryo, they can divide indefinitely and, under appropriate conditions, be coaxed to form many types of tissues. These cells are termed *pluripotent*. Pluripotent stem cells were also isolated from primordial gonadal tissue obtained from an aborted fetus.[16] In the former case, the cells were extracted from the blastocyst stage, the stage at which an embryo is implanted to produce a child after IVF. Currently, embryonic stem pluripotent cells can be harvested only from aborted fetuses or embryos that are killed to obtain their cells.

This discovery was revolutionary because stem cells have unlimited capacity for self-renewal and can differentiate into many cell types such as skin, liver, heart, cartilage, bone, kidney, and neurons and other cells found in the brain and spinal cord. Hopefully, these cells can be used to repopulate damaged organs and even to produce large fragments of tissue or organs that could be used for transplantation. Additionally, scientists could gain a great deal of basic information about the regulation of cell division that might help in understanding what causes uncontrolled growth or cancer.

These findings, however, ignited a fiery public debate. Following Dr. Harold Varmus's (Director of the National Institutes of Health [NIH]) support of the use of embryonic stem (ES) cells in research, seventy Congressman wrote a letter of protest. In response, a group of seventy-three scientists (including sixty-seven Nobel laureates) wrote a letter to the journal *Science* in March 1999. The letter supported studies on stem cells, claiming that the decision by Dr. Varmus "protects the sanctity of life without impeding scientific research."[17] This conclusion was reached primarily on the basis of utilitarian ethics. The American Association for the Advancement of Science prepared a position paper in favor of stem-cell research and held a public meeting in August 1999. In July 1999, another group of scientists, religious leaders, and ethicists with a different viewpoint held a press conference objecting to this utilitarian approach. They argued that such research was unnecessary, immoral, and illegal. Their position papers were made available through a web site developed by the "Do No Harm" coalition (www.stemcellresearch.org).

As the debate rages within the scientific and public communities, three seminal landmarks should be highlighted. First, the General Counsel of the Department of Health and Human Services offered a legal opinion that the congressional ban on embryo research did not apply to embryonic stem cells because the cells themselves do not meet the statutory medical or biological definition of a human embryo. Subsequently, Dr. Varmus, ruled that, under certain conditions, cells harvested from a preimplantation embryo could be used in research. At the time of this writing, the ban on embryo research remains in effect. However, Senator Arlen Spector has held hearings on the use of stem cells to determine whether the ban should be lifted and the NIH permitted to fund embryonic stem-cell research.

The second major advance was the discovery of the widespread existence of stem cells in adult humans.[18] When ES cells were first cultured, little was known about adult stem (AS) cells. The discovery that AS cells can differentiate into a variety of tissues was not only unexpected but also revolutionary. Essentially, in organs of adults are stem cells that can repopulate and repair a damaged organ. Not only will they supply pluripotent cells to the organ in which they are located but also they can develop into many tissues. Vogel reported that organs such as brain, muscle, and bone marrow have stem cells that can differentiate into tissues. For example, AS cells from muscle can differentiate into cartilage, bone cells, fat cells, muscle cells, hematopoetic support cells, and astrocytes. These stem cells are responsible for the self-renewal of adult tissues following injury. Although a number of

AS cells can produce many types of tissues, others, such as epithelium, have stem cells that usually are involved in producing only normal regeneration and renewal of skin following injury (wound healing).[19] The mechanism of control of differentiation of these AS cells remains obscure. These and many other studies demonstrate that AS cells can theoretically be used to produce many types of tissues in the same fashion as ES cells.

Third, President Clinton requested on November 14, 1998, ". . . that the [National Bioethics Advisory] Commission undertake a thorough review of the issues associated with such human stem cell research, balancing all ethical and medical considerations." The NBAC reported its deliberations in September 1999 in a publication titled "Ethical Issues in Human Stem-Cell Research."[20] The report discussed three types of stem cells: (1) ES cells harvested by killing preimplantation embryos, (2) ES cells derived from gonadal tissue of aborted fetuses, and (3) AS cells obtained from adult humans. All of these cells are pluripotent and can develop into many types of tissue. The Commission acknowledged that "therefore embryo research that is not therapeutic is bound to raise serious concerns and heighten tensions between two important ethical commitments: to cure disease and protect human life."[21] After acknowledging that many people strongly object to the sacrifice of the embryo to obtain cells to treat the living, the Commission concluded, "[o]n this issue [the moral status of the embryo], the commission adopted what some have described as an intermediate position, one with which many would agree: that the embryo merits respect as a form of human life, but not the same level of respect accorded persons." A concise summary of the more relevant recommendations is presented in Figure 3. The reader is referred to the NBAC report for a more detailed analysis.[22]

The report to President Clinton by NBAC recommended a major departure from the congressional ban on harmful research involving embryos. Essentially, it recommends that "spare embryos" left over from IVF be used for research if the parents consent and requires that the research be conducted under recommended guidelines. With a nod to the dignity to be accorded to the embryo based on its human nature, the embryo was afforded no protection.

THE ETHICAL QUESTIONS

Pluripotent stem cells are likely to produce significant scientific and medical advances. Should embryos be sacrificed for as yet unrealized promises of major medical discoveries and therapies based on utilitarian ethics? Should research be permitted only with human AS cells? Should a moratorium on research of ES cells and EG cells be implemented until the ethical and religious concerns are addressed and a consensus is reached?

Lessons Learned

The primary focus in the rDNA debate was on the safe use of the technology. The ethical concerns were deliberately avoided. Instead, the scientific community provided the major force behind this technology. Although some people in the religious community worried about "man playing God," the

Figure 3

1. Research involving the derivation and use of human embryonic germ (EG) cells from aborted (cadaveric) fetal tissue should continue to be eligible for federal funding. Ethical safeguards were offered.
2. Research involving the derivation and use of human ES cells from embryos remaining after infertility treatments should be eligible for federal funding. An exception should be made to the present statutory ban on federal funding of embryo research to permit federal agencies to fund research involving the derivation of human ES cells from this source under appropriate regulations that include public oversight and review.
3. Federal agencies should not fund research involving the derivation or use of human cells from embryos made solely for research purposes using IVF.
4. Federal agencies should not fund research involving the derivation or use of human ES cells from embryos made using SCNT into oocytes.
5. Prospective donors of embryos remaining after infertility treatments should receive timely, relevant, and appropriate information by which to make informed and voluntary choices regarding disposition of embryos. Options of preservation and adoption should be offered before they are used for research.
6. In federally funded research involving embryos remaining after infertility treatments, researchers may not promise donors that ES cells derived from their embryos will be used to treat patient subjects specified by the donors.
7. Embryos and cadavaric fetal tissue should not be bought or sold.
8. DHHS should establish a National Stem-Cell Oversight and Review Panel to ensure that all federally funded research on ES or EG cells is conducted in conformance with the ethical principles and recommendations contained in this report.

fears in the minds of most Christians generally were overcome by the stewardship of dominion given to man by God as described in Genesis 1:28. Furthermore, the rapid rate of scientific progress precluded much involvement. Regretfully, little discussion occurred within the various faith communities. Few scientific experts were also able to articulate the theological concerns. Additionally, opinions were sought largely from those who agreed with the direction that science was going. More recently, some proponents of rDNA in the religious community actually termed mankind as "cocreator," endeavoring to legitimize mankind's role in genetic manipulation and elevate man's responsibility beyond that of a steward.[23] Thus, in the absence of any major call for an ethical framework, the regulatory process in the United States took over and led to resolution of most concerns based on safety.

However, the climate of opinion has changed. In a report of the twenty-fifth anniversary of the Asilomar conference, Barinaga noted that the public trust is not easily won today and that scientists must reflect on the ethical considerations. Currently, an ethical framework is formed by consensus.[24] Therefore, we must use our God-given talents to present clearly the Christian worldview in the marketplace of ideas. Christian representation and influence in politics by highly skilled scientists, physicians, clinicians, and bioethicists is essential to the protection of the dignity of human life.

How to Proceed

The Christian believes that God created the universe, the earth, and all that is therein. Men and women are created in God's image. After their creation, Adam and Eve were told to "be fruitful, and multiply; fill the earth and subdue it; have dominion over the fish of the sea, over the birds of the air, and over every living thing" (Gen. 1:28 NKJV). Here is a legitimate opening in the door to scientific research, although it is far from being *carte blanche* in nature. The first couple was given the requirement of obedience that, if followed, would protect them from the harmful influence of evil; nonetheless, they decided to trust in their own intuition (Gen. 2:17; 3:1–7). Their disobedience resulted in the corruption of the human body, soul, heart, and mind (Jer. 17:9) Fellowship with God was broken and the physical and spiritual effects of fallenness engulfed humanity; therefore, the potential for ethical violations in research of any kind was inevitable without divine guidance. But God provided redemption through His only begotten Son, Jesus Christ, who once and for all personally paid the penalty of death with His own blood for those whom God calls. This salvation is through grace and not of one's own merit.[25] Yet, as noted in Ephesians 2:10, ". . . we are His workmanship, created in Christ Jesus for good works, which God has prepared beforehand" (NKJV) for us to do. God, not science (or more specifically, genetic engineering), is Creator, Redeemer, and Savior. Science might temporarily assist us and serve us well in the physical world, but the complete and lasting healing of the human condition is ultimately God's work. This is why His view of the dignity of human life and our responsibility to represent this view of life (good works) publicly is so critical in ethical thinking. Human beings are genuine reflections of God, and we bear within us a law that He has written on the hearts of each of us (Rom. 2:12–15). Science can only stray when its research is conducted without an immeasurable regard for human life.

Furthermore, the Christian worldview contends that the Bible holds the truths necessary for life even many centuries after the close of the canon of Scripture. Molecular genetics, cloning, and embryo manipulation were not taught in Scripture, but Scripture contains an abundance of principles that enable us to address these issues.

Principles

- God is Creator and sustainer of the universe. While there might be different opinions about the mechanism, the role of Creator is a fundamental belief (Gen. 1–2).

- Human beings are creatures created in God's image and function as stewards—not as cocreators—of God's creation.
- Because humans are created in God's image, human life is sacred.
- Conflict exists within each human being (a person often does what his or her conscience knows, or at least thinks, to be wrong (cf. Rom. 2:14–15; 7).
- Our devotion should be first and foremost to God, but we also have responsibilities to governments. God establishes governments to promote and sustain social order (Rom. 13).
- Christians should recognize that their view will be a minority view in society yet one that must be enunciated clearly and through the available channels. We are admonished to be salt and light in the world (Matt. 5:13–16).
- Life on earth is finite. It is appointed for men to die once (Heb. 9:27). Therefore, eternal life with God is more important than temporal life on earth.
- Part of dominion over creation is the ministry of healing and relieving suffering. Yet, we must remember that even the Great Physician, Jesus, did not heal all people; in fact, divine healing was primarily a representation of His powers as the Son of God.

Jesus clearly explains that believers should render unto God what is God's and to Caesar what is Caesar's.[26] Therefore, involvement in the theological and political spheres of life is obvious. But as Christians, our loyalty is first to God, whom we are to love with all of our heart, soul, mind, and strength (Deut. 6:4–5; Matt. 22:37–8). Second, we are to love our neighbors (whether believers or unbelievers) as we love ourselves (Matt. 22:39–40). Therefore, *we have an ethical responsibility to bring biblical truths to bear on contemporary issues for the glory of God and for the benefit of all humanity.* Involvement in public affairs is really not an option.

A CASE STUDY: DISINTEGRATION OF EMBRYOS TO OBTAIN STEM CELLS FOR RESEARCH AND THERAPY

Theological and ethical guidance. The use of stem cells harvested from embryos raises great ethical and theological concerns. A number of the previously mentioned biblical principles can be used to address this decision from a Christian perspective. First, because the embryo is alive at the time that the stem cells are harvested, the harvesting results in death and, therefore, violates the sixth commandment (Exod. 20:13). Second, the embryo as a living entity bears the image of God (Gen. 1:26; 5:26). Third, the violation of an image bearer is an act of violence against the Creator (Gen. 9:6) Fourth, human beings are given unique responsibilities to glorify God, defend the dignity of humankind, and properly care for the world over which we have been given authority (Ps. 8). Finally, the book of Jeremiah clearly states that God intimately knows a person before he or she is formed (Jer. 1:5).[27] Because IVF techniques of necessity involve a preimplantation embryo, and because a woman does not pay for the introduction of "dead matter" into her uterus, it is difficult to argue that a preimplantation embryo is not alive.

As noted by Hoekema, Genesis 1:26–28 describes a threefold relationship between God and man.[28] First, humans are directed toward God and completely dependent on Him. We are not to act contrary to His will and character. Second, human beings are not to be isolated from or indifferent to one another; rather, they are to benefit and complete one another as exemplified by God's creating a "suitable helper" (Gen. 2:18). Third, humans are rulers over nature (i.e., they are to subdue and have dominion over God's creation). Thus, human beings have a special relationship both to God and to creation. Although the Fall distorted this relationship, it did not destroy the love of God for His creation. Therefore, the respect for the sanctity of human life is an overarching principle. However, the gift of eternal life with God looms much larger as it is the grace of God. The brevity of temporal life, which certainly will end in death, is overshadowed by this glorious hope.

Ethically, the treatment of living human embryos as mere objects of experimentation to extend the life of the living causes one to speculate that human embryos could be developed by SCNT for spare parts (i.e., through cloning). Although this end was not approved in the recommendations within the NBAC report on stem-cell research, it is important to note the report's conclusion: "[A]t this time, because other sources are likely to provide the cells needed for the preliminary stages of research, federal funds should not be provided to derive ES from SCNT. Nevertheless, the medical utility and scientific progress of this line of research should be monitored closely." Is this an example of scientific incrementalism? Asked another way, has the door been left ajar for future reconsideration?

Medical guidance. An important principle in bioethics is "Do no harm," and this concept is clearly enunciated in both medicine and Scripture. In fact, the Christian worldview has encouraged medical research throughout the centuries. As noted by Hollinger, "If genetic therapy can be a form of healing and a procedure that does not cave into base intentions or unethical procedures, then we should accept it as a good gift from God."[29] Because AS cells can be used to meet most of the objectives of basic and clinical research, why should embryos be sacrificed for experimentation at this or any other time? To counter this argument, some people have suggested that these are spare embryos that will probably be destroyed; therefore, the research is viewed as merely a salvaging mission, that is, getting something rather than nothing. Perhaps regulation of the number of embryos produced in IVF and guidelines for adoption of frozen embryos could resolve this apparent excess.

Legal protection. Laws that protect life exist in all fifty states. The death of a pregnant woman with an embryo less than one month old was considered a double homicide by the law. Some states have laws specifically designed to protect the embryo. Additionally, because the embryo is outside the uterus, *Roe v. Wade* does not apply.[30] Finally, Congress has prohibited embryo research since 1993, and this prohibition still exists. However, Senator Spector's proposal

(S2015-Stem-Cell Research Act of 2000) would permit obtaining human stem cells from embryos that could otherwise be discarded at IVF clinics.

On the basis of these facts, many people have concluded that human embryo research is unnecessary, immoral, and illegal. Because it is important to resolve the ethical and theological issue first, a time for restraint was recommended.[31] Therefore, a moratorium on research with human ES and GS cells was proposed. During this time the scientific advances in ES, GS and AS cells could be documented and their potential assessed. Research funding for studies on human and animal AS cells and on animal ES cells should be enhanced. Particular emphasis should be given to AS cell research to determine whether a need exists for ES and GS cells for therapies to enhance organ function. Most importantly, the ethical concerns should be enunciated and the theological ramifications defined. Unless the ethical and theological concerns are addressed first, the controversy is likely to harden into fixed positions where meaningful dialogue is not possible. At this time, it is important not to rush headlong into this research.

WHAT CAN YOU DO?

Recognizing that the Christian worldview is a minority position, how does a person make this view known to policymakers? What levers and knobs of government can be used to influence the formation of policy?

First and foremost, you must ensure that you understand the scientific, ethical, and theological issues. Pray and study both the pertinent academic data and the Scripture before embarking on a course of action. You have a number of ways to be informed. In addition to books and journals, one can visit the web site of the National Library of Medicine (www.nlm.nih.gov). Under the section on Health Information, it is possible to access abstracts from 4300 biomedical journals. The NIH houses the Human Genome Project. This web site (www.otnl.gov/techResources) includes information on ethical, legal, and social issues as well as scientific information. Information about bills in Congress can be obtained through the web site http://thomas.loc.gov, and administration initiatives can be followed through the White House web page (www.whitehouse.gov) or through departments such as the DHHS (www.dhhs.gov). For those who wish to subscribe to a scientific journal, the journal *Science*, published by the American Association for the Advancement of Science, is one of the more timely technical publications. For instance, the February 25, 2000, issue devoted twenty-five pages to stem-cell research and ethics.

Second, one can correspond with lawmakers at the local, state and federal levels on particular bills and subjects. At the federal level, these opinions are usually shared with the Administration. If your congressman or senator is a sponsor of a bill that affects one of your concerns, correspond with that person and, if possible, visit the local office of your representative. Phone calls and telegrams are also effective. Thoughtful letters are much more influential than a name on a petition or a postcard response as part of an organized campaign. If you are adequately prepared and God provides the opportunity, testify at a congressional hearing or submit a letter for the record on the subject of a particular hearing.[32]

Third, be familiar with the way the Administration processes work. For example, the FDA makes rules through a process of steps. First, usually there is the Notice of Proposed Rule Making. After comments are received and incorporated, the second step is the Proposed Rule, and, after comments are considered, a Final Rule is promulgated. Because each of these steps permits public comment, ample opportunity exists for input (by regulation each comment must be considered). Surprisingly, the public in general and the Christian community in particular, makes few comments. Perhaps this lack of input relates to their ignorance about the procedures to get information. One of the best sites to correct this problem is the web site of the Government Printing Office (www.gpo.gov#info), which lists the various document resources such as the *Federal Register*, the publication that records all federal regulations and guidelines.

Guidelines promulgated by the NIH follow a different and less formal path than those of the FDA. Essentially, the proposed guidelines are published in the *Federal Register* with an invitation for comment. If the topic is highly controversial, such as the guidelines developed by the NBAC, public meetings may be held. A list of public meetings, reports, and other useful information may be found at the web site: www.bioethics.gov.

Fourth, communicate with decision-makers in the Administration through the appropriate departments and agencies. Your comments should be well thought out and address the issues. Remember, the system responds best when the issue is one of current importance.

Fifth, be prepared to comment on guidelines and position papers. The American Association for the Advancement of Science analyzed the stem-cell research and ethics issue and presented a paper titled "Stem-Cell Research and Applications: Monitoring the Frontiers of Biomedical Research" for comment at a public meeting.[33] Many people from the audience were able to make remarks. If you do make a statement, be sure that it is in writing. It can be prepared in a style similar to, though less technical than, the statement I made before a Senate Appropriations Committee (see Appendix at the conlusion of this chapter).

Sixth, join a coalition that addresses your concern, if one exists. If not, consider forming one. For example, Do No Harm is a coalition of Americans for research ethics. You may visit the web site at www.stemcellresearch.org. Because our government responds to grass roots organizations, this is an important opportunity. Your opinion can also be made known through speeches, journal articles, and letters to the editors of newspapers.

Finally, I would encourage interested Christians to prepare academically and engage fully in research in genetics, embryology, molecular biology, and immunology, where many of these controversial discoveries will be made. It is imperative to develop a generation of Christians in science who can address with expertise both the scientific issues and a Christian worldview. To do less will leave us out of the most central discussions and issues. We must be armed spiritually and intellectually to engage in the ethical and theological battles of our time.

CONCLUSION

Scientific and technologic advances are occurring at an unanticipated rate. Less than fifty years ago, the structure of DNA was unknown. Twenty-five years ago, a meeting of scientists occurred at Asilomar to determine how to proceed safely with recombinant DNA technology. Now we are on the threshold of manipulating human life. The actions taken in the next few years on research with human embryos will, in large measure, define our view of human nature. Religion in general and Christianity in particular have much to offer. It provides a framework of truth that is not present in the empiricism of science. We can ill afford to be silent. This case study provides general principles that will serve to enable us to participate. In the last analysis, however, God is sovereign and our participation is a privilege.

APPENDIX

Statement
Before the Senate Appropriations Committee on
Labor, Health and Human Services,
November 4, 1999
Frank E. Young

Mr. Chairman and Members of the Appropriations Subcommittee:

Thank you for the opportunity of participating in this hearing concerning the controversial ethical issue of research on human embryos to optimize the procedures for harvesting embryonic stem cells and the federal funding of research on stem cells derived from human embryos. Allow me to state the question clearly: should we destroy living human embryos in order to experiment with their cells for the potential benefit of the living? The Executive Summary of the Report of the National Bioethics Advisory Committee (September 1999) aptly summarized the Congressional intent. "The current ban on embryo research is in the form of a rider to the appropriations bill for the Department of Health and Human Services (DHHS), of which the National Institutes of Health (NIH) is a part. The rider prohibits use of the appropriated funds to support any research ' in which the embryo [is] destroyed, discarded, or knowingly subjected to risk of injury greater than that allowed for research on fetuses in utero. This is not an unexpected controversy. As early as 1982, the President's Commission for the Study of Ethical Problems in Medicine and Biomedical and Behavioral Research issued a report entitled "Splicing Life: A Report on the Social and Ethical Issues of Genetic Engineering with Human Beings." Yet, there has been little sustained development of consensus policies regarding the ethics of the new genetics and cell biology on the National level with the notable exception of recombinant DNA (rDNA) technology.

In 1999, the level of the intellectual and societal playing fields were changed by recent advances in the cloning of animals and manipulation of embryonic cells and by a decision of DHHS. On January 26,1999, Dr. Varmis, in testimony before the Appropriations Subcommittee, stated that the General Counsel of DHHS concluded that DHHS funds can be used to support research using human pluripotent cells derived from human embryos because the statutory ban does not apply. It was posited that "the statutory prohibition does not apply to research utilizing human pluripotent stem cells because pluripotent stem cells are not embryos." In response to this decision, early in 1999, 70 members of the Congress signed a letter that called upon DHHS to reverse the NIH Director's decision to allow funding for research on pluripotent stem cells. In a letter in Science, a group of 73 scientists offered support for the Director Varmus' decision to fund this research (*Science*, 283:1849–50, 1999). It is important to emphasize that this research on embryos is one of the most controversial societal concerns today. It will be a proxy for our view of the essence of the meaning of life in the twenty-first century.

To understand the issues fully, we must clearly realize that while science measures and explores the known world, religion embodies a devotion to God and the meaning of life. Thus, there will be different worldviews within our society, and each one must be heard respectfully and considered carefully. As noted by Professor Gould, science and religion are two "Non-Overlapping Magisteria." Both make major contributions to society. But these contributions are different.

In this testimony, I shall present an analysis of this dilemma and offer a recommendation to resolve it.

Throughout my scientific career as a molecular geneticist, I have been involved in the ethical issues confronting biotechnology and cellular biology as well as medical advances. I was present at the Asilomar Conference where 150 scientists from 18 nations first met to debate the safety of rDNA technology and also consider the ethics of the research. Careful attention to both safety and scientific inquiry was incorporated into the NIH Guidelines that resulted from the Asilomar meeting. A deliberately careful approach was taken to this research and the guidelines were relaxed as scientific and social concerns permitted. As a member of the first Recombinant DNA Advisory Committee, I participated in deliberation on the development of this technology and was keenly aware that public confidence in this new field of biotechnology was imperative. This rDNA research using microbes and animal cells to produce medicines led to the establishment of the biotechnology industry as we know it today. For many years, I participated in recombinant DNA research and in policy deliberations on implementation of guidelines for conducting rDNA research. As the Commissioner of the Food and Drug Administration, I led in the development of regulations nationally and internationally that ushered in the current era of biotechnology. However, I must emphasize that this research and industrial development did not involve the disintegration of human embryos. Instead it used or "enslaved" bacterial yeast and animal cells to produce large amounts of desired products. As Commissioner, I was conscious that the ethical considerations, as well as safety and effectiveness, must be considered carefully in order to ensure public support.

Today, we are considering embarking on an equally significant revolution in cellular biology. The use of stem cells to produce tissues such as blood vessels, brain cells and heart cells could result in the partial regeneration of organs. Unlike the development of biotechnology, which uses bacteria, yeast and adult tissue culture cells to produce products, the research on embryonic stem cells is dependent on disintegration of human embryos. Ethical problems abound. I contend that killing embryos by disintegration to harvest stem cells is illegal, immoral, and unnecessary.

Analysis of postulated benefits and inherent liabilities of research on embryonic pluripotent stem cells:

1. The potential benefits are clearly enunciated in the March 19,1999 letter in Science. These hypothetical benefits range from research to clinical medicine. It must be emphasized that these abundant research promises have yet to be realized even in experimental animals on a broad scale. Furthermore, history is replete with over promises as evidenced by the "War on Cancer" and the rapid development of a vaccine for AIDS. The risks, however, are real. An embryo, which could have a chance to live, is destroyed.

2. The Executive Summary of the Report of the National Bioethics Advisory Committee (September 1999), recommends that Embryonic Stem (ES) Cells be harvested from "excess or spare" embryos remaining after infertility treatments. Recommendation 2 states: "research involving the derivation and use of human ES cells from embryos remaining after infertility treatments should be eligible for federal funding. An exception should be made to the present statutory ban on federal funding of embryo research to permit federal agencies to fund research involving the derivation of human ES cells from this source under appropriate regulations that include public oversight and review." At first glance this looks to be an attractive option. Why not use an unwanted embryo to benefit the living? However, there are a number of objections. First, there are no existing regulations on In Vitro Fertilization procedures. Congress might wish to promulgate a law to regulate this industry including production of spare embryos, standards for preservation, record keeping and options for adoption. Second, serious consideration should be given to developing procedures for adoption of embryos. Third, there is enormous peer pressure in science to "support the current ethos or risk loss of funding or intellectual denigration." Therefore, objectors could be cautious in expressing contrary opinions.

3. The NBAC proposed voluntary guidelines and possible regulations to cover this research. However, the safeguards recommended by the NBAC are neither sufficient nor enforceable. The problem is clearly seen in a report in The Washington Post on November 3,1999. In an

article entitled "Gene Research Moves Toward Secrecy," Deborah Nelson and Rick Weiss reported that there were 8 deaths in gene therapy that were neither reported to patients nor properly communicated to the regulatory and scientific community. A loss of public confidence could drastically curtail research and development. In the early days of the recombinant research, there were reports of individuals leaving the country to find a location where research not approved in the US could be conducted. Steps were rapidly taken to prevent these ethical infractions.

4. The DHHS proposal and the NBAC recommendations enable the research to go forward expeditiously. However, there is an inherent conflict of interest when academicians comprise the vast majority of the membership. A special interest group that stands to "profit" through grants, industrial contracts, or research on the ethical concerns, thereby engendering notoriety, should not propose the recommendations. Any Commission that represents public interest should have broad participation including people with opposing views. Did the scientists learn from the rDNA regulations that public participation is cumbersome and should be avoided? Finally, once the research is initiated there is no turning back. An ethical position should be established first. While not challenging the credentials of any committee member, I contend that the NBAC was not sufficiently independent and sufficiently broad to fulfill this mandate.

5. Recommendation 2 in the NBAC report implies that the extra embryos described have no legal status nor affords them any. This legal issue raises many questions that demand further analysis. For example, can the donors of the sperm and egg that were used to produce an embryo legally give it away? Our Declaration of Independence states that "we hold these truths to be self-evident, that all men are created equal, that they are endowed by their Creator with certain unalienable Rights, that among these are Life, Liberty and the pursuit of Happiness." I contend that the embryo should receive such protection no matter how it is conceived. It is important to note that the embryo is accorded legal protection in many states. Finally, the harvesting of an embryo and the subsequent use of its cells for research might violate the Fourteenth Amendment. Throughout American history, our nation has striven to protect the vulnerable. The Americans with Disabilities Act, our efforts in Kosovo, and the recent Clinton Administration's Conference on Mental Health are contemporary examples of our National commitment in this regard.

6. The NBAC report focuses primarily on ES and Embryonic Germ (EG) cells. In science there is an ethos of the imperative, "if it can be done, try to do it", or, stated differently, "research is a First Amendment right." However, we live in a society where the cardinal principal is do no harm, whether in medicine or to the environment. Therefore, the use of adult stem cells should be fully explored and investigated prior to reversing the moratorium on human embryo research. Recent

studies have demonstrated that these cells might be a suitable substitute for ES and EG cells.

We are at a critical junction in society and faced with a serious dilemma. The problem of conflicting human desires was stated clearly by Arthur A. Leff in the *Duke Law Journal*, December 1979, page 1229. "I want to believe, and so do you, in a complete transcendent and immanent set of propositions about right and wrong, findable rules that authoritatively and unambiguously direct us how to live righteously. I also want to believe, and so do you, in no such thing, but rather that we are wholly free, not only to choose for ourselves what we ought to do, but to decide for ourselves, individually and as a species, what we ought to be. What we want, heaven help us, is simultaneously to be perfectly ruled and perfectly free, that is, at the same time to discover the right and good and to create it."

APPENDIX CONCLUSIONS

The issues are contentious and difficult. Our population is divided on the ethical appropriateness of the use of ES cells. The scientific imperative impels us ever forward. But there are major costs. These are the same considerations that we had at FDA as we embarked on the approval of biotechnology products and developed regulatory policies. We need to have the confidence of the people and to be concerned for the social, religious, medical, environmental and scientific interests of our citizens. Once we lose credibility, all chance for acceptance of the adequacy of the public health system is eroded. Under such conditions, the fruits of biotechnology would have rotted in the laboratory. However, we succeeded admirably! Following the pattern of the successful development of the biotechnology industry, I contend that the rush to engage in embryonic pluripotent stem cell research is foolhardy. We need to settle the ethical concerns first.

Since I have moved from medicine into pastoral ministry, I have become more aware than ever of the need to ensure the dignity of each person. As a scientist, I am fascinated with the complexity of life and the capacity to develop medicines that can alleviate the suffering of mankind. As a physician, I am committed to promoting health and providing care to the living. Now as a pastor, I know that we are made in the image of God (Gen. 1:26–27) and as image bearers we must respect the sanctity of life. Because each of us will die, it is imperative that we know the meaning of life and live accordingly. Maintaining the endowment by the Creator "with certain unalienable rights, that among these are life, liberty and the pursuit of happiness" is as important for the embryo as for the adult. The utilitarian ethical stance of promoting the greatest good could lead to a new eugenics and the sacrifice of the vulnerable to relieve the pain and suffering and extend the life of the living.

RECOMMENDATIONS

1. To ensure a broad representation of the citizens of the country, I recommend that Congress and the Administration appoint a

Commission to review the current progress in ES, EG and Adult Stem cells. This Commission should be charged to hold public meetings and to report annually to Congress and the President. Additionally the Commission should develop an ethical framework for research with stem cells and propose a well-designed way to communicate with the public. The Commission should also recommend policy questions for analysis by the Administration and Congress. To ensure representation of all points of view, five members should be appointed by the President, five by the Senate and five by the House of Representatives. The membership should consist of at least two of each of the following: public representatives, scientists, physicians, ethicists and theologians. The term of service should be limited to three years.

2. A moratorium for three years to enable the Commission to report to the Administration and Congress.

3. The Commission should be adequately funded through an independent budget to accomplish its tasks.

4. In the interim, as an added layer of safety, the FDA should examine whether additional guidelines and regulations are required for in vitro fertilization. FDA should report to Congress on the adequacy of regulations to meet the new responsibilities and the adequacy of the staff resources to accomplish the expectations of the public.

5. In the meantime, there should be sufficient funding for research on human adult stem cells and animal embryonic and germinal stem cells to enable this technology to continue to be developed during the moratorium on human pluripotent stem cells.

I will be pleased to answer any questions you have regarding my testimony. If you wish, I shall provide more in depth recommendations about the proposed Commission and additional insights into the commercialization of biotechnology that occurred on my watch as Commissioner of FDA. Thank you for your attention and concern.

ENDNOTES

1. T. B. Kornberg and M. A. Krasnow, "The Drosophila Genome Sequence and Implications for Biology and Medicine," *Science* 287 (2000): 2218.
2. M. S. Frankel, "In Search of Stem Cell Policy," *Science* 287 (2000): 1397.
3. J. A. Robertson, "The Scientists Right to Research: A Constitutional Analysis," *Southern California Law Review*, 1978, 1278.
4. S. J. Gould, "Rocks of Ages: Science in the Fullness of Life," *New York: Library of Contemporary Religious Thought* (Baltimore: Baltimore Publishing Group, 1999), 9. Gould commented on the contributions of each as follows: "If religion can no longer dictate the nature of factual conclusions residing properly with the magisterium of science, then scientists cannot claim higher insight into moral truth from any superior knowledge of the world's empirical constitution."
5. F. Griffith, "Significance of Pneumococcal Types," *J. Hygiene* 27 (1928): 113–59.

6. O. T. Avery, C. M. MacLeod, and M. McCarty, "Studies on the chemical nature of the substance inducing transformation by a deoxyribonucleic acid fraction isolated from pneumococcus type III," *J. Exptl. Med.* 79 (1944): 137–58.
7. P. Berg, et al., "Potential Biohazards of Recombinant DNA Molecules," *Science* 185 (1974): 303.
8. For more information, see National Institutes of Health, Department of Health, Education, and Welfare, "Recombinant DNA Research Guidelines," *Federal Register*, 7 July 1976, 37902–43. An example of a notice for public comment on the coordinated federal guidelines can be obtained in "Coordinated Framework for Regulation of Biotechnology; Announcement of Policy and Notice for Public Comment," *Federal Register* 51 (1986): 23302.
9. Organization for Economic Cooperation and Development, *Safety Evaluation of Foods Derived by Modern Biotechnology: Concepts and Principles* (Paris, France: Organization for Economic Cooperation and Development, 1993).
10. L. E. Rosenberg and A. N. Schechter, "Gene Therapist, Heal Thyself," *Science* 287 (2000): 1751.
11. E. D. Zanjani and W. F. Anderson, "Prospects for In Utero Human Gene Therapy," *Science* 285 (1999): 2084.
12. M. A. Abram, chairman, *Splicing Life: A Report on the Social and Ethical Issues in Genetic Engineering* (Washington, D.C.: Library of Congress, 1982). This is the first commission to consider some of the religious concerns; however, little of substance was included.
13. SCNT is a process in which an egg is harvested from an ovary, and, while held by suction, the nucleus, containing one copy of the chromosomes of the individual, is removed. A nucleus from a cell in an individual's body containing two copies of each chromosome is introduced into the egg. This procedure provides the necessary two copies of chromosomes essential for a mammal that are normally produced by a sperm carrying one copy fertilizing an egg caring another copy. The egg is stimulated to divide and produce an embryo. The embryo is grown to the appropriate stage *in vitro* and then introduced into the uterus of an animal of the same species. This is the process that was used to clone Dolly. For more information, see F. E. Young, "Worldviews in Conflict," in *Genetic Engineering: A Christian Response*, ed. Timothy J. Demy and Gary P. Stewart (Grand Rapids: Kregel, 1999), 71–85.
14. National Bioethics Advisory Commission, *Cloning Human Beings* (Rockville, Md.: National Bioethics Advisory Commission, 1997), Executive Summary i–v. Also, see chapters 3 and 4 for religious and ethical Considerations, respectively.
15. J. A. Thompson, et al., "Embryonic Stem Cell Lines Derived from Human Blastocysts," *Science* 282 (1998): 1145–47.
16. M. J. Schamblott, et al., "Derivation of Pluripotent Cells from Cultured Human Primordial Germ Cells," *Proceedings of the National Academy of Sciences* 95 (1998): 13726–31.
17. R. P. Lanza, "Science over Politics," *Science* 283 (1999): 1849–50. The article is an example of many promises as yet unrealized, but designed to influence public opinion. Note the following statement: "We join with other scientific organizations and patient groups in our belief that the DHHS current position is both laudable and forward thinking. It succeeds in protecting the sanctity of human life without impeding biomedical research that could be profoundly important to understanding and treatment of disease. In addition to helping to unravel processes underlying cell differentiation and biological development

(which, in turn, could lead to new ways to prevent and treat birth defects and cancer), the use of human pluripotent stem cells could potentially reduce the number of animal studies and clinical trials required for drug development and testing. The implications of this research for clinical medicine are equally enormous." Few, if any, advocate groups are omitted! No explanation was given for the contention that sacrificial killing of embryos protects the sanctity of human life.

18. G. Vogel, "Can Old Cells Learn New Tricks?" *Science* 287 (2000): 1418–19; Frank Gage, "Mammalian Neural Stem Cells," *Science* 287 (2000): 1433–41; and F. M. Watt and B. L. Hogan, "Out of Eden: Stem Cells and Their Niches," *Science* 287 (2000): 1427–30.

19. J. M. Slack, "Stem Cells in Epithelial Tissue," *Science* 287 (2000): 1431–33.

20. National Bioethics Advisory Commission, Executive Summary, *Ethical Issues in Human Stem Cell Research*, (Rockville, Md.: National Bioethics Advisory Commission, 1999). Also available at http://bioethics.gov/cgi-bin/bioeth-counter.pl; INTERNET.

21. Ibid., ii.

22. National Bioethics Advisory Commission, *Ethical Issues in Human Stem Cell Research*.

23. The reader is referred to an excellent discussion on, "Redemptive Technology and Participating in Creation" by Cole-Turner. R. C. Cole-Turner, *Theology and the Genetic Revolution* (Louisville, Ky.: John Knox, 1993).

24. M. Barinaga, "Asilomar Revisited: Lessons for Today," *Science* 287 (2000): 1584.

25. Ephesians 2:8–9: "For it is by grace you have been saved, through faith and this not from yourselves, it is the gift of God, not by works, so that no one can boast."

26. Matthew 22:15–21: "Then the Pharisees went out and laid plans to trap him in his words. They sent their disciples to him along with the Herodians. 'Teacher,' they said, 'we know you are a man of integrity and that you teach the way of God in accordance with the truth. You aren't swayed by men, because you pay no attention to who they are. Tell us then, what is your opinion? Is it right to pay taxes to Caesar or not?' But Jesus, knowing their evil intent, said, 'You hypocrites, why are you trying to trap me? Show me the coin used for paying the tax.' They brought him a denarius, and he asked them, 'Whose portrait is this? And whose inscription?' 'Caesar's,' they replied. Then he said to them, 'Give to Caesar what is Caesar's, and to God what is God's.'"

27. Jeremiah 1:5: "Before I formed you in the womb I knew you, before you were born I set you apart; I appointed you as a prophet to the nations."

28. A. A. Hoekema, *Created in God's Image* (Grand Rapids: Eerdmans, 1986), 75–82

29. D. P. Hollinger, "A Theology of Healing and Genetic Engineering," *in Genetic Engineering: A Christian Response*, 295–303.

30. For a detailed discussion, the reader is referred to C. D. Forsythe, "Human Cloning and the Constitution," in *Valparaiso University Law Review*, 1998, 469–542.

31. F. E. Young, "A Time for Restraint," *Science* 287 (2000): 1424.

32. An example of a testimony before Senator Spector on stem cells is provided as appendix 1 at the conclusion of this chapter.

33. A copy of this paper may be obtained at: http://www.aaas.org/spp/dspp/sfrl/projects/stem/report.pdf; INTERNET.

PART 3

CONTEMPORARY PERSPECTIVES
ON POLITICS AND PUBLIC POLICY

An Overview

Rather than help society, the growth of evangelicalism has mostly abandoned society to its own mores by removing its citizens (now captured—or better, rescued—by the gospel) from intellectual and influential positions of cultural authority. We have so focused on the lives of the redeemed that we have neglected to engage appropriately the society within which the redeemed operate. Therefore, evangelicals no longer have any legitimate reason to express shock over its current philosophical and moral condition and have no credibility that allows them to protest or be critical of what society has developed without their influence. Don Eberly clearly and succinctly describes America's autonomous society and the compromising effects it has on law and politics in a democracy. His insights into American culture rightly see law and politics as products of society's virtue and character. It is culture, and not politics, that needs reform if recovery is possible. And it is into culture that evangelicals must wisely and compassionately go, not to "Christianize America," but to influence it for the good of all people and to create an environment that sees Christian principles as valuable or even essential to societal interests. The "good news" of the gospel of Jesus Christ is broad enough to benefit the unredeemed as well as the redeemed.

Chapter Twelve

THE PLACE OF LAW AND POLITICS IN A CIVIL SOCIETY

Don Eberly

BEFORE MY APPEARANCE BEFORE THE House Judiciary Committee (May 13, 1999) on the role of popular mass culture in producing youth alienation and school violence, a panel of students gave their observations. They were led by an articulate twelfth grader from a large suburban high school whose function at the hearing was simply to describe her school. What distinguished her high school, she said, was that "no one was in charge"—not the teachers, not the parents, not even the security guards. She added that in the midst of this chaos the school kept adding more and more rules, even though the rules that did exist were never enforced.

Knowing that a picture such as this was worth a thousand words, I dispensed with my planned remarks and merely urged the thirty-five-plus representatives to reflect long and hard on the vivid portrayal they had just witnessed of institutions with their most basic authority hollowed out. Here, in this one public high school, was a microcosm of the entire society.

RADICAL AUTONOMY

Welcome to the "Republic of the Autonomous Self," where the individual is the only real sovereign, where "mediating" structures have been leveled, and where rules proliferate and yet lack legitimacy. Those who point to legitimate social authority as an essential ingredient in a well-ordered society and who would prefer less individualism and more community often have the charge of nostalgia leveled against them. But the rise of what Robert Bellah called a "radically unencumbered and improvisional self"[1] and the resulting social collapse produce the ugly tensions, discord, and national disharmony that we must now endure everywhere we turn. The results of this radically emancipated self are anything but progressive or pleasant.

One consequence is that we are transformed from "one nation, indivisible" to a balkanized place of endless divisibility, a process historian Arthur Schlesinger aptly describes as "the fragmentation, resegregation, and tribalization of American life."[2] A related result is that people become more self-centered. Social analyst and pollster Daniel Yankelovich has spent his entire adult life studying the shifting sands of American moral attitudes, and concluded that the vast changes in our society can be explained by one underlying seismic shift. We have moved, he said, from a sense of "duty to others" to a "duty to self."

Collapsing under the weight of radical autonomy is any notion of the common good. Yankelovich's observation tracks with what I found in doing extensive research on citizen attitudes for a book on the state of American civil society. In surveying the description of society by citizens themselves, I repeatedly found them using words such as *fraying, fracturing*, and *fragmenting* to describe the world around them. Citizens were saying essentially that too many people are out for themselves. "What chills me about the future," wrote one person, "is a general sense of the transformation of our society from one that strengthens the bonds between people to one that is, at best, indifferent to them." There is "a sense of an inevitable fraying of the net of connections between people at many critical intersections, of which the marital knot is only one. Each fraying accelerates another. A break in one connection, such as attachment between parents and children, puts pressure on other connections such as marriage." With enough fraying, individuals lose "that sense of membership in the larger community which grows best when it is grounded in membership in the small one."

Fraying communities, fractured families, a fragmenting nation— journalists, scholars, and citizens alike seem to agree that American society is, in too many ways, pulling apart at the seams. Public surveys likewise reveal a precipitous decline in social trust. Where does the citizen come by the capacity to be helpful, respectful, and trustful toward others? Mostly through involvement in functioning social institutions, *especially the family*. The fact that only 35 percent of the American people indicate that they can trust most people most of the time is a function of more than flawed democratic institutions; it is a function of social breakdown. It is hard to imagine how children who have been betrayed by the persons in whom they thought they could put their intimate trust—namely, their own parents—are ever going to become public trust-builders.

DEMOCRACY ON THE SKIDS

The result is an increasingly self-centered, litigious, and arbitrary society. The social space where decisions are made on the basis of self-interest, competition, and the struggle for power expands, while the space that is truly voluntary and consensual, where people of good will and civilized values can join together in rational deliberation, shrinks. The handshake gives way to the omnipresence of the law. The law, in turn, becomes overworked and arbitrary. Society feels like an engine running low on oil—things heat up.

When cultural reformers are not being accused of nostalgia, they are being lectured on how culture is a private sphere where we make thousands of individual choices, operating safely beyond the scope of public concern. After all, we are reminded, if we object to our ten-year-old being subjected to soft porn on prime time, we can just "change the channel." Any other approach would be a direct assault on the First Amendment. But culture affects democracy in hundreds of ways, large and small. As Mary Ann Glendon of Harvard put it, "If history teaches us anything, it is that democracy cannot be taken for granted. There are *social and cultural* conditions that are more or less favorable to its success."[3] Democracy requires a capacity for trust and collaboration, at least on the small scale of face-to-face community. America's founders talked about the ingredients of civic virtue, such things as sentiments, affections, manners, and duty to the common good. These core qualities are the first link in a long series of steps whereby, as Edmond Burke put it, "we develop our love for mankind" generally. In other words, the outer order of society is directly linked to the inner order of our souls.

Most democratic reforms today, however, are directed toward fixing the procedural state (outer order) without addressing the underlying cultural and social crisis (inner order). The problems of money, declining participation, and the uneven distribution of power are indeed serious problems, but democracy is fragile in a way that no campaign finance reform and no amount of increased voter participation can cure. The more serious problems of American democracy have to do with the erosion of democratic character and habit. *A society in which men and women are morally adrift and intent chiefly on gratifying their appetites will be a disordered society no matter how many people vote.* We must recover the democratic citizen through restored communities, functioning social institutions, and a renewed culture.

To thrive, democracy needs the help of nongovernmental sectors, including strong social institutions and a healthy culture. Can anyone doubt that today's toxic culture of crass consumerism, cynicism, and utilitarian values is cheapening our respect for the human person and eroding the foundations of democracy? Cultural excess awakens an appetite for things that no viable democracy can offer—the simultaneous expansion of the law and a widening search for freedom from the abuses of the law. The law is forced to enter where gentler forms of governance such as manners and social norms retreat, ultimately eroding human dignity and freedom.

This restless search for human progress through legal reforms creates a politicized society and a state that expands radically even as its competence and legitimacy ebb. The law degenerates into an arbitrary tool of the politically organized. A right conferred upon one group becomes an obligation imposed on another. One person's gain is another person's loss. The legal system is forced to find ever-finer balances and boundaries between conflicting parties and claims. People expect the law simultaneously to confer the light of sexual freedom and freedom from sexual assault; to guarantee gender and racial advantages for some and the protections against reverse discrimination for others; to protect the rights of criminal offenders and the rights of their victims; to guard the rights of free speech while initiating new rights against the insult of hateful speech; to defend the rights of both individuals and communities; and so on.

Never before has the law been called upon to split conflicting demands with such exasperating precision. The justice system begins to resemble a harried referee who has the impossible task of policing a sport that is both choked by rules and overwhelmed by infractions. The pursuit of a just society is reduced to a perpetual fight over what the rules should be.

DISORDERED LIBERTY

The first cousin of rights-based individualism is the pernicious idea that "the personal is political," which was brought to the American debate first by the feminist movement and since by any number of "identity politics" factions. Recently, a libertarian friend described how a homosexual associate of his decided to inform his office colleagues of his sexual orientation and to use a staff meeting to announce boldly his exit from the closet. Apparently expecting his colleagues' approval as a matter of right, the person instead got a range of mixed opinion, including some firmly stated disapproval. After a contentious struggle ensued inside the organization over the handling of the matter, the disgruntled staffer left. My response to this story was to inform my friend that his homosexual colleague, by demanding that others suspend their deeply held moral and religious beliefs to guarantee an approving atmosphere for his lifestyle, demonstrated that he was not a libertarian but a totalitarian. At issue was not his constitutional protection, which few would argue against, but his explicit attempt to coerce a change in the moral beliefs of his office peers.

The story illustrates powerfully the extent of America's cultural transformation; the ramifications for our public order and constitutional system could not be more profound. Ironically, those who most ardently advocate the right to conduct themselves freely in private have no concept of the meaning of private as distinct from public space, even when the most intimate aspects of life are involved. What they want is simultaneous protection from intrusion into the bedroom while being assured broad public validation for what takes place there. The most private aspects of one's life become the grounds for one's public identification. When only the law and politics arbitrate human affairs, everything becomes politicized—even the most basic and private forms of human association and action, such as one's sexual practices. The private, sacred, and mystical aspects of life become the basis for social and political agitation.

What we see around us is the steady replacement of an ordered liberty with the libertarianism of John Stuart Mill, in which freedom is absolute, the self is unbounded by even private morality and convention, and one's actions are protected even from social disapproval. Whereas liberty was once conceived of as having properties beyond the self, bound by morality and religion and tied to the interests of the commonwealth, today "the individual is the sole repository and arbiter of all values," as historian Gertrude Himmelfarb put it, and is thus in "an adversarial relationship to society and the state." This is a liberty, says Himmelfarb, which "is a grave peril to liberalism itself."[4]

UNDERMINING AUTHORITY

What must be acknowledged is that many of the most corrupting viruses are now being borne along not by sinister politicians but by an entertainment and information media culture and that this omnipresent culture is displacing the core social institutions that once shaped and molded the democratic citizen. Whereas parents, pastors, and pedagogues once presided over the socialization of the young, now television, film, music, cyberspace, and the celebrity culture of sports and entertainment dominate this process of shaping youthful attitudes and beliefs. Popular mass culture largely informs our most basic understanding of society, our public life, our obligations to each other, and even the nature of the American experiment.

The culture naturally both reflects and influences what people think is right and proper. American culture has usually stressed moral rectitude but has always permitted latitude for abnormal beliefs and behavior to operate freely at the margins of society, as long as it stayed there. We had "red light districts," for example, which one was free to frequent, albeit at the risk of exposure and public shame. But even these mild social constraints crumble when everybody is electronically hardwired and what is marginal becomes mainstream at the flip of a TV remote or the click of a computer mouse.

Much of what passes for culture today is, in fact, anticulture. Its chief aim is to emancipate, not restrain, to give free reign to human appetite, not to moderate it. The role of entertainment, we are frequently told by entertainers themselves, is to challenge and stretch standards. "Break the rules!" "Have no fear!" "Be yourself!" are the common themes within mainstream cultural programming, and they are designed to discredit traditional forms of authority.

Which takes us back to the Congressional hearings on school violence. Without a healthy culture maintaining the conditions for human flourishing, we evolve steadily into a mildly authoritarian custodial democracy in which more and more transactions are supervised by the state. The anarchy of the school is but a passing phase that creates the desire for more laws and restrictions. This is how social conflict erodes freedom. *People are ruled either by character and civility or by cops and lawyers.* Anarchy produces injury, which produces lawsuits followed by a thickening layer of defensive measures. Not many years ago, parents from small towns would have recoiled in horror to think that electronic surveillance would become commonplace in our schools, much less that uniformed police would one day roam the halls. "These are schools" they would probably have said, "not prisons." Today, by contrast, polls show that most parents now embrace these symbols of a police state.

Such is the course of freedom's erosion. Gone is freedom of the most precious kind—the freedom of parents to send their children to schools where safety and order are maintained through instruction in the gentle virtues of respect and civility, not the chilling presence of weapons detectors and armed police. Gone is the freedom of children to proceed through life unharrassed and unhurried, enjoying the innocence of youth as long as it should be theirs to enjoy.

This is the delusion of the modern libertine. When social institutions and authority collapse and the capacity to govern human affairs through voluntary, consensual means erodes, all roads lead to the state—especially the courts and innumerable social agencies forced by default to become the caretakers of fragile families and poorly socialized individuals, the unruly children of the underclass, and the spoiled and dysfunctional suburban latchkey kids. *The fragmentation round about us, which libertarians of all stripes tend to view benignly, is leading inevitably and ironically to the very statism that they claim to oppose.* A society in which atomized and poorly socialized individuals continually organize to use the state against each other is a society in which the individual and the state are advancing but civil society, a place of consensual and voluntary action, is in rapid retreat.

THE CHRISTIAN RESPONSIBILITY

As proponents of civil society, the responsibility of the Christian community is not to retreat from the political square altogether (spiritual isolation), nor is it to accept the status quo (moral toleration). The debate should focus not on methods of retreat but on new models for engagement and new strategies that focus more on culture than on politics in the decades to come. The issue is not that politics is unimportant; it is that even if one succeeds in building working majorities, the lawmaking process can at best suppress the symptoms of cultural disorder. It can do very little about the underlying causes. The most one can hope for in politics is to ensure that government "do no harm," an objective that will keep many good people busy in politics for a long time to come, to be sure.

But politics cannot begin to put the "connecting tissue" back in society. It is ill-equipped to reconstruct traditional moral beliefs. The best policies cannot recover courtship or marriage, make fathers responsible for their children, restore shock or shame where it once existed, or recover legitimate social authority to institutions that have been hollowed out by a pervasive ideology of individual autonomy. The vast majority of moral problems that trouble us cannot be eradicated by law.

Some people imagine the nation in a state of political crisis and long for a Churchill figure to set things right. But our crisis is cultural. Even in the unlikely event that such a figure were to emerge, politics cannot confront a debauched culture in the same fashion that it can offer bold action in the midst of war or depression. In a disordered society, a heavy reliance on political authority to renew the nonauthoritative sector of culture can quickly become more disease than cure. In fact, the most promising possibility in the debate that Weyrich and Thomas/Dobson[5] have triggered is the emergence of a new politics of prudence, a politics that will be both more realistic in its expectations and more sustainable. The problem has not been expecting too little of politics but expecting far too much.

True conservatism brings a natural skepticism to the reforming possibilities of politics. It sees as its first job the long-term cultivation of character, culture, and community. It views politics as "downstream" from culture, *more reflecting it than shaping it.* Conservatism avoids excessively politicizing religion or religionizing politics because genuine religious faith stirs allegiances that transcend nation and ideology. The Scriptures would counsel even more skepticism about both the possibilities of politics and the form in which it should be practiced.

Before very recently, the mainstream of evangelical opinion looked askance at the now common practice of uniting or fusing biblical faith with American ideologies of the Left or Right. The greatest fallacy that has emerged in recent years is the expectation that national politicians and other civil authorities should take the lead in restoring biblical righteousness or, worse, using political power to create a "Christian America." This smacks of the idolatry of Constantinianism and is guaranteed to fail on the American scene, as even seventeenth-century Puritans discovered. Public statesmen today should imagine themselves as called to serve, *not in a predominantly Christian nation*, but one that more resembles the conditions that Paul encountered in Athens, where he invoked the literature and philosophy of the times to make his point without imagining a large sympathetic majority standing behind him.

The appeal to create a "Christian America" represents a misreading of our times, American history, and, I would argue, the Scripture itself. The late English historian Christopher Dawson said that the idea "that the spiritual life of the society should be ruled by a political party would have appeared to our ancestors as a monstrous absurdity." This perspective is not only theologically sound but also where the people are. The American people have registered stratospheric levels of concern about moral values, but they don't see moral renewal coming predominantly from politics. In fact, when moral renewal becomes completely synonymous with political takeovers and legislative agendas, it awakens an intense fear of state intervention in people's private lives. One can see this as either more evidence of America's moral corruption or as an impulse as old as America itself, illustrated best historically by the rush to repeal the brief experiment with Prohibition.

Religious conservatives, in other words, have put their stock in a model for moral renewal that awakens a deep, native resistance. Strategies that invest heavily in prohibitionist logic will almost always fail. If individual behavior is to be regulated, it should be regulated through the re-establishment of real social and moral norms in communities. Many exceptions to this exist, of course, as opponents of this argument will quickly point out (e.g., the current battle over legalized gambling).

Christians are understandably dismayed that the culture has become unhitched from its Judeo-Christian roots. What many people refuse to acknowledge is that, in a thousand ways, *this unhitching was produced by a massive retreat of Christians from the intellectual, cultural, and philanthropic life of the nation*. Although evangelicals count millions of members among their grassroots political groups and are now, if anything, over-represented in the legislative arena, the number of evangelicals at the top of America's powerful culture-shaping institutions could be seated in a single school bus! The watching world is understandably chagrined by the interest evangelicals have shown in power while simultaneously showing so little interest in the noncoercive arenas of society where one's only weapon is persuasion.

More than anything, Christians need a model for engagement that combines the preceding principles. Perhaps the most helpful historical model is that of the British statesman, William Wilberforce, a politician who ultimately succeeded in outlawing the slave trade but who did so by first acknowledging the limits of the law absent the reform of manners and morals. Over the course of more than forty years, Wilberforce created sixty-seven councils and commissions to bring about social and moral reform, some religious and some secular. His model had all of the preceding ingredients in perspective, especially the subordinate relationship of politics to the culture. Wilberforce organized grassroots as well as "gatekeeper" reform movements operating in intellectual and influential professions and fields. He saw the need to transcend ideology; anyone who was useful on a particular issue was enlisted, whatever his religious or political creed.

This approach happens also to be deeply American. Any American movement that starts with the law, not culture, will fail. In the past, when citizens have reacted to the general disregard for social standards and obligations, they organized society-wide social movements that effectively moved people toward restraint and social obligation. At various times in history, America witnessed an explosion of new voluntary aid and moral-reform movements aimed at improving cultural conditions.

Finally, what is needed within the Christian community right now is a debate, deep and wide, regarding cultural and policy matters, and we can thank Paul Weyrich, Cal Thomas, and Ed Dobson for getting that long-overdue conversation started. Too many people have behaved as though politics is on a par with the church in the life of the Christian, placing matters that are filled with practical considerations on a par with biblical doctrine. The Christian community cannot avoid this debate, and it will have to be accompanied by a profound outpouring of understanding, wisdom, and grace to be effective (see chap. 9 by Stephen Hoffmann in this volume, p. 139).

ENDNOTES

1. Robert Bellah et al., *Habits of the Heart: Individualism and Commitment in American Life* (New York: Harper & Row, 1985), 83.
2. Arthur Schlesinger Jr., *The Disuniting of American Reflections on the Multicultural Society* (New York: W. W. Norton, 1992), 17.
3. Mary Ann Glendon, *Seedbeds of Virtue: Source of Competence, Character, and Citizenship in American Society,* ed. Mary Ann Glendon and David Blankenhorn (Lanham, Md.: Madison Books, 1995), 2.
4. Gertrude Himmelfarb, *On Looking into the Abyss* (New York: Knopf, 1994) 106.
5. Paul M. Weyrich, "Separate and Free," *The Washington Post,* 7 March 1999, B7; and Cal Thomas and Ed Dobson, *Blinded by Might* (Grand Rapids: Zondervan, 1999).

An Overview

Could the American system of government have survived if the Constitution had been framed on something other than a biblical understanding of human nature and law? What role, if any, did Christianity play in the minds of the founders of American democracy? Kerby Anderson candidly interacts with the original thoughts of these founders, clearly communicates their commitment to establish a government by the people and for the people (as Abraham Lincoln later described their creation), and points out their credible concerns about innate human leanings that have the potential to threaten and possibly undo such a government. Whether America could actually be described as being or becoming a "Christian nation" is easily debatable; however, the fact that America's democratic government was *founded on and depends upon* Christian principles is indisputable and, therefore, cannot long last without them.

Chapter Thirteen

A CHRISTIAN PERSPECTIVE ON AMERICAN GOVERNMENT

Kerby Anderson

THE FOUNDING OF THIS COUNTRY and the framing of the key religious documents rest upon a Christian foundation. That doesn't necessarily mean that the United States is a Christian nation, although some framers used that term. But it does mean that the foundations of this republic presuppose a Christian view of human nature and God's providence. Consider just a few famous quotations from a variety of sources.

AMERICA'S CHRISTIAN ROOTS
The framers of our government explicitly stated that the government they were forming rested upon a Christian foundation. Patrick Henry, known for his fiery rhetoric, made this claim about the Christian roots of this country: "It cannot be emphasized too strongly or too often that this great nation was founded, not by religionists, but by Christians, not on religion, but on the gospel of Jesus Christ!"

James Madison is often called the "architect of the Constitution" because of his central role in drafting the Constitution, defending the Constitution (through the *Federalist Papers*), and drafting the Bill of Rights. If anyone understood the foundation of our government, James Madison did. He said, "We have staked the whole future of the American civilization, not upon the power of government, far from it. We have staked the future of all of our political institutions on the capacity of each and all of us to govern ourselves, to control ourselves, to sustain ourselves, according to the Ten Commandments of God." He understood the need for Americans to govern themselves instead of looking to a federal government to dictate or control their passions and behavior.

John Adams also saw the need for religious values to provide the moral base line for society. He said, "Our constitution was made only for a moral and religious people. So great is my veneration of the Bible that the earlier my children begin to read it, the more confident will be my hope that they will prove useful citizens of their country and respectful members of society."

John Adams wasn't the only founding father to talk about the importance of Christian values and the Bible. Consider this quotation from George

Washington: "Reason and experience both forbid us to expect that national morality can prevail in exclusion of religious principle. . . . It is impossible to govern rightly without God and the Bible."

Two hundred years after the establishment of the Plymouth colony in 1620, Americans gathered at that site to celebrate its bicentennial. One of the most eloquent speakers at this 1820 celebration was Daniel Webster. He reminded those in attendance of this nation's origins. "Let us not forget the religious character of our origin. Our fathers were brought hither by their high veneration for the Christian religion. They journeyed by its light, and labored in its hope. They sought to incorporate its principles with the elements of their society, and to diffuse its influence through all their institutions, civil, political, or literary."

CHARACTER AND GOVERNMENT

The framers of this government also believed that the American people should elect and support leaders with character and integrity. George Washington expressed this concern in his Farewell Address delivered in 1796. He said, "Of all the dispositions and habits which lead to political prosperity, religion and morality are indispensable supports."

Benjamin Rush talked about the religious foundation of the republic which demanded virtuous leadership. He said, "The only foundation for . . . a republic is to be laid in Religion. Without this there can be no virtue, and without virtue there can be no liberty, and liberty is the object and life of all republican governments."

The British commentator Edmund Burke warned both the British and the Americans of what would occur if they did not elect leaders with character: "Vice incapacitates a man from all public duty; it withers the powers of his understanding, and makes his mind paralytic."

Daniel Webster understood this foundation as well: "Our ancestors established their system of government on morality and religious sentiment. Moral habits, they believed, cannot safely be entrusted on any other foundation than religious principle, not any government can be secure which is not supported by moral habits. . . . Whatever makes men good Christians, makes them good citizens."

John Jay was one of the authors of the *Federalist Papers* and also America's first Chief Justice of the Supreme Court. He was also the President of the American Bible Society. He understood the relationship between government and Christian values. "Providence has given to our people the choice of their rulers," he said, "and it is the duty, as well as the privilege and interest, of a Christian nation to select and prefer Christians for its rulers."

Historian C. Gregg Singer, therefore, makes the following summary observation in his book *A Theological Interpretation of American History*:

> Whether we look at the Puritans and their fellow colonists of the seventeenth century, or their descendants of the eighteenth century, or those who framed the Declaration of Independence and the Constitution, we see that their

political programs were the rather clear reflection of a consciously held political philosophy, and that the various political philosophies which emerged among the American people were intimately related to the theological developments which were taking place. . . . A Christian world and life view furnished the basis for this early political thought which guided the American people for nearly two centuries and whose crowning lay in the writing of the Constitution of 1787.[1]

A Christian perspective influenced not only our earlier documents, but also the Declaration of Independence and the Constitution. Let's look at that influence in more detail.

A CHRISTIAN PERSPECTIVE ON
THE DECLARATION OF INDEPENDENCE

On June 7, 1776, Richard Henry Lee introduced a resolution to the Continental Congress calling for a formal declaration of independence. But even at that late date, the resolution faced significant opposition. So, Congress recessed for three weeks to allow delegates to return home and discuss the proposition with their constituents while a committee was appointed to express the congressional sentiments. The task of composing the Declaration fell to Thomas Jefferson. His initial draft reflected his deistic philosophy. He left God out of the manuscript entirely, except for a vague reference to "the laws of nature and of nature's God." Yet, even this phrase makes an implicit reference to the laws of God.

The phrase "laws of nature" had a fixed meaning in eighteenth century England and America. It was a direct reference to the laws of God in a created order as described in John Locke's *Second Treatise of Civil Government* and William Blackstone's *Commentaries on the Laws of England*.

But what Jefferson was content to leave implicit, other members of the committee made more explicit. They changed the language to read that all men are "endowed by their Creator." Later, the Continental Congress added phrases which further reflected a theistic perspective. For example, they added that they were "appealing to the Supreme Judge of the World for the rectitude of our intentions" and that they were placing "firm reliance on the protection of divine Providence."

The founders of this nation built their framework upon a Reformation foundation laid by such men as Samuel Rutherford and later incorporated by John Locke. Rutherford wrote his book *Lex Rex* in 1644 to refute the idea of the divine right of kings. *Lex Rex* established two crucial principles: first, that there should be a covenant or constitution between the ruler and the people; and second, that because all men are sinners, no man is superior to another. These twin principles of liberty and equality are also found in John Locke's writings.

Legal scholar Gary Amos believes that Locke's *Two Treatises of Civil Government* is simply Rutherford's *Lex Rex* in a popularized form and that it, too, was written to refute the concept of the divine right of kings. Amos writes in his book *Defending the Declaration* about Locke's understanding of the laws of nature and of God, which preclude a king from governing according to the dictates of his own will. The ruler, like his subjects, was equally responsible and accountable to God.

> Locke explained that the "law of nature" is God's general revelation of law in creation, which God also supernaturally writes on the hearts of men. Locke drew the idea from the New Testament in Romans 1 and 2. In contrast, he spoke of the "law of God" or the "positive law of God" as God's eternal moral law specially revealed and published in Scripture.[2]

This foundation helps explain the tempered nature of the American Revolution. The Declaration of Independence was a bold, but not a radical, document. The colonists did not break with England for "light and transient causes." They were mindful that they should be "in subjection to the governing authorities," which "are established by God" (Rom. 13:1 NASB). Yet, when they suffered from a "long train of abuses and usurpations," they argued that "it is the right of the people to alter or to abolish [the existing government] and to institute a new government."

A CHRISTIAN PERSPECTIVE ON THE CONSTITUTION

After the Constitution was written, fifty-five men emerged from the State House in Philadelphia. A woman approached Benjamin Franklin and asked, "Dr. Franklin, what have you given us?" The statesman replied, "A republic, madam, if you can keep it."

One key to the keeping of the republic is a proper understanding of the foundation upon which the republic rests. James Madison argued in *Federalist Paper #51* that government must be based upon a realistic view of human nature.

> But what is government itself but the greatest of all reflections on human nature? If men were angels, no government would be necessary. If angels were to govern men, neither external nor internal controls on government would be necessary. In framing a government which is to be administered by men over men, the great difficulty lies in this: you must first enable the government to control the governed; and in the next place oblige it to control itself.[3]

Framing a republic requires a balance of power that liberates human dignity and rationality and controls human sin and depravity.

> As there is a degree of depravity in mankind which requires a certain degree of circumspection and distrust, so there are other qualities in human nature, which justify a certain portion of esteem and confidence. Republican government presupposes the existence of these qualities in a higher degree than any other form.[4]

A Christian view of government is based upon a balanced view of human nature. It recognizes both human dignity (we are created in God's image) and human depravity (we are sinful, self-centered individuals). Because both grace and sin operate in government, we should neither be too optimistic nor too pessimistic. We should view governmental affairs with a deep sense of biblical realism. A people's desire to trust in government must always be tempered by a deeper desire to trust in the Lord. "It is better to take refuge in the LORD than to trust in man. It is better to take refuge in the LORD than to trust in princes" (Ps. 118:8–9).

Most political theorists in Britain and the United States accepted this balanced view of human nature. Edmund Burke, an English Christian, developed his description of what government should be in his *Reflections on the French Revolution* based upon a balanced view of human nature. So did the founders of the American form of government. Although many of them were not Christians, they were frequently influenced by the Christian milieu. This does not mean that Christians must support every aspect of the American governmental system. *The Constitution represents a compromise of Christian principles and humanistic principles from the Enlightenment.* And it is unfortunate that Christians have sometimes misunderstood this fact and, therefore, been guilty of substituting a civil religion for biblical principles. Nevertheless, the American political experiment has been successful because it is based upon a balanced view of human nature that avoids the dangers of utopian experiments in human government.

Madison concluded from his study that governments are destroyed by divisive factions. Such factionalism was due to "the propensity of mankind to fall into mutual animosities" *(Federalist Paper #10)*, which he believed were "sown in the nature of man." Government, he concluded, must be based upon a more realistic view that also accounts for the sinful side of human nature. A year before the Constitutional Convention, George Washington wrote to John Jay, "We have, probably, had too good an opinion of human nature in forming our federation." From now on, he added, "We must take human nature as we find it."

We can see the wisdom of the American political system. Madison and others realized the futility of trying to remove passions (human sinfulness) from the population. Therefore, he proposed that human nature be set against human nature. This was done by separating various institutional power structures. *First*, the church was separated from the state so that ecclesiastical functions and governmental functions would not interfere with each other's religious and political liberty. *Second*, the federal government was delegated certain specified powers while the rest of the powers resided in the state governments. *Third*, the federal government was divided into three equal branches: executive, legislative, and judicial.

This division of the federal government provides that each branch is given separate but rival powers, thus preventing the possibility of concentrating power into the hands of a few. Each branch has certain checks over the other branches so that there is an equal distribution and balance of power. In addition, the people are given certain means of redress. Elections and an amendment process are designed to keep power from being concentrated in the hands of governmental officials. *Each of these checks is motivated by a healthy fear of human nature.* The founders believed in human responsibility and human dignity, but they were not overly confident in human nature. Their solution was to *divide* power into three branches and, therefore, *conquer* human nature by vesting each branch with competing or rival power.

The effect of this system was to allow ambition and power to control itself. Each branch is given power, and as ambitious men and women within each branch seek to extend their sphere of influence, they are kept in check, if need be, by equally ambitious men and women within the other branches. This idea is what has often been referred to as "countervailing ambitions." For example, the executive branch cannot independently take over the government and rule at its whim because the legislative branch has been given the power of the purse. Congress has the power to approve or disapprove budgets for governmental programs. Consequently, a president cannot wage war if the Congress does not appropriate money for its execution.

Similarly, the legislative branch is also controlled by this separation of powers. It can pass legislation, but it always faces the threat of presidential veto and judicial oversight. Because the executive branch is responsible for the execution of legislation, the legislature (Congress) cannot exercise complete control over the government. Undergirding all of this is the authority of the ballot box, that is, the vote of the people.

Modern democratic systems (whether the American form of government or the British form of parliamentary rule) function well because they protect liberty and allow the greatest amount of political participation. A benevolent dictator might be more efficient, but would probably be less objective and less keen at adjudicating rival interests. Each of us has biases, and the potential for being corrupted by power is very great in a dictatorship. But the greatest fear would be that a benevolent dictator might be replaced by a malevolent dictator. An effective democratic government prevents the unleashing of human sinfulness that might occur through concentrations of power. A healthy democracy describes a political system in which bad men do the least amount of harm and good men have the freedom to do good works. Unlike other political systems, it takes human sinfulness seriously and, thereby, protects it citizens from major abuses of power. Madison was accurate in his assessment that government should follow a policy of supplying "opposite and rival interests" *(Federalist Paper #51)* through a series of checks and balances. This theory of countervailing ambitions both prevented tyranny and provided liberty.

In fact, it was this liberty or freedom to do good that made this nation great. For the republic was established not only for the protection against evil but also for the promotion of virtue. Madison understood the importance of virtue in government. "To support that any form of government will secure liberty or happiness without any virtue in the people is a chimerical idea," that is, an unrealistic and fanciful idea. Yet, the promotion of morality and religion, though a crucial element in the vitality of the republic, was not prescribed by the government. In fact, the Constitution says almost nothing about religion because *it tacitly assumes the ubiquitous nature of religion*, that is, its influence is naturally expected. Instead, churches, families, and individual citizens were expected and free to cultivate and promote the moral life of the republic.

One of the greatest flaws in the American form of government is the tendency to assume that the public good is the sum total of all special interests. In this regard, we have been excessively influenced by utilitarianism (the greatest happiness for the greatest number of persons). We have focused *too much* on pragmatic policies and questions of majority rule and *not enough* on public justice. Interest-group politics dominates the political landscape. Each special group of individuals in society has a desire to see its competitive interests represented in public policy. As a result, interest-group politics often predominate over the just and moral action that should be taken. Rather than consider the normative (what should be done), we frequently focus on the strategic (what can be done with the political forces involved). Not only did the American government rest upon a Christian foundation and a particular structure of government but also the framers presupposed a moral foundation for law and justice.

THE MORAL BASIS OF LAW

Law should be the foundation of any government, and a particular view of law provided the foundation for the American government. Whether law is based upon moral absolutes, changing consensus, or totalitarian whim is crucial. Until fairly recently, Western culture held to a notion that common law was founded upon God's revealed moral absolutes. As one legal scholar put it, "There never has been a period in which common law did not recognize Christianity as laying at its foundation."[5] In a Christian view of government, law is based upon God's revealed commandments. Law is not based upon human opinion or sociological convention. Law is rooted in God's unchangeable character and derived from biblical principles of morality.

By contrast, a political theory that rests on a naturalistic world view rejects the idea of revelation and presupposes a different set of legal assumptions. In naturalism, human beings replace God as the source of law. Law is merely the expression of the human will or mind. Because ethics and morality are manmade, so also is law. In naturalism, however, law is rooted in human opinion and, therefore, is relative and arbitrary.

Two important figures in the history of law are Samuel Rutherford (1600–1661) and William Blackstone (1723–1780). As was already mentioned, Rutherford's *Lex Rex* had a profound effect on British law (and subsequently American law) because it challenged the foundations of seventeenth-century politics by proclaiming that law must be based upon the Bible rather than upon the word of any man. Up until that time, the king had been the law. *Lex Rex* created a great controversy because it attacked the idea of the divine right of kings, which held that the king or the state ruled as God's appointed regent. Thus, the king's word had been law. Rutherford properly argued, from passages such as Romans 13, that the king (as well as anyone else) was under God's law and not above it.

William Blackstone was an English jurist in the eighteenth century, but he is best remembered for his *Commentaries on the Law of England*, which embodied the tenets of Judeo-Christian theism. According to Blackstone, the two foundations for law are nature and revelation through the Scriptures. Blackstone believed that the fear of the Lord was the beginning of knowledge (Prov. 1:7) and thus taught that God was the source of all laws. Interestingly, even the humanist Rousseau noted in his *Social Contract* that one needs someone outside the world system to provide a moral basis for law. He said, "It would take gods to give men laws." Unfortunately, our modern legal structure has been influenced by relativism and utilitarianism instead of moral absolutes revealed in Scripture by God. Relativism provides no secure basis for moral judgments because there are no moral absolutes upon which such judgments can be made or an objective and secure legal foundation can be built.

Utilitarianism looks merely at consequences (results or ends) to determine right from wrong rather than following an established set of moral principles. Our legal foundation has been further eroded by the relatively recent phenomenon of sociological law, by which law is based upon relative sociological standards. However, no discipline is more helpless without a moral foundation than is law. Law is a tool, and it requires a jurisprudential foundation. Just as contractors and builders must have the architect's blueprint to build trustworthy structures, so legislators must have theologians and moral philosophers to make good laws.

American government was founded on Christian principles. This fact doesn't mean that every aspect of American political theory could be considered to rest on Christian principles or to be distinctly Christian. Far from it. The founding documents were forged in a political context of compromise and expediency. Nevertheless, *the success of the American governmental system lies in its acceptance of a biblical perspective of human nature, government, and law.*

ENDNOTES

1. C. Gregg Singer, *A Theological Interpretation of American History* (Nutley, N.J.: Craig Press, 1964), 284–85.
2. Gary Amos, *Defending the Declaration* (Brentwood, Tenn.: Wolgemuth and Hyatt, 1989), 57.
3. James Madison, *Federalist Papers*, no. 51 (New York: New American Library, 1961), 322.
4. Madison, *Federalist Papers*, no. 55, 346.
5. Statement by Joseph Story in his 1829 inaugural address as Dane Professor at Harvard. Quoted in Perry Miller, ed., *The Legal Mind in America* (New York: Doubleday, 1962), 178.

An Overview

Are the words we once relied upon to direct and protect America's moral compass being retooled to promote social and political agendas that have historically been unacceptable not only in America but also in the world at large? Harold O. J. Brown discloses the subtlety and power of the language that has been and is still being used by many lobbyists and politicians to justify, or to numb, the general population's moral sensitivities to abortion, euthanasia, adultery, homosexuality, and war. If truth continues to be suppressed by the strong and persuasive words of the powerful, the populace will gradually become more subservient and compliant and less thoughtful and engaged. Without a precise understanding of the way words are being used to promote new ideas and behaviors, we unthinkingly become passive participants in a morally perilous cultural shift and eventually become perpetrators of behaviors that once were, and still are, unthinkable.

Chapter Fourteen

LANGUAGE RULES
The Importance of Language in the
Political and Ethical Discussion

Harold O. J. Brown

WHAT ARE THE MOST SIGNIFICANT ISSUES for the moral, ethical, medical, and spiritual conflicts of our day? The questions of biomedical ethics are paramount: life and death, terminal care, assisted reproduction, partial-birth abortion, fetal research, cloning, stem-cell research, and many more. We do not even need to look at other areas that are also important—such as the vaunted sex revolution, the AIDS epidemic, homosexuality, "gay marriage," and the like—to sense the confusion that prevails in ethical discussion. And finally, recent events in the spring and early summer of 1999—air "campaign," "genocide," "ethnic cleansing," "peacekeepers,"—add to the confusing mass of details out of which it is indeed difficult to isolate a clear and coherent ethical position.

Many factors contribute to this situation, and surely one of the main factors is illuminated by the apostle Paul in Romans 1:22: "Professing to be wise, they became fools (NASB)." But, of course, they are not foolish fools or gibbering idiots. They are learned fools, talking in language that sounds good, that wins adherents, but that in effect deprives the auditors and users of the ability to think. Moral discourse becomes vain. In the area of ethics generally and in the ethics of medicine and biology particularly, the old presuppositions can no longer be taken for granted.

Words can no longer be trusted to mean what we always thought they meant. They are not important for what they mean, for their correspondence to truth, to any objective reality, but for what they do. George Orwell, in *Nineteen Eighty-Four*, tells of Newspeak; Hannah Arendt, in *Eichmann in Jerusalem*, speaks of language rules. There is "true language," which instructs because it relates directly to reality, and "powerful language," which manipulates because it persuades people to act without understanding, to do without really asking why. Such powerful language manipulates not only those who hear it but also, ultimately, those who use it.

"Is language only a simple means of communicating thought, or is it equally the means of power?" After asking this question, Aaron-Arnaud Upinsky continues,

Language is the measure of everything: it is our representation of the world. It is language that filters reality and lets only "authorized" images through; it is language that imposes the prejudices of its models on us; it is languages that dictates to us the just and the unjust, the legitimate and the illegitimate, acquiescence of revolt. How are we to take accurate measure of the world with a standard meter that is false?

Manifestly, our language is no longer *representative*. It is urgently necessary to find another one. Confronted with the great questions of our epoch, we would love to understand and to come to solid conclusions. But where are we to begin? How can we cut through this mass of data, the immense quantity of which incessantly increases their *insignificance*? We possess the data, certainly, but not the language that would enable us to sort them out.

Our modern means of communication, computers, image and voice synthesizers, data banks are diabolical machines for the infinite multiplication of data without doing a thing to foster a true debate about ideas. We are weighed down with lists without head or tail, ambiguous figures and deceptive statistics. We might as well look for a needle in a haystack. Isn't this hyperinformation the ideal ruse of disinformation? Who would have the courage to acknowledge his powerlessness to exploit such apparently rich material?[1]

In his interesting study, Upinsky delineates the problem that dominates so many of the questions that we regularly confront in the area of ethics and public policy. A major source of our problem is the old battle between reality and abstraction, between the language of truth, which is used to convey reality, and the language of power, which is useful to manipulate minds and bodies. The "language rules" of our own era no longer speak of "resettlement in the East" to conceal the reality of extermination, as the Nazi rules did, but we have similar rules. The degree to which even the best-intentioned among us succumb to them may give us a more sympathetic understanding of the "good Germans" who believed Hitler and his propaganda until it was too late, until they were not merely enmeshed in his evil but actually became perpetrators themselves. We use language rules in our own discussions and debates; woe to him who disregards them for he will be cut out of the discussion. *But woe to them who unthinkingly follow them, because they will lose the power to discern the true from the false, the real from the illusory.*

Where language rules prevail, everyone must accommodate himself to them. If one fails or refuses to do so, one is no longer in the discussion; he or she is figuratively, or perhaps literally, "off the field." Nowhere is this situation more evident than in three of the fields where, to paraphrase Churchill, never have so few done so much to so many, namely, medical ethics, sexual ethics, and the ethics of war and peace. All of these areas are related to the fundamental issues of life itself because sex generates life, medicine seeks to preserve life, and war takes life.

THE LANGUAGE OF LIFE

In the preamble to its 1975 abortion decision, the *Bundesverfassungsgericht* (Germany's highest court) observed that abortion raises questions of not only a medical and biological nature but also of an anthropological, philosophical, and theological nature. Unfortunately, as I shall seek to show, the deepest level of these questions has not even been touched because language rules have prevented it and predetermined the outcome. From the beginning, the abortion debate has been dominated by "powerful language"—the politically correct, tactful language that trumps the language that truly conveys reality.

Early on, opponents of abortion protested the substitution of the technical-sounding word *fetus* for *baby*. *Baby* would be true, but it is not acceptable because it renders inevitable the conclusion that abortion is homicide (as indeed the German court declared). To use the word *baby*—the truth—is to give the battle away. To insist on *fetus*—a valid technical term but one that in the context conceals the reality—is to win the day. After the minor antiabortion victory of *Webster* in 1988, the proabortionists, who had already been making use of powerful language, hit on the expression *choice*. The success of this word in molding minds is a graphic illustration of our thesis: *he who controls the language controls the debate*.

The word *baby* refers to an ontological reality, a real, tiny, human being. That this human being is already present in the womb was evident in earlier times; the common law used the French expression *l'enfant en ventre de sa mère*, literally, "the baby in its mother's stomach." When someone suggests to a woman with an unwanted pregnancy that she give up the child for adoption, one sometimes gets the response, "I could never give my baby away." But rather than do that, some will—to use the crude but true language of Dr. Laura Schlesinger—"suck it into a sink."

The word *choice* refers to an abstraction. *Choice is nothing in itself*; everything depends on what one is able to choose. But the word had become universal, and through it the antiabortion cause is virtually predestined to defeat. As one assistant to a pro-life senator commented in a Capitol Hill meeting during the 1992 election campaign, "Even our supporters in Congress use the language 'pro-choice.'" Indeed, supporters of abortion regularly identify their opponents as "anti-choice," and the media repeat it after them.

A baby is a reality; choice is a function, an abstraction. Its significance clearly depends on the context within which the choice is offered. It is not a powerful word when it comes to smoking cigarettes on an airliner; smoking is considered an evil and a public health menace, and when one is willing to accept or to promote the idea that something is evil, the word *choice* is not used. To use it in the abortion controversy is precisely to say that abortion is not an evil, in other words, to beg the question and to predetermine the outcome. Such is the power of "strong language," and unless a better language can be found, the truth will never win.

AND AT THE EDGE OF LIFE

Similarly, in the discussion surrounding euthanasia proposals, language rules prevail. The old synonym for euthanasia, mercy killing, which was unashamedly used by the early euthanasia advocates, told the truth. Killing is what it is, with mercy as the reason presented. Selling this to the general public proved difficult because the general public is not yet prepared to accept the principle of killing (true language). Therefore, we resort to two techniques, the first of which is the creation of a false continuum. Actions that are medically, legally, and ethically acceptable, namely, the withholding of treatment considered useless—"extreme measures"—are tied to the word *euthanasia* and called "passive euthanasia."

Allowing the patient to die when nothing can be done for him or her is not euthanasia and should not be called such because it habituates the public to the term and makes the next stage, active euthanasia, acceptable whereas the honest terminology, *mercy killing*, would not be. Other terms have also been substituted, such as *death with dignity* and *natural death*, but one has clearly won the day: *physician-assisted suicide*. Curiously, this particular action, the giving of a deadly drug, is the one that is explicitly forbidden by the Hippocratic Oath, but it is the one that has become popular and that may win the day for the thanatophiles. Physicians are good and assistance is good, so who can object to physician-assisted suicide when two-thirds of the language is good?

Abortion and euthanasia have this in common, as Vienna Professor Hans Millendorfer says: they are methods in which killing represents a solution. But who dares speak this true language?

EXTREMISM

In the current warm-ups for the presidential races of the year 2000, some candidates who are reputed to be "pro-life" seek to avoid the label "extremist" by submitting fully to the language rules. In his losing race against President Lyndon B. Johnson in 1964, Senator Barry Goldwater foolishly said, "Extremism in defense of liberty is no vice." That was enough to stamp him, fatally for his campaign, as an "extremist," a very powerful word that, when used to characterize an individual or an opinion, makes him or it unacceptable to the modern public.

One candidate, asked whether he would appoint only pro-life judges, replied, "I will not have a litmus test." *Litmus test* is another bit of strong language that is used to demolish any person with firm principles. What if such a candidate replied to the questioner with his own question: "Should I not care whether a judge values human life?" Surely such a question cannot be answered, "No, human life doesn't matter." It would throw the questioner back on the common resource of the proabortionists, "Who can say when life begins?" or "Who can say what is human?" But as bizarre as such questions may be, that debate can be intellectual and moral; litmus testing cannot.

Both questions, often cast into the teeth of the pro-lifers, clearly are relevant only in the abortion controversy and are not capable of being used in general. No defense attorney for an accused murderer would argue concerning the victim, "Who can say whether human life had begun or whether he was human?" But the language rules and their powerful language are so strong that no major pro-life candidate has been willing to break them, or, if one does, he immediately qualifies himself as an extremist and pushes himself out of the discussion.

By saying, "I will not have a litmus test," the respondent joins the "moderates," in the process tacitly accepting the proposition that human life is not important and signaling that he can accept any attitude toward abortion on the part of a judge. Would anyone say, "No litmus test" when asked if he would accept a judge who was open to a bribe? The powerful language phrase *litmus test* is clearly a metaphor and does not apply literally. It is plainly not the language of reality. Nevertheless, it is sufficiently powerful to permit a candidate to avoid facing the true language that would convey what is actually at stake: whether a judge truly has respect for human life.

One successful senatorial candidate, running in a fairly conservative and generally pro-life state, announced that he did not favor partial-birth abortion. But, he added, if the President were again to veto a ban on partial-birth abortions, as he had already done twice, this candidate would not vote to override the veto. This is to say, in effect, that he ascribes to the President the right to decide for the life, or rather the death, of thousands or tens of thousands of almost-born babies. Of course, he would not say *that*. But, hypnotized by strong language, the media never ask. The inability of the public to acknowledge that partial-birth abortion kills a human child, or, if it recognizes it, to hold its officials responsible when they permit such a thing, makes one aware of the degree to which strong language stifles true discourse and creates an immature electorate.

OTHER "AFFAIRS": SEXUAL ETHICS

In sexual matters, facts are obscured or totally obliterated by powerful language. This fact is abundantly evident with respect to adultery, for which a new term has been found. When a president was accused of marital infidelity and of a perverse kind of sexual expression, much of the potential damage was avoided by the skillful use of powerful words such as *judgmental*. To be judgmental is bad; to be tolerant is good—at least within the chosen area of discourse. If one condemns racism, which is generally acknowledged as an evil, one is not called judgmental, nor will he be asked to be tolerant. Nor will one be called judgmental for condemning cigarette smoking. To use the word *judgmental* is essentially to justify the action or attitude under consideration, to beg the question. The use of the word *consensual* is to justify, by implication, conduct that might have been described as adulterous or unnatural. It is even increasingly used in efforts to legitimatize pedophilia.

The importance of language rules is particularly evident in the discussions of homosexuality. The older expressions—*unnatural, perversion,* and *deviant*—are implicitly critical and condemnatory terms that certainly had at least some statistical claim to truth. They were replaced by *gay*, a term without pejorative (i.e., derogatory) connotations. In the typical academic environment, it is not permissible even to consider treating homosexual conduct as a moral issue. The rather scientific and neutral-sounding term *orientation* replaces conduct; one must not discriminate (a bad word) against "orientation."

Orientation cannot normally be observed; conduct can. But once *orientation* has replaced *conduct* as the term of choice, then virtually all conduct can be excused as indicative of one's orientation. To object to any particular manifestations of the orientation is to be not merely "judgmental" but also "homophobic" and thus doubly reprehensible.[2] In fact, even to refer to them as possible subjects for moral criticism is homophobic. The use of the wrong words—true words but not correct words—automatically means that one is no longer in the discussion.

The controversies about the creation of "gay marriage" are also useful examples. First, one speaks of "legitimizing" the "homosexual marriage," which presupposes that such a thing exists, but something that does not exist cannot be legitimized. Opponents have brought up prudential arguments, such as the valid contention that a "normal" marriage (i.e., between one man and one woman) is the best environment for the raising of children. But they have lost in advance to the strong language of their opponents. Even to venture onto this terrain is to accept as true that which cannot be true, namely, that such a thing as gay marriage exists, that it is not per se a contradiction in terms. The basic problem with homosexual "marriage" is not that it is bad for children but that it *is* not, that it cannot exist. Not that the conventions of the law do not recognize it, but that marriage is not something created by courts or conventions. Rather, it is part of the order of nature, as the Prayer Book says, "an honorable estate, established by God, regulated by His commandments." By the mere acceptance of the powerful language as a basis for discussion, one has effectively given up the best arguments against the proposal.

The Supreme Court of Canada, dealing with the law of the Province of Ontario that defines *spouse* as either the male or female partner in a marriage, has ruled such a law a violation of the Canadian constitution. To rule for reality would deny "equality," a powerful word, an abstraction, in favor of a word that is merely true. In other words, the mathematical abstraction, equality, trumps the biological reality on which marriage is based, the difference between the sexes.

Perhaps the decision of the Canadian court is not as self-evidently absurd as it would be to pronounce dogs legally equal to cats, but it is of rather the same nature. Absurd though it seems today even to suggest that a court could rule that dogs are legally cats, it really is no more absurd than saying that two men are each other's "spouses." If the dog-equals-cat decision is ever handed down—and given the insanity of the present world, there is no guarantee that it will not be—it will not help the canines to climb trees. On that level, reality will triumph over what purports to be law.

RECENT PARALLELS

The recent actions of the United States in Yugoslavia offer another example of the ability of strong language to stifle serious consideration of moral issues or existing law. The United States Constitution gives the power to make war only to Congress, and the War Powers Act places specific limitations on the ability of the President to commit American forces to military action on his own. The French Constitution has a similar provision. The United Nations Charter forbids member nations to commit aggressive actions against other members without a Security Council resolution; the NATO Charter defines the alliance as defensive in nature and provides that the forces of member nations will be engaged if and only if a member is attacked. But never mind, strong language takes precedence over true language. "Genocide" was there,[3] as was "ethnic cleansing." That strong language clearly overruled the statements of constitutions and charters.

Officially, of course, Messrs. Clinton, Blair, Jospin, and Schröder did not make *war*. Officialdom did not say *war* because they had no authority to do so. In fact, there are no more war departments and ministries of war, only of defense. In this case, aggression was not war; it was defense. Although the media regularly called it war, and for the victims it was exactly like war, officially it was only a "campaign," an "operation." Now fifty thousand or so troops of the alliance are to be lodged on the territory of Kosovo, while the troops, officials, and police of the legal sovereign, the Federal Republic of Yugoslavia, have been expelled. In earlier times, this would be called an occupying army, but now it is "peacekeepers."

CONCLUSION

A few more words from Upinsky are in order: "In *Mathematical Perversion: The Eye of Power* (1985), we have already made the observation that our great modern systems operate on the basis of the inversion of language: the majority is nothing but a minority; equality implies discrimination; the 'general will'[4] is nothing but the will of one party; the presumption of the innocence of the accused is nothing but a myth; representation in government, a fiction, etc." The author of these lines, Arnaud-Aaron Upinsky, expounds in some detail how what we are calling "strong language," including statistics, is used to suppress "true language" and to blind the members of the public to reality. This makes them subservient to the will of those in power. In effect, their heads are severed, for although they are still on their bodies, they cannot be used to think.[5]

Upinsky contends that the entire history of mankind can be interpreted in terms of a merciless war between what he calls realism and nominalism: the realists are those who believe in the *truth* of words; the nominalists are those who believe in the *power* of words. The nominalists are political optimists—actually, Utopians—who believe in the myth of the "Good Savage" promoted by Rousseau. The realists believe, instead, that man has a "cannibal nature," which leads to a pessimistic view of politics but one that is much closer to reality.

Government policy-making, indeed all moral discourse, in the areas we have been considering—abortion, euthanasia, assisted suicide, homosexuality, and war—is now dominated, corrupted, and manipulated by powerful language. To demystify this perversion of language and to put language back on the solid ground of the real and the true has become a question of physical and spiritual survival in our era. It can be done although surely not all at once. But it is possible, and it must be attempted, if the tasks to which we devote ourselves as Christians in the political and ethical arena are even to begin to be accomplished.

ENDNOTES

1. Aaron-Arnaud Upinsky, *La tête coupée* (s.l., Le Bec, 1998), 165–66. Translation by the present writer.
2. *Homophobia*, viewed etymologically, would mean "fear of the same, or of sameness, or at the extreme, of homosexuality," but, as the reader will know, it has come to mean "hatred" of homosexuals and is one of the worst forms of intolerance, extremism by its very nature.
3. Actually, only after the "campaign" began, and much less extensive than the NATO spokesmen alleged.
4. An allusion to Rousseau's *volonté générale*.
5. Upinsky, *La tête coupée*, 106.

An Overview

One of the most debated public issues of the last twenty-five years has been that of abortion. The debate has crossed social, ideological, and political boundaries, and it extends beyond abortion to other issues regarding human life and human rights. Although much attention has been (and will continue to be) given to the Republican Party and its internal struggle over its national platform language, the content of the plank in question—mistakenly referred to as the "abortion plank" by both supporters and critics—is rarely, if ever, challenged by pro-choice forces that are calling for it to be removed. In this chapter, the author argues that this situation is largely the result of opponents, supporters, and media members not having carefully read and understood the language, implications, and moral logic of the text. Consequently, when partisans and media say that the plank in question deals primarily with abortion and/or a woman's right to choose, they are not speaking accurately, and they clearly are not addressing their observations and criticisms to the essential claim put forth by the planks' authors: fetuses are members of the human community and deserve to be protected from unjust harm.

Chapter Fifteen

DISAGREEMENT WITHOUT DEBATE

The Republican Party Platform and
the Human Life Amendment Plank[1]

Francis J. Beckwith

"John Stewart [sic] Mill once said, 'there is always hope when people are forced to listen to both sides of the issue,'" Ann Stone, of Republicans for Choice, in an open letter to the delegates of the 1992 Republican National Convention in Houston.

IN THE 1990S, REPUBLICAN PRO-CHOICE governors George Pataki (NY), William Weld (MA), Christie Todd Whitman (NJ), and Pete Wilson (CA), joined by many rank-and-file Republicans, came out publicly in support of removing their party's pro-life plank. In fact, the 1996 platform included an appendix that contained alternatives to the plank suggested by delegates. These alternatives (all of which were either rejected by the platform committee or withdrawn from consideration) ranged from acknowledging disagreement on abortion among party members to calling for the shoring up and nurturing of social and civic institutions that would result, according to its authors, in abortion becoming rare (RNC 1996, appendix I). All of the alternatives, however, fell short of what the platform language called for: a human life amendment (HLA) to the U.S. Constitution.[2]

The media, of course, enjoy this bickering. When I was a delegate from Nevada at the 1992 national convention in Houston,[3] I was approached by at least six network correspondents (including Dan Rather) who asked me if there was anything in the party platform or convention speeches that made me uneasy. I responded to them by saying that I was disappointed that there was nothing in the Republican Party platform condemning the gagging of pro-life spokesmen (such as former Pennsylvania Governor Robert Casey) at the Democratic National Convention in New York.[4] Needless to say, the network correspondents moved on to search for more cooperative malcontents.

DISAGREEMENT WITHOUT DEBATE

What stands out about this intramural G.O.P. debate is that for all of the talk about Republican disagreement about abortion, one rarely, if ever, *actually*

234 CONTEMPORARY PERSPECTIVES ON POLITICS AND PUBLIC POLICY

sees or hears pro-choice Republicans arguing for the merits of their position, a position which, if correct, would entail that the *content* of any HLA, as called for by the platform, is mistaken. Although one might hear *affirmations* of the pro-choice position (e.g., "A woman's right to choose is a fundamental right"), there is near total silence when it comes to proponents *actually defending* their position or the media requiring them to do so. Certainly, one hears from both pro-life and pro-choice proponents much about the political ramifications of their positions. For example, pro-lifers point out that Ronald Reagan's 1980 and 1984 landslides as well as George Bush's 1988 victory occurred while the party's presidential standard bearer stood firmly for the pro-life position. They also argue that in 1994 pro-lifers running for Congress were overwhelming victors resulting from a large number of pro-life voters who, through both their activism and their voting preference, played a large part in the Republican takeover of Congress.

Of course, pro-choicers have a different interpretation of these and other political events. For example, some pro-choicers argue that the Republican takeover of Congress was the result of the American people's fondness for "The Contract with America," which was virtually devoid of any mention of "social issues" such as abortion. The consecutive presidential victories of Bill Clinton, a strongly pro-choice Democrat with moderate economic policies, as well as the decrease of the Republican Congressional majority resulting from the 1998 mid-term elections, are cited as evidence that the American people are rejecting the G.O.P.'s pro-life message. Making the political argument among party faithful, Ann Stone and her group, Republicans for Choice (RFC), maintain in their literature that more than 71 percent of all registered Republicans are pro-choice.[5]

Although political concerns no doubt are important, the very nature of the abortion question makes it nearly impervious to political resolution. Most partisans on the issue believe that their position is grounded in some fundamental nonnegotiable right, whether it is the right to life (pro-life) or the right to personal autonomy (pro-choice). Nonnegotiable perspectives do not lend themselves to the typical compromises that are necessary for the pacification of contrary factions in the rough and tumble world of party politics (see Hunter 1991). For instance, pro-choice Republicans William H. Hudnut III, former mayor of Indianapolis, and his wife, Beverly Hudnut, advocate an uncompromising and yet principled position: "It seems to us that under traditional minimalist Republican policy, government would choose *not* to interfere with a woman's right to make her own decision about whether or not to bear a child" (Hudnut and Hudnut 1996). The Hudnuts seem to be saying that even if espousing the pro-choice position were a political liability, the members of the Republican Party should *encourage* their elected officials to support this fundamental right.[6] Ann Stone affirms this principled position in the postscript of a 1992 open letter to Republican delegates to the national convention in Houston: "The Supreme Court . . . reaffirmed that a woman's right to choose is essential for women to participate equally in society. Our party platform is in contradiction with the Court" (Stone 1992).[7]

The pro-life position is equally resistant to political inoculation. For most pro-lifers, the fetus is a human person from the moment of conception or at least during virtually all of her development in her mother's womb (see Beckwith 1993; Lee 1996; Moreland and Rae 2000; Schwarz 1990). Therefore, the fetus deserves at least as much protection (perhaps more because it is so vulnerable and defenseless) as those who were fortunate enough to have been born. This is why pro-lifers are unmoved by the typical arguments one hears propounded by pro-choice advocates. For example, it is often argued that before legal abortion, women resorted to unscrupulous doctors who performed illegal abortions on them; consequently, these women were harmed (and sometimes died). Therefore, abortion ought to remain legal. Of course, if the fetus is *not* a human person, this is a legitimate concern. But if the fetus *is* a human person, this argument is tantamount to saying that because people die or are harmed while killing other people, the state should make it safe for them to do so. Thus, the pro-choicer begs the question because he has not refuted the one premise which, if true, makes virtually all of his arguments unsound: the fetus is a human person.[8] But this flaw is found in nearly every popular pro-choice argument, whether it is the argument from poverty, from "choice," from familial inconvenience, from fetal handicap, or from single parenthood. Without first begging the question as to the fetus's nonpersonhood, virtually none of the pro-choice arguments work (see Beckwith 1993; Lee 1996; Schwarz 1990). This is why author and social critic Gregory P. Koukl is fond of saying, "If the unborn is not a human person, no justification of abortion is necessary. However, if the unborn is a human person, no justification for abortion is adequate" (Koukl 1996, 4).

None of this means, of course, that political compromises are impossible. It just means that abortion is not *merely* a political issue. For it touches on the most important philosophical questions of our time, including but not limited to the meaning of liberty; what it means to be a human person; and whether law, with all of its assumptions about property, freedom, and rights, can be divorced from metaphysical questions about the nature of such things. One does not ordinarily *choose* a position on abortion; it is typically thrust upon oneself by how one has *already first answered* (whether consciously or unconsciously) these metaphysical questions.[9]

WHAT THE "ABORTION PLANK" REALLY SAYS

Although the media continue to say that there is a plank in the Republican platform calling for "a constitutional amendment banning abortion,"[10] there is simply nothing in either the 1992 or 1996 platforms that calls for such an amendment. What is typically and incorrectly referred to as the "abortion plank"[11] is the section of the 1992 and 1996 platforms that calls for a constitutional amendment to protect all human life regardless of venue or level of maturity. The 1992 plank reads as follows:

> We believe the unborn child has a fundamental right to life which cannot be infringed. We therefore affirm our support for a human life amendment

to the Constitution, and we endorse legislation that the Fourteenth Amendment's protections apply to unborn children. (RNC 1992, 39)

The 1996 plank provides a different reading:

> We oppose the non-consensual withholding of health care or treatment because of handicap, age, or infirmity, just as we oppose euthanasia and assisted suicide, which, especially for the poor and those on the margins of society, threaten the sanctity of human life. The unborn child has a fundamental individual right to life which cannot be infringed. We support a human life amendment to the Constitution and we endorse legislation to make clear that the Fourteenth Amendment's protections apply to unborn children. (RNC 1996)

The text in which both the 1992 and 1996 planks reside deals with issues of race relations, bigotry, the civil rights of women, the rights of the handicapped, and the rights of the unborn. In fact, this portion of the 1992 platform, which is under the general heading of "Individual Rights," begins with these sentences: "The protection of individual rights is the foundation of opportunity and security. The Republican Party is unique in this regard. Since its inception, it has respected every person, even when that proposition was universally unpopular. Today, as in the day of Lincoln, we insist that no American's rights are negotiable" (RNC 1992, 38).[12]

For the pro-life Republican, both the 1992 and 1996 planks call for extending our nation's moral progress toward the elimination of unjust discrimination to those who are the most vulnerable in the human family, the unborn. Consequently, when Republicans, such as the Hudnuts and Ann Stone, refer to this section of the platform as primarily referring to abortion and/or a woman's right to choose,[13] they simply are not speaking accurately, and they are clearly not addressing their criticisms to the essential claim put forth by the planks' authors: the unborn are members of the human community and deserve to be protected from unjust harm.

The remaining portion of the 1992 HLA plank reads: "We oppose using public revenues for abortion and will not fund organizations which advocate it. We commend those who provide alternatives to abortion by meeting the needs of mothers and offering adoption services. We reaffirm our support for appointment of judges who respect traditional family values and the sanctity of innocent human life" (RNC 1992, 39). The only time abortion is opposed in the 1992 platform is in terms of government funding, which is hardly a call for a total ban on abortion.

The 1996 platform, in comparison to its 1992 predecessor, has more to say immediately following its call for a human life amendment:

> Our purpose is to have legislative and judicial protection of that right against those who perform abortions. We oppose using public revenues for abortion and will not fund organizations which advocate it. We support the

appointment of judges who respect traditional family values and the sanctity of innocent human life.

Our goal is to ensure that women with problem pregnancies have the kind of support, material and otherwise, they need for themselves and for their babies, not to be punitive toward those for whose difficult situation we have only compassion. We oppose abortion, but our pro-life agenda does not include punitive action against women who have an abortion. We salute those who provide alternatives to abortion and offer adoption services. Republicans in Congress took the lead in expanding assistance both for the costs of adoption and for the continuing care of adoptive children with special needs. Bill Clinton vetoed our adoption tax credit the first time around—and opposed our efforts to remove racial barriers to adoption— before joining in this long overdue measure of support for adoptive families.

Worse than that, he vetoed the ban on partial-birth abortions, a procedure denounced by a committee of the American Medical Association and rightly branded as four-fifths infanticide. We applaud Bob Dole's commitment to revoke the Clinton executive orders concerning abortion and to sign into law an end to partial-birth abortions. (RNC 1996).

The only time abortion is opposed in the 1992 platform is in terms of government funding, which is hardly a call for a constitutional amendment to ban abortion. Although abortion is mentioned more explicitly in the 1996 platform, an anti-abortion constitutional amendment is nowhere to be found. Like its 1992 version, the 1996 platform both calls for the ending of public funding for organizations that advocate abortion and commends and supports those who provide abortion alternatives such as adoption. The 1996 platform, however, discusses the latter in greater detail and makes the point that the party's call for protecting the unborn will not translate into punishment for women seeking abortions if this protection were to become part of the Constitution. The platform does call for the punishment of physicians and others who abridge the right to life of the unborn by performing procedures whose *sole* purpose is the destruction of prenatal human beings. In addition, the plank is critical of both President Clinton's vetoing of the partial-birth abortion ban and his initial resistance to certain adoption measures put forth by the Republican majority in Congress.

Certainly, it would be correct to infer that if a human life amendment were to become part of our Constitution, statutes and court decisions (such as *Roe v. Wade*) that permit virtually unrestricted abortion would be unconstitutional. However, this is merely *an inference* from the passage of such an amendment.[14]

The reason why neither the 1992 nor the 1996 platform mentions a direct ban on abortion is because its authors no doubt understood, and their opponents are reticent to admit, that what is doing the moral work in the question of abortion is the status of the fetus. Everything else is simply beside the point. This is why there was a call for a human life amendment to the Constitution in the 1992 and 1996 Republican platforms and *not* a call for a constitutional amendment to ban abortion totally.

WAYS TO AVOID DISCUSSING FETAL PERSONHOOD:
A CRITICAL ANALYSIS

Clearly, if pro-choice Republicans want to address the content of the plank with which they find disagreement, they must address the question of fetal personhood. Pro-choice Republicans may employ a number of tactics to avoid confronting this question. These tactics seem to come in two varieties: (1) appeals to pluralism and/or tolerance, and (2) appeals to agnosticism concerning fetal status.

1. Appeals to pluralism and/or tolerance. In an attempt to maintain an apparently "neutral" posture on the question of fetal personhood, pro-choice Republicans may argue in the following way: because people disagree about abortion, we ought simply to permit each person to decide for himself or herself whether the fetus is a human person and/or whether abortion is immoral. Consequently, if pro-lifers believe that abortion is homicide, that is fine. They need not fear state coercion to have an abortion or to participate in the procedure. On the other hand, if some people believe that abortion is not homicide and/or it is morally permissible, then they need not fear state coercion to remain pregnant.[15] This view, according to conventional wisdom, is the tolerant position one ought to take in our pluralistic society.

The problem with this reasoning is that it misses the point of why people oppose abortion. That is to say, it does not seriously engage the opposition's case. Perhaps an example will help. During the 1984 presidential campaign when questions of Geraldine Ferraro's Catholicism and its apparent conflict with her pro-choice stance were prominent in the media, New York Governor Mario Cuomo, in a lecture delivered at the University of Notre Dame, attempted to give the tolerance argument intellectual respectability (Cuomo 1984). He tried to provide a philosophical foundation for Ferraro's position. But it is not clear that Cuomo gained any ground politically or philosophically. For one cannot appeal to the fact that we live in a pluralistic society, as Cuomo argued, when the very question of *who* is part of that society (that is, whether it includes fetuses) is itself the point under dispute. Cuomo lost the argument because he begged the question.

To tell pro-lifers, as many Republican supporters of the tolerance argument do, that "they have a right to believe what they want to believe" is evidence of a failure to grasp the pro-life perspective.[16] Think about it. If *you* believed, as the pro-lifers do, that a class of persons were being unjustly killed by methods that include dismemberment, suffocation, brain-suctioning, and burning, wouldn't you be perplexed if someone tried to ease your outrage by telling you that you didn't have to participate in the killings if you didn't want to?[17] That's exactly what pro-lifers hear when pro-choice supporters tell them, "Don't like abortion? Don't have one," or "I'm pro-choice but personally opposed to abortion." In the mind of the pro-lifer, this argument is like telling an abolitionist, "Don't like slavery? Don't own a slave," or telling Dietrich Bonhoeffer, "Don't like the Holocaust? Don't kill a Jew." Consequently, for the defender of the tolerance argument to request that pro-lifers "should not force their pro-life belief on others" while claiming that "they have a right to believe what they want to believe" is to reveal a gross misunderstanding of the pro-life position.[18] Keep in mind that for the pro-lifer, a fetus is no less a member of the human community simply because it happens to be living inside Ann Stone, Whoopi Goldberg, Eleanor Smeal, or Kate Michelman. All fetuses deserve protection, even if they happen to reside in the wombs of citizens who do not embrace the pro-life viewpoint.

Perhaps the pro-choice Republican will reply to this critique by giving his argument a theological twist and argue that the pro-life position is a "religious position," and, in the interest of "pluralism," the pro-lifer ought to refrain from imposing her religious views on others.[19] In fact, one piece of pro-choice literature claims that "personhood at conception is a religious belief, not a provable biological fact" (NARAL 1983). What could this assertion possibly mean? Is it claiming that no aspect of a religious worldview has scientific import? If it is, it is incorrect, for many religions, such as Christianity and Islam, maintain that the physical world literally exists, which is a major assumption of contemporary science. On the other hand, some religions, such as Christian Science (Eddy 1875) and certain forms of Hinduism (Hackett 1979), deny the literal existence of the physical world. Moreover, some of the arguments used to support the view that life begins at conception, or any other view on abortion for that matter, are not even remotely religious because they involve the citing of scientific evidence and the use of philosophical reasoning and reflection (see Beckwith 1993; Brody 1975; George 1997; Lee 1997; Moreland and Rae 2000; Schwarz 1990).

But maybe this assertion is claiming that biology can tell us nothing about values. If such is the case, it is right in one sense and wrong in another sense. It is right if it means that the brute facts of science, without any moral reflection, cannot tell us what is right and wrong. But it is wrong if it means that the brute facts of science cannot tell us *to whom* we should apply the values of which we are aware. For example, if I don't know whether the object toward which I am driving my car is a living woman or a mannequin, biology is important in helping me to avoid committing an act of homicide. Running over mannequins is not homicide, but running over a woman is homicide.

Maybe this assertion is saying that when human life should be valued is a *philosophical* belief that cannot be proven scientifically. Maybe, but this argument cuts both ways. For isn't the belief that a woman has *abortion rights* a *philosophical* belief that cannot be proven scientifically and over which people disagree widely? But if the pro-life position cannot be reflected in the Republican party platform and/or enacted into law because it is philosophical (or religious), then neither can the pro-choice position be so enacted. The pro-choice advocate might respond to this by saying that this fact alone is a good reason to leave it up to each individual woman to choose whether she should have an abortion. But this begs the question, for this is precisely the pro-choice position, a disputed moral viewpoint. Furthermore, the pro-lifer could reply to this pro-choice response by employing the pro-choicer's own logic. The pro-lifer could argue that because the pro-choice position is a

240 CONTEMPORARY PERSPECTIVES ON POLITICS AND PUBLIC POLICY

disputed philosophical position over which many people disagree, society should permit each individual unborn human being to be born and make up his or her own mind as to whether he or she should or should not continue to exist.

The tolerance argument, then, seems not to be as neutral as its proponents believe. For to say that a woman should have the "right to choose" to terminate the life of the fetus she is carrying is tantamount to denying the pro-life position that fetuses are human persons worthy of protection. And to affirm that fetuses are human persons with a "right to life" that ought to be protected by the state is tantamount to denying the pro-choice position that a woman has a fundamental right to terminate her pregnancy because such a termination would result in a homicide. Consequently, when pro-choice Republicans, in the name of tolerance and pluralism, call for the elimination of the HLA plank and to replace it with either nothing[20] or a pro-choice plank,[21] they are calling for the party to acquiesce to the legal status quo, namely, that fetuses are not full-fledged members of the human community and therefore are not entitled to protection by the state. It seems, then, that the tolerance argument is inadequate in resolving the current debate over the HLA plank in the Republican party platform.

2. Appeals to agnosticism concerning fetal status. An example of such an appeal can be found in Justice Blackmun's often-quoted comments in *Roe v. Wade:* "We need not resolve the difficult question of when life begins. When those trained in the respective disciplines of medicine, philosophy, and theology are unable to arrive at any consensus, the judiciary, at this point in the development of man's knowledge, is not in a position to speculate" (U.S. Supreme Court 1973, 160).

Justice Blackmun is arguing that because experts disagree as to when life begins the Court should not come down on any side. That is, because experts disagree about when and if the fetus becomes a human life, then abortion should remain legal.

In popular debate, pro-choice advocates often put forth Justice Blackmun's claim when they affirm that "no one knows when life begins" and from that affirmation conclude that abortion ought to be legally permitted. Republicans for Choice, for example, maintains that the claim that human life begins at conception is "a fact still widely disputed" ("Oklahoma's Massive Challenge," 1992, 2). There is a difference, however, between claiming that "no one knows when life begins" and "experts disagree as to when life begins." My guess is that when people use the former argument in popular debate, they are in fact arguing that it is justified by the latter argument:

1. Experts disagree as to when life begins.
   Therefore,
2. No one knows when life begins.

Of course the second proposition does not necessarily follow from the first proposition. It might be that experts disagree as to when human life begins but that some of them are wrong whereas others do, in fact, know when human life begins. This situation would not be surprising because historically some faction of experts usually turns out to be correct about a disputed issue, such as in the cases of slavery, women's suffrage, and the position of the earth in the solar system. In some cases, expert disagreement can be accounted for by some factions ignoring contrary evidence or alternate theories because of a prior commitment to a worldview that the expert judges to be properly basic to knowledge about the world and thus ought not be discarded unless an alternative worldview has more explanatory power.[22] In other cases, expert disagreement might result from holding an irrational belief, clinging to a religious or secular dogma, or not wanting to appear politically incorrect. By treating all expert disagreement over fetal personhood as philosophically and scientifically indistinguishable, giving the impression that all of the arguments of all of the factions in the personhood debate are equally compelling, and simply appealing to expert disagreement rather than wrestling with the actual arguments put forth by these experts and evaluating these arguments for their logical soundness, the Court was able simply to discard the issue of fetal personhood while pretending to take it into consideration.

The claim, however, that "no one knows when life begins" is a misnomer because virtually no one seriously doubts that individual biological human life is present from conception.[23] Thus, what pro-choicers probably mean when they say that "no one knows when life begins" is that no one knows when the personhood or full humanness is attained in the process of human development by the individual in the womb. That is to say, no one knows when the fetus becomes a member of the human community and worthy of protection.[24]

In light of this fact, it is interesting to note the conclusions of a U.S. Senate subcommittee that interviewed numerous scientific and bioethical authorities in conjunction with its study and analysis of the 1981 Human Life Bill. It concluded that "no witness [who testified before the subcommittee] raised any evidence to refute the biological fact that from the moment of conception there exists a distinct individual being who is alive and is of the human species. No witness challenged the scientific consensus that unborn children are 'human beings,' insofar as the term is used to mean living beings of the human species." On the other hand, "those witnesses who testified that science cannot say whether unborn children are human beings were speaking in every instance to the value question rather than the scientific question. . . . [T]hese witnesses invoked their value preferences to redefine the term 'human being.'" The committee report explains that these witnesses "took the view that each person may define as 'human' only those beings whose lives that a person wants to value. Because they did not wish to accord intrinsic worth to the lives of unborn children, they refused to call them 'human beings,' regardless of the scientific evidence" (U.S. Senate 1981, 11)

Thus, Justice Blackmun and pro-choice Republicans are likely arguing in the following way:

1. Experts disagree about when human life becomes valuable (or a person or fully human, as some ethicists have put it).
   Therefore,
2. No one knows when human life becomes valuable (or "begins").
   Therefore,
3. Abortion should remain legal.

This argument has many problems, but consider just the following two.

1. The argument from agnosticism is difficult if not impossible to maintain in practice. Recall what Justice Blackmun said in *Roe v. Wade:* "We need not resolve the difficult question of when life begins. When those trained in the respective disciplines of medicine, philosophy, and theology are unable to arrive at any consensus, the judiciary, at this point in the development of man's knowledge, is not in a position to speculate" (U.S. Supreme Court 1973, 160). Hence, the state should not take one theory of life and force those who do not agree with that theory to subscribe to it, which is the reason why Blackmun writes in *Roe,* "In view of all this, we do not agree that, by adopting one theory of life, Texas may override the rights of the pregnant woman that are at stake" (U.S. Supreme Court 1973, 163). Thus, for the pro-life advocate to propose that non-pro-life women should be forbidden from having abortions on the basis that individual human personhood begins at conception or at least sometime before birth is clearly a violation of the right to privacy of non-pro-life women.

But the problem with this reasoning is that it simply cannot deliver on what it promises. To claim, as does Justice Blackmun, that the Court should not propose one theory of life over another and that the decision to abort should be left exclusively to the discretion of each pregnant woman *is* to propose a theory of life that hardly has a clear consensus. It has all of the earmarks of a theory of life that morally segregates fetuses from full-fledged membership in the human community, for it in practice excludes fetuses from constitutional protection. Although verbally the Court denied taking sides, part of the theoretical grounding of its legal opinion, regardless of whether it admits to it, is that the fetus in this society is not a human person worthy of protection.

Thus, the Court actually did take sides on when life begins. It concluded that the fetus is not a human person, because the procedure permitted in *Roe,* abortion, is something that the Court itself admits it would not have ruled a fundamental right if it were conclusively proven that the fetus is a human person: "If the suggestion of personhood [of the unborn] is established, the appellant's case, of course, collapses, for the fetus' right to life is then guaranteed specifically by the [Fourteenth Amendment]" (U.S. Supreme Court 1973, 157–58).

Imagine if the Court were confronted with the issue of enslaving African-Americans and delivered the following opinion: "We need not resolve the difficult question of whether blacks are human persons. When those trained in the respective disciplines of medicine, philosophy, and theology are unable to arrive at any consensus, the judiciary, at this point in the development of man's knowledge, is not in a position to speculate." Suppose that the Court on that basis *allowed* white Americans to own blacks as property, concluding that slave ownership is a fundamental right. It would appear that although the Court would be making a verbal denial of taking any position on this issue, the allowance of slavery and the claim that it is a fundamental right would for all intents and purposes be morally equivalent to taking a side on the issue, namely, that blacks are not human persons. Likewise, the Court's verbal denial of taking a position on fetal personhood is contradicted by its conclusion that abortion is a fundamental constitutional right and that fetuses are not persons under the Constitution.

Republicans for Choice employs reasoning similar to the Court's in its commentary on a 1992 Oklahoma Initiative: "The Initiative, putting the rights of the fetus above those of the woman, declares 'The life of each human begins at fertilization'—a fact still widely disputed" ("Oklahoma's Massive Challenge" 1992, 2). But if we are to accept the Supreme Court's holding in *Roe*, as RFC does,[25] and agree with Justice Blackmun that the right to abortion is contingent upon the status of the fetus (U.S. Supreme Court 1973, 157–58), then the allegedly disputed fact about life's beginning means that the right to abortion is disputed as well. For a conclusion's support—in this case, "abortion is a fundamental right"—is only as good as the veracity of its most important premise—in this case, "the fetus is not a human person." So, RFC's admission that abortion rights is based on a widely disputed fact, far from establishing a right to abortion, entails that it not only does not know when life begins but also does not know when, if ever, the right to abortion begins.

2. The argument from agnosticism is contrary to the "benefit-of-the-doubt argument." If it is true that no one knows when life begins, this is an excellent reason *not* to permit abortion because an abortion *may* result in the death of a human entity who has a full right to life. If one killed another being without knowing whether the being is a person with a full right to life, such an action would be negligent, even if one later discovered that the being was not a person. If game hunters shot at rustling bushes with this same mind-set, the National Rifle Association's membership would become severely depleted. Ignorance of a being's status is certainly not justification to kill it. This position is called the benefit-of-the-doubt argument because we are giving the fetus the benefit of the doubt.

The agnostic argument as employed by Justice Blackmun and pro-choice Republicans seems to imply that the different positions on fetal personhood all have able defenders, persuasive arguments, and passionate advocates, but none of them really wins the day. To put it another way, the issue of fetal personhood is up for grabs; all positions are in some sense equal; none is better than any other.[26] But if such is the case, then one can safely say that the odds of the fetus being a human person are 50/50. Given these odds, society would seem to have a moral obligation to err on the side of life and, therefore, legally to prohibit virtually all abortions.

CONCLUSION:
WHAT THE PLATFORM DEBATE IS REALLY ABOUT

One could conclude from what has been written so far that the debate in the Republican Party over its platform is a dispute between two factions that hold incommensurable value systems. But one would be mistaken, for these factions hold many values in common.

First, each side believes that all human persons possess certain inalienable rights regardless of whether their governments protect these rights. That is why both sides appeal to what each believes is a fundamental right. The pro-life advocate appeals to "life" whereas the pro-choice advocate appeals to "liberty" (or "choice"). Both sides believe that a constitutional regime, to be just, must uphold fundamental rights.

Second, each side believes that its position best exemplifies its opponents' fundamental value. The pro-choice advocate does not deny that "life" is a value but argues that his position's appeal to human liberty is a necessary ingredient by which an individual can pursue the fullest and most complete life possible.[27]

On the other hand, the pro-life advocate does not eschew "liberty." He or she believes that all human liberty is limited by another human person's right to life. For example, one has a right to pursue freely any goal one believes is consistent with one's happiness, such as attending a Los Angeles Lakers basketball game. One has, however, no right to pursue this goal freely at the expense of another's life or liberty, such as running over pedestrians with one's car so that one can get to the game on time. And, of course, the pro-life advocate argues that fetuses are persons with a full right to life. And because the act of abortion typically results in the death of the unborn, abortion, with few exceptions, is not morally justified, and for that reason it ought to be illegal.

The pro-choice advocate does not deny that human persons have a right to life. He just believes that this right to life is not extended to fetuses because they are not human persons. The pro-life advocate does not deny that people have the liberty to make choices that they believe are in their best interests. He or she just believes that this liberty does not entail the right to choose abortion because such a choice conflicts with the life, liberty, and interests of another human person (the fetus) who is defenseless, weak, and vulnerable and has a natural claim upon its parents' care, both pre- and postnatally.

Thus, when all is said and done, the debate over the HLA plank is not even really about conflicting value systems. After all, imagine if the plank had said, "The Republican Party affirms a woman's right to terminate her pregnancy if and only if it does not result in the death of her unborn child." Disagreement over such a plank would not be over the morality of killing persons or even the morality of abortion; it would be over the metaphysical question of whether the unborn human is a full-fledged member of the human community.

What, then, is one supposed to conclude from this essay? First, most politically active Republicans, both pro-life and pro-choice, along with most members of the media and most Republican candidates, seem not to have read the national platform. Not surprisingly, then, most of them do not seem to understand what the platform debate is supposed to be about. It is supposed to be about *the plank*, a plank that calls for our Constitution in its text to assert clearly and unequivocally that the human community includes both the born and the unborn from the moment of conception until natural death, and, for that reason, unborn persons, like their postnatal brethren, should be protected from unjust harm.

Second, if pro-choice Republicans want to dislodge *that plank* from their party's platform, and if pro-life Republicans want their party's platform to retain *that plank*, and if the media want to report accurately the debate over *that plank* to their viewership, readership, and listenership, then the content of *that plank* is the only appropriate topic of debate. For, as we have seen, everything else is simply beside the point.

What, then, is the platform debate really about? It is about the nature and order of things. It is about who and what we are. It is, in the end, whether we like it or not, a testimony to that inescapable truth penned by Aristotle over two millennia ago: "Statecraft is soulcraft."

REFERENCES

"Attention." *Choice News: The Bi-Monthly Newsletter Produced by Republicans for Choice* 1, no. 4 (July–August 1992).

Beckwith, Francis J. *Politically Correct Death: Answering the Arguments for Abortion Rights.* Grand Rapids: Baker, 1993.

———. "Personal Bodily Rights, Abortion, and Unplugging the Violinist." *International Philosophical Quarterly* 32 (March 1992).

Bedate, C. A., and R. C. Cefalo. "The Zygote: To Be or Not to Be a Person." *Journal of Medicine and Philosophy* 14 (1989).

Boonin-Vail, David. "A Defense of 'A Defense of Abortion': On the Responsibility Objection to Thomson's Argument." *Ethics* 107, no. 2 (January 1997).

Brody, Baruch. *Abortion and the Sanctity of Human Life.* Cambridge, Mass.: MIT, 1975.

Clouser, Roy. *The Myth of Religious Neutrality: An Essay on the Hidden Role of Religious Belief in Theories.* Notre Dame, Ind.: University of Notre Dame Press, 1991.

Cuomo, Mario. "Religious Belief and Public Morality: A Catholic Governor's Perspective." *Notre Dame Journal of Law, Ethics, and Public Policy* 1 (1984).

Dworkin, Ronald. *Life's Dominion: An Argument About Abortion, Euthanasia, and Individual Freedom.* New York: Knopf, 1993.

Eddy, Mary Baker. *Science and Health with Key to the Scriptures.* Boston: The First Church of Christ, Scientist, 1875.

Englehardt, H. Tristram, Jr. "The Ontology of Abortion." *Ethics* 84 (1973–1974).

George, Robert P. "Public Reason and Political Conflict: Abortion and Homosexuality." *Yale Law Journal* 106 (June 1997).

Hackett, Stuart C. *Oriental Philosophy: A Westerner's Guide to Eastern Thought*. Madison: University of Wisconsin Press, 1979.

Hunter, James Davison. *Culture Wars*. New York: Simon & Schuster, 1991.

Hudnut, Beverly G., and William H. Hudnut III. "We're Good Republicans—and Pro-Choice," *The New York Times*, 29 May 1996.

Kamm, Frances M. *Creation and Abortion: A Study in Moral and Legal Philosophy*. New York: Oxford, 1992.

Koukl, Gregory P. *Precious Unborn Human Persons*. San Pedro, Calif.: Stand to Reason, 1996.

Kuhn, Thomas. *The Structure of Scientific Revolutions*. 2d ed. Chicago: University of Chicago Press, 1970.

Laudan, Larry. *Progress and Its Problems: Towards a Theory of Scientific Growth*. Berkeley: University of California Press, 1977.

———. *Science and Values: The Aims of Science and Their Role in Scientific Debate*. Berkeley: University of California Press, 1984.

Lee, Patrick. *Abortion and Unborn Human Life*. Washington, D.C.: Catholic University of America Press, 1996.

Marquis, Don. "Why Abortion Is Immoral." *The Journal of Philosophy* 86 (April 1989).

McDonagh, Eileen. *Breaking the Abortion Deadlock: From Choice to Consent*. New York: Oxford, 1996.

Moreland, J. P., and Scott B. Rae. *On Human Persons: Metaphysical and Ethical Reflections*. Downers Grove, Ill.: InterVarsity, 2000.

National Abortion Rights Action League (NARAL). "Choice—Legal Abortion: Pro and Con." Prepared by Polly Rothstein and Marian Williams. White Plains, N.Y.: Westchester Coalition for Legal Abortion, 1983.

News Hour. "Campaign'96—AbortionPlank." 1996. Database on-line. Available from <www.pbs.org/newshour/bb/election/june96/abortion_6-11.html> (4 April 1999).

"Oklahoma's Massive Challenge." *Choice News: The Bi-Monthly Newsletter Produced by Republicans for Choice* 1, no. 4 (July–August 1992).

Pavlischek, Keith. "Abortion Logic and Paternal Responsibilities: One More Look at Judith Thomson's Argument and a Critique of David Boonin-Vail's Defense of It." In *The Abortion Controversy 25 Years After Roe v. Wade*. 2d ed. Ed. Louis P. Pojman and Francis J. Beckwith. Belmont, Calif.: Wadsworth, 1998.

Pojman, Louis P. "Abortion: A Defense of the Personhood Argument." In *The Abortion Controversy 25 Years After Roe v. Wade*. 2d ed. Ed. Louis P. Pojman and Francis J. Beckwith. Belmont, Calif.: Wadsworth, 1998.

"Pro-Choice Minister Booed." *Choice News: The Bi-Monthly Newsletter Produced by Republicans for Choice* 1, no. 4 (July–August 1992).

Rawls, John. "The Idea of Public Reason Revisited." *University of Chicago Law Review* 64 (summer 1997).

Republican National Committee (RNC). *The 1996 National Republican Platform*. 1996. Database on-line. Available from <www.gopnm.org/gopnm/platform.html> (4 April 1999).

Republican National Committee (RNC). *The Vision Shared: Uniting Our Family, Our Country, Our World—The Republican Platform 1992.* Washington, D.C.: The Republican National Committee, 1992.

Republicans for Choice (RFC) Home Page. 1999. Database on-line. Available from <www.rfc-pac.org> (4 April 1999).

Republicans for Choice (RFC) Home Page. "Welcome." 1999. Database on-line. Available from <www.rfc-pac.org/welcome.html> (3 April 1999).

Stone, Ann. "A Message from Ann Stone." Republicans for Choice Home Page. 1999. Database on-line. Available from <www.rfc-pac.org/ann.html> (4 April 1999).

———. "Open Letter from Ann Stone to the Delegates and Alternates to the 1992 Republican National Convention," 1992.

Suarez, Antoine. "Hydatidiform Moles and Teratomas Confirm the Human Identity of the Preimplantation Embryo." *Journal of Medicine and Philosophy* 15 (1990).

Sullivan, Lynn K. "Gearin' Up for Houston." *Choice News: The Bi-Monthly Newsletter Produced by Republicans for Choice* 1, no. 4 (July–August 1992).

Sumner, L. W. *Abortion and Moral Theory.* Princeton: Princeton University Press, 1981.

Thomson, Judith Jarvis. "A Defense of Abortion." *Philosophy and Public Affairs* 1, no. 1 (1971).

Tooley, Michael. *Abortion and Infanticide.* New York: Oxford, 1983.

———. "In Defense of Abortion and Infanticide." In *The Abortion Controversy 25 Years After Roe v. Wade.* 2d ed. Ed. Louis P. Pojman and Francis J. Beckwith. Belmont, Calif.: Wadsworth, 1998.

Tribe, Laurence. *Abortion: The Clash of Absolutes.* New York: W. W. Norton, 1990.

U.S. Senate. *The Human Life Bill—S.158; Report Together with Additional and Minority Views to the Committee on the Judiciary, United States Senate, Made by Its Subcommittee on Separation of Powers.* Washington, D.C.: U.S. Government Printing Office, 1981.

U.S. Supreme Court. *Casey v. Planned Parenthood* 505 U.S. 833 (1992).

U.S. Supreme Court. *Roe v. Wade* 410 U.S. 113 (1973).

Warren, Mary Ann. "On the Moral and Legal Status of Abortion." In *The Problem of Abortion.* 2d ed. Ed. Joel Feinberg. Belmont, Calif.: Wadsworth, 1984.

Wilcox, John T. "Nature as Demonic in Thomson's Defense of Abortion." *The New Scholasticism* 63 (autumn 1989).

ENDNOTES

1. This essay, which differs only slightly from the original, was first published under the same title in *Nexus: A Journal of Opinion* (Chapman University School of Law) 4, no. 1 (spring 1999).
2. An example of what such an amendment would look like is S.158, which was proposed by the U.S. Congress in 1981. A portion of it follows:

SECTION 1. (a) The Congress finds that the life of each human being begins at conception.

(b) The Congress further finds that the fourteenth amendment to the Constitution of the United States protects all human beings.

SECTION 2. Upon the basis of these findings, and in the exercise of the powers of Congress, including its power under section 5 of the fourteenth amendment to the Constitution of the United States, the Congress hereby recognizes that for the purpose of enforcing the obligation of the States under the fourteenth amendment not to deprive persons of life without due process of law, each human life exists from conception, without regard to race, sex, age, health, defect, or condition of dependency, and for this purpose "person" includes all human beings.

SECTION 3. Congress further recognizes that each State has a compelling interest, independent of the status of unborn children under the fourteenth amendment, in protecting the lives of those with the State's jurisdiction whom the State rationally regards as human beings. . . . (U.S. Senate 1981, 1–2)

3. I was also delegate to the Nevada Republican state conventions in 1990 and 1992 as well as a delegate to the Clark County (Nevada) Republican conventions in 1992 and 1994. In the 1992 county convention, I served as chair of the platform committee.

4. Ironically, some delegates suggested addressing this issue in the 1996 platform. Following is a portion of a suggested change that was considered but not accepted by the platform committee: "As Republicans, we acknowledge and respect the honest convictions that divide us on the question of abortion. Unlike the Democratic Party, we will not censor members of our party who hold opposing views on this issue. We are a party confident enough in our beliefs to tolerate dissent." (RNC 1996, appendix I)

5. On its web site, RFC asserts, "71% of Republicans nationwide are pro-choice. That pro-choice majority wants to replace the plank with one which recognizes Republicans can differ on this issue, and that abortion should not be a litmus test for candidates or Party members." ("Welcome" 1999).

6. For a defense of abortion as a fundamental nonnegotiable legal right, see Dworkin (1993) and Tribe (1990).

7. Although Stone's point is factually correct, it is unclear how her point would persuade those who think that the Court is mistaken about abortion. After all, these noncompliant Republicans can always argue that the G.O.P. came of age while resisting another controversial U.S. Supreme Court decision: the party's 1860 platform—the one on which Abraham Lincoln ran—contradicted the most controversial Court decision of Lincoln's time, *Dred Scott*.

8. Some people challenge this claim that the nature of the fetus is what is doing or ought to be doing the moral work in the disagreement over abortion. For defenses of this perspective, see Thomson (1971); Tribe (1990), chapter 6; Boonin-Vail (1997); and McDonagh (1996). For replies to this perspective, see Beckwith (1992); Lee (1996), chapter 4; Pavlischek (1998); and Wilcox (1989). Although this is an important and influential perspective, it falls outside the scope of this essay. The focus of this discussion is a plank in the Republican Party platform that calls for amending the Constitution to include a human

life amendment. The purpose of such an amendment, as I understand it, is to respond directly to the conditional challenge put forth by Justice Blackmun in *Roe v. Wade*: "The appellee and certain amici argue that the fetus is a 'person' within the language and meaning of the Fourteenth Amendment. In support of this, they outline at length and in detail the well-known facts of fetal development. If this suggestion of personhood is established, the appellant's case, of course, collapses, for the fetus' right to life would then be guaranteed specifically by the Amendment. The appellant conceded as much on reargument. On the other hand, the appellee conceded on reargument that no case could be cited that holds that a fetus is a person within the meaning of the Fourteenth Amendment." (U.S. Supreme Court 1973, 157–58). Consequently, the political and legal reality is that fetal personhood is doing all of the moral work, although some moral philosophers and legal and political theorists argue that it does not and/or should not.

9. For an interesting defense of the view that political and social perspectives are the result of certain ultimate (or religious) commitments, see Clouser (1991).

10. Consider the following comments from Margaret Warner in a story that appeared on the June 11, 1996, edition of PBS's News Hour: "Abortion is a potentially explosive issue for Republicans this year. The 1992 party platform called for a constitutional amendment banning abortion, and pro-life forces within the party want the '96 platform to remain the same, but pro-choice Republicans, including some powerful governors, have threatened a convention fight unless the anti-abortion plank is struck or radically amended." (News Hour 1996). Later in the program, in her interview with Ann Stone and Phyllis Schlafly, Warner makes the same mistake again in a discussion with Stone:

> STONE: We appreciate the fact that [Bob Dole's] welcoming the majority [i.e., pro-choice advocates] back into the party, but we do have to go beyond this, and for his own sake, and we are very concerned about keeping the human life amendment in the platform as we look to fall because I think Bill Clinton laid out his strategy will be a fight over should there be a constitutional amendment or not, and that—
> WARNER: You're talking about an amendment to outlaw abortion?
> STONE: Right. Outlaw abortion, and if that is the discussion in the fall campaign, Bob Dole will lose that discussion. Once people understand what such an amendment would include, it would be a real problem for us. (News Hour 1996)

11. On numerous occasions during the 1996 presidential campaign, Republican candidate Bob Dole referred to the HLA plank as "the abortion plank." See, for example, Dole's comments in News Hour (1996).

12. This section of the 1996 platform reads a little differently, although the meaning is the same as in the 1992 version: "We are the party of individual Americans, whose rights we protect and defend as the foundation for opportunity and security for all. Today, as at our founding in the day of Lincoln, we insist no one's rights are negotiable." (RNC 1996)

13. The Hudnuts (1996) write: "Why should political parties, our party in particular, stake out a position on abortion? Why borrow trouble on a matter on which

people are so seriously divided? It seems to us that under traditional minimalist Republican policy, government would choose *not* to interfere with a woman's right to make her own decision about whether or not to bear a child." Stone writes (1992): "You see, to be Republican and Pro-Choice does not mean you are advocate of abortion. It simply means that you feel the best way to solve the problem is through inspiration and leadership, rather than legislation." In an interview (June 11, 1996) on PBS's News Hour, Margaret Warner asks Stone the question, "You're talking about an amendment to outlaw abortion?" Stone replies: "Right. Outlaw abortion . . ." (News Hour 1996). The Republicans for Choice web page states: "We will fight at our Party's National Convention to remove the anti-choice plank and nominate a pro-choice Vice-Presidential candidate. We must be viewed as a Party of inclusion and not one of exclusion. Continuing to maintain the anti-choice plank in our Party's platform and ignoring GOP pro-choicers will continue to drive away many Americans who would normally support us" ("Welcome" 1999).

14. The Congressional authors of the failed 1981 Human Life Amendment (S.158) understood the moral logic of this inference. After Sections 1 through 3 in which abortion is *not* mentioned (see n. 2), the amendment reads:

> SECTION 4. Notwithstanding any other provision of law, no inferior Federal court ordained and established by Congress under article III of the Constitution of the United States shall have jurisdiction to issue any restraining order, temporary or permanent injunction, or declaratory judgment in any case involving or arising from any State law or municipal ordinance that (1) protects the rights of human persons between conception and birth, or (2) prohibits, limits or regulates (a) the performance of abortions or (b) the provision at public expense of funds, facilities, personnel, or other assistance for the performance of abortions: *Provided*, That nothing in this section shall deprive the Supreme Court of the United States of the authority to render appropriate relief in any case.
>
> SECTION 5. Any party may appeal to the Supreme Court of the United States from an interlocutory or final judgment, decree, or order of any court of the United States regarding the enforcement of this Act, or any such law or ordinance. The Supreme Court shall advance on its docket and expedite the disposition of any such appeal.
>
> SECTION 6. If any provision of this Act or the application thereof to any person or circumstance is judicially determined to be invalid, the validity of the remainder of the Act, and the application of such provision to other persons and circumstances shall not be affected by such determination. (U.S. Senate 1981, 2)

15. Stone asserts (1992): "[W]e do not and will not ask President Bush, or anyone else, whose views differ from ours, to change their position. Nor do we advocate that our Party not welcome, or support candidates who represent the pro-life/anti-choice position. While *they* [i.e., pro-lifers] have invited us [i.e., pro-choicers] out of our party, *we welcome them* with open arms. We respect their right to hold a position that differs from ours. *That is their choice*." (Emphasis is the author's.)

16. Recall Stone's concession to pro-life Republicans (1992): "[W]e do not and will

not ask President Bush, or anyone else, whose views differ from ours, to change their position. . . . *That is their choice.*" (Emphasis is the author's.)

17. Political and legal philosopher John Rawls (1997, 798–99) seems to be saying something similar when he writes: "Some may, of course, reject a legitimate decision, as Roman Catholics may reject a decision to grant a right to abortion. They may present an argument in public reason for denying it and fail to win a majority. *But they themselves need not themselves exercise the right to abortion.* They can recognize the right as belonging to legitimate law enacted in accordance with legitimate public institutions and public reason, and therefore not resist it with force. Forceful resistance is unreasonable: it would mean attempting to impose by force their own comprehensive doctrine that a majority of other citizens who follow public reason, not unreasonably, do not accept." (Emphasis added.) Of course, the pro-lifer (Catholic, Protestant, or whatever) believes that the state's allowance of feticide and it's requirement that the pro-lifer not interfere with the performance of feticide is using it's force to establish a particular comprehensive doctrine, one that entails certain philosophical conclusions about the nature of persons and the nature of things. Among these conclusions is the belief that the properties necessary to declare something a full-fledged person are absent from fetuses.

18. Stone seems to affirm both of these assertions:

> [W]e do not and will not ask President Bush, or anyone else, whose views differ from ours, to change their position. . . . We respect their right to hold a position that is different from ours. . . . The Supreme Court just declined to overturn *Roe* and affirmed that a woman's right to choose is essential for women to participate equally in society. Our party's platform is in contradiction with the Court—a Court mostly selected by Republican Presidents. Let's return our Party Platform to the basic Republican Philosophy of less government in our lives. (Stone 1992)

> How can we reconcile our goal to take government out of the daily life of business, but yet thrust government into this most personal and private individual decision? (As quoted in Sullivan 1992, 5)

19. Pro-choice Republicans sometimes subtly make this argument when they describe their opponents in language that conveys the message that pro-life Republicans are *religious* extremists. In one article, pro-life Republicans are called "anti-choice fanatics" and "anti-choice zealots." ("Pro-Choice Minister Booed," 1992, 4)

20. The Hudnuts write (1992): "Granted, we are pro-choice, but why not simply leave abortion out of the platform, which has opposed abortion in recent years. As soon as a party or politician or citizen takes a stand on abortion, an 'us against them' situation is set in place, leaving little room for dialogue or diversity of opinion." In an announcement for new members, RFC states, "Help us take abortion out of politics" (RFC Home Page 1999).

21. Sometimes it appears that pro-choice Republicans are not merely calling for the pro-life plank to be dropped, but to replaced with a pro-choice one. On the RFC web page, a portion of the welcome statement reads: "Republicans for Choice believes that in accordance with the basic fundamental principles of the

Republican Party, we must protect individual rights, including a woman's right to choose." ("Welcome" 1999). Stone writes:

> That Statement of Principles reads: The Republican Party wants "[a]n America with a smaller less burdensome government that trusts its people to decide what is best for them . . . [a]n America where freedom of expression, individual conscience, and personal privacy are cherished and respected." Apparently, these principles apply only to men.
>
> The new Statement of Principles would be comical if it weren't so insulting. How can anyone take these principles seriously when the Platform abortion plank specifically says the Party doesn't trust a woman to make the right decision, disrespects her individual conscience, and intends to intrude into her private life with a Constitutional amendment that could help put her behind bars? It's no wonder the GOP has a female gender gap problem.

Stone, in her testimony before the 1992 Republican Platform Committee, asserted: "How can we reconcile our goal to take government out of the daily life of business, but yet to thrust government into this most personal and private individual decision?" (Sullivan 1992, 5). Although it is not clear from RFC literature whether it merely wants to remove the HLA plank or replace it with a pro-choice one, its rhetoric to justify the former sometimes seems to lead inexorably to an obligation to do the latter as well.

22. Some philosophers of science have argued that a scientist's worldview or scientific paradigm has a very strong influence upon the process of discovery and theory-making as well as other aspects of the scientific enterprise. See, for example, Kuhn (1970); Laudan (1977); and Laudan (1984). It does not take much imagination to conclude from this that political, social, and legal theories may also be shaped largely by one's worldview or paradigm commitments. See Clouser (1991).

23. This view has been challenged by Bedate and Cefalo (1989). Their case, however, is seriously flawed. See Lee (1996), 98–102; and Suarez (1990).

    Some people have argued that the phenomena of twinning and possible recombination count against human individuality beginning at conception. Although there is good reason to believe this conclusion to be flawed (see Beckwith [1993], 97; and Lee [1996], 90–98), even if it were correct, its practical effect would be negligible, for virtually all pregnant women discover their pregnancy long after these phenomena would have occurred.

24. Note that some pro-choice scholars argue that they *do know* when human life becomes morally valuable. They maintain that at some decisive moment during pregnancy or after birth, the fetus (or newborn) acquires certain properties that make him a human person (or moral human being) rather than merely a human being (or genetically human). For defenses of a variety of views on when after conception this decisive moment occurs, see Brody (1975); Englehardt (1973–74); Tooley (1983); Tooley (1998); Pojman (1998); Sumner (1981); and Warren (1984). For critiques of these and other views, see Beckwith (1993); Brody (1975); Lee (1996); Moreland and Rae (2000); and Marquis (1989).

25. Stone writes (1992): "The Supreme Court just declined to overturn *Roe* and reaffirmed that a woman's right to choose is essential for women to participate equally in society. Our party platform is in contradiction with the Court—a

Court mostly selected by Republican Presidents." See also the brief analysis of *Casey v. Planned Parenthood* (U.S. Supreme Court 1992) by RFC in "Attention" (1992), 1.

26. Although this is a logical conclusion of the Court's reasoning, it is clear that the Court's permission of abortion, as I argued earlier, is inconsistent with this logical conclusion.

27. More sophisticated pro-choice advocates argue that fetuses are not human persons. And for this reason, fetuses do not have a right to life if their life hinders the liberty of a being who is a person (i.e., the pregnant woman). See Dworkin (1993); Englehardt (1973–74); Tooley (1983); Tooley (1998); Pojman (1998); and Warren (1984). Of course, in debate over the HLA plank in the Republican platform, one rarely, if ever, hears an argument that defends this sophisticated pro-choice claim and takes on the plank's content: fetuses are human persons entitled to the state's protection.

An Overview

"All politics are local" is a slogan that is frequently cited by those wishing to highlight economic and community ramifications of government, law, and public policy. To the extent that this maxim is true, enormous social and racial considerations are also involved. At the heart of many communities is the local church. What then are the opportunities and responsibilities of Christians and churches at the grass roots level of politics? In this essay, Darrell Bock looks at racial reconciliation as one means of bridging some of the divisions within local communities. If Christians are to have any lasting positive influence in the realm of politics and public policy, there must first be peace, respect, and cooperation within the church. It may well be that the most effective witness the church can provide in the political realm is that of internal reconciliation.

Chapter Sixteen

RECONCILIATION
Witness to a Prepared and Redeemed People,
Invitation to Real Community

Darrell L. Bock

FOR MANY CHRISTIANS, social and racial issues are for politicians, not believers. Christians are called to do evangelism and save souls. Concerns about reconciliation and diversity are not a part of the church's call or the theological task. Although this view is often well motivated by a concern that the main thing, Jesus, stay the main thing, it is a particularly short-sighted way to read Scripture. Every now and then, such as with Promise Keepers, there are hints that such concerns are an element of the church's concern. Such impulses should be encouraged.

This essay has two goals. First, I want to make a theological case for the importance of reconciliation and an affirmation of diversity in the midst of unity for the theological task, including evangelistic concerns. Second, I want to discuss some practical aspects of pursuing goals in this area for the church by discussing my own experience related to such efforts in both a seminary and a church context. Seeking to develop community in Christ that reflects the racial range within the body is not an easy pursuit. In fact, many people argue against it in practice by consciously establishing homogeneous communities where cultural expectations are shared and social perspectives are similar. This approach is certainly the easiest and least bothersome route to take in pursuing community. It also may be necessary in certain contexts to accomplish evangelistic goals. However, as we shall argue, it also risks cutting believers off from experiencing the richness of the body that Christ has formed, if that is all that such communities expose themselves to in their pursuit of ministry.

A THEOLOGICAL CASE FOR RECONCILIATION
TO LOVE GOD AND TO LOVE ONE'S NEIGHBOR

It is not a profound theological observation to argue that love for God and love for one's neighbor is one of Jesus' most fundamental ethical teachings. Whether one considers the teaching of the parable of the Good Samaritan (Luke 10:29–37) or Jesus' discussion with the scribe (Mark 12:28–34), Jesus clearly saw a link between the love of God and the love for one's neighbor.

He even argued that these were the two greatest commandments. In fact, the roots of this idea are part of the Old Testament (Deut. 6:5; Lev. 19:18). The theme is deeply biblical, being affirmed across the whole of Scripture. A similar perspective is seen in Paul's commendations in his letters when he commends the saints for their faith in Jesus and their love for the saints (Eph. 1:15). Their vertical dependence on God has translated relationally and horizontally into their relationships in the community. In the Ephesian community, the background involved a mixed church of Jews and Gentiles (Acts 19:1–41; 20:17–35). Many of the letters of the New Testament concern themselves with issues of how Jews and Gentiles can function together as a part of the new community Jesus brings. It was not a simple task. Combining people of diverse backgrounds is never simple.

Two texts deserve special attention, for they show how central this theme is to the witness of the church. The first text is Luke 1:16–17, when the task of John the Baptist is set forth, like Elijah, as a forerunner of the coming Messiah. It is said that John's call is to "make ready a people prepared for the Lord" (v. 17). A closer look at that text shows how they will be prepared. First, he will turn people to the Lord God, a reference to calling them back to the Father from their spiritual unfaithfulness, which had led to Jewish exile under Babylon and now under Rome (v. 16). It is the second part of the passage, however, that often goes unnoticed. In turning them to God, other effects will be evident. The hearts of the parents will be turned to their children. The disobedient will be turned to the righteous. Now there is nothing about racial diversity here, but what is significant is that a turn to God results as well in a turn of people back to one another. The passage argues that turning to God and being prepared for God is shown in our relationships with others as we are mutually drawn back to righteousness. If this is what being ready for God's coming meant when he sent Jesus, is it not the case that it should characterize those to have welcomed His coming?

A second text, Ephesians 2:11–22, says this even more explicitly and makes the racial point directly. In this passage, Paul takes the perspective of the previously excluded Gentiles, noting how they were outside the promise. With Christ's coming, those who were "far off" were brought near. Now not only were they brought near to God but also He became "our peace" for Jew and Gentile. Now this phrase should not be read as arguing that Jesus brings peace between Himself and each individual believer, although that certainly is true. Rather, the point is that the Lord has removed the enmity that stood between Jew and Gentile so they now can relate to one another in a way that shows that the two are reconciled as one. Jesus has done this by creating one "new man," that is, the new community Christ is building into a holy temple. Thus, at the very essence of the identity of the new community is their shared oneness in Christ across racial lines but in a way that allows the whole world to see that Jew and Gentile are now reconciled to God and to each other. Here is a potentially powerful way in which the church can witness itself to be different than the world. In a world where each ethnic group often contends for itself against other groups, here is a community that can affirm both Jew and Gentile, yet in a way that shows that they are reconciled. Most of the rest of Ephesians is concerned with detailing in a specific way how this unity can be preserved and maintained in a hostile world.

The way the New Testament does this is also very significant. Jews could remain Jews in practice, custom, and form while coming to Christ. Jewish identity was consistent with trusting in Christ. Assimilation into Gentile practices was not required. Just a reading of the book of Acts shows how Jewish were some Jewish Christians. On the other hand, some Jews had somewhat assimilated to the larger Hellenistic or Gentile world. They also lived within the church in a style that paralleled their background. Finally, Gentiles were not to become Jews but could live as Gentiles. When tensions became particularly high, the church met in Acts 15 and asked only that Gentiles be sensitive to the Jewish brethren with respect to certain practices that could be offensive to them.

The point in all of this is that when God reconciles Jew and Gentile, he does not ask them to become exactly like one another. Rather, they are to get to know one another in such a way that they can respect differences between them that are not theologically substantive. One of the ways the church grows in community is to appreciate the fact that although Jew and Gentile are one in Christ, and although there is no Jew or Greek in Christ, it is as Jew and Gentile that they are reconciled. It is their ethnic identity and the union of those identities that makes for the beauty of the body's diverse unity, showing the very tapestry of the reconciliation God has made.

So we see that reconciliation, not just to God but to each other, is a major theme that identifies and marks out the church as having been affected by God's redeeming work. It is a part of what marks out the "new man" as sanctified by God. Thus, not only were people preparing for the Lord's coming during John the Baptist's time called to be reconciled but also those redeemed by Him were formed into a reconciled people as a way of showing God's work had really taken place. That characteristic is part of what marked them out as a holy place of God, as a work wrought by divine hands.

If such reconciliation is a mark of a redeemed community, then an important question becomes how we evidence this reality in our larger communities. Note how I have presented the issue in terms of internal relationships within the church. It is in this place that such reconciliation should be most evidenced as an evidence of God's work in our midst. Here, I turn to practical expression and note my own experience in this area in communities that have attempted to embrace these dimensions of corporate spirituality. I wish to make the point that one of the more potentially powerful means of giving credibility to our evangelistic efforts will be to evidence what God designed us to be.

SOME PRACTICAL EFFORTS AT PRACTICING
RECONCILIATION AND SOME LESSONS TO NOTE

In looking at the practical side of this question, I wish to describe my own personal experience in two subcommunities that make up a significant portion of the church in the United States. They are the Jewish-Christian and African-American Christian communities. Over the last several years, I have had the fortune of association with church and seminary programs tied to the African-American community in Dallas. This association has involved a consciously pursued "sister" church relationship with two predominantly African-American churches, one our church helped to plant and another, down the block from us, with whom we are developing an ongoing relationship. On another front, as a part of my work in spiritual formation at Dallas Theological Seminary, our formation group has hooked up informally with Baylor Hospital's nursing school and one inner city job training and housing ministry. We sought to give what little help we could to ministry efforts among some of our neighbors in Dallas. These ministries are located only a few blocks from the seminary. We thought it only appropriate to see how we could be good neighbors as we pursued our own spiritual growth. Finally, my association with Chosen People ministries has exposed me to the world of evangelism to the Jewish community.

Each of these experiences, operating within existing structures, has stretched the communities of which I am a part, as well as spurring my own spiritual growth. None of these ministries is exactly the same; each has its own lessons.

In the Church

My church is only a little more than twenty years old. It is located in Richardson, Texas, a relatively affluent suburban city just north of Dallas. When we had been in existence for only five years, we knew that we wanted to be involved in church planting. But anyone who knows Dallas knows that it is filled with many good churches. We did not want merely to multiply the placing of pews. Our goal then was to seek to plant a church in an area of the city that lacked a good community church. In God's providence, we had an African-American who was training for ministry and wanted to go back and minister in the environment where he was raised. So we looked for the poorest area in Dallas that lacked any solid community church. Our church was not big enough on its own, being new itself, to sustain the initial phases of such an effort. So we sought out other like-minded churches and put together a group of five of them who offered to help in planting this church. In fact, as is often the case, out of the five original partners, two communities ended up bearing most of the burden, but that is to be expected in such an effort. Such a ministry is hard work and requires perseverance.

Today, about seventeen years later, this planted church is doing very well. It is self-sustaining, has a gym used for community outreach, and operates a private school where children are getting a solid education. It is located across the street from some of the Dallas housing projects. Dallas has had a bad reputation in racial relations. Yet, this church and its work in the community, including the cooperation among the ethnic groups in the city, has received press attention in *The Dallas Morning News* as an example of how cooperative relationships take place in a city known for more destructive patterns of behavior. A few times a year, we exchange pulpits with this community, and occasionally we worship together. We have held men's and women's retreats together, where each church has an equal role. We also have shared in a basketball league, which is held in their gym. For years, many of the women from our church have gone into the other community to help tutor kids at their school or elsewhere in their community. The opportunities for service are multiple and rewarding.

The result has been that many of our members understand life on the "other side" of town with much more appreciation for how some of our brothers and sisters in Christ live. We have also come to see and appreciate the diversity of how people live and worship our Lord, gaining insight into race relations first hand with guides who could help us see our own blind spots.

About ten years after this first effort, our church learned that a predominantly African-American church had relocated near us, about four blocks away. Our pastor made an initiative to get to know the pastor at this other church, meeting with him on occasion simply to encourage each other in their work. This church had an exploding ministry to both affluent African-Americans and racially mixed couples. They were growing so fast that they could not build facilities fast enough to keep up with attendance and programs. Their leadership, still developing, was being stretched thin. Yet, in the midst of their growth, their pastor and ours decided that it would be good for each community to get to know each other.

This relationship was launched with elders meeting with each other over meals and with a joint congregational picnic. Everyone involved regarded that event as a success. At their request, one of our elders moved to their church to help them with their leadership development. The relationship has grown and leveled off. We have attempted a couple of combined small groups with limited success. We have successfully conducted joint men's and women's meetings as well as evangelistic efforts. They have also joined with the other African-American church in three-way efforts of various sorts. We have even had between us very frank discussions about how race functions in America. These very difficult discussions often have been the means of the greatest growth for our group.

I do not want to romanticize these efforts. They require much patience and understanding. Suspicion, which has been culturally nurtured and sustained over decades, is hard to work past to a point where trust comes naturally. As an Anglo-American, I have found there is much to learn from an African-American brother who lives in a world where the mere color of one's skin makes one an automatic object of suspicion for many. I have never lived my life in that kind of a microscope. Values about planning, scheduling, and the use of time in doing joint events mean compromise for both sides in working together. Some individual efforts had less success because the gaps could not be closed. But each community values the stretching that God has brought to each of us as we have continued to work alongside each other. In the learning and continued working through the kinks comes the growth.

There never has been an intention to combine congregations. Rather, the goal has been a "sister" church relationship, affirming our oneness in joint outreach events and other select gatherings. When we do evangelistic outreach or other joint projects together, it does not take long for someone walking in on our joint events to realize that this is not a normal situation. In pursuing reconciliation, we give a powerfully visible foretaste and preview of what God will one day complete.

In the Seminary and Spiritual Formation Groups

Our seminary formation group experience has been the most difficult logistically. First, the group itself meets for only one hour each week with its own detailed program to pursue. Second, the participants in the various ministries in the area are away at training when our group is meeting. Third, our time together as a formation group means that we can go out together only every so often, on the average, every other week. Nonetheless, the premise with which we work seems sound. Talking about spiritual formation and our private walk with God is enhanced by engaging in a stretching ministry experience, working side by side as servants.

Again, by God's providence and by keeping our eyes open for an opportunity, we discovered that Baylor's nursing school, which also was located only a few blocks away, had a semester-long internship program required of their nurses at a medical storefront set up at an inner city Dallas police station. Twice a week, the police station opened up a wing for a doctor and a team of nurses who cared for cases in the neighborhood. They came as walk-ins or from word-of-mouth referrals. In this part of town, many refugees from Asia and Africa have moved in and often lack any kind of medical care. Sometimes the foreign field is not an ocean away. The nurses have a circuit of apartments that they regularly visit to find out if anyone needs care. Interpreters of various nationalities are necessary to make the Baylor program work.

Every other week, we simply offered our services to them to be of whatever help we could. This effort meant pretty basic assistance. Could we accompany the nurses when they went to the apartments? In some cases, could we make rounds or escort a particular family to the locale so they could get care? Could we help move an elderly family who had no means of moving from one apartment complex to another? Through all of this activity, my students and I were exposed to living conditions and a way of life that was foreign to us. We learned that we could go into such areas and minister to people at basic human levels. We learned that scores of existing organizations lack good volunteers and could use help in their worthy work. We learned what being a neighbor might really mean. Some of the students have had a chance to share Christ, and a couple of them have decided on long-term ministry here.

One connection is an illustration of the effort. We have been engaged with them for the last two years. We stumbled over this ministry as we walked through the neighborhood with the nurses. This organization is dedicated to helping get men and women off drugs, training them for a vocation, and giving them the skills to be self-sufficient. It has been fascinating to see people's lives transformed as they discover basic life skills and grow in the Lord. Their students live on-site for a period of several months. This group had daily worship each evening with a pastor and a few volunteers directing the work. They were stretched thin. Our schedule would not allow us to meet with them for worship at night, although we did visit a service one Friday evening to get a sense of their work. What they wanted was help in encouraging their trainees in personal Bible study. So now we are working on simple personal Bible study notes for their people (a kind of basic question-and-answer study guide through individual books). Each year my group teams up to write notes to cover one biblical book. When we are done, we deliver the materials to the pastor and visit the ministry. This is what the pastor really needs from us to give support to his teaching ministry. Our hope is to raise a few volunteers to lead studies. We simply serve them and give them support. Many of my students have commented that this experience showed them that such an outreach was possible. They had not thought or had been too afraid to consider it, or they thought that they would have to begin such a ministry from scratch. Now the fear of the unknown is gone. They appreciate the fact that many worthy organizations already exist that simply need help. All it took was a little vision, some initiative, and a little follow through.

In a Parachurch Context

My exposure to Jew-Gentile issues had been largely theoretical until last year. I would often come to the numerous texts on Jew-Gentile questions and treat them as issues of the past now transformed into racial issues involving black, Hispanic, or Asian communities. Nothing could be further from the truth. Not only are these issues alive but also the reason they are so prevalent in the New Testament is that genuine reconciliation within individual groups of Christians and across the entire church was a major topic of early church practice. The early church appreciated the difficulty of such cross-cultural efforts and their importance as a statement of how God transforms patterns in the world.

I have now come to appreciate that Jew-Gentile questions are still quite alive today. The texts that discuss these issues in the early church have much to teach us about how we address such problems today. About 250,000 Jewish believers exist today. One of the hardest issues they face is trying to reach out to their own families and people after they come to the Lord. For a Jew to trust Christ often means that he or she is disowned by the family, but that does not mean that the one coming to Christ has ceased to care or pray for one's relatives. Often, when Jewish believers are fully assimilated into the church, they lose the ability to reach out to relatives. They are perceived as having defected, not only religiously but also culturally. The result is that many messianic congregations have sprung up across the country to show Jewish people that believing in Jesus is consistent with Jewish identity.

The problem is not new. Anyone reading the book of Acts can discover that many Jewish believers remained quite Jewish in practices that did not interfere with their embrace of Jesus (or Yeshua) as Messiah. Other more

Hellenistically rooted Jews, were less reflective of their Jewish roots, which also was acceptable in the church. The beauty of this variegated portrait is that the church took a view that said, "Let us affirm both the Jew as Jew and the Gentile as Gentile in their practice, even as we affirm their oneness in Jesus." Variety of practice is fine as long as one group does not force the other group to become something that they are not and as long as the gospel remains clear (Acts 6; 15; 21; Rom. 14:15; 1 Cor. 7:18–20). We recognized that for Jewish believers to reach other Jews might require that they be sensitive to Jewish practices as they reached out with the gospel and that sometimes this sensitivity might also extend to Gentiles when they were in contact with Jews (Acts 15).

To most Gentile believers, all of this kind of discussion is a foreign world, a cultural context to which they have never been exposed. The communities in the church have grown so far apart that many believers do not even know the needs of their Jewish Christian brothers and sisters. The sad thing is that this isolation shows just how disunified the body has become. So much of the church has little clue what another segment of the church is experiencing. Reconciliation need not mean uniformity, but neither is it isolationism.

Fortunately, parachurch ministries exist that seek to bridge the gap. (That is often why God raises up parachurch groups, that is, to do what the more formal churches are failing to do.) Chosen People Ministries and Jews for Jesus are two of the more visible groups that attempt not only to engage in evangelism to Jews but also to keep the predominantly Gentile church sensitive to issues that involve Jewish believers in the church. Here, pursuing reconciliation might involve as simple an initial step as inviting someone who is engaged in such work to explain what a ministry in such a context involves. The goal is to make us sensitive to our own blind spots as we work in the church. Pursuing reconciliation often begins with a simple conversation in which listening to another group's perspective helps to build the bonds to better relationship.

Sometimes an objection is raised that such ethnically constructed churches are wrong. I know numerous Asian churches also form on this basis. But the reason such churches often exist is that the dominant group in a community is not sensitive enough to the concerns and needs of one of its minority elements. The normal church group struggles to meet the needs of such groups. So ethnically focused churches form. They often provide services in their own language for people who do not know English and help them assimilate to a new home and country. Such ethnically sensitive division of labor is seen in Acts 6. This approach seems fine as long as these churches do not become so isolated that they do not have contact with other communities. All of our communities need more sensitivity to such issues. Drawing on these parachurch groups is one small first step.

My point here is that sometimes the different compositions of our churches is not a bad thing but rather a practical necessity. The tragedy occurs when any group is allowed to function and struggle on its own as an island community. In the United States—whether one thinks of Jewish, Asian,

Hispanic, or other ethnic communities—the church is not really evidencing itself as the church, Jew and Gentile in one body, unless it reflects the reconciliation that God has brought to humanity through Christ.

CONCLUSION

Any lasting influence that Christians and the church have in the realm of politics and public policy will have to be biblically based from the beginning. The credibility and efforts of Christians will be greatly enhanced if reconciliation and unity exist within the body of Christ. Perhaps the greatest influence we can have in addressing social and political issues in our culture is the daily visible witness and example of reconciliation within the church. When Christians reach across racial, ethnic, and other cultural boundaries within the body of Christ, they are preparing a solid foundation for exerting influence beyond the body of Christ into society. In a sense, such efforts are prepolitical. From the perspective of political action and public policy, they are desirable; from a biblical perspective, they are not only essential but also commanded.

None of the efforts that I have mentioned here are administratively top heavy or expensive. They are all simple steps going in a direction that says that my church will not be a spiritual island concerned about only itself or its own ethnic or socio-economic group. In churches that use small groups, such an outreach could be chosen and organized by one group. Reconciliation is a means by which the church can visibly reveal what God has done for people in Christ. It can show how God designed a diverse community to function. Caring and sensitivity come with the territory of building such relationships, deepening one's spirituality by causing us to look beyond ourselves. It can show that being a neighbor means being like the Good Samaritan (i.e., without consideration of another's race). It also is a means by which we can keep ourselves from being spiritually self-focused, which is really a contradiction in terms. But most importantly, moving toward and embracing reconciliation in the church means experiencing the body in its diverse fullness as God designed it to be. It is the witness of a redeemed people, willing to cross old boundaries built up by sin, prejudice, or just plain ignorance.

God's redemption is for all humanity, Jew and Gentile alike. The place where we are to see evidence of its reality most visibly displayed is the church. What better visible expression of our faith can there be than showing our love for God by showing our love for those who are made in His image, especially for those who are now our brothers and sisters in Christ? The beauty of such expression is that in moving toward such community, we are the ones who grow and benefit. We experience a fullness of community with a unified diversity that we could have only imagined before. Maybe that is what God had in mind all along in designing the body.

An Overview

Should Christians be involved at all in politics and public policy? If so, to what extent should they be involved? In this essay, law professor and theologian H. Wayne House argues that political activism is consistent with a biblical worldview. He contends that the attempt to dichotomize the Christian life into the now and the later is an unacceptable dualism and is in many respects an eschatological Gnosticism in which the later is real and important whereas the now is trivial and mundane. Christians have a definite role in politics and public policy. Christians are called to be faithful in their service and in their stewardship. Many of the issues that we face are long-term social concerns, and it is easy to become disheartened if we expect a quick victory or easy success. However, we must not lose heart because the final victory will be God's.

Chapter Seventeen

WHAT IN THE WORLD IS THE CHURCH SUPPOSED TO BE DOING?

H. Wayne House

ARE CHRISTIANS SUPPOSED TO BE INVOLVED in the temporal issues of this life? Or are we called to only eternal pursuits such as preaching the gospel, developing our "spiritual" life, and waiting for the Lord to take us away in the Rapture? Segments of the church have chosen the former option with little emphasis upon gospel proclamation whereas the evangelical arm of the church has usually taken the second route with little concern for societal issues or extraecclesiastical questions. Both of these positions are unacceptable for the individual Christian and the corporate Christian community.

ARGUING AGAINST ACTIVISM

Those who discourage either individual Christians or the church from being involved in society and politics use several arguments. One approach is to say that attempts at such temporal changes as may be achieved by the Christian are futile in view of the downward spiral of corruption in the world in anticipation of the Lord's soon coming. This view is the "don't-polish-the-brass-on-a-sinking-ship" approach. Another method within this approach is to claim that time and energy invested in social action takes away from the more important task of preaching the gospel. A third strategy is to point out that social concern puts the individual Christian or the church in a position of compromising with the world or involvement with politics that is contrary to the Christian life because (it is said) Satan controls the state.

A second approach is sometimes offered. Some people advocate individual Christian involvement with society and in politics but deny that the corporate body of Christians should ever speak on controversial questions. As individual citizens, we may seek to be influential, it is said, but the church should concern itself with only the Great Commission or other such "spiritual" matters. After all, total harmony about certain issues being debated in the public arena might not exist in the local church. Moreover, the Internal Revenue Services allows only a small amount of corporate action from the church if it is to retain its tax exemption. We must be careful, some say, lest we step over that line and be subject to government reprisal.

The two preceding approaches to disparaging Christian activism in contemporary society are certainly not all of the arguments that might be leveled, but they are representative of often-expressed views, and they should be addressed straightforwardly.

POLITICAL ACTIVISM AND THE CHRISTIAN WORLDVIEW

Without question, the efforts that we make in changing the world in which we live and the attempts to correct wrongs and promote justice might seem to pale in light of some loftier eternal standard, but I believe that to be so involved gives cohesiveness to the Christian worldview. As I see it, the attempt to dichotomize the Christian existence into the now and the later is an unacceptable dualism and is in many respects an eschatological Gnosticism in which the later is real and important whereas the now is trivial and mundane. Moreover, it is the establishment of a practical Deism. Unlike the Deists of the past, who believed that God withdrew after Creation, this God ceased to be involved (other than in some personal way) after the closing of the apostolic age. God has ceased to be a God of history now and is reserved either for the biblical days of the past or for one of the apocalyptic visions of the future. He really is not seen as acting out His will discernibly today, at least not in a way in which His people are active with Him. However, we should realize more than some (and I write as a dispensationalist) that God is a God of history as well as a God of the future.

One who holds a view that compartmentalizes time so that certain works are "spiritual" and other works are mundane has established a difficult task for himself or herself. Clearly, the preaching of the gospel is a major task for each Christian, but all of life is God's work. Spending time with my son might be as spiritual an activity as attending a missions conference. Praying with someone who is discouraged might be as much God's will as preaching to a multitude. And picketing an abortion clinic protesting the child sacrifices to the god of convenience might be as much God's work as handing out tracts. All of the facets and concerns of our lives are to be dedicated to God. It is not up to us to judge the relative importance of each part as though we were calculating a mathematical formula.

The view that society is evil and politics is dirty has many shortcomings. All that touches humanity (except for the Incarnation) suffers from the malady of sin. To be sure, reaching out to the poor and wretched in society is not glamorous work, but it emulates our Lord. It is as significant to minister a loaf of bread with a word of hope in Christ as it is to preach in the largest church. To stand to speak righteousness in the political world is reminiscent of our Lord's criticism of the adulterous affair of Antipas. To be a Christian might require getting dirty. But if we seek to escape such ministry, we would need to abandon home and church, for sin dwells there, too. God has established all three entities, and they are all our concern.

Whether social action should be corporate or only individual is more problematic. The ministry of the local church and the individual Christian would seem to be unrelated. Let me illustrate. Worship occurs in private and with other believers. The Great Commission to the church was to be expressed through individual action but may also be a corporate effort. Being a Good Samaritan is an example of individual concern, but it should not be excluded from corporate action. The church is the corporate Christian magnifying individual actions to and in the world.

A BIBLICAL PRESENTATION FOR CHRISTIAN ACTIVISIM

Jesus and Activism

Christians are citizens of a new and different kingdom. But does this truth preclude the attempt of Christians to establish justice and Christian perspectives in the kingdom in which we live daily? I have already set forth in general terms some perspectives of how many Christians view the interrelationship of Christians and society. In this section I will examine a biblical basis of Christian involvement in society.

When we desire to find biblical support for the social involvement of Christians, the person of Jesus Christ becomes our best example. He was a man who was part of His world. We must be careful not to view the Lord gnostically, seeing Him in some mystical, spiritual way, unattached to His earthly existence. Nor should we restrict His concerns for His immediate world—Judea—by making Him an apocalyptic Christ who was looking only for the establishment of His future kingdom. The writers of the Gospel did not envision Him in such terms, and we must not let spatial and temporal separation from the historical Jesus dim our vision of Him.

Christ said that Christians were not to be of the world but that we were to be in the world (John 17:6–19). He demonstrated this principle a number of times in his association with the people of Judea. He mixed freely with all classes of people—rich and poor, religious leaders and prostitutes, Jews and Samaritans. Paul, following Christ, developed a similar line of thinking in 1 Corinthians 5:9–11, where he commented that when he said for Christians not to mix with immoral people he was not speaking of non-Christians but of those who claimed to be believers; otherwise, we would have to go out of the world and isolate ourselves.

Christ often had struggles with the political leaders of the day. Whenever He criticized the Sadducees, He was speaking against the political as well as the religious elite. The Sadducees were part of the civil governmental powers in Roman-dominated Judea, yet this fact never stopped Jesus from speaking forth the truth for fear of becoming embroiled in politics. Moreover, He made a point to decry the immorality of the king, Antipas, even though He certainly had no earthly way to cause him to change his marriage practices or to remove him from office. Christ so interacted with the society in which He lived that some scholars have even seen Him (wrongly) as a revolutionary. Although He was not a zealot, and although His kingdom was not of this world, He lived fully and actively in the world in which He lived until His work here was finished.

The Apostles and Activism

The real problem arises not from Christ's obvious involvement with society but from the absence of specific calls to political or social action in the apostles' letters. The apostles, notably Paul and Peter, inform Christians on how to act toward other believers; no epistolary author urges Christians to seek to change the world around them. I think that too much has been made of this absence. We must be realistic about the world in which the New Testament arose. In the first century, to call for freedom for slaves or the abolition of abortion or infanticide simply would have been futile. No mechanism to achieve such goals existed other than direct revolution, which was not acceptable. Christians were small in number, only gradually gaining acceptance of their message and lives among the people.

However, we do have specific passages in which the apostle Paul encourages charity for both Christians and non-Christians (Gal. 6:10). He urged the believers in Ephesus to pray for the king so that they might not be harassed as they attempted to live godly lives (1 Tim. 2:1–2). He told slaves that if the opportunity came for them to become free (manumission), they should take it (1 Cor. 7:21–24). And he persuasively moved Philemon toward freeing his slave Onesimus. Paul exercised fully his rights of Roman citizenship in Phillipi, Jerusalem, Caesarea, and Rome (Acts 16:35–40; 22:23–29; 25:10–12; 28:11–20).

I seriously believe that if Paul were with us today in a democratic country like America, he would not hesitate to be active in society. He would urge Christians not only to pray for the king but also to vote for or against the king. He would admonish leaders to follow the proper dictates of government as he gave them to the Romans (Rom. 13:1–4). He would exercise all of the rights afforded him as an American to abolish social evils and to provide a political setting in which he could preach unfettered the gospel of Jesus Christ. The actions of Paul in Acts and the teachings in his letters indicate as much, and the actions of Jesus in Judea leave little doubt as to how Paul would act today.

A THEOLOGICAL FOUNDATION FOR ACTIVISM

Being created in the image of God brings forth tremendous privileges that are not shared by the rest of God's creation, but it also brings many important duties. We have been called to tasks that tax our mental and emotional capacities whereas other living things have established and virtually invariable living patterns. I mention this point because a theology of humanity is basic to an understanding of how we should relate to God, to others, and to the world around us. We simply do not accept the way things are, as do animals, but we have been called to create, to change, to cause conformity to our wills. And this activity is proper. We have been given the task of dominating the earth (Gen. 1:26–28), although we should understand this task in the sense of stewardship and not squander or pilfer our resources.

The Christian has a great responsibility to be involved in his world. The theological basis for such action is essentially the nature of God and man. I want to draw our attention to some important issues of the day, especially regarding the importance of making responsible and correct decisions regarding candidates for the presidency and for legislative positions at both the state and the federal levels. I will not propose to instruct anyone on how to vote—you are responsible to God for that—but I believe that thinking Christians should use certain touchstones in determining which candidates they will support. The Bible has not left us helpless in these matters. Principles on the proper function of government are abundant, and we should be careful not to miss them, or we do so to our own peril. Until such time as Christ takes the church away from this earth, He is using common grace to sustain human government, and with it an orderly society, and to restrain evil in the world. We as Christians should be cooperating with this work of God, not resisting it or begin indifferent toward it.

CONTEMPORARY CONCERNS

The State and the Defense of Its Citizens

A primary function of government is to defend its people from aggression, both inside and outside its boundaries. Whereas many other functions performed by government often could be performed by the other two divine institutions, the church, and the home, only government has the capability of efficient military and police action. Romans 13:1–4 demonstrates the police power of the state, the power of the sword. Individuals are to refrain from retribution but the state may exercise God's vengeance because it is specifically ordained by God to do so. The government has as its divine task to commend good and punish evil (Rom. 13:3–4; 1 Peter 2:14). This concern of the state covers both personal crime and societal crime, such as industrial offenses. In maintaining the protection of the country it serves, a given government also may exercise its power in military and/or diplomatic action. As George Ladd has said, "At root it makes little difference whether this force is exercised through local police punishing wrongdoers with the community, or in international terms through armies enforcing justice among nations."

A couple of practical contemporary observations may be made that I believe flow from an understanding of how God expects the state to do good and resist evil for the benefit of the people it serves. Government is acting irresponsibly when it fails to punish crime adequately and to protect the populace from criminals. Quick probation for dangerous felons causes the citizenry to lose confidence in the seriousness of government retribution against evil.

The State and Fiscal Responsibility

Nobel laureate economist Milton Friedman and Rose Friedman, in their book *Free to Choose*, speak of four classifications regarding the frugality one has in spending money. If you spend your own money on yourself, you are more Spartan than if you spend your own money on someone else. If you spend your own money on someone else, you are more frugal than if you spend someone else's money on yourself. If you spend someone else's money on yourself, you are more thrifty than if you spend someone else's money on someone else. The last classification is the one that we find often practiced by our representatives in the state and national legislatures. Because of this situation, we must be careful to call them to account for the use of our money. If I were to go to a bank to borrow money for items that I desired for my house, but at the same time I had outstanding debts that I needed to pay off, I would be viewed as irresponsible. Yet, this is exactly what the federal government is doing through the actions of Congress. They go to a private bank, the Federal Reserve, and borrow more and more money without even having paid previous loans, to finance special-interest projects of different legislators. Such action will have a dramatic impact on the economy, ultimately causing a tailspin that will hurt practically everyone in the country. If they print more money to flood the economy, they will be using "false weights" that make our money increasingly useless. We as Christians have a responsibility to encourage the moral use of money in which the currency is backed by a legitimate and just standard that will not be robbing from the citizenry the fruits of their labors. Moreover, we should not be "hocking" future generations, that is, our children.

The State and Concern for the Poor and Oppressed

The proper function of government is to protect the innocent in society, both from foreign invaders and from persons within the society who would act criminally. This, not the provision of education or social services, is the main purpose for the state. On the other hand, the state may encourage the people toward productive lives. The federal and state governments should be providing mechanisms by which private enterprise can help the poor, rather than seeking to perform such services itself. Lyndon Johnson's "Great Society" has never materialized. In fact, it has become progressively worse.

Solutions do exist. Perhaps the government should provide additional tax benefits to companies so that they can offer child care for the workers who need it. Regulations should be rewritten to encourage grocery stores to give edible food to the poor rather than throw it away. Government programs should emphasize job training rather than "handouts." The gleaning principle in the Old Testament provides a possible model for some of these ideas. Enterprise zones to encourage new businesses in depressed areas would do much to build the inner cities. Voucher systems for social and educational services could also be practiced. Welfare programs should encourage families to take care of their own (1 Tim. 5:8) and, in some cases, make it a violation of the law not to do so, rather than having government do it at taxpayers' expense. Welfare laws should be rewritten so as not to encourage the breakup of families when a husband is not working in a family that is receiving federal assistance. Many possibilities and opportunities exist to promote justice and alleviate suffering within our society, and Christians must be active in such endeavors.

We all desire a just society in which the homeless, hungry, and poor are given sustenance and a new hope. The question is whether the federal government has been able to, or even can, provide such benefits and be seen as the primary catalyst for change. Rather, I believe, these tasks should be returned to the control of the local communities and put back into the hands of churches, charities, and private enterprise as was the case before the Roosevelt era, when, as economist Thomas Sowell argues, almost all charity was done by the private sector with much better results.

BASIC FREEDOMS FOR CHRISTIANS TO PRESERVE

Nations vary in securing for their citizens God-given rights. Jefferson and his corroborators, writing in the Declaration of Independence, declared that God-given rights were self-evident and were to be secured by government. Notice that the rights are not granted or created by government; they are to be protected by the state because they come from God.

Often, we hear someone say that Christians essentially have no rights because they are to surrender their rights for the sake of others. Certainly there is place for the selfless surrender of rights (1 Cor. 8:9–13; 9:1–23; 10:23–11:1). But this idea is not a universal rule (this argument may easily be become a *reductio ad absurdum*) nor is it a virtue when dealing with government (as the following examples will demonstrate). The government, according to Paul in Romans 13, is a divine institution (like the family and the church), intended by God to commend the good works of its citizens and to punish evil works. When it does so, it is functioning as God's servant. Paul's statements cannot be stretched to say that government is God's servant for our good when it commends the evil and punishes the good, although government itself is ordained by God. At that point, it runs afoul of God's will.

When governments have asked for obedience contrary to the will of God, the faithful of God have consistently refused to obey such godless law, for example, as in the command for Hebrew midwives to kill the Hebrew male children (Exod. 1:15–22), or the prohibition of prayer (Dan. 6:6–24), or the demand for worship (Dan. 3:1–30), or the prohibition of the proclamation of the gospel (Acts 4:18–20; 5:27–32). Similarly, when government leaders or agencies seek to infringe on the rights of parents to educate their children in the way of God, for churches to train children in a godly manner by licensing (controlling) day-care centers or Sunday schools, by limiting the pastor in his biblical roles to his people of counseling or preaching, to mention only a few examples, believers should resist (albeit nonviolently) the government.

We see in the life of Paul how a Christian can exert his or her rights before government. The Roman government, unlike most other ancient and even some contemporary governments, was stable and afforded many rights to its citizens. As a Roman citizen, Paul could not be whipped or imprisoned without due process of law. When the apostle was in Jerusalem, he confronted the Roman soldier who was about to use the whip on him, stating that such treatment was a violation of his rights as a Roman citizen. When Paul was in Philippi, he and Silas were sent to jail without a hearing of charges. Upon their release the next morning, they made known manifestly that their due process rights under Roman law had been violated, and they would not leave the jail until the civil magistrates came to the prison to lead them out.

Under the U.S. Constitution, citizens are entitled to basic God-given rights, which rights are provided in the Constitution, by the limited nature of the government, and in the Bill of Rights, which are addressed against the state. The First Amendment secures the rights of religion, speech, press, association, and redress of grievances. Other amendments protect the citizenry from unlawful and unreasonable intrusions upon their homes, property, and person. Due process is required before any right can be abridged lawfully. The Ninth Amendment asserts that other traditional rights are recognized in our culture that need not be enumerated to be protected. These rights would include marriage, bearing of children, rearing of children, etc. When governmental leaders or government agencies seek to intrude upon these rights, they must be judged in view of the supreme law of the land, the Constitution. Some Christians believe that they should surrender their rights to whatever the government requests. However, the law is the Constitution, not a human official. The Constitution says, WE THE PEOPLE, not THEY THE GOVERNMENT. To obey an unjust law is to uphold injustice and lawlessness and, ultimately, to denigrate law itself. To disobey an unjust law is to honor law itself.

When we look to the next presidential and congressional and legislative elections, we must seek to support the candidates who recognize the preceding rights. A candidate who rejects protection of the unborn is an unworthy candidate. A candidate who seeks to intrude into the home and control parental training is an unworthy candidate. A candidate who desires to force nontraditional/antibiblical rights such as homosexuality is an unworthy candidate. A candidate who does not support the right of children to gather with other children to pray voluntarily in the public schools is an unworthy candidate. A candidate who wants to invade the churches and demand conformity to the latest social perversion is an unworthy candidate.

American Christians have waited much too long in asserting their God-given rights. (Readers who might not be citizens of the United States should seek to implement the principles stated herein.) We have an obligation to assert our rights and to fight for them because we are the government under the Constitution. Not to do so is to abdicate our responsibility as servants of God and, thus, to disobey God. Most of the social ills—such as abortion, hardcore pornography, homosexuality, euthanasia, licensing of Christian ministries, etc.—are making an impact in our society largely because individual and corporate Christians have withdrawn from society and have failed to assert the influence that we legally possess.

A PERSONAL CALL FOR ACTIVISM

More than a quarter century has passed since the tragic decision of *Roe v. Wade*, and we are now in a new century with the decision firmly in place. This situation has caused me to ponder my involvement in this cause over the last twenty years. Sometimes, so little progress seems to have been made that I should resign myself to this evil. Yet, to do so would be to neglect my duties as a Christian to come to the defense of the helpless (Luke 10, the Good Samaritan) and the requirement to seek justice. The teachings of the prophets (Deut. 12:31; 14:29; Ps. 146:9; Isa. 1:17, 23), the spirit of James's teaching (James 1:27), and the teaching (Matt. 25:34–40) and example of our Lord guide us to our ethical duty in this regard.

January 22, the anniversary of the Supreme Court's *Roe v. Wade* decision, would not normally seem like a significant day unless maybe it were my birthday. On this day in previous years, I have taught classes and spoken at pro-life rallies at the city hall. Often in my ponderings, my mind has gone to events in history of which I would have liked to have been a part.

I sometimes think how exciting it would be to experience the many wonderful moments in history: to be with Moses as the Red Sea split asunder with the stretching out of his rod; to stand with Francis Scott Key and see Old Glory still waving after the night's barrage of cannon fire; and to witness a list of other events too many to enumerate but the most important of which would be to see Christ calm the terrible storm with but a single word and to touch Him after His resurrection.

I sometimes think that if I had been present at such moments of truth when Christians have had opportunity to express dignity and courage against tyranny and the denigration of humanity, surely I would have been willing to stand and be counted. Surely I would not have denied our Lord as Peter did. Surely I would rail against the chains of slavery that bound our brothers and sisters in the painfully too recent past. Surely I would have resisted the evil of the camps at Buchenwald and Auschwitz. Yet, good intentions or untried moments are worth little in the hall of heroes.

Sometimes, I might question why God did not put me in those great moments. But in His own wisdom and timing He has placed me here to capture those treasures of events that I have before me every day, moments for me to guard, to cherish, and to use. Moments like today! As the wise man Solomon once said,

> If you falter in times of trouble,
>   how small is your strength!
> Rescue those being led away to death;
>   hold back those staggering toward slaughter.
> If you say, "But we knew nothing about this,"
>   does not he who weighs the heart perceive it?
> Does not he who guards your life know it?
>   Will he not repay each person according to what he has done?
>   —Proverbs 24:10–12

The fight for justice and liberty never brings with it the promise of easy victory.

The life-long struggle by William Wilberforce against slavery in England did not bring him immediate popularity, and victory alluded him in this life, but the results of his efforts were realized soon after his death. We have waited many long years for an end to the "slaughter of the innocents." But we must remember that we have not been called by God to instant success. Instead, we have been summoned to faithful service. Eventually, He will vindicate our actions and will judge abortionists for their evil, just as He will judge all people. Such is not our responsibility; we are called to be faithful.

But until then, let us see this as our moment, our time to express courage, our time to show faithfulness in the midst of tribulation. And let us pray that God will soon bring this national tragedy to an end. Believers are commanded to be the salt and the light to this world. The political arena in America has never been so tasteless and dark as we see it today. It is time to gather the shakers and beacons from the church pantry and do what we are told.

An Overview

In this chapter, Ed Hindson views the history and the premises of both evangelical avoidance of politics and evangelical engagement. He argues that Christians have not only a civic obligation but also a spiritual obligation to participate in the political process and public discourse of our nation. Hindson also contends that one's views of prophecy and eschatology do not give one biblical justification for avoiding the realm of politics or for abstaining from participation in it.

Chapter Eighteen

EVANGELICALS, POLITICS, AND THE DAWN OF THE NEW MILLENNIUM

Ed Hindson

THE CURRENT CONFLICT BETWEEN religion and politics is not merely a political issue. Rather, it is the last wave of the conflict that raged between Christianity and anti-Christianity throughout the last century. The first waves of this conflict were philosophical and then theological. As the philosophies of relativism and secularism began to dominate thinking in the late nineteenth century, they soon influenced theology as well. This influence gave rise to theological liberalism and the eventual ecclesiastical controversies between fundamentalism and modernism in the early twentieth century.[1]

PHILOSOPHICAL FOUNDATIONS OF THE CONTEMPORARY CONFLICT

As the concepts of relativism and secularism gained control of institutionalized religion, they provoked a theological debate that, in turn, led to ecclesiastical power struggles to control the ideology of the mainline denominations. Thus, the argumentation shifted to the issue of ecclesiastical control. When conservatives were unable to prevent liberalism from infiltrating and eventually controlling the theological institutions, they withdrew, forming new denominations and new institutions. This left liberalism entrenched in the mainline institutions. As time passed, succeeding generations of theological students became increasingly secularized so that today one cannot easily distinguish a liberal theological agenda from a secular agenda.

The influence of nearly a century of liberal preaching has now filtered down to the level of the common person in society. Popular literature, television, and movies all tend to reflect this mentality. As the liberal mindset gained a grip on society, it also influenced the political process through legislative and judicial change. Political decisions began to reflect the values of secularism.

This process of the *filtration of ideas* was first brought to the attention of evangelicals by the late Francis Schaeffer.[2] He viewed philosophy as the wellspring from which popular culture derived. As philosophical concepts

277

filter down through the culture, they first affect the elite and eventually become popularized by society in general.

Schaeffer argued that the philosophical concepts of Kant and Hegel gave rise to a whole new way of thinking that resulted in relativism. He suggested that this concept spread geographically from Germany to Holland and Switzerland before it caught on in England and America. As an American living in Switzerland, Schaeffer realized that American culture was moving in the same direction as European culture, although at a slower pace. God was simply being eliminated as a serious intellectual option. Schaeffer also observed that relativism affected the intellectual classes first and was passed on to the workers by the mass media, bypassing the middle class. He observed, "The middle class was not touched by it and often is still not touched by it."[3]

The strength of the evangelical church in America is our greatest deterrent to relativism and secularism. Were it not for the thousands of evangelical churches and schools representing millions of members, secularism would have swept America long ago. Therefore, a great void still exists between Evangelical and liberal churches today. Not only does our theology differ but also our entire response to modernity rests upon totally different philosophical foundations.

What was unique about the twentieth century, however, was the ability of the mass media to translate secular values to every level of society through television, films, books, and magazines. Our inability to think critically and objectively while being entertained—especially by television, movies, or videos—leaves even the Christian community vulnerable to the influence of secularism. We can watch a program that challenges or contradicts the very values that we hold dear and never even realize that those values have been attacked!

POLITICS: CHRISTIANITY'S LAST STAND

The grip of secularism on our society is so tight that its influence is being felt in nearly every area of American life. The secularization of education, morality, and public policy eventually results in the politicization of those beliefs through the legislative and judicial process. The end result will be the legalization of secularism and the disenfranchisement of Judeo-Christianity.

Politics, in the broadest sense of human governance, is the last line of defense for religion in our society. The filtration of secularism is now so nearly complete that it dares to enshrine itself through the political processes. For example, when evolutionists argued for academic freedom to present the theory of evolution in the public schools at the time of the Scopes Trial in 1925, both sides in the debate assumed that creationism would also be allowed to be taught. In fact, that assumption was so widely held that no one seriously questioned it. All that the evolutionists wanted at that time was the opportunity to gain a fair hearing for their position. But in the decades that passed, secularism gained such control of public education that the teaching of creation is now forbidden by law. Creationists do not even have the same fundamental academic freedom for which evolutionists once begged.[4]

A more recent example of the controversy between secularism and religion was the Civil Rights Restoration Act of 1987, popularly known as the Grove City bill. The issue involved the right of Grove City College, an evangelical Presbyterian institution, to dismiss a homosexual staff member for violation of the church school's code of moral conduct. When initial attempts to pass the bill failed, liberal members of Congress attached it to other proposed legislation, and President Reagan vetoed it.

In the controversy that resulted, various religious organizations headed by Jerry Falwell, James Kennedy, Tim LaHaye, and James Dobson pressured Congress to support the President's veto. In reaction, the American Civil Liberties Union (ACLU) and Norman Lear's People for the American Way took out full-page advertisements in major newspapers and lobbied the Congress to override the veto, which they did.

Evangelicals opposed the bill because they believed that it was an attempt by secularists to force non-Christian morality on the Christian community. Ironically, the ads that were run against this evangelical backlash implied just the opposite! Because the bill prevented the use of federal funds by institutions that discriminated against women, minorities, and homosexuals, the secularists actually criticized Christians for trying to use federal funds to finance their intolerance, when that was not the reason for the evangelical reaction at all. They were trying to get the secularists to leave them alone.

One of the peculiarities of a democracy is that it is always in a state of flux. Any particular group can potentially propose new legislation at any time. Therefore, democracies are rarely static; there is nearly always a state of fluidity in the exchange of ideas. Unfortunately, most Christians tend to forget this fact. We think that things will continue as they have always been. As a result, we live in a naive moment of false security in which we have forgotten the whole history of the world.

A PUBLICLY IRRELEVANT FAITH

While acknowledging his personal concerns about the illusion of political power brokering, Charles Colson admits that we have come to a time when many people are advocating a privately engaging but publicly irrelevant faith.[5] He argues that two extreme positions dominate Christian thinking on the issue of religion and politics. On the one hand, he sees a politicized faith that tends to seek political solutions to spiritual problems while neglecting the church's real spiritual mission. On the other hand, Colson observes a privatized faith that "divorces religious and spiritual beliefs from public action."[6]

Colson observes that the political left, including mainline religion, has a "morbid fear of religion encroaching on the secular realm."[7] Evangelicals have an equally morbid fear of secularism encroaching on religious freedoms. This point is exactly where the controversy between religion and secularism lies today. While mainline religion has an innate fear of imposing religious values in a pluralistic society, evangelicals have an innate fear of allowing secularists to impose antireligious values on that society.

Colson criticized former New York Governor Mario Cuomo for a publicly irrelevant position on abortion. Colson noted that the ex-governor was a practicing Roman Catholic who held to his church's belief that abortion is wrong. However, as a public official, Cuomo acknowledged in a speech at the University of Notre Dame in 1984 that he not only could not impose his views on others but also that he was under no obligation to advocate such views. Such a position, Colson says, is "impotent to reverse the tides of secularism."[8]

Where do the extremes of privatization or politicization leave us? Unfortunately, they tend to leave us in confusion. On the one extreme are Christians who believe that we must take over the government to enforce religious values. On the other extreme are Christians who pietistically want to avoid all public or political issues. I believe that the church can have a proper balance between these two extremes. We must become a voice of conscience to our society or forever forfeit any spiritual influence in matters of public policy. The fact that religious, spiritual, and moral issues have become a subject of political debate simply indicates how far secularism has already advanced in our society.

DRAWING A LINE OF DEFENSE

Much of the evangelical involvement in political issues has been little more than drawing a line of defense against the encroachment of secularism. For the most part, evangelicals have not advocated taking rights away from secularists or humanists. Conservatives have merely insisted that secularists not deny their rights to live by the moral values and principles that they believe to be valid. For example, evangelicals are not calling for the elimination of existing rights for anyone; they simply oppose extending those rights to include the imposition of a nonbiblical morality upon the church or church-related institutions.

If we do not draw a line of defense at this point of the debate, we will end up sacrificing everything we believe in the area of public policy. This view does not mean that the church cannot survive in a hostile society. In some cases, as in ancient pagan Rome and modern atheistic communist states, true Christianity has actually flourished. However, in other cases, such as under the sword of Islam, it has been all but eradicated.

Conservative Christians are merely calling the church to awaken to its responsibilities in this new century. We have no excuse for losing our religious freedoms in a democratic society. If such does happen, we will have no one to blame but ourselves. The irrelevance of a privatized pietism is as dangerous to the health of Christianity as is the apathy of a self-indulgent church.

Regardless of whether we like it, we have come to religion's last stand in American culture. The political debate is the final attempt of secularism to prevail over religion in our society. The implications of this debate have eternal consequences. For secularism, all human values must be understood in the present whereas the biblical worldview is eternal. R. C. Sproul rightly observes, "This is precisely where Christianity and secularism collide. This is the point of conflict"[9] Sproul observes that "right now" counts forever in

Christianity. What we do has eternal significance because our existence is related to God Himself.

THE GOSPEL ACCORDING TO POWER

Jesus' preaching of the kingdom of God contradicted every prevailing view of religion and politics of His day. He rejected the asceticism and isolationism of the Essenes. He refused to play the games of political accommodation that characterized the Sadducees and the Pharisees. He totally confounded the Herodians and refused to give cause to the Zealots (see Matt. 22:15–46). He stood alone with a uniquely new message, emphasizing that the kingdom of God was within the hearts of true believers. Thus, they were free from the suppression of political domination or the corruption of political compromise. They were citizens of heaven as well as of earth, and their mission on earth was to make people citizens of the kingdom of God.

Jesus offered the people of His day a whole new way of looking at politics and power. He clearly announced, "My kingdom is not of this world" (John 18:36). Ironically, His own disciples struggled with this issue. At the time of His Ascension, they asked, "Lord, are you at this time going to restore the kingdom to Israel?" (Acts 1:6). He reminded them that He had another priority and that was the preaching of the gospel to the whole world (v. 8). By the end of the book of Acts, we find the apostle Paul "preach[ing] the kingdom of God" free from all political entanglement (see 28:31).

In time, the very government of Rome that had persecuted Jews and Christians alike became "Christian" under Constantine in the fourth century A.D. One would expect that those who had been so severely persecuted that they were driven into the catacombs would have resisted the temptation to misuse power themselves, but they did not. It was not long until the powerless became the powerful and the persecuted became the persecutors.

The whole history of the church reveals that the seduction of power has all too often drawn her off course from her spiritual mission. Wars have been fought, crusades undertaken, inquisitions established, and people burned at the stake because someone capitulated to the illusion that spiritual goals could be accomplished by political means. When the church has seized power in the name of Christ, the very principles of Christ have often been destroyed.

In this same manner, our Lord reminded Pilate, "My kingdom is not of this world" (John 18:36). When Pilate became frustrated in questioning Jesus, he threatened, "Don't you realize I have power either to free you or to crucify you?" Our Lord replied, "You would have no power over me if it were not given to you from above" (John 19:10–11).

The word *power* in this passage translates the Greek word *exousia* (power in the sense of authority). The more familiar word *dunamis* (power in the sense of force or might) is not used in this passage. Therefore, Christ is not threatening Pilate with a display of force; rather, He is reminding him that all human authority is delegated authority whereas the *exousia* of God is absolute and unrestricted. Thus, true power in the world derives from divine authority and not from political force.

WHAT POWER?

The threat of political power being used against them causes most evangelicals to want to influence or control that power. We tend to be monarchists at heart. We think that if "our" person is in control, then all will go well for us. Many of us forget that our very entrance into politics might degenerate into the use of force (*dunamis*) in the form of political coercion rather than in the pursuit of spiritual power (*exousia*). Without spiritual authority, we cannot hope for much change.

We who claim to trust in the sovereignty of God may at some point have to put that trust to the ultimate test of faith. Just because a professing Christian is running for office does not guarantee the success of his endeavor. Nor does it necessarily mean that he or she is the best candidate for the job. An individual may be a sincere believer but an incompetent politician.

The Scriptures also remind us that there are times that God places the worst of people into political power to accomplish His own goals and purposes. In Daniel 4:17 we read, "The Most High is sovereign over the kingdoms of men and gives them to anyone he wishes and sets over them the lowliest [*basest*, KJV] of men." This fact, however, in no way eliminates our personal responsibility for influencing government any more than it did for Daniel.

In fact, Scripture is filled with a wide variety of responses to politics and governance. The judges, for the most part, were miserable failures at human government. Saul lacked the character and skills of leadership. David and Solomon were relatively successful rulers, but each sowed the seeds of future destruction within his own administration. Most of the prophets had strong political opinions about their rulers' personal lives and their administration of justice. Nathan, Elijah, Elisha, Isaiah, and Jeremiah were directly involved in giving advice to political rulers. Daniel, Ezra, Nehemiah, and Esther also served in places of responsibility within hostile pagan governments.

By the time of Christ, people were divided over issues of politics. The pious wanted to avoid all contamination of contact with Rome. The Herodians promoted total involvement, and the Pharisees and Sadducees preferred limited relations to further their own ends. On the extreme, the Zealots wanted to overthrow the government by force and usher in the Messiah with an earthly kingdom.

THE DIVINE ENIGMA

Jesus stood above them all. Like a divine enigma on the landscape of humanity, He seemed to treat the political as mundane. When asked if He would pay the Roman tax, He asked to see the tribute coin. When it was produced, He asked, "Whose is this image and superscription?" (Matt. 22:20 KJV). When He was told that it was Caesar's, He merely responded, "Render therefore unto Caesar the things which are Caesar's; and unto God the things that are God's" (Matt. 22:21 KJV).

Jesus always made clear that the spiritual supersedes the political and that the political derives its authority from the spiritual. No wonder that He who was the embodiment of divine authority confounded His captors, accusers, and even the political governor who sentenced Him to die. "I am innocent of the blood of this just person," Pilate protested, as he attempted to wash his hands of the whole matter (see Matt. 27:24 KJV). But no one has ever believed that excuse; indeed, we should not, for the Bible clearly teaches that we are our brother's keeper and responsible under God for the governance of human affairs.

This is the vital truth to which evangelical Christians must adhere above all else. Might does not necessarily mean that we are right. We have often viewed ourselves as a religious minority holding forth against the dragon of unrestricted secularism. But we dare not blow the opportunity by becoming entangled in the mundane affairs of power politics, forgetting that true power (authority) is from God. He is the ultimate source of authority, and He communicates that authority to us when we determine to please Him.

EMPOWERED TO WITNESS

Much is to be said in favor of political involvement by the Christian community. Politics, simply defined, is the life of the city (*polis*) and the responsibilities of the citizen (*polites*). British evangelical John Stott states that, in its broadest sense, politics is concerned with "the whole of our life in human society." Therefore, it is "the art of living together in community." In a more narrow sense, he also observes, it is the "science of government" whereby the adoption of specific policies are "enshrined in legislation."[10] In this regard, he argues, true Christianity cannot—indeed, it dare not—become isolated from society.

Richard Neuhaus has stated that "religion is the heart of culture, culture is the form of religion, and politics is a function of culture."[11] In this sense, religion and politics are inseparable expressions of human culture. He further argues that the culture-forming enterprise in America can be traced back to the nation's Puritan beginnings. However, evangelical Christians have been largely absent from the process of defining America or setting the moral agenda. But with the abdication of mainline religion from the task of legitimizing the American experiment, Neuhaus believes that the opportunity has passed to the evangelicals.

When Jesus gave to His disciples the Great Commission to evangelize the world, He said, "All authority [Gr., *exousia*] in heaven and on earth has been given to me" (Matt. 28:18). On the basis of that divine authority, He commissions us to be His representatives here on earth. As such, we can neither abdicate the sociopolitical consequences of discipleship, as did the medieval monastics, nor hope to bring about His kingdom on earth by the mere use of political or legal force. Therein lies the tension between religion and politics, and therein must come the solution.

Notice that Jesus said, "All authority . . . has been given to me. Therefore go and make disciples of all nations . . . and surely I will be with you always, to the very end of the age" (Matt. 28:18–20). The power of authority was given *to Him*, not us. We are to take His gospel to the world based on His merits, not our own. In Acts 1:8, Jesus told His disciples, "But you will receive power [Gr., *dunamis*, "force"] when the Holy Spirit comes on you; and you will be my witnesses . . . to the ends of the earth."

Notice the proper place of power in the gospel. First, Jesus Christ alone has the authority to send us into the world, and He promises to be with us until the end of this age. Second, He empowers our witness by the baptism of the Holy Spirit so that we will recognize that whatever power we seem to have in doing His work is not of ourselves but of Him. This is the only transmission of power that can change the course of history, and it is not limited to political institutions, although it can transform every area of society.

WHAT CAN WE DO?

We stand at this great moment of history. Concerned about the unprecedented advance of secularism in our society, we cry out against it. But can we really stop it? Evangelical social involvement has brought many issues to the forefront of the public policy debate. Some progress has been made by groups such as Focus on the Family, the Christian Coalition, and the Liberty Alliance. But little legislative change has been effected that could not be undone by a different administration.

All of this should not surprise us. Believers are citizens of two kingdoms, one heavenly and one earthly. That is why Jesus taught us to pray, "Your will be done on earth as it is in heaven" (Matt. 6:10). As long as we are living on earth, we have a God-given mandate to do all we can to influence this world for the cause of God and Christ. We cannot give up on society merely with the excuse that these are the "last days," so it doesn't matter. We don't know for sure how much time we have left; therefore, we dare not presume on God's timetable.

Jesus told us to evangelize the world until the end of the age (Matt. 28:20). That commission still applies to us until He calls us home. Meanwhile, secular society is rapidly moving farther away from God and may well be beyond the point of no return.

Let me illustrate this tension between our present responsibility and our ultimate inevitability. Ultimately, this world will vanish away, so why should we be concerned about it? That is like saying, "Why paint your house? It will only need painting again." "Why mow your lawn? It will all burn up one day." "Why exercise? You are going to die anyway." Let's take this a step further. "Why vote? Eventually, the Antichrist will rule the world anyway." "Why evangelize? People really don't want to hear it. Besides, eventually they will all be deceived."

The tension between the here-and-now and the hereafter is as old as the church itself. The apostle Paul had to remind the believers of his day not to become alarmed over this very same thing (2 Thess. 2:1). As God's people, we perceive the growing deception of the evil one in our society. Therefore, we must speak out against it. At the same time, however, we realize that the deceiver will eventually win out during the Tribulation. Meanwhile, we cannot fatalistically resign ourselves to failure. Christ Himself has commissioned us to make a difference in this world until He calls us home.

ENDNOTES

1. For a history of this conflict, see Ed Dobson, Ed Hindson, and Jerry Falwell, *The Fundamentalist Phenomenon* (Garden City, N.Y.: Doubleday, 1981), 47–77.
2. Francis Schaeffer, *Escape from Reason* (Chicago: InterVarsity, 1968).
3. Ibid., 43–44.
4. See Richard J. Neuhaus, "Religion: From Privilege to Penalty," *Religion and Society Report* (March 1988): 1–2.
5. Charles Colson, *Kingdoms in Conflict* (Grand Rapids: Zondervan, 1987), 220–23.
6. Ibid., 221.
7. Ibid. He quotes James Wall in the *Christian Century* without a specific reference.
8. Ibid., 222.
9. R. C. Sproul, *Lifeviews* (Old Tappan, N.J.: Revell, 1979), 35.
10. John Stott, *Involvement: Being a Responsible Christian in a Non-Christian Society*, vol. 1 (Old Tappan, N.J.: Revell, 1984), 31.
11. Richard J. Neuhaus, "The Post-Secular Task of the Churches," in *Christianity and Politics*, ed. C. F. Griffith (Washington, D.C.: Ethics and Public Policy Center, 1981), 1–18.

PART 4

INTERNATIONAL PERSPECTIVES
ON POLITICS AND PUBLIC POLICY

An Overview

Religion is increasingly in not only the local and national headlines but also the international headlines. Sadly, much of this news pertains to religious persecution. In this essay, one of the world's leading authorities on religious persecution reports that not only does such persecution continue worldwide but also it is more brutal and more widespread than the Western media have led us to believe. Whether in East Timor, the Balkans, the Middle East, China, Latin America, or the Sudan, people of faith are undergoing persecution because of their faith. The freedom and privileges we often take for granted are ones for which others around the globe continue to be persecuted. Marshall urges Christians to make religious rights prominent among human rights. If we do so, we should also understand and react to world politics more clearly and consistently.

Chapter Nineteen

KEEPING THE FAITH
Religion, Freedom, and International Affairs

Paul Marshall

AT THE END OF 1997, FORMER *New York Times* executive editor A. M. Rosenthal confessed, "I realized that in decades of reporting, writing, or assigning stories on human rights, I rarely touched on one of the most important. Political human rights, legal, civil, and press rights, emphatically often; but the right to worship where and how God or conscience leads, almost never."

The habit of ignoring religious persecution is all too common in the West. On August 22, 1998, for example, seven leaders of underground churches in China released an unprecedented joint statement calling for dialogue with the communist government. The U.S. media virtually ignored the statement, despite the fact that these leaders represent the only nationwide group in China not under government control. Their membership of fifteen million is several times larger than the population of Tibet and hundreds of times larger than the number of China's democracy and human rights activists. But the press just isn't interested in them.

Nor is it interested in religious persecution in Sudan, the largest country in Africa, which still practices crucifixion. After enduring more than forty years of civil war, the predominantly Christian population in southern Sudan is subject to torture, rape, and starvation for its refusal to convert to Islam. Christian children are routinely sold into slavery. Muslims who dare to convert to Christianity are faced with the death penalty.

In the last fifteen years, Sudan's death toll of more than 1.9 million is far greater than that of Rwanda's (800,000), Bosnia's (300,000), and Kosovo's (1,000) *combined*. The United Nations' special rapporteur on Sudan, Gaspar Biro, produced fine official reports documenting the carnage, declaring "abuses are past proving . . . these are the facts." He resigned when his reports were consistently ignored.

Not a week goes by that Freedom House's Center for Religious Freedom does not learn of major stories of religious persecution abroad. Christians are usually the victims, but so are many others, such as Buddhists in Vietnam, Baha'i's in Iran, and Shiite Muslims in Afghanistan. Yet, these stories rarely make headlines or penetrate the consciousness of journalists and foreign political professionals.

SECULAR MYOPIA

One main cause for this ignorance is what I call "secular myopia," that is, "an introverted parochial inability even to see, much less understand, the role of religion in human life." It is a condition that afflicts mainly the "chattering classes," which include diplomats, journalists, political commentators, and policy analysts. As a strategic theorist, Edward Luttwak has observed, the chattering classes are eager to examine economic causes, social differentiations, and political affiliations, but they generally disregard the impact of faith upon the lives of individuals and the lives of nations.

Secular myopia can have painful consequences. Remember how little the United States knew about the Ayatollah Khomeini and his followers in Iran during the late 1970s? Luttwak notes that only one proposal suggested that the Central Intelligence Agency (CIA) examine "the attitudes and activities of the more prominent religious leaders," and that proposal was vetoed as an irrelevant exercise in sociology.

As the Shah's regime was collapsing, U.S. political analysts kept insisting that everything was fine. True to their training, they focused on economic variables, class structure, and the military, and they concluded that because businessmen, the upper classes, and the military supported the Shah, he was safe. Of course, many mullahs (religious teachers and leaders) were arousing Islamic sentiment, but the analysts believed that religious movements drew only on folk memories, were destined to disappear with "modernization," and were irrelevant to the real forces and institutions of political power. Consequently, the United States did not clear its embassy of important documents or staff. When Khomeini seized power, his followers captured both. They used the former to attack American personnel throughout the Middle East and the latter to precipitate a hostage crisis that paralyzed our nation for two years.

According to Luttwak, during the Vietnam War, "every demographic, economic, ethnic, social, and, of course, military aspect of the conflict was subject to detailed scrutiny, but the deep religious cleavages that afflicted South Vietnam were hardly noticed." He added that the "tensions between the dominant Catholic minority [and] a resentful Buddhist majority . . . were largely ignored until Buddhist monks finally had to resort to flaming self-immolations in public squares, precisely to attract the attention of Americans so greatly attentive to everything else in Vietnam that was impeccably secular."

Similar tales can be told of our myopic view of conflicts in Bosnia, Nicaragua, Israel, Lebanon, India, Indonesia, and the Philippines.

MISUNDERSTANDING RELIGION

Religion as Ethnicity

In 1997, when Malaysian Prime Minister Mahathir Mohamed railed against speculators with the outrageous claim, "We are Muslims, and the Jews are not happy to see the Muslims progress," the *Los Angeles Times* described him as "race-obsessed." Perhaps the *Times* took its cue from media descriptions of former Yugoslavia. In this tortured land, the war that is raging between the Muslims, Catholics, and Orthodox Christians is always referred to as "ethnic," and attacks on Bosnian Muslims are always referred to as "ethnic cleansing."

Many such examples of media misunderstanding exist. The *Economist* headlined a 1997 story about attacks on twenty-five churches and a temple in eastern Java that were prompted by a Muslim heresy trial as "Race Riots." A 1998 *New York Times* editorial on rampant violence in Indonesia cited "tensions between Indonesia's Muslim majority and Chinese" as if there were no Chinese Muslims and no non-Muslims except for the Chinese.

Religion as Irrationality

Western opinion makers and policy makers consider themselves the heirs of the "Enlightenment," an eighteenth-century intellectual movement that stressed rationalism and science over faith and other forms of "superstition." To them, all contemporary peoples, events, and issues fall into Enlightenment categories, which are most often political or ideological.

Muslims are identified as "right-wing," even when they advocate leftist economic controls. Hindus who propose to build a temple on the site of the Babri mosque in India and Jews who propose to build a Third Temple on the site of the Dome of the Rock in Jerusalem are also labeled "left-wing" or "right-wing" without any regard to religious context.

When the vocabulary of "left" and "right" has run its tired course, we are left with that old standby *fundamentalist*—a word dredged up from the American past, despite dubious provenance. What *fundamentalist* means when applied to Christians, Buddhists, Hindus, or Muslims is hard to understand. Using the term is a sign of intellectual laziness. If what believers believe does not easily fall into an Enlightenment category, then it is assumed that they must be "irrational." Thus, *fundamentalist* is now merely shorthand for "religious fanatic," someone who is to be categorized rather than heard, observed rather than comprehended, dismissed rather than respected.

Religion as Sublimated Anxiety

When ethnicity and psychology fail to subsume religion, the alternative is to treat it, in quasi-Marxist fashion, as the sublimation of drives that supposedly can be explained by poverty, economic changes, or the stresses of modernity. Of course, these factors do play a role, but, all too often, what we encounter is an *a priori* methodological commitment to treating religion as secondary, as a mildly interesting phenomenon that can be explained but that is never an explanation in and of itself.

So great is this bias that when the *Journal of International Affairs* devoted its 1996 edition to studies of religious influences, it apologized in part for even mentioning faith with the admission, "Religion may seem an unusual topic for an international affairs journal." The editors added that "it is hardly surprising that scholars . . . have, for the most part ignored [religion]."

TAKING RELIGION SERIOUSLY

Religion and War

If we *do* start to take religion seriously in international affairs, then we will learn a great deal about war, democracy, and freedom of all kinds. Religion scholars noted long before political scientist Samuel Huntington's book *The Clash of Civilizations and the Remaking of World Order* [1996] that chronic armed conflict is concentrated on the margins of the traditional religions, especially along the boundaries of the Islamic world. The southern Sahara, the Balkans, the Caucasus, Central Asia, and Southern Asia are where Islam, Christianity, Judaism, Buddhism, and Hinduism intersect. It is also where most wars have broken out in the last fifty years.

These wars are not explicitly religious wars. But because religion shapes cultures, people in these regions have different histories and different views of human life. Regardless of the triggers for conflict, they are living in unstable areas where conflict is likely to occur, in religious fault zones that are also prone to political earthquakes.

Religion and Democracy

Religion also shapes governments. In Eastern Europe, authoritarian governments are finding it easier to hold on in areas where the Orthodox Church, with its long history of association with the state, has had special influence. The new boundaries of Eastern and Western Europe are tending to fall along the old divide between Orthodox and Catholic/Protestant.

Huntington makes a strong case that, in the 1970s and the 1980s, a "third wave of democracy" swept over Portugal, Spain, Eastern Europe, Latin America, and the Philippines in part because of important changes in the dominant nongovernment institution—the Catholic church. (He concludes that changes made after the Second Vatican Council inspired a major movement toward democracy and human rights.)

The role of the church in the fall of communism might not be clear to Western observers afflicted with secular myopia, but it is all too clear to Chinese government officials. As brutal practitioners of communism, they are perversely aware of the power of human spirituality, and so they regard religion with deadly seriousness. In 1992, the Chinese press noted that "the church played an important role in the change" in Eastern Europe and the former Soviet Union and warned, "If China does not want such a scene to be repeated in its land, it must strangle the baby while it is still in the manger."

Underground church or "house church" leaders consistently report that the current government crackdown is due to fears prompted by religious events in the former Soviet bloc. Even Chinese government documents actually implementing the crackdown state that one of their purposes is to prevent "the changes that occurred in the former Soviet Union and Eastern Europe."

Each year, Freedom House conducts a comparative survey of political rights and civil liberties around the world. The 1998–1999 survey found that of the eighty-eight countries rated as "free," seventy-nine "are majority Christian by tradition or belief." Clearly, correlations are not causalities, so this statistic does not imply any direct link between Christianity and democracy (the survey also finds a connection between Hinduism and democracy). However, the existence of such a relationship is significant, not least because it is far greater than material factors such as economic growth, on which theorists and analysts lavish attention.

Politics and the Nature of the Church

One reason for the modern correlation between Christianity and political freedom lies in the nature of the church. From the beginning Christians, although usually loyal citizens, necessarily have an attachment to "another king" and a loyalty to a divine order that is apart from and beyond the political order.

In the Latin churches of the West, the two realms of *sacerdotium* (church) and *regnum (state)* emerged; henceforth, there were two centers of authority in society. As political philosopher George Sabine reminds us, the Christian church became a distinct institution, independent of the state, entitled to shape the spiritual concerns of mankind. This, he adds, "may not unreasonably be described as the most revolutionary event in the history of Western Europe, in respect both to politics and to political thought."

It is not that the church or the state directly advocated religious freedom or any other freedom—they did not, and often inquisitions were defended. But people in both realms always believed that there *should be* boundaries, and they struggled over centuries to define them. This meant that the church, whatever its lust for civil control, had always to acknowledge that there were forms of political power which it could not and should not exercise. And the state, whatever its drive to dominate, had to acknowledge that there were areas of human life that were beyond its reach.

The very existence of the modem church denies that the state is the all-encompassing or ultimate arbiter of human life. Regardless of how the relationship between God and Caesar has been confused, it now at least means that, contra the Romans and modern totalitarians, *Caesar is not God.* This confession, however mute, sticks in the craw of every authoritarian regime and draws an angry and bloody response.

Faith and Freedom

This confession also suggests that people interested in democracy should heed religion. For example, attention to China's courageous prodemocracy activists is certainly deserved, but it must be remembered that their following is quite small. Therefore, more attention should be paid to China's dissident churches, which, at a conservative estimate, number some twenty-five million members (apart from fifteen million members in official churches) and which are growing at a rate of 10–15 percent a year.

In a 1997 cover story, "God Is Back," the *Far East Economic Review* quoted the words of one Beijing official: "If God had the face of a 70–year-old man, we wouldn't care if he was back. But he has the face of millions of 20-year-olds, so we are worried."

Clearly, the rapid growth of the only nationwide movement in China not under government control merits political attention.

RELIGION AND INTERNATIONAL RELATIONS

Apart from some of the horrific situations already described in Sudan, the Balkans, and elsewhere, the following religious trends also merit political reflection.

- The rise of large, militant religious parties such as the Welfare Party in Turkey and the Bharatiya Janata Party (BJP) in India and the growth of radical Islam all over the world.
- The rapid growth of charismatic Protestantisim and Catholicism in Latin America. As Cambridge sociologist David Martin has shown, these indigenous developments represent one of the largest religious changes of the century. They also produce personal reform and provide a major impetus toward entrepreneurial activity.
- The pattern of violence and warfare along the sub-Saharan boundary from Nigeria to Ethiopia. This constitutes a huge Christian/Muslim breach that must be addressed before peace is possible.
- Massive rates of Christian conversions in Korea (now 25 percent of the population), China (a minimum of forty million, up from one million in 1980), Taiwan, and Indonesia.
- Increasing religious tensions in trouble spots such as Nigeria and Indonesia. Widespread religious violence has occurred in the northern and central regions of Nigeria, with thousands of people dying in recent years. All-out religious war could occur. In Indonesia, escalating religious strife preceded and has some separate dynamics from recent anti-Chinese violence: two hundred churches were destroyed in Java alone in a recent fifteen-month period, and most of them were not attended by ethnic Chinese. Such incidents threaten to undermine what has been one of the world's best examples of interreligious toleration and cooperation. In both of these regions, instability and violence possibly will spread far beyond the religious communities themselves.
- The exodus of Christians from the Middle East—some two million in the last five years. Currently some 3 percent of Palestinians are Christians, compared to an estimated 25 percent fifty years ago. Similar mass flight has occurred from Egypt, Syria, Lebanon, Turkey, and Iraq.
- The emergence of the Orthodox Church as a unifying symbol in Russia, the Balkans, and other parts of the former Soviet Union.
- The increasing prominence of religion in the conflicts between India and Pakistan, which now possess nuclear weapons.

I am not making the absurd suggestion that religion—apart from other cultural, ethnic, economic, political, or strategic elements—is the only or the key factor in international affairs. Societies are complex. But I am saying that it is absurd to examine any political order *without* attending to the role of religion. We must deal consistently with religion as an important independent factor. Analyses that ignore religion should be inherently suspect.

THE CENTRALITY OF RELIGIOUS FREEDOM

In the West, hopeful signs of a new awareness of the importance of religion and religious freedom are evident. On October 9, 1998, the U.S. Senate passed the landmark International Religious Freedom Act. The following day, the House did the same. On October 27, President Clinton—a strong opponent of the bill—cut his losses and signed the act, which establishes a commission appointed by Congress and the White House to monitor global religious persecution and recommend responses. This is a small step, but it *is* a step in a vital area where few have trod. It is vital that *we* as concerned citizens take similar steps.

We must support policies, programs, and organizations that promote and defend religious freedom. We must support people such as Pope John Paul II, a man with no military or economic resources who is nonetheless daily aware of the spiritual dynamics of the world and who, for this reason, is perhaps its most important statesman.

We must make religious freedom the core element of "human rights." This issue is not a parochial matter. Historically, it is the first freedom in the growth of human rights, and it is the first freedom in the First Amendment to the U.S. Constitution.

Although all human rights pressures make "geopolitical realists" nervous, religion carries the additional burdens of touching on deeply felt commitments, of facing confused domestic claims about "separation of church and state," and of feeding fears that the United States is an imperial Christian power. But this is no reason to hesitate. Religious rights must be at the forefront of any sound human rights policy; unless we understand this point, our ability to fight for any freedom at all is compromised.

An Overview

Why should Christians be concerned about international politics? A comprehensive Christian worldview requires that we think about politics and public policy on not only local, state, and national levels but also on an international level. Without question, the world has changed dramatically in the last decade with regard to nationalism, order, and globalization. What is less clear is what the outcome of these changes will mean for international relations, the nation-state, and the promotion of biblical perspectives globally. Will the nations move toward fragmentation and chaos or unity and order? This essay demonstrates the challenge of applying the Christian perspective, especially justice, in the complex realm of international relations. Lawrence Adams examines three competing approaches to analysis of the international system: political "realism"; various "world order" and "integration" models; and "international polyarchy," an attractive intermediary paradigm. Polyarchy is a promising framework but lacks sufficient justification to be adopted; it nevertheless offers goals for international politics that promise proximate justice in a post-Cold War international structure. Christian engagement globally is a demanding task, and any hope of effectiveness requires clear thinking about and a willingness to wrestle with difficult issues. "It is," contends Adams, "a sphere for Christian engagement and obedience, not rejection and separation."

Chapter Twenty

FOUNDATIONS FOR POST-COLD WAR INTERNATIONAL JUSTICE
Creation, Polyarchy, and Realism

Lawrence Adams

IN THE YEARS SINCE THE COLLAPSE of the Union of Soviet Socialist Republics and the Soviet bloc, and with it the bipolar "Cold War" international structure, policy makers and scholars alike have striven to describe and classify the new international system. Is the world now politically "multipolar," evolving into a system similar to those of the Great Power eras of the eighteenth and nineteenth centuries? Is it being transformed by economic and cultural "interdependence" into a more orderly system? Is war more or less likely as patterns of interdependence and cooperation are challenged by disintegrative, fragmentary forces pursuing exclusivist goals at the expense of opposing ethnic groups or economic interests? To claim that the old models do not apply, that the good guys and the bad guys are not easily distinguished, and that "everything has changed but our thinking" have become clichés.

In the study of international relations, two dominant approaches have emerged as competing frameworks for analysis. The first approach, known as political "realism," is the traditional school, which assumes a continued game of competitive power politics among states—albeit with new or altered players—in a situation of global anarchy. Henry Kissinger's monumental work *Diplomacy*[1] illustrates the continued power and viability of realism among policy elites. A second general approach includes various "world order" and "integration" models that perceive (or insist upon) emerging patterns of community and assume a restructuring of global politics.

A third option, which some people have labeled "polyarchy," is a variant on the second approach and pays homage to the first approach, offering an attractive alternative model that is being increasingly accepted.[2] It suggests the emergence of multiple forms of political authority that variously compete and cooperate, not fully integrated but constituting a qualitatively different situation from the passing three hundred fifty-year-old system that is dominated by independent, sovereign nation-states. Intergovernmental organizations (IGOs), international nongovernmental organizations (INGOs), multinational corporations, and loose functional "regimes" join states to undertake the management of international concerns. Scholars and policy makers who accept the significance of these developments embrace Michael Walzer's call that new theoretical formulations are needed to examine politics, which is at the same time both more globally integrated and more particularized and locally empowered.[3]

In this essay, I examine the polyarchy hypothesis for its empirical and normative justification. Does it offer an adequate theoretical conception useful for the study and practice of international politics? In normative terms, does it offer a foundation for Christian ethical engagement with the international realm? Above all, can the claims of justice be met in a polyarchical international environment? Therefore, I undertake three tasks in this essay. In Part I, I examine in summary form the competing approaches to international politics, highlighting their merits and deficiencies. In Part II, I examine more closely the polyarchy construct, finding it promising but lacking in sufficient justification to be adopted as a framework for research and policy without reservation. Finally, in Part III, I nevertheless suggest that polyarchy offers a reasonable normative structure for Christian engagement—a set of goals for international politics with which Christians could work for the realization of proximate justice as the search for a post-Cold War structure continues.

This essay is part of a larger attempt to outline an approach to understanding international politics from the basis of the presuppositions of the Christian tradition. It relies on the rich heritage of Christian reflection on the nature of and possibilities for politics in light of the overriding truth of the kingdom of God. These reflections seek no less than to establish a framework for teaching world politics and for the analysis and evaluation of international policy.

I have undertaken this essay to clarify for myself guiding principles for teaching, researching, and making the presentations I am sometimes invited to give on "Christian approaches to foreign policy." The essential question is why Christians should bother at all with international politics? This particular investigation does not seek to cover many of the specific policy questions that arise in the study of international politics. Rather, it asks whether it is possible to sketch a satisfying framework within which to think about it; or, as it is often put, this is paradigm-building. The undertaking also echoes what many people have found as they reflect on the political aspects of life: that the study of politics and international relations is of interest not only in itself but also for its compelling demonstrations of human nature and of relationships of humans both with each other and with the Creator and Redeemer.

REALISM OR WORLD ORDER

Discussions of international relations typically start from a set of assumptions about the modern nation-state and the system of states' interaction, which is the basic structure of international politics. For more than three centuries, since the Peace of Westphalia ending the Thirty Years War and reducing the pan-European scope of the Holy Roman Empire in 1648, "the State" has been the recognized, authoritative, "sovereign" entity that has international standing.

It is understood to be the legitimate actor in international policy. *Statesmen* and diplomats do not represent themselves but act in the interests of particular states. States alone legitimately apply force and wealth for specific ends, and they alone can combine those efforts in alliances or collective arrangements (such as the North Atlantic Treaty Organization [NATO], the United Nations [UN], or the European Union [EU]).

Realism, the dominant school of interpretation in the study of international relations, sees international politics as a "self-help" system, much like the free market, of independent states pursuing their own interests and seeking to maximize benefits to themselves—primarily by maintaining and expanding their power. It is a system in which conflict is the norm, and cooperation occurs only because of a coincidence of interests or the need to join forces to balance the power of expanding states. No permanent conditions of amity or enmity between states exists in this view. Furthermore, the structure of the states system changes historically according to the distribution of power among states, and it is described in terms of power distributions. A system can be multipolar, tripolar, bipolar, or even unipolar.

Proponents of the primary rival to realism hold that the emergence of a more fully developed, transformed international realm can be charted by many factors, all pointing to the increasing internationalization, interdependence, and even integration of some functions of human society, especially economic and political functions. These factors include the following.[4]

- *Economic interdependence:* seen in the proliferation of common markets and regional organizations, such as the European Union, the North American Free Trade Agreement [NAFTA], and the new World Trade Organization emerging under the General Agreement on Tariffs and Trade. Many multinational corporations operate quite free of the shackles of state political power and enable wealth creation to cut across political divisions.
- *Security interdependence:* seen in the multilateral uses of force to respond to outbreaks such as in the Persian Gulf, Somalia, Haiti, and the Balkans. States rarely pursue their security goals autonomously anymore. In international law and in practice, the legitimacy of intervention by force in regional security problems and localized disorders depends upon it being in the form of multinational response sanctioned by mutual agreement.
- Internationalization of *environmental problems and regulation:* seen in recent covenants such as those delineated at the Earth Summit in Rio de Janeiro in 1992.
- Universalization of *human rights:* seen in the Universal Declaration of Human Rights and other international covenants.
- Development of *"international civil society":* seen in nongovernmental, organized means of human endeavor, through international religious organizations, economic enterprises, the arts and many other associations (e.g., Amnesty International, unions, and professional bodies).

Furthermore, transformationalists hold that sovereign states, formerly the predominant international political actors, now share their authority with, and themselves have interests in, globally cooperative arrangements. *The international realm now functions somewhat like a loosely structured political confederation of multiple institutions.* This new system, in infancy before World War II, developed during the Cold War period and has appeared more fully after the systemic revolution of 1989–91.

Simultaneously, the concept of the state itself is undergoing major revision, in part as a result of the collapse of centralized, authoritarian states and in part as a result of the global dispersal of power away from national centers. The venerable concept of "civil society" has been recovered to describe the ongoing development of multiple institutions within states that have come to compete with the state for functional authority. The image of *hierarchy* no longer serves the description of the state, even though many leaders still cling to authoritarian models and interests still abound that demand centralized management. This trend toward *diffusion of power* is most notable in economic policy and in demands for accountability, democratic participation, and access being placed on all governments. Speculations on "the demise of the nation-state," or the fundamental alteration of its nature, abound in political literature[5] and present one of the major questions for political thought in this day.

The broad transformational/interdependence perspective presents a significant challenge to the dominant realist school. Realists describe international relations as a system of *anarchy* analogous to the "state of nature."[6] Thomas Hobbes's phrase" war of all against all" is often used to summarize realist explanations of international relations. The depiction of the international system as anarchy, however, does not necessary imply chaos, but it is used according to its precise definition to convey that no overarching authority runs the world and that power is dispersed to states that are perpetually competitive. States themselves maintain the system by balancing power and by each pursuing its interests in a complex mix of competition and collaboration.

Thus, realists respond to their challengers that states remain the most potent and durable political entities and that power shifts and struggles did not disappear with the Cold War, nor were they created by states. This view is surely the case. The recent conflicts in the Balkans, the Transcaucasus, Rwanda, and elsewhere demonstrate both this continuing feature of human existence and the persistence of the forces of particularity against the demands of universality.[7]

Some contemporary commentators have noted these trends and posed the question as to which is the stronger international force, fragmentation or globalization/integration? Will the world break up into smaller units or merge into larger ones, either regionally or globally?[8] Apparently, the answer is that neither world government nor total "tribalization" constitutes the global future; rather, a more complex framework that considers both patterns is necessary.

POLYARCHY AS ALTERNATIVE MODEL

Because of these conflicting trends and the inadequacy of both realism and its challengers to develop a satisfactory model, some scholars have adopted an alternative model acknowledging change but still attentive to continuing actors and patterns. Both states and the international system are changing significantly. Seyom Brown, one of the major proponents of the polyarchy hypothesis claims,

> The post-Cold War era features a wide diversity of alignments and adversary relationships, formed around a myriad of issues: jurisdictional and territorial, economic, ecological, cultural, and moral. Lacking a dominant axis of cooperation and conflict, yet featuring both regional and functional enclaves of order, some coercively imposed, some voluntaristic, the world polity is more than ever a *polyarchy* in which national states, subnational groups, and transnational special interests and communities are vying for the support and loyalty of individuals, and in which conflicts are prosecuted and resolved primarily on the basis of ad hoc power plays and bargaining among combinations of these groups—combinations that vary from issue to issue.[9]

One way to describe these ostensible changes is to suggest that the state is becoming more like the traditional international system, and the international system is becoming more like the historical state: the state is less hierarchical, and the international system more organized. This is a very fluid situation in which roles and relationships are still sorting out, and which does not lend itself to easy classification. To pose the extreme case for purposes of illustration, were the tendencies within either system to achieve full realization, either the states would be absorbed into a single world state or a primitive, fragmented chaos would result. (See Figure 1.)

Figure 1: Competing Contemporary Trends

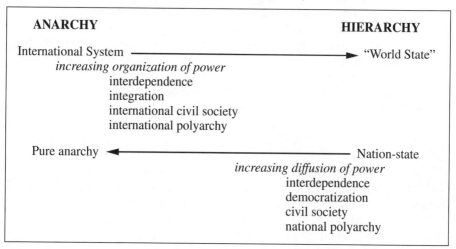

No evidence exists to indicate that either extreme case will result. However, as each field moves toward its own form of *polyarchy*, or *structured pluralism*, it is possible that they will converge in a new form of governance that is global in nature but highly diffused and differentiated. Proponents of this analytical model have labeled this scenario *international polyarchy*.[10] (See Figure 2.)

Figure 2: Possible Synthesis of Trends

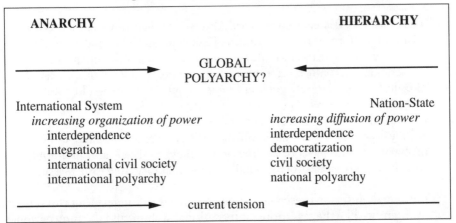

Diversity and Plurality: The Essence of International Polyarchy

In a polyarchic system it is necessary to think in terms of diversity or plurality of components; in other words, the international system is composite, not unitary. Nations and states are real entities, not mere subsets of the international sphere. This is also true of smaller, more organic communities. The traditional Catholic term *subsidiarity* offers a useful depiction of this situation if it describes a pluralistic situation under some overarching principles of law and justice.[11]

The ongoing process of change, described here, means that the emerging international mode of governance is variegated, perhaps more analogous to medieval Europe than to the modern sovereign nation-state period. Multiple actors, institutions, and associations follow an invisible choreography to make up the whole. Sovereignty is shared; "world authority" issues from a variety of settings as the function warrants. International politics is a much more pluralistic, or polyarchic, endeavor. Furthermore, the content of international obligation is expressed in multiple covenants and practices, according to the categories of international functional concern (human rights, trade, security, etc.)

The international polyarchy model has significant implications then for both policy making and analysis if it accurately describes a new system of international politics. It means that foreign policy must account for a multitude of relationships and requires multiple negotiations and maneuvers. The complexities of attempts to deal with the current Balkan war is a case in point, involving more than one international organization (NATO, the UN, the EU, the OSCE), many nongovernmental organizations (relief, religious, and human rights organizations) and fluid policies of other states (Russia, the United States, and European powers are all players).

The model also suggests some positive trends that make it attractive to those who have ethical concerns guided by Christian assumptions. One of the appeals of the model is that it has a place for everything; it is inclusive of all particular concerns and interests. In this model, global politics has simply added a dimension of interdependence to other "thicker," more "organic" realms and offers possibilities for some harmonization among competing realms. Thus, nations and ethnic communities are granted freedom, space, authority, and the right to exist and flourish for a time. Nations and their governments also have obligations to God, who gave them their existence and sustains them, and obligations to other nations that also have legitimate existence. They all are equally under authority and are under judgment and restraint because they all inevitably exhibit patterns of sin and rebellion. Apparently, particular national and community identity are not fading away; indeed, they are perhaps even more significant in this new situation. Perhaps they will function better without the full burdens of statehood as they provide other goods and local expressions of human solidarity in a polyarchic system.

Another aspect of increasing diversity is that world politics is—and should be—diffused and differentiated, not centralized. States share some of this authority, as do international organizations, nonstate associations, religious groups, and other aspects of international civil society. As has already been shown, this "international polyarchy" potentially captures the best features of both anarchy (characteristic of the states system) and hierarchy (characteristic of "the state"). It also indicates that opportunities for international and domestic tyranny alike might be reduced, given the diffusion of power inherent in polyarchy.

Continuing differentiation indicates that the nature of the state is also undergoing revision along with the international realm. States must become less hierarchical and guided less by national self-interest if the international realm is becoming less anarchical. The consequences of the emergence of civil society, both within states and in international civil society, are at work. Thus, a Christian view can accept and applaud the slow movement toward a true global polyarchy as it seems to offer some address to timeless concerns of injustice, war, and deprivation.

Limitations to the International Polyarchy Model

However, we must conclude that the potential situation of global polyarchy is not actually realized and is far from realization. It remains a hypothetical case, as are those of the world state and of pure anarchy. The contemporary situation is one of confusion and dialectic between internationalization and localization, and it is a situation in which the prevalence of states and the anarchic states system are likely to succeed again, as they have for centuries. Authorities and functions overlap, and contending institutions vie for influence; yet, one cannot dismiss the ancient tendency of power to concentrate.

Many problems exist with this approach, and many points must be clarified before a full adoption of the model can be realized. Each objection shows that the model requires further elaboration and testing before a satisfactory resolution can be realized. Primarily, acceptance of the model would require resolution of the following challenges that address the persistence of the problem of power—its necessity and its misuse—in international politics.

1. Proclamation of the emergence of polyarchy might be overreaching in response to meager contemporary evidences of international harmony, closer collaboration, and the expansion of democracy that represent the interested perspective of confirmed internationalists. The world might simply be going through a transitory phase to a new power balance with new hegemonic alliances pursuing competing interests. It is too easy to "jump the gun" in declaring new ages.
2. Many contrary, fragmentary forces are at work, particularly virulent nationalism, and many culture-breaking forces challenge social cohesion. Particularity could overwhelm the integrative tendency. Most national governments are reluctant to give up sovereignty willingly, and pluralism has proven to be chaotic and, at times, violent. Nationalism and inter-ethnic conflict abound, and nuclear proliferation reinforces fragmentation. Some states, such as China and perhaps even the United States, show signs of wanting to achieve regional and even global hegemony.[12]
3. Conversely, the increasing concentration of power internationally might go beyond the limited level indicated by polyarchy to a new state of global tyranny. The development of the global sphere could in time become an extension of unitary power, as in a global empire. Or, more likely, as new technological *means* allow for the extension of influence, the persistent patterns that realists identify are simply being taken into new arenas for the same old ends. The insidious side of globalization, so feared by some Christians, should not be dismissed.
4. The recognition of "world community" (to use St. Thomas's phrase) still has a much thinner basis than thick, immediate "natural community"; thus, it might not have much of a foundation. The recent writings of the communitarian school make a convincing case that humans need community, and that community is an interwoven pattern of relationships, traditions, and habits of the heart. "International polyarchy" and international civil society are much more prosaic than the appeals of blood, soil, tongue, and historical memory. Universal moral standards can seem abstract and disembodied if they are given a burden too great to carry. For most people, international institutions are distant, complex, and experienced only indirectly.

   At the same time, a pluralistic, polyarchic sphere might not provide sufficient ground for the heavy demands of justice. Does not justice, particularly if it is based on appeals to natural law and *jus gentium*, require a distinct and clear *telos* to stand? The purposes of the sphere and its characteristic relationships must be clear. What is owed to the identified entities in a polyarchic system?

In contrast, one might be historically justified to say that previous eras, particularly medieval Christendom and the nineteenth century European balance of power, had a firmer basis for international community because they had a clearer moral consensus and a common worldview. Pluralism, as we experience it, offers little hope of such consensus.

5. The development of international cooperation is not the same as the achievement of "peace"; indeed, conflict continues to be a feature of all fallen realms until the completion of redemption. Polyarchy is not a "world order scheme";[13] it is an attempt to explain new phenomena. Some analysts are subject to the temptation to see in the development of international community the answers to persisting dilemmas of violence and desire. Proclaiming the emergence of international polyarchy might be another case of raising false hopes.

6. The values of a pluralistic system are ill-defined and amorphous. Currently, the concept of cultural contextualization of rights and expectations has great appeal, potentially watering down the development of universal standards and rights. For example, the Bangkok Declaration effort by Islamic and communist states to water down the universal interpretation of human rights through demands for "cultural contextualization" at the 1993 Vienna UN Conference on Human Rights represents powerful political sentiments. This effort has continued with the propagation of an "Asian way" in politics and human rights by many states that are seeking to avoid adherence to the prevailing "Eurocentric" understanding of human rights.[14]

7. Many of the institutions necessary for the realization of international obligations are still quite weak. This situation is especially true of the judicial function, which would challenge the tendency of executive and legislative bodies to abuse power and protect particular interests. Although the standards of international justice might be articulated clearly, the means of realizing them are not yet clear.

8. This approach could be misappropriated for sentimental globalism (for example, "I am a child of the universe," "I am a citizen of Earth," or "Love your Mother"). Such themes seem to be quite appealing to certain segments of the Christian community. Polyarchy, to its credit, rather assumes the hard necessity of governance and the harsh realities of incompatibilities that must be given some structure to avoid total chaos.

POLYARCHY AS A MORAL FOUNDATION

In spite of the limitations in the concept of *international polyarchy*, it points to the possibility that more solid foundations for claims to international morality and justice can be established. Although it is not fully realized, sufficient evidence can be shown to support the potential for something like international polyarchy to become the prevailing international system. And it offers a reasonable set of goals for those who are concerned with change and justice in international affairs—structural objectives to create conditions in which proximate substantive justice could be realized. I suggest that a Christian position toward international change is to encourage the trend toward polyarchy.

To define such goals is not a futile task. If this time in history is indeed a turning point, analogous to other major crossroads in the international system, then such claims have a valid place in the process of international restructuring. Principles and goals have been part of previous periods of creation. The architects of the Concert of Europe in 1815, the Versailles system in 1919, and the post-1945 system created new structures and patterns under the guidance of identifiable principles, along with their experiences and particular interests. I argue that a polyarchic structure is a worthy objective as we contribute to the discussion of international politics in its new phase. To make the complete argument requires the clarification of some normative principles drawn from Christian reflection on politics.

The desirability of a polyarchic system is built on two appeals consonant with the Christian tradition. First, such a system resonates with a creation/redemption-founded ethic, particularly in its indication of ongoing differentiation in creation and the continued work of God in history and in judgment and common grace. Second, such a system aims toward harmonization of the tensions between universality and particularity in that it recognizes an international realm that speaks of global good and checks exclusive interests while it gives room for particular interests within a larger framework. Specifically, it provides a means for restraining states and their pursuit of national interests at the expense of others while providing checks on the excessive accumulation of power in a global tyranny.

The Creation/Redemption Ethic and the International Realm

An expansive view of Creation understands that if the realm of international politics exists as such, it must have its ultimate origin in God; that is, it is embedded in His Creation. It is neither the result of accident, at least not in the senses of this term that indicate either chance development or the by-product of other processes, nor is it artifice, as in simply human invention—for example, the deliberate construction of exploitive structures by a particular class or nation.

This claim appeals to an apologetic/dogmatic rationale: the believer must presume that all that exists is from God. This bedrock premise follows from the prior understanding that God is Creator, which comes with the conversion of knowing and is in part "personal knowledge."[15] God is in control of all that he has made, and is drawing every aspect of creation into the kingdom of Christ through redemption. Elaboration of the argument draws from the following essentials of the Christian tradition.

1. God created all things, not only bringing them into existence but also establishing their essential structure. He declared His Creation good and upholds it by His power and love.
2. As St. Augustine, St. Thomas, Calvin, and Luther understood and as various twentieth-century reformational thinkers believe, Creation is not static, and the unfolding good of Creation is tainted but not obliterated by the Fall.[16]
3. The "cultural mandate" is both descriptive and prescriptive; that is, human society is structurally set upon the task of organizing the Creation and operating within it according to its normative designs.
4. The differentiation or unfolding of Creation can yield new historical relationships, institutions, and patterns. Many Christian scholars have contributed to spelling out the nature of this differentiation and its implications for social pluralism.[17]
5. Furthermore, Christ has been revealed as Lord of all, for whom all things were created. The recognition of His lordship is the vocation of the Christian, who is by definition totally committed to the kingdom of God. Obedience to this Lord means apprehending and serving Him within the entirety of His realm.

"Politics," then, can be identified as a legitimate and intentional aspect of created order. It is the development of ordered means of collective action toward common ends or the common good. The political realm is subject to creational norms and is limited in scope. Such is also true of world politics, the ordered means of international collective action toward common ends.

A creational conceptualization of politics emphasizes that *governance* stands in the same creational order as, and is interactive with, other aspects of Creation such as individual thought and choice, family life, economic activity, religion, and aesthetics. But it is not the same as those aspects, nor is it an extension of those aspects, nor are those aspects extensions of governance. It does have the function of maintaining order among those aspects, and its distinctive end (purpose) is justice: that each of these modes of created human existence receives its due freedom and is rightly related to the others. Governance is subject to judgment according to the norms of its existence, that is according to its purposes and its competence.

Governance also, like all of creation, is under the effects of the Fall: human and cosmic sin and rebellion against the Creator. Its characteristic sin is idolatry of power, and the tendency of those "in power" is to expand it. Government, therefore, can be tyrannical or weak and insufficient. It is incomplete and imperfect until the consummation of all things under Christ. It reflects God's nature in the sense that the human "kingdom" is an aspect of human stewardship of earthly creation, and it discloses the fuller kingdom of God. But human governance cannot "bring in the kingdom" nor accomplish righteousness. Governance must be limited and counterbalanced.

Whereas governance is a permanent creational reality, particular *governments* are not. They are temporal, constantly changing, and limited.

Change is the rule and stability is the exception in political order. Thus, not surprisingly, governance could take new forms that have international dimensions.

Applying these concepts to international relations could mean that new forms of international politics are emerging as Creation continues its differentiation and as humans have acted to develop the institutions necessary to the original creational mandate. Patterns of sin and rebellion are manifested in the international realm, with frightening consequences, as are patterns of pursuit of the good. Although humans have always interacted across cultural and national lines, the institutionalization and regularization of these pursuits gives the international realm its independent identity. A contemporary example of these normative patterns is the emergence of universal standards of human rights. Participation in and encouragement of this further differentiation might also be a means of furthering the possibilities for justice in international relations.

Consequences of the Emergence of Polyarchy: Universality and Particularity

1. Theoretical and Historical Consequences

Development of a polyarchic international system would mean that international affairs is no longer simply a function of national government or an extension of the responsibilities of the state (as most current realist and evangelical treatments of international relations now assume[18]). It would be more than "relations among states" and become more an "international society." Regime theory as developed in recent years, which depicts the development of cooperative "regimes" among states and other bodies for specific purposes, offers some descriptions of rudimentary forms of polyarchy that could be expanded,[19] as do models of international society.

Throughout the modern period of international relations, the effort either to design or to find some foundation for *international society* has been a central part of the study and practice of international politics. One school of interpretation holds that historical development can be explained as the evolution of international society.[20] Cicero's Stoic universal community, Dante's *de Monarchia*, Kant's democratic community, and Rousseau's confederation, were extensive efforts at delineating various constitutions for international society. The continuous Western tradition of international law—propounded by Grotius, Vitoria, Suarez, and Vattel and carried into this century—has sought to establish a normative basis for international interaction. Many other approaches to international institutionalization, such as David Mitrany's functionalism, have been articulated, and some of them, obvious among them the League of Nations and the United Nations, have been tried. In the twentieth century, the primary effort among international "reformers" has been the attempt to find a basis and structure for international society. The tragic triumphs of Napoleon, Hitler, and Stalin were also in their own ways attempts to establish international communities. The impulse to

extend particular human experience to universal dimensions has never been absent.[21]

St. Thomas expressed well this impulse toward universalization: "the community of a province includes the community of a city; and the community of the kingdom includes the community of a province; and the community of the whole world includes the community of a kingdom."[22] Those who reflect upon or act within the reality of international life regularly desire to find the means of binding together that which is separated. If the foundation of such community can be made much "thicker," then these means might be both more legitimate lasting.

2. Institutional Consequences: World Authority

A polyarchic international society would exhibit a particular "authority" manifested in distinct patterns. Provision of this authority would mean simply that the realm would be enabled to do what it is intended to do. The source of this authority is ultimate. Power is unified in God, but He distributes it throughout Creation to enable the accomplishment of the purposes for which entities are created. The instruction of St. Paul that "those authorities that exist have been instituted by God . . . [they are] God's servant for your good" applies in this arena as well. For the international realm, this aspect could be called "world authority." Appropriate mechanisms for the exercise of this authority, both political and nonpolitical, under the limitations of God's sovereignty, ought to be developed and encouraged and monitored. *International civil society* is a label that some people now apply to express the internationalization of various human practices, including social, economic, and political functions, particularly those outside of governmental control.

3. Political Consequences

With the development of polyarchy, one could speak of pursuing the international common good and even of the establishment of an international public square in which the multiple actors meet and interact. The purposes of international authorities, be they states or other entities, would be related to larger purposes than their own interests because they would have to operate in coordination rather than independently. As well, important checks would be placed on the ability of these entities to aggregate power or to pursue ends hostile to others. These tendencies, however, would not disappear altogether.

4. Moral Consequences

If the international system took on a more differentiated form, it, too, would be subject to the claims of the lordship of Christ. Christians would understand the natural obligation of the actors in the international realm to God, who created the realm and enables it to function. The terms of this obligation must be spelled out in clearer detail, but it can be generally described as fulfilling the good for which the realm exists. International public justice could be further defined and understood as giving what is due to those within the system. So morality, to the surprise of many realists, would be seen more clearly to apply to international politics. But the moral nature of the realm must be understood: making the moral claim is not the same as attempting the simple application of "personal morality" to politics, as so many moral-reductionist critics claim.

The articulation of international standards of morality has always been difficult for scholars and political leaders; yet, the question of whether international relations constitutes a moral field always appears in study and practice.[23] Ethics and norms require the existence of some community that upholds common memory, myth, and heritage, in other words, *culture*. Realists, in particular, recognize that nothing so robust has been true at the international level. Thus, since Thucydides realists have demanded that we pay attention to the actual patterns (of interest and power) that dominate rather than to our preferred "moral" hopes. The realist approach dominated international politics in the Cold War period, with analyses of the causes of World War II pointing to the blindness brought by "idealism" and with the realization that the UN global order scheme was doomed by the ideological and power competition of the Cold War. If international society is truly emerging in the post-Cold War period, then some more solid ground for upholding international morality would be found.

Another significant moral consequence of the development of polyarchy would be that "just war criteria," the most commonly understood aspect of Christian reflection on the international realm, although still valid, would become insufficient as the sole moral consideration in international affairs. It forms the core of Christian reflection, but it is based on the foundation of a thinner international community in which only a few rudimentary mutual obligations could be pronounced. Just war theory assumes that nations will engage in peaceful commerce and otherwise leave each other alone unless certain principles are violated. Then, such principles must be defended. A polyarchic international realm would be filled with many more sinews of interconnection, and thus a more robust sense of obligation. Some of the consequent content of international justice, made more firm in a situation of polyarchy, can then be elaborated.

A Foundation for International Justice in International Polyarchy?

A polyarchic international realm requires development of a set of principles and obligations, analogous to a constitution, that gives it some coherence. A polyarchic structure potentially could provide a setting for the realization of proximate or intermediate claims of justice. It offers possibilities within the understanding that we live between the times, that perfect justice is "not yet."

For those informed by revelation, the obligations of the created to the Creator are fundamental. A renewed appreciation of *jus gentium* and *jus naturale* would be warranted if a new level of community is developed to sustain it. It is neither a coincidence nor merely the effects of dominant cultural power that the basis for much of what is recognized as international law is summarized in the principles of the Christian natural law tradition. If these principles follow from the apprehension of the nature of Creation, then they will be true to revelation as well. For example, commitment to human rights, the limited sovereignty of the state, the requirements of justice for the use of force, and universal environmental stewardship are emerging as central principles of international obligation and embodied in international covenants and treaties, although they are not lacking in challenges and setbacks.

What is the content of international obligation or justice in a polyarchic system? Are international actors to obey the Ten Commandments and the Sermon on the Mount? Are they to act in love of their neighbors? How can "natural law" or creational normativity be expressed dynamically and purposefully?

The content of international justice cannot be left with moralism or look to such simple, detached ethical maxims to be complete. It requires a robust development of the obligations of justice, of the nature and limits of the polyarchic authority, and even a sense of collective virtue. The demands of justice in every structure must be applied through the comprehension of prudence by those given the offices of leadership. These demands also must be embodied in actual associations and institutions.

Thus, "world politics," the means of organizing international polyarchy according to international justice, would be guided by the following points:

1. the recognition of the universal nature of humanity, including human dignity and diversity; provision of a universal reference point for human freedom; articulation and promulgation of human rights standards; and monitoring and enforcement of these standards;
2. the establishment of clear purposes in enabling the functional, cultural, religious, and scientific associations that transcend national/local identity to carry out their responsibilities;
3. the obligation to enable provision and distribution of goods through the structures of production and trade;
4. the demand for structures for joint stewardship of global resources, especially water, the atmosphere, and the biosphere;
5. the resolution of conflicts and the enforcement of international standards against unjust uses of force (security); and
6. the provision and enforcement of avenues of participation and access to the centers of authority, that is, democratic enhancement, election monitoring, etc. This aspect must be evident to prevent the unjust concentration of power potential in this new realm.

In general, polyarchy would define justice in part as limitation on centralized power and as serving the international common good cooperatively. World politics is *not*—and should not be—about many things, including managing local services, determining and guiding individual choices, education, and enforcing religious compliance. These tasks are within the proper jurisdiction of other authorities. But the day of the supremacy of the state would be over in a polyarchic system, and the claims of absolute sovereignty by states would no longer stand.

An Objection Considered

If the suggested relationship between the doctrines of sovereign creation and the emergence of international forms of authority is invalid, then it must be the case that the institutions of international relations are artificial constructs designed according to power, utility, or contract. They are sin-driven creations of "this world" doomed for destruction, and they should be subjects of prophetic resistance. This critique does not necessarily invalidate their existence, but it assesses them functionally and requires ethical analysis by casuistry and consequentialism or by a more critical, ideological perspective. Neither polyarchy nor anarchy or hierarchy are essentially better than other structures, none more or less likely to be "just," as no essential purpose for them can be identified.

On this point, many modern ethicists—such as John Rawls, Jeffrey Stout, and Richard Rorty—argue that no foundation is really necessary to ground rights and obligations but that these can be developed through practice and reflection on practice.[24] Others, with whom I am more sympathetic, insist on the necessity of communal and ontological moorings for normative claims.[25] Thus, to give credible moral challenge to these emerging international institutions, one must find a sound reason for their existence and a sense of what they ought to be, which is the point of this essay. Polyarchy offers a reasonable structural goal within which such normative claims could be realized.

CONCLUSION

Major international political developments always elicit theological, ethical, and grand historical reflections. In some circles, they elicit sweeping speculations and even flights of fancy. Witness the apocalyptic pronouncements at the time of the Gulf War, the ecumenical embrace of the United Nations as bringing a millennium of peace in the mid-1940s, the embrace of Stalinism by Christian socialists in the 1930s, and heightened expectations for the age of democracy and "the end of history" in the early 1990s.

That global change is met with extensive reflection is not surprising because it encompasses matters the significance and sweep of which are unmatched on earth. Those who approach the field with Christian assumptions naturally will consider the larger patterns that these changes might reflect. If God is active in history, and if we are to avoid either sweeping generalizations or narrow preoccupations about that activity, careful attention and theological grounding must offer a foundation for discerning it. In the course laid out in this essay, one conclusion about that activity is that it involves both judgment and redemption, both tearing up and preservation. Yet, it is activity with a clear end—the fulfillment of the kingdom of God.

In an understanding of international politics as embedded in the normative differentiation of Creation, the international realm is to be encouraged, embraced, prayed over, and worked within for good. It is also to be viewed critically, as it is subject to corruption and in need of continual reformation according to its normative purposes. It can be an arena of both (great) good and (great) evil. It is a sphere for Christian engagement and obedience, not rejection and separation.

Furthermore, the development of international institutions that fulfill their limited purpose within the boundaries set by justice is a rational and felicitous pursuit. Resistance to those structures that go beyond these bounds is imperative. It is a Christian activity to be involved in international politics. It is necessary for fulfilling the command of Jesus to "go into all the world."

A more tenuous proposition in conclusion: because the story of creation is the story of the summing up of all things in Christ, the gathering of the nations into His kingdom, and the bringing of all things under His feet, is it possible that this time in history indicates the emergence of another "stage" in that cosmic process? This possibility would be no indication of immediacy, for "a thousand years is as one day. . . ." That the greater integration of the world also is subject to sin and death, to the pretensions of the antichrist spirit, as is all Creation, must also be noted. So while the development of the international realm does point to the end of times, to the day of the Lord, and perhaps hastens that day, this age still must be considered "between the times," as is all of human existence as we know it historically. Perhaps the most important contribution of the study of international politics is to set our minds upon that greater hope of the rule of Christ over all of the nations, of which the current age is merely a pale reflection.

ENDNOTES

1. Henry Kissinger, *Diplomacy* (New York: Simon and Schuster, 1994).
2. This awkward term, meaning "many forms of rule," is defined and elaborated more fully later.
3. "I would guess that the interest of political theorists over the next decades will lie, as it were, above and below the level of the nation (and the nation-state). It will lie in transnational formations of different sorts and in civil society." Michael Walzer, "Between Nation and World," *The Economist*, 11 September 1993, 49.
4. See Richard Rosecrance, "A New Concert of Powers," *Foreign Affairs* 71, no. 2 (spring 1992): 64–82.
5. "Goodbye to the Nation State?" *The Economist*, 23 June 1990, 11.; James Rosenau, *Turbulence in World Politics* (Princeton: Princeton University Press, 1990); and John C. Garnett, "States, State-Centric Models, and Interdependence," in *Dilemmas of World Politics: International Issues in a Changing World*, ed. John Baylis and N. J. Rengger (Oxford: Clarendon, 1992).
6. For an excellent overview of the development of international theory as articulated by the seminal twentieth century scholar Martin Wight, see David S. Yost, "Political Philosophy and the Theory of International Relations," *International Affairs* 70, no. 2 (1994): 263–290. See also Paul R. Viotti and Mark V. Kauppi, *International Relations Theory: Realism, Pluralism, Globalism,* 2d ed. (New York: Macmillan, 1993); and Michael Donelan, *Elements of International Political Theory* (Oxford: Clarendon, 1992).
7. The most insightful treatment of this dilemma remains that of Reinhold

Niebuhr, *Children of Light and Children of Darkness* (New York: Charles Scribner's Sons, 1944).

8. John Lewis Gaddis, "Toward the Post-Cold War World," *Foreign Affairs* 70, no. 2 (spring 1991); Joseph S. Nye, "What New World Order?" in *The Future of American Foreign Policy*, ed. Eugene Witkopf, 2d ed. (New York: St. Martins Press, 1994); and Francis Fukuyama, "Against the New Pessimism," *Commentary*, February 1994, 25–29.

9. Seyom Brown, *New Forces, Old Forces and the Future of World Politics* (New York: HarperCollins, 1995), 140.

10. The term *polyarchy*, meaning "many forms of rule," is not a commonly used term, but it is a useful term to describe a simultaneously nonhierarchical and nonanarchical situation. Robert Dahl used it as his preferred label for modern democracy, and an emerging group of international theorists have used it. Robert A. Dahl, *Democracy, Liberty and Equality* (New York: Oxford University Press, 1988). See also Donelan, *Elements of International Political Theory*, 20. Seyom Brown of Brandeis University has been the chief exponent of polyarchy in the study of international politics *(New Forces, Old Forces)*. See also the unpublished paper by Justin Cooper, "International Polyarchy," presented to the Calvin Center Conference on Morality and International Relations, 30 September 1994.

11. See James Skillen and Rockne M. McCarthy, *Political Order and the Plural Structure of Society* (Atlanta: Scholars Press, 1992), for background on terminology. Also, note the modern use of subsidiarity in current Catholic social teaching, led by the 1991 papal encyclical *Centesimus Annus:* "a community of a higher order should not interfere in the internal life of a lower order, depriving the latter of its functions, but rather should support it in case of need and help to coordinate its activity with the activities of the rest of society, always with a view to the common good." *Centesimus Annus* (Quebec: Editions Paulines, 1991), sec. 48, p. 87.

12. Robert D. Kaplan, "The Coming Anarchy," *The Atlantic Monthly* 273, no. 8 (February 1994), 44–76; and John J. Mearshimer, "Why We Will Soon Miss the Cold War," *The Atlantic Monthly* 266, no. 2 (August 1990): 35–50.

13. Stanley Hoffman, "Delusions of World Order," in *At Issue: Politics in the World Arena*, ed. Steven L. Spiegel and David J. Perrin, 7th ed. (New York: St. Martin's, 1994), 13–27.

14. See discussion in Fareed Zakaria, "A Conversation with Lee Kwan Yew," *Foreign Affairs* 73, no. 2 (March–April 1994): 109–126; and Eric Jones, "Asia's Fate: A Response to the Singapore School," *The National Interest*, no. 35 (spring 1994): 18–28.

15. Michael Polanyi, *Personal Knowledge* (London: Routledge and Kegan Paul, 1958). A helpful exposition of this perspective and its application to social analysis can be found in Lesslie Newbigin, *The Gospel in a Pluralist Society* (Grand Rapids: Eerdmans/WCC, 1989). See also Drusilla Scott, *Everyman Revisited: The Common Sense of Michael Polanyi* (Grand Rapids: Eerdmans, 1995).

16. A diverse range of Christian thinkers who differ on much have this point in common. I mention Abraham Kuyper, Herman Dooyeweerd, J. N. Figgis, William Temple, Oliver O'Donovan, John Courtney Murray, Jacques Maritain, Richard J. Neuhaus, George Weigel, and Michael Novak. Skillen and McCarthy, *Political Order and the Plural Structure of Society*, is an excellent source for exemplary selections from some of these thinkers.

17. Richard Mouw and Sander Griffioen, *Pluralism and Horizons* (Grand Rapids:

Eerdmans, 1993), develop the distinctions between descriptive and normative pluralism, each with directional (value and choice), associational, and contextual (racial, ethnic, geographic, etc.) dimensions to depict diversity. See also Joseph Runzo, ed., *Ethics, Religion and the Good Society: New Directions in a Pluralistic World* (Louisville: Westminster/John Knox, 1992), for a variety of contemporary views. See also Skillen and McCarthy, *Political Order and the Plural Structure of Society.*

18. Dean C. Curry, *A World Without Tyranny* (Westchester, Ill.: Crossway, 1990); and Doug Bandow, *Beyond Good Intentions* (Westchester, Ill.: Crossway, 1988). Substantial treatments of Christian ethics also tend to place international matters solely as activities of states. See Ernst Troeltsch, *The Social Teaching of the Christian Churches* (Louisville: Westminster/John Knox, 1992); and Reinhold Niebuhr, *Moral Man and Immoral Society* (New York: Charles Scribner's Sons, 1947).

19. Regime theory has been one of the more important descriptive schemes for the study of international politics and particularly international political economy in the last twenty years with the influence of the works of Joseph Nye, Robert Keohane, and Stephen Krasner. An international regime is considered to be a loosely organized, temporary functional relationship among states. Examples are the "international trade regime" and the "arms control regime." See Donald J. Puchala and Raymond Hopkins, "International Regimes: Lessons from Inductive Analysis," in *The Theoretical Evolution of International Political Economy*, ed. George Crane and Abla Amawi (Oxford: Oxford University Press, 1991), 266–82.

20. Adam Watson, *The Evolution of International Society* (London: Routledge, 1992); Hedley Bull and Adam Watson, *The Expansion of International Society* (Oxford: Oxford University Press, 1984); Hedley Bull, *The Anarchical Society* (London: Macmillan, 1977); and Martin Wight, *Systems of States* (Leicester, U.K.: Leicester University Press, 1977).

21. Mark Kauppi and Paul Viotti, *The Global Philosophers: World Politics in Western Political Thought* (New York: Lexington, 1992), provide excerpts and descriptive commentary on the historical development of international political thought.

22. St. Thomas Aquinas, *Commentary on the Sentences of Peter Lombard*, book 4, distinction 24, question 3.

23. See George Kennan, "Morality and Foreign Policy," *Foreign Affairs* 64, no. 2 (winter 1985–86): 205–218; and Reinhold Niebuhr, *Children of Light and Children of Darkness* (New York: Charles Scribner's Sons, 1944), for significant examples of the dilemmas posed by the postwar generation in relating moral standards to international policy. Excellent recent treatment of the problem can be found in essays by Alberto Coll, James Finn, and George Weigel in Michael Cromartie, ed., *Might and Right After the Cold War: Can Foreign Policy be Moral?* (Washington, D.C.: Ethics and Public Policy Center, 1993). This work includes excerpts on the concept of moral prudence from Aristotle and Aquinas. See also George Weigel, *Idealism Without Illusions* (Grand Rapids: Eerdmans, 1994), for a well-argued example of a Christian response to changing global circumstances.

24. See Richard Rorty, "Human Rights, Rationality, and Sentimentality," *Yale Review* 80, no. 1 (winter 1994): 1–20; John Rawls, *A Theory of Justice* (Cambridge, Mass.: Harvard University Press, 1971); and Jeffrey Stout, *Ethics After Babel: The Languages of Morals and Their Discontents* (Boston: Beacon, 1988).

25. Alisdair MacIntyre, *After Virtue*, 2d ed. (Notre Dame: University of Notre Dame Press, 1984). See also, among others, the work of Josef Pieper, George P. Grant, Charles Taylor, Michael Sandel, Os Guiness, and Jean Bethke Elshtain.

An Overview

The ramifications of politics and public policy are many and far-reaching. The Prussian military theorist Carl von Clausewitz is well known for his dictum that "war is nothing but the continuation of policy with other means." Tragically, religion is often more of a catalyst for war than for peace. In this essay, Timothy J. Demy surveys the role of religion in contemporary conflict around the world. He argues that religion can easily become a sociological force in warfare that is too often used and abused by both supporters and detractors of religion. An understanding of the role of religion in international affairs and in the events that ensue when peace is absent can enhance the Christian worldview and give an appreciation of global trends. Although we Christians must always distinguish between that which is biblical and that which is religious but unbiblical, it is important that we also have an understanding of and appreciation for the sociological dynamics of religion and the role that it plays in national and international affairs.

Chapter Twenty-One

HOLY HATRED
The Return of Religious Nationalism
and Future Global Conflict

Timothy J. Demy

For God doth know how many now in health
Shall drop their blood in approbation
Of what your reverence shall incite us to.
Therefore take heed how you impawn our person,
How you awake our sleeping sword of war.
—Henry V to the Archbishop of Canterbury
Henry V (Act 1, Scene II)
William Shakespeare

"GOD IS GREAT! DEATH TO AMERICA!" Such was the chant and rallying cry in a recent clash between Palestinians and Israeli authorities in the highly volatile West Bank. What do we see in these words and in this incident? Palestinians in Israel, probably Muslims, engaged in conflict, embracing religion, demonstrating for the creation of a new nation-state, and condemning the world's remaining superpower because of its alliance with Israel—in short, religion, conflict, nationalism, and international relations.

In his acclaimed and controversial work, *The Clash of Civilizations and the Remaking of World Order*, former National Security Council advisor Samuel Huntington asserted, "In the modern world, religion is a central, perhaps the central, force that motivates and mobilizes people."[1] Similarly, Thomas L. Friedman noted, "In the post-cold war world, the combustible cocktail of weapons proliferation, religious extremism, rogue states and free markets is becoming the biggest threat to U.S. interests."[2] Regardless of whether one agrees completely with these statements, they are certainly worthy of pause and reflection. Religion might not be the cause of every future international incident or revolution, but it will be the cause of some of them. Indeed, sociologist Peter Berger has warned, "Those who neglect religion in their analyses of contemporary affairs do so at great peril."[3]

THE DARK AND BLOODY CROSSROADS

In the early Middle Ages, the Christian theologian Tertullian raised the question, "What has Athens to do with Jerusalem?" The relationship between the temporal and the eternal, the political and the religious has been a recurring dilemma in Western thought. Although Tertullian's remark might appear at first glimpse to be simply a theological, philosophical, or academic question, it is one that is worth the time and thought of strategic thinkers and policy makers, not because they might believe it to be valid but because many others in the world believe it to be valid and act upon that belief.

For those in the increasingly secularized West, it might seem antiquated to link religion, politics, and force. However, for much of the world, it is a growing trend and a daily reality. Sociologist Mark Juergensmeyer observes, "It has become increasingly clear that religious nationalists are more than just religious fanatics; they are political activists seriously attempting to reformulate the modern language of politics and provide a new basis for the nation-state."[4]

In a cultural climate in which many U.S. citizens and social forces are doing all they can to separate religion and the state, they would do well to remember that such a dichotomy and worldview is not the cultural norm for much, perhaps the majority, of the world. In fact, just the opposite is true. A "mental map" of the globe, for many, includes a strong religious element that readily mixes religious enthusiasm and political fervor. Douglas Johnston writes of the American politico-religious myopia that

> the rigorous separation of church and state in the United States has desensitized many citizens to the fact that much of the rest of the world does not operate on a similar basis. Foreign policy practitioners in the United States, for example, are often inadequately equipped to deal with situations involving other nation-states where the imperatives of religious doctrine blend intimately with those of politics and economics. At times, this has led to uninformed policy choices, particularly in our dealings with countries of the Middle East. . . . Because of the degree to which we as Americans separate our spiritual lives from our public lives, we face a certain difficulty in comprehending the depths to which religious and political considerations interact in shaping the perceptions and motivations of individuals from other societies.[5]

The religious impulse of which Johnston speaks can be both a force for peace and a force for war. This essay addressed the latter of these two forces.[6] More specifically, we will address what Gertrude Himmelfarb has called "the dark and bloody crossroads where nationalism and religion meet."[7]

What has occurred at this crossroads in recent years? Among the more prominent incidents, we have witnessed the bombings of embassies in Africa, the bombing of the World Trade Center in New York by Muslim nationalists, the destruction of India's Ayodhya mosque by Hindu nationalists, the Sikh revolution in Punjab, the quelling of the incipient Muslim government in Tajikistan, the rise of the Taliban in Afghanistan, the violent reactions of Muslim and Jewish extremists to the Israeli-Palestine Liberation Organization accords, Muslim aggression against Christians in the Sudan, secular and Muslim political clashes in Algeria, the ongoing conflict between predominately Muslim Pakistan and Hindu India (both now nuclear powers), the conflict in Chechnya between the Russian military and largely Muslim nationalist rebel forces, and the continued political strife in the former Yugoslavia that appeals to ethnic, nationalist, and religious heritage.[8] These are not the only examples, and they are not all East-West clashes. But what underlies all of them is the volatile mixing of religion and politics, faith and force.

BACK TO THE FUTURE?

In 1977, British scholar Hedley Bull argued that a model of the future might look more like the past than something new. Recognizing the potential rise of "a new medievalism," he wrote,

> It might . . . seem fanciful to contemplate a return to the medieval model, but it is not fanciful to imagine that there might develop a modern and secular counterpart of it that embodies its central characteristic: a system of overlapping authority and multiple loyalty.[9]

What is this threat of a "new medievalism?" It is the emergence of an international system "in which interstate relations of power are deeply submerged under overlapping supranational, transnational, subnational, and national processes and institutions, and in which individuals identify themselves not just or even primarily with the state, but instead with groups or networks other than states."[10]

Religion might well be one of the key ingredients or the only major ingredient that comprises such a system. What we see in the growth of religious nationalism around the globe might confirm this perspective. To the extent that it does, the contemporary rise of religious nationalism is, in reality, a return to the international environment of three hundred and fifty years ago. It is a return to a pre-Westphalian world in which religious conflict and religious nationalism are prevalent-in one sense, a new medievalism.

As scholars and political leaders attempt to discern future trends and geopolitical realities, there are many models from which to choose. To the extent that thinkers such as Samuel Huntington, Robert Kaplan, and Ralph Peters address religious values and loyalties, policy planners and practitioners would do well to consider their arguments and models.[11] Unfortunately, these writers are often labeled as extreme and therefore readily dismissed. Yet, they are among the few thinkers who consider the political aspects of faith and force in international relations.

Barry Rubin writes the following of the rising role of religion in international affairs:

> For several decades, the prevailing school of thought underlying U.S. foreign policy has assumed that religion would be a declining factor in the life of states and in international affairs. However, experience has shown and projections indicate that the exact opposite is increasingly true. To neglect religious institutions and thinking would be to render incomprehensible some of the key issues and crises in the world today.[12]

Mark Juergensmeyer presents a similar view:

> There has been a religious connection to virtually every other case of public
> violence in recent years. Clearly, the rise of religious nationalism around
> the world has created a threat to global security. By fueling terrorist assaults,
> supporters of religious nationalist movements have toppled political regimes,
> altered the outcomes of elections, strained relations between nations, and
> made the world dangerous for international travel.[13]

One must consider both the long-term and the short-term effects of
religious nationalism. In the short-term are concerns regarding the continued
use of terrorism, as evidenced in both the recent efforts of Osama bin Laden
and the immediate power struggles such as those involving the Taliban in
Afghanistan. Interestingly, one recent correspondent wrote of the "medieval
ethos" of the Taliban's philosophy and practices.[14] Similar struggles are present
in nearby Uzbekistan and the more distant nations of Algeria and the Sudan.[15]

In the long-term, however, religious nationalism must be viewed on a larger
geopolitical scale. On this level, the questions are not solely those of strategic
threat but also those of ideological compatibility. Values have consequences,
and philosophical and religious values can have dramatic political and military
ramifications. The question that must be asked is a variation of "are
democracies more or less likely to go to war with each other?" It is "are
religiously-controlled nations and groups more or less likely to go to war
with each other and with secular states?" Policy-makers, strategists, and
diplomats must understand and evaluate issues of theological exclusivism and
philosophical compatibility. Juergensmeyer astutely observes, "In the long
run the question is whether nations that adopt a religious basis for political
order will be able to coexist peacefully within the family of nations."[16] Are
the values and virtues of secular Western democracy compatible with those
of the various varieties of religious nationalism? How compatible are Athens
and Jerusalem, a democracy and a theocracy?

Just as religion has the power to reduce violence, it also has the power to
produce violence. No major religion eschews violence under all conditions,
and when religious violence is initiated, religion has the capacity to inspire
ultimate commitment.[17] By raising past and present disputes to a spiritual
level, religion can be a significant impediment to achieving peace, as evidenced
in war-torn Lebanon. Because it validates the struggle in which the faithful
are embroiled, religion is often a deterrent to peace.

> Religion is a powerful force in tribal warfare, and it can reinforce ethnicity
> in making a conflict more intractable and cruel. Like ethnicity, religion is
> not a simple guide to a tribal conflict. Muslims have fought Muslims, and
> Christians have fought Christians. In Lebanon they formed cross-religion
> alliances: the Christian Franjiyahs aligned with the Muslim Syrians against
> their co-religionists.[18]

White had also noted the following.

In a political-geographic microclimate like those in Lebanon, Somalia, or Kurdistan, understanding is elusive. Shifting patterns of family, tribal, religious, economic, and military relations overlaid on specific geography produce a complex, dynamic, and uncertain analytic environment—one likely to make intelligence analysts cautious and policymakers and commanders uncomfortable and vulnerable.[19]

Failure to address or understand the religious dimensions of international relations and warfare can be disastrous. Because the religious rivalries are often centuries old and flow from deep religious conviction, they can make achieving an effective peace particularly challenging. Thus, David C. Rapoport observes,

All major religions have enormous potentialities for creating and directing violence, which is why wars of religion are exceedingly ferocious and difficult to resolve. When a religious justification is offered for a cause which might otherwise be justified in political or economic terms, the struggle is intensified and complicated enormously. There are many reasons why this happens, perhaps the most important being that religious conflict involves fundamental values and self-definition; and struggles involving questions of identity, notoriously, are the most difficult to compromise because they release our greatest passions.[20]

Religion can exacerbate warfare just as easily as it can ameliorate it.

COSMIC WARFARE IN EARTHEN VESSELS

A difference exists between wars justified by religion and religious wars. It is one thing when the moral sanction of religion is brought to bear on such worldly and non-spiritual matters as political struggles. It is quite another thing when the struggles themselves are seen primarily as religious events in which a spiritual struggle is occurring on social and political planes. In the latter case, reason and logic might not be adhered to; therefore, planners and strategists must consider unorthodox as well as rational courses of action of potential adversaries. Once a cause is elevated to the level of a spiritual struggle, a new logic and perspective prevails.[21]

The logic of religious violence, whether in a crusade or a terrorist act, raises the conflict or incident to a cosmic struggle played out in history. Acts of violence become infused with cosmic significance and are performed with the same commitment as participation in a religious rite or sacrament. The religious sanction of violence creates a strong motive, whether it be just war or *jihad*, that is unlikely to be thwarted by secular reasoning. In such cases, appeals to logic, public opinion, humanitarianism, or international outrage are likely to have little, if any, consequence. In short, spiritual battle is being enacted on a physical battlefield.[22] In such cases, spiritual warfare will likely lead to human bloodshed.

First, the blending of nationalism and religion is significant because it entails a conscious rejection of both secular democracy and socialism. All political perspectives and frameworks other than the divine are abandoned. Second, mixing nationalism and religion creates a new social force with extremely powerful political and psychological potentials. Religion and nationalism are two forces that have historically been able to give moral sanction to martyrdom and violence.[23] Separately, either of these two forces is capable of gaining fatal allegiance. When they are combined, one wonders if there might not be an exponential effect that creates a powerful new force. Additionally, in any culture the appeal of religion and religious violence to those who are marginalized can result in a sense of empowerment that was previously unknown. In such cases, religious violence becomes a justification for attempts at achieving both social equilibrium or social dominance and spiritual victory. In the struggle is the quest for both religious and social advancement, with each fanning the flames of the other.

A GLOBAL CULTURE WAR?

Religious nationalism is not confined to any particular religion, although we are probably most aware of its manifestations in Islam and its effects throughout the Middle East. In the United States, the rise of the militant aberrations of the "Religious Right" since the late 1970s and other elements within conservative Protestantism provide proof that this view is not simply an idea emanating from the Middle East. It is, in fact, a global phenomenon that cuts across most religions.[24] Thus, we find clashes between Hindu and Buddhist nationalism and extremism in Sri Lanka and Kashmir; Sikh separatism and Hindu nationalism in India; Islamic fundamentalism and nationalism in countries such as Algeria, Afghanistan, Iran, and Indonesia; Buddhist monks and secular socialists Myanmar; Christian liberation theology in Central and South America; and the rise of aberrant Christian militants in the United States, to mention but a few. And, of course, Israel and Ireland are not to be overlooked. Like Baskin-Robbins ice cream, religious nationalists are a diverse lot that come "in 31 flavors." They are Hindu and Christian, democratic and socialist, pacifist and violent, high-tech and low-tech, terrorists and "prayer warriors." Their theologies are diverse, but the political and sociological visions they have often see a common enemy in either the secular state or the state of a religious opponent. "What they have in common is what they oppose."[25] The manifestations of religious nationalism are many, but the opposition to a nonreligious or other-religious enemy is shared.

"THE GREAT SATAN" (AND HIS RELATIVES)

The single thread that runs through the various forms of religious nationalism is a belief in the moral decline of culture as a result of secular forces or religious views others. In some instances the aversion to secularism is based on a perception that the values of secularism are responsible for the difficulties of the culture, society, and nation of the religious adherent. All social, moral, and ethical decline is viewed as stemming from the influx and influence of secularism. In other cases, especially in formerly colonized countries, unfulfilled expectations of social and economic prosperity, which were anticipated on the basis of secular values, lead to an overthrow of those values and replacement with religious ideology. This view is often the perspective of religious nationalists in South Asia.[26]

In the former instance, secularism is perceived as a threat, whereas in the latter instance, it is seen as a failure. And in both instances, the religion may be the same. Such is the case of the Muslim Brotherhood in Egypt, where secularism failed, and Shi'ite politics in contemporary Iran, where secularism is a threat.[27] In cases where Marxism and the influence of the former Soviet Union prevailed, the demise of those political structures and ideologies has set the stage for confrontations of allegiance between secular and religious nationalists. In areas such as Central Asia, where Islam was repressed by the Soviet Union, and in Mongolia, where Buddhism was stifled by both China and the Soviet Union, there is today renewal of religious interest that might lead to conflict.[28]

In Central Asia, the issues of religious nationalism deal with the mobilization and unification of religious forces. Will Central Asia replicate the events of Afghanistan, and will it be politically unified by religion? Juergensmeyer writes,

> Thus the issue of religious nationalism in Central Asia is really two issues. One is whether Muslim nationalists within each of the five Central Asian nations have sufficient force to challenge the secular order-the order that is often led by old Communists who have adopted a new, democratic posture. The other is whether the various religious nationalists in the region will be able to come together under a common banner, even if it is a loose federation of states.[29]

To the extent that such forces are mobilized, effective, and unified, observers and potential participants must be aware of the nuances of both religious nationalism as a political phenomenon and the religious beliefs that energize individuals and masses of people.

RELIGIOUS CERTITUDE AND STRATEGIC UNCERTAINTY

As we consider the geopolitical future and the role of religion in international relations, what does the globe look like? In western medieval cartography, it was common practice to place Jerusalem at the center of earth. Such a practice recognized the Judeo-Christian heritage of the West as well as the rise of Islam as a political force, especially in relation to its control of Jerusalem during much of the period of the crusades. In the seven hundred years after the death of Muhammad the Prophet, Islam spread throughout much of the world. Are we to expect the same in the twenty-first century? Are we to expect future cartographers to place Jerusalem (or Mecca) at the center of the maps they create? Or might it be some city in Africa, Afghanistan, Tibet, Central Asia, or Central America? With regard to religious nationalism and models of the future, can there be any certainty?[30]

If we create a spectrum of possibilities and at one end draw a map for religious nationalism in which global domination by one perspective or several perspectives covers the globe, then, at the other end, we should have a world of international political entities or boundaries that are devoid of religious control. It doesn't seem reasonable that either of these will prevail, and historically no such cases exist. We are then left with the middle and the attempt to place religious nationalism somewhere on the spectrum or to determine how much of the globe to paint a specific color (or colors). How shall we decide? Having ruled out "all states (or areas)" and "no states," to which ones shall we look for coloring. Shall we look at models of failing states, pivotal states, clashing civilizations, emerging states, states of anarchy, or historic powers? Will religious nationalism be promulgated in a unipolar, bipolar, multidominated, or chaotic world? Such questions will generate much debate and discussion, but they must be considered. If we grant that religious nationalism will be a reality and a force, then we must ask the questions of where, when, and under what conditions. The next and perhaps most crucial question will be that of compatibility. How compatible will future religious nationalism be with the secular West? And, furthermore, what will (or can) the West do about it? Juergensmeyer notes,

> Increasingly the world is forced to come to terms with the possibility that the ayatollahs, the radical bhikkhus, the Bhindranwales, the Kahanes, and the liberation priests will not quickly fade from the scene. The critical question is whether we can live with what appears to many secular Westerners to be a hostile force, as alien as the communist ideology of the old Cold War.[31]

The benefits of understanding the presence and, potentially, the permanence of religious nationalism can be enormous for those who are concerned with grand strategy. Stanton Burnett, senior adviser at the Center for Strategic and International Studies, writes of the following implications for strategy and statecraft:

> Strategic thinking needs information, analysis, and insight-insight from all of the relevant sources contributing to an understanding of human interaction. It needs the capacity to predict, but prediction about the person or the community that is playing by different rules. . . . an incapacity to see, understand, and make proper use of spiritual/religious factors will involve even higher future costs because of an increase in the number of conflicts and instances of political turmoil in which these phenomena will be an important part of either the problem or the possible solution, usually both. U.S. diplomacy, by consciously widening its vision, can achieve much greater suppleness and effectiveness.[32]

Ralph Peters is a little more blunt in his analysis and predictions:

> We never thought the [religious] fundamentalist problem through. . . .
> Nationalism and fundamentalism are not separate problems. They are
> essentially identical. If their rhetoric differs, their causal impulses do not.
> Their psychological appeal to the masses is identical. Nationalism is simply
> secular fundamentalism. To the extent they differ at all, religious
> fundamentalism may even become the preferable disease from the U.S.
> standpoint. In any case, these are twin enemies. And we are going to have
> to struggle with them, on many fields, for a very long time.[33]

As the twenty-first century comes to a close, strategic planners hopefully will
heed these words, for the threat of conflict that is inherent in religious
diversity is very real.

If present trends continue, the future interaction between religion and
politics is going to be strong around the globe. A generation ago, Hans
Morgenthau observed but dismissed this dynamic:

> The supernatural forces, such as universal religions, humanitarianism,
> cosmopolitanism, and all the other personal ties, institutions, and
> organizations that bind individuals together across national boundaries, are
> infinitely weaker today than the forces that unite people within a particular
> boundary and separate them from the rest of humanity.[34]

In the post-Cold War era, such a statement would not be reasonably made.

In the coming era, religion will continue to be a powerful force in global
politics just as it has been in recent years as evidenced in both widespread
movements as noted throughout this essay and the work of religious leaders
striving for peace such as John Paul II and the Dalai Lama. The degree of
violence and militancy that will be advocated is unknown. Robert Wuthnow,
a well-known and respected sociologist of religion, has observed:

> The relations between religious institutions and their host societies are
> unlikely to be static. That assumption may be more appropriate in some
> societies than others. Certainly, it appears that the position of religion in a
> great many societies has taken new and unexpected turns in recent years.
> The specific turns cannot be predicted beforehand; indeed, to think they
> can is to misunderstand the purpose of social theory. But the factors
> influencing these twists and turns must be examined and interpreted if we
> are to grasp their meaning.[35]

Similarly, Gertrude Himmelfarb writes of today's world:

> These are the paradoxical realities of our time. In an international world,
> nationalism is rife. And in a secular world, religion is alive and well-and
> not only the kind of religion that is denigrated as "fundamentalist," but

the time-honored religions that continue to command intellectual respect as well as pious devotion. There is no point denying these realities, and every reason to admit them, if only to be realistic in trying to meliorate and conciliate them in the interests of a humane, pacific, civil order.[36]

It is incumbent on strategists and planners to heed this advice. Failure to do so, thus neglecting the religious dimension of international relations, could prove disastrous.

In the introduction to a recent issue of *Orbis* devoted to the topic "Religion in World Affairs," editor Walter A. McDougall made the following observation:

> The interplay of religion and politics has been and remains more complicated than conventional wisdom suggests. In some cases, apparent religious conflicts-from early modern times to the Northern Irish and Bosnian strife today-can be interpreted as familiar turf battles in which religious prejudice has played the role of "force multiplier," inspiring greater zeal and sacrifice from the masses. By the same token, the origins and outcomes of apparent political conflicts-from the Crimean and Russo-Japanese wars to the recent war in Afghanistan-were powerfully influenced by religion, with results that astounded the world. It was Napoleon, after all, who recognized that "In war, the moral is to the material as three is to one."[37]

Regardless of whether we like it, McDougall is probably right in both his interpretation of history and his concerns for the future. A generation before Napoleon, another leader, Frederick the Great, observed that "religion becomes a dangerous arm when one knows how to make use of it."[38]

The fact that such military and political leaders as Napoleon and Frederick the Great should speak of the relationship between religion and politics should not surprise us. The blending of the two has been present from at least the days and writings of Plato. The abuse of religion and politics can hinder the proper functioning of the two entities with conflict, chaos, and the death of many being the results. In geopolitical affairs around the globe, the future may indeed look more like the past, for did not another leader, Jesus, ask us, "Or what king, when he sets out to meet another king in battle, will not first sit down and take counsel whether he is strong enough with ten thousand men to encounter the one coming against him with twenty thousand?" (Luke 14:31 NASB).

ENDNOTES

1. Samuel P. Huntington, *The Clash of Civilizations and the Remaking of World Order* (New York: Simon and Schuster, 1996), 21.

2. Thomas L. Friedman, "Missile Myopia," *New York Times*, 20 October 1997, A-25.

3. Peter L. Berger, "The Desecularization of the World: A Global Overview," *in The Desecularization of the World: Resurgent Religion and World Politics,* ed. Peter L. Berger (Washington, D.C.: Ethics and Public Policy Center, 1999), 18.

4. Mark Juergensmeyer, *The New Cold War? Religious Nationalism Confronts the Secular State* (Berkeley, Calif.: Univ. of California Press, 1994), xiii.

5. Douglas Johnston, "Introduction: Beyond Power Politics," in *Religion: The Missing Dimension of Statecraft,* ed. Douglas Johnston and Cynthia Sampson (New York: Oxford Univ. Press, 1993), 5.

6. For more on religion as a force for peace, see R. Scott Appleby, "Religion and Global Affairs: 'Religious Militants for Peace,'" *SAIS Review* 18, no. 2 (summer-fall 1998): 38–44; and Judith A. Mayotte, "Religion and Global Affairs: The Role of Religion in Development," *SAIS Review* 18, no. 2 (summer-fall 1998): 65–69.

7. Gertrude Himmelfarb, *Looking into the Abyss: Untimely Thoughts on Culture and Society* (New York: Vintage Books, 1994), 107.

8. In view of contemporary events in Kosovo, three pertinent works on religion and the Balkans are as follows: Branimir Anzulovic, *Heavenly Serbia: From Myth to Genocide* (New York: New York Univ. Press, 1999); P. H. Liotta and Anna Simons, "Thicker Than Water? Kin, Religion, and Conflict in the Balkans," *Parameters* (winter 1998–99): 11–27; and Warren Zimmerman, "The Demons of Kosovo," *The National Interest* (summer 1998): 3–11.

9. Hedley Bull, *The Anarchical Society: A Study of Order in World Politics* (New York: Columbia Univ. Press, 1977), 254–55, 264–76.

10. Bradley H. Roberts, *World Order in the Post-Post Cold War Era: Beyond the Rogue State Problem?* (Alexandria, Va.: Institute for Defense Analyses, 1996), 5–6. Interestingly, this concept is being considered in other disciplines as well, notably economics. See Stephen J. Korbin, "Back to the Future: Neomedievalism and the Postmodern Digital World Economy," *Journal of International Affairs* 51, no. 2 (spring 1998): 361–86.

11. Samuel P. Huntington's volume, *The Clash of Civilizations and the Remaking of World Order,* and Kaplan's "The Coming Anarchy" and subsequent volume, *The Ends of the Earth,* are well known. Such is not the case with the writings of Ralph Peters, whose works are always guaranteed to be lively and controversial. Especially pertinent to this essay are "Vanity and the Bonfire of the 'isms,'" *Parameters* (autumn 1993): 39–50; and "The New Warrior Class," *Parameters* (summer 1994): 16–26.

12. Barry Rubin, "Religion and International Affairs," in *Religion: The Missing Dimension of Statecraft,* ed. Douglas Johnston and Cynthia Sampson (New York: Oxford University Press, 1994), 33.

13. Mark Juergensmeyer, "Religious Nationalism: A Global Threat?" *Current History* (November 1996): 372.

14. Pamela Constable, "Into the Land of the Taliban," *Washington Post,* 27 September 1998, A-1.

15. In each of the struggles noted, Islam is the dominant religion. This does not mean, however, that there is a unified Islamist perspective on issues of politics and religion. Although there is a common bond and a sense of the umma that is present throughout Islam, the political understanding of Islam has different manifestations. For an overview of Islam, politics (especially the Islamic Renaissance Party), and nationalism in Central Asia, see Pinar Akcali, "Islam as a 'Common Bond' in Central Asia: Islamic Renaissance Party and the Afghan Mujahidin," *Central Asian Survey* 17, no. 2 (1998): 267–84.

16. Juergensmeyer, "Religious Nationalism," 372.
17. David C. Rapoport, "Some General Observations on Religion and Violence," *Terrorism and Political Violence* 3, no. 3 (autumn 1991): 119.
18. Jeffrey B. White, "Some Thoughts on Irregular Warfare," *Studies in Intelligence* 39, no. 5 (1996): 53.
19. Ibid., 52. A similar observation comes from Ralph Peters, "The New Warrior Class," in which he writes as follows: "We also need to struggle against our American tendency to focus on hardware and bean-counting to attack the more difficult and subtle problems posed by human behavior and regional history. For instance, to begin to identify the many fuses under the Caucasus powder keg, you have to understand that Christian Amenians, Muslim (and other) Kurds, and Arabs ally together because of their mutual legacy of hatred toward Turks. The Israelis support Turkic peoples because Arabs support the Christians (and because the Israelis are drawn to Caspian oil). The Iranians see the Armenians as allies against the Turks, but are torn because Azeri Turks are Shi'a Muslims. And the Russians want everybody out who doesn't 'belong.' Many of these alignments surprise U.S. planners and leaders because we don't study the hard stuff. If electronic collection means can't acquire it, we pretend we don't need it—until we find ourselves in downtown Mogadishu with everybody shooting at us" (23–24).
20. David C. Rapoport, "Comparing Militant Fundamentalist Movements," in *Fundamentalisms and the State*, ed. Martin E. Marty and R. Scott Appleby (Chicago: The Univ. of Chicago Press, 1993), 446.
21. On this issue, especially as it relates to terrorism, see Mark Juergensmeyer, *Terror in the Mind of God: The Rise of Global Religious Violence* (Berkeley: Univ. of California Press, 2000).
22. Mark Juergensmeyer, "The Logic of Religious Violence," in Inside Terrorist Organizations, ed. David Rapoport (New York: Columbia Univ. Press, 1988), 185–86, 189–90. This is not to imply that all religious nationalists engage in terrorism or that all terrorists are religious. Rather, it is arguing that religion can push politics, violence, and warfare into a sphere where standard protocols and responses may be irrelevant or of little value. Once a divine mandate is believed to be in effect, then one has incidents and experiences in which the instigators claim divine permission for their acts and the results are cast into a context and environment of terrorism, human rights violations, and genocide. For additional information on religious terrorism, see also Bruce Hoffman, *Holy Terror: The Implications of Terrorism Motivated by a Religious Imperative* (Santa Monica, Calif.: RAND, 1994); and Mark Juergensmeyer, "Terror Mandated by God," *Terrorism and Political Violence* 9, no. 2 (summer 1997): 16–23.
23. Juergensmeyer, *The New Cold War?* 15.
24. The social, political, and theological dimensions of contemporary religious fundamentalism have been addressed in the recent Fundamentalism Project begun at The University of Chicago in the late 1980s and culminating in the massive five-volume *Fundamentalism Project*, edited by Martin E. Marty and R. Scott Appleby and published by The University of Chicago Press. Of particular value to readers of this essay are volumes 3 and 5, *Fundamentalisms Comprehended*, vol. 3 (1993); and *Fundamentalisms and the State: Remaking Polities, Economies, and Militance*, vol. 5 (1995).
25. Juergensmeyer, "Religious Nationalism," 372.
26. See Juergensmeyer, *The New Cold War?* 78–109.

27. Juergensmeyer, "Religious Nationalism," 373. For a detailed analysis of these two cases, see Ann Elizabeth Mayer, "The Fundamentalist Impact on Law, Politics, and the Constitutions in Iran, Pakistan, and the Sudan," in *Fundamentalisms and the State*, 110–51, and Abdel Azim Ramadan, "Fundamentalist Influence in Egypt: The Strategies of the Muslim Brotherhood and the Takfir Groups," in *Fundamentalisms and the State*, 152–83.
28. See Juergensmeyer, *The New Cold War?* 110–50. For an overview of contemporary religious dynamics in China, see Arthur Waldron, "Religious Revivals in Communist China," *Orbis* 42, no. 2 (spring 1998): 32–34. Akcali writes of the sense of "Homo Islamicus" in Central Asia and a common hatred of the Soviet heritage (267–69). Although not all elements of Islam in Central Asia have been antinationalist (favoring the umma instead), antidemocracy, or anti-West, a strong fundamentalist Islamic perspective exists in the Islamic Renaissance Party (IRP). For an overview on the pro- and antidemocracy perspectives in relation to Islam in Central Asia, see Mehrdad Haghayeghi, "Islamic Revival in the Central Asian Republics," *Central Asian Survey* 13, no. 2 (1994): 249–66; and Ahmed Rashid, *The Resurgence of Central Asia: Islam or Nationalism?* (London: Zed Books, 1994).
29. Ibid., 125–26.
30. Hugh Courtney, Jane Kirkland, and Patrick Viguerie, "Strategy Under Uncertainty," *Harvard Business Review* (November–December 1997): 67–79.
31. Juergensmeyer, *The New Cold War?* 194.
32. Stanton Burnett, "Implications for the Foreign Policy Community," *in Religion: The Missing Dimension of Statecraft*, 294. For practical suggestions on how to remedy current shortcomings of insight on religious factors, see Edward Luttwak, "The Missing Dimension," *in Religion: The Missing Dimension of Statecraft*, 9–19.
33. Peters, "Vanity and the Bonfires of the 'isms,'" 40–41. Although he paints with a broad brush and writes with a sharp pen, I think he is generally correct in his interpretation of nationalism and religious fundamentalism. His portrayal of fundamentalism contains some caricature and he misses some of the theological distinctions, but on the whole, it reflects the social dynamics as we read of them today. Strategists will smile at his comment, "To paraphrase [Carl von Clausewitz], the most thoughtful soldier who ever learned to write, 'Nationalism is merely the continuation of fundamentalism by other means'" (50).
34. Hans Morgenthau, *Politics Among Nations* (New York: Knopf, 1950), 312. Quoted in Burnett, "Implications for the Foreign Policy Community," 297–98. Burnett notes that this citation was repeated without change in the editions of 1954, 1967, 1972, and 1985, although other elements of the same chapter were revised (305, n. 25).
35. Robert Wuthnow, "Understanding Religion and Politics," *Dædalus* 120, no. 3 (summer 1991): 18.
36. Himmelfarb, *Looking into the Abyss*, 120–21.
37. Walter A. McDougall, "Introduction," *Orbis* 42, no. 2 (spring 1998): 162.
38. Cited in Charles W. Freeman, ed., *The Diplomat's Dictionary* (Washington, D.C.: National Defense Univ. Press, 1994), 330.

An Overview

Christian social responsibility extends beyond the communities in which we live and transcends national boundaries. If we are truly to have a Christian worldview, then we must have an awareness and appreciation of international relations and the forces that shape global headlines. Throughout history, people of all cultures have experienced consistently the recurring themes of war, social upheaval, and political unrest on both the national and the international. A biblical understanding of these phenomena provides a framework within which to place political endeavors for goals such as justice, security, and human rights. Christianity provides a point of reference for both analysis and action. Christian realism maintains that the effects of the sinful nature of humanity are wide-ranging and touch every area of human existence and creation. These areas include politics, public policy, and international relations. It also affirms that Christianity offers all people principles and a perspective that should be applied in the realms of public discourse and international relations. Christianity is not silent regarding statecraft; rather, it has informed participants throughout the centuries that enduring principles exist that should be remembered and applied.

Chapter Twenty-Two

SOME CHRISTIAN REMINDERS FOR THE STATESMAN

Alberto R. Coll

MORALLY, NO LESS THAN POLITICALLY, international relations is truly a realm of "groping" and of seeing "through a glass darkly." Yet, a Christian view of reality suggests some reminders that can serve as helpful sources of general guidance in the conduct of foreign policy. These reminders are the value of history, the ubiquity of tragedy, and the importance of prudence or practical wisdom in narrowing the ever-present gap between moral goals and sinful human beings and institutions in a broken world.

They are not exclusively Christian reminders because other traditions such as Judaism and Greek philosophy have also contributed to our awareness of them. But in the history of Western civilization Christianity has been an important conveyor of these insights, and in the modern world it stands as a key source of their continuous application to the political world.

HISTORICAL CONSCIOUSNESS

The Christian faith is rooted in historical consciousness and a historical witness spanning millennia. Christians derive their intellectual anchors from the Old and New Testaments, which are the magnificent story of God's relationship with His people, a historical testimony to His judgment and justice and His mercy and grace. The Old and New Testaments are also the story of man's sin and of the depths of evil and irrationality to which man is capable of sinking. Thus, Christianity, in spite of its own idealistic and messianic strains, which often compel Christians to seek to build the kingdom of heaven on earth, cannot but turn its attention to man's repeated political failures and limitations as demonstrated in all of their rich and sad variety by thousands of years of recorded human experience. The Bible complements great masterpieces of secular history—such as Thucydides's *Peloponnesian War*, Polybius's *History*, and Gibbon's *Decline and Fall of the Roman Empire*—in reminding modern society of the chaos of international politics, the pervasiveness of human sin and lust for power, and the wisdom of not trusting the common humanity or the good will of adversaries for one's national defense.

In our own century, Christian philosophers and historians such as Nikolai Berdyaev, Christopher Dawson, and Herbert Butterfield have underlined the character of history as cataclysmic.[1] Man lives closer to the edge of the Abyss, to the border of disintegration and chaos, than he likes to admit. This situation is true of both our personal lives and our communities' corporate lives. Underlying the delicate edifice of civilization are powerful forces of hubris, self-seeking, and moral anarchy, which threaten to erupt at any moment. This, in turn, makes coercion and violence inevitable features of political life in most communities. Violence itself, or the threat of it, is necessary to keep under control the primeval urgings toward chaos stirring beneath even the most refined social structures. Christian writers such as Pascal and Dostoevski have drawn attention to the way in which man's creativity and intense desire to fulfill and experience his own freedom are at the root of his perpetual restlessness.[2] Politically, this restlessness translates itself into dissatisfaction with existing boundaries to one's individual power or that of one's community. It also expresses itself in the quest to explore continuously one's potentialities and give free rein to what Kenneth Thompson has called "the vitalities of life." As Professor Thompson explains,

> Greek tragedy, compared with Greek philosophy, finds that human life in its effort to be creative is also destructive. Despite the counsel of Greek philosophers calling for restraint and moderation, Greek tragedy tends to confirm Friedrich Nietzsche's observation: "Every doer loves his deed more than it deserves to be loved." Thus there is no resolution, or at most a tragic resolution, between the vitalities of life and the principle of measure; the various vitalities in life remain permanently in conflict not only with Zeus but with one another.[3]

Thus, long-term plans for enhanced domestic stability or international peace, no matter how rational or desirable, are fragile at best. The forces of anarchy and self-seeking repeatedly break out in violent struggle against institutional limitations seeking to contain them, and violence (or the authority of law effectively backed by the credible threat of violence) is necessary to push those forces beneath the fabric of everyday social life.

The study of long periods of history suggests that in international relations man is always at the edge of chaos. War, sudden upheaval, and man's inhumanity to man are powerful, recurrent themes. After a lifetime of study, the nineteenth-century Swiss historian Jacob Burckhardt lamented,

> . . . at times, evil reigns long as evil on earth, and not only among Fatimids and Assassins. . . . There are (or at any rate there seem to be) absolutely destructive forces under whose hoofs no grass grows. The essential strength of Asia seems to have been permanently and forever broken by the two periods of Mongol rule. Timur in particular was horribly devastating with his pyramids of skulls and walls of lime, stone, and living men. Confronted with the picture of the destroyer, as he parades his own and his people's self-seeking through the world, it is good to realize the irresistible might with which evil may at times spread over the world. . . . Even old times present a

picture of horror when we imagine the sum of despair and misery which
went to establish the old world empires, for instance. Our deepest
compassion, perhaps, would go out to those individual peoples who must
have succumbed to the kings of Persia, or even to the kings of Assyria and
Media, in their desperate struggle for independence. All the lonely royal
fortresses of individual peoples (Hyrcanians, Bactrians, Sogdanians,
Gedrosians) which Alexander encountered marked the scenes of ghastly last
struggles, of which all knowledge has been lost. Did they fight in vain?[4]

For a glimpse at the cataclysmic character of international relations, one
can look at the Assyrians' lightning wars of conquest against their neighbors,
at the emergence of the Roman Empire and its downfall under hordes of
barbarian invaders, at the suddenness with which the Spanish conquistado-
res overwhelmed the highly advanced civilizations of the Aztecs and the Incas
and in a generation exterminated most of them,[5] and at the millions of Afri-
cans carried away to slavery halfway around the world. In our own century,
one could contemplate the massacre of millions of Armenians by neighbor-
ing Turks: the speed and relative ease with which a frustrated Austrian artist
almost gained dominion over the world, leaving in his path tens of millions
of victims of his fury and ambition; and the narrowness with which the United
States and the Soviet Union escaped from plunging the world into nuclear
war in October 1962. The cataclysmic nature of history suggests that a state
is morally justified in taking extensive precautions to protect itself against
foreign dangers, reduce its vulnerability to would-be aggressors, and generally anticipate the unexpected. A statesman who in the name of universal love
and self-sacrifice downplays the importance of strategy and military power,
thereby reducing his people's "margin of safety," is acting immorally by exposing them to increased levels of international political risk and intimida-
tion from adversaries. The historical record and a historical perspective on
international politics can be helpful in outlining some general limits to the
statesman's benevolence and idealism.

THE TRAGIC CHARACTER OF HUMAN EXISTENCE

A second reminder that the Christian tradition issues to the student and
practitioner of foreign policy concerns the tragic character of human existence
generally and of much of international politics in particular. Human sin seems
to ensure that even the loftiest political endeavors are tainted by self-interest
and that the best-intentioned deeds often produce results that are the opposite
of those that are expected. Moreover, at both the individual and the societal
levels, the peculiar virtues and strengths of a people are also at the root of its
defects and weaknesses. In the United States, for example, the dynamic
individualism and freedom that helped to turn a once-small nation into a great
power are partly responsible today for the breakdown of community and the
moral decay that are throwing in doubt the nation's future preeminence. One
of the key political manifestations of tragedy is the sin of pride—the tendency
of a nation, as it prospers and grows powerful, to imagine that there are few

limits to its capacity to change the rest of the world. The sin of pride, as explicated in traditional biblical doctrine, grows out of precisely the most exalted virtues and abilities. It develops out of beauty, true greatness, and genuine achievement. After all, Satan was the most beautiful of God's angels. The classical Greek counterpart to the Christian notion of sinful pride was hubris, the desire to reach beyond one's limits. Few testimonials to the workings of hubris in international relations are as poignant as Thucydides's *Peloponnesian War*. Hubris is inevitably linked to tragedy. A nation's effort to soar above the gods has a tragic outcome for both its hapless victims and itself. The alienation and corruption brought about by its own success are inevitably followed by defeat and destruction at the hands of another state.

Yet another indication of the tragic character of international politics is the paradoxical relationship of ethics and power. All Christians agree that power should be guided by ethical objectives and that as a nation's power expands so should the scope of its international moral responsibilities. But throughout history, Christians in the tradition of St. Augustine and of political realism have also reminded us that the obverse is equally true: the fulfillment of ethical objectives in international relations requires a degree of power, be it economic, political, or military, and preferably a combination of all of these areas. The more ambitious one's ethical objectives, the more power that is required to achieve them. As Professor Michael Howard notes,

> To concern oneself with ethical values to the total exclusion of any practical activity in the dimension of power is to abdicate responsibility for shaping the course of affairs. To accumulate coercive power without concern for its ethical ends is the course of the gangster, of St. Augustine's robber bands. . . . Obsession with ethical values with no concern for their implementation is ultimately unethical in its lack of *practical* concern for the course taken by society; concern for coercive capability without the legitimization of moral acceptance leads ultimately to impotence, and disaster at the hands of an indignant and alienated world. Thus political action, whether in the international or any other sphere of activity, needs to be *diagonal*. Ethical goals should become more ambitious as political capability increases. The political actor, be he statesman or soldier, needs to grow in moral awareness and responsibility as he grows in power. The moralist must accept that his teaching will not reach beyond the page on which it is written or the lectern from which it is expounded without a massive amount of complex activity by men of affairs operating on the plane of their own expertise. The more ambitious and wide-ranging the ethical goals, the greater the power-mechanisms required to achieve them.[6]

The tragic element in the relationship of ethics and power is as follows. The effort to increase our power so as to fulfill ever higher ethical objectives carries with it the danger that as our power grows our moral and political vision is increasingly corrupted together with our use of that power. The dilemma is inescapable because the alternative is equally tragic. Renunciation or reduction of one's power for the sake of maintaining inner moral purity overlooks the reality of sin and corruption in the midst of weakness, while it leaves oneself dangerously exposed to the ravages of adversaries. While power may tend to corrupt, weakness by itself does not necessarily purify. Today's Greeks are weaker than those of Thucydides's time, but they are not any better for it morally.

The tragic character of international politics implies that the statesman ought not to hold any overly ambitious expectations about the possibility of bringing about God's Kingdom on earth or radically transforming the world as it exists. To quote Kenneth Thompson again,

> Tragedy is distinguished by its realization of the unbridgeable gulf between human aspirations and attainments. Such an awareness points to the necessity to live in an imperfect world with fear and uncertainty. The human drama never reaches a wholly successful conclusion or a single triumphal ending. Its little acts and scenes go on with unending trials and the need for testing, each full of despair as well as momentary exaltation. Learning to live with fear and uncertainty is another facet of the tragic sense.[7]

THE IMPORTANCE OF PRUDENCE

A third reminder of the Christian tradition is the importance of prudence, or practical wisdom, in the conduct of foreign policy. As a process of moral reasoning concerned with accommodating moral goals with the less-than-moral realities of international politics, prudence is used to the contours of a tragic world. While it was Aristotle who gave prudence its classical definition,[8] the notion has strong biblical roots, especially in the books of Proverbs and Ecclesiastics; in Jesus' clear differentiation between the work of the kingdom of God, which He enjoined, and messianic political activism, about which He was curiously indifferent; and in St. Paul's repeated acknowledgments of the special character of the political realm, in which rulers were to guide their policies not by a literalist application of the Sermon on the Mount but through a careful balancing of the demands of justice with the needs of maintaining order in a turbulent world. Others also recognized the political indispensability of prudence, including St. Augustine; the medieval theologians, who considered it one of the Dominical virtues; Luther and Calvin; and the Roman Catholic Church through its inclusion in the just war tradition.[9]

Prudence, or practical wisdom, is a Christian virtue as well as a process of moral reasoning. It is the mediator between morality and politics, the instrument by which moral ideals are approximated in an imperfect world. To use Aristotelian language, pure moral ideals, or "theoretical wisdom," indicate the ends that we should seek in politics. Practical wisdom helps us to balance and choose among competing ideals and suggests means of actually fulfilling them or coming as close to them as possible.

The first question that prudence raises regards the ends that we ought to seek. Must these ends be weighed and balanced against one another? This balancing process might require reducing the ambitious scope of some of our ends. Practical wisdom requires that moral analysis revolves around not one single value but many competing values. As Professor Thompson argues,

> ethical choice involves arbitrating not only between the good and evil but between *rights* and *rights*. Moral principles compete, often clashing and colliding with one another. We want to do what is right—but what is right? Choice involves moral dilemmas that confront men every time they seek to be virtuous. The devoted father seeks to do right for his family and children. . . . Will he choose success in business to the neglect of the solidarity of his family and the ever-present emotional needs of his children? Or will he strive to be a loving father at the price of business advancement? . . . How will the national leader resolve his dilemma of promoting the nation's economic health and general welfare at home while safeguarding its security and helping the poor around the world whose worsening condition can only increase the chances of global conflict? In every sector of personal, national, and international life, dilemmas multiply, expressed in the inevitable tension between freedom and order, justice and power, or security and change.[10]

Such dilemmas are endless in foreign policy.

Once one has decided on the ends to be pursued, prudence raises the question of means. How do we get there? What means are not only effective but also morally appropriate? Prudence also calls for moral reasoning to play a major role in this step. Sometimes, less-than-perfect moral means must be used to accomplish worthwhile moral ends; in some situations, the ends *do* justify the means. Thus, a nation may go to war to prevent enemies from conquering and destroying it, and a politician may cut deals with special-interest groups to save a good piece of legislation. Yet, the means have to be considered very carefully because, beyond a certain point, gross immorality or inhumanity in one's means begins to affect the intrinsic moral growth of one's ends. This is why for the Christian, unlike for the Marxist-Leninist, the proposition that "the ends justify the means" is not absolute. Some means—such as genocide, mass murder of innocents, direct assassination of foreign leaders, and treachery—are so morally repulsive that it is difficult to conceive of ends that would justify them.

Prudence's concern with means is also valuable in another respect. The world's "fallen" condition, the finiteness, and the unpredictability of history often limit the range of means that are effectively available for reaching certain ends, no matter how worthy they might be. To take the goal of complete disarmament as an example, the ambitiousness of one's ends might have to be reduced or trimmed a bit simply because the means are unavailable, insufficient, or have negative side-effects or consequences of their own that we might want to avoid.

Practical wisdom is more concerned with particulars than with universals.[11] Its objective is not so much the knowledge of generalizations, which after all are useful in politics only to a limited degree, as an awareness of particulars and of the complex multiplicity of variables in political life. No man ever knows all of these variables, but the prudent statesman tries to acquaint himself with as many particulars as are relevant to the decision he is pondering. Therefore, experience is an essential requirement of practical wisdom.

Experience gives a person intimate knowledge of the possibilities open to human action. An experienced statesman, such as Winston Churchill when he assumed the office of prime minister in 1939, has seen much of what political reality is capable of throwing on the statesman's lap; therefore, he is less likely to be caught completely unaware by the sudden twists and turnings of the human drama. The experienced statesman will pursue flexible and open-ended policies, eschewing rigidity of mind and action. He will recognize the amorphous texture of politics for what it is and will try to anticipate the un-expected shapes this amorphous mass may take. Long acquaintance with particulars also will give the statesman an intuitive feeling for the situation he faces and the means necessary to cope with it. For Aristotle, as well as for Christian thinkers such as Pascal and Butterfield, intuition is intrinsic to political wisdom and experience the most important contributor to enlight-ened intuition.

Other companions of prudence are deliberation and good sense. One of the marks of prudent men is their ability to deliberate well. According to Aristotle, "excellence in deliberation will be correctness in assessing what is conducive to the end, concerning which practical wisdom gives a true conviction."[12] Deliberation is intrinsic to moral reasoning. Insofar as slogans, ideologies, and Orwellian doublespeak, or for that matter, rigid legal analysis, replace deliberation and tighten their grip on all forms of political reasoning and discourse, moral and political reasoning wither.

Good sense, which Aristotle defined basically as sympathetic understand-ing, plays a broad role in prudence. It has two dimensions. One dimension is the ability to make a "correct judgment of what is fair and equitable." The other dimension is a "sense to forgive" and to put oneself in somebody else's place. "To say that a person has good judgment in matters of practical wis-dom implies . . . . that he has sympathetic understanding; for equitable acts are common to all good men in their relation with someone else."[13] The two dimensions of sympathetic understanding are intimately related. A "correct judgment of what is fair and equitable" requires ultimately putting oneself in somebody else's place; moreover, such a judgment often calls us to for-give. As Butterfield was fond of saying, when one understands the predica-ments facing those with whom one deals, their weaknesses and limitations, it is easier to let bygones be bygones and "forgive."

The fairness and equity to which sympathetic understanding lead are far removed from strict legal demands that the last ounce of flesh be paid and that justice be done even if the heavens fall. As Aristotle and numerous thinkers in the Jewish and Christian traditions have insisted, equity and fairness are a higher and more perfect form of justice than strict legal justice as commonly understood.[14] Equity and fairness adapt the requirements of justice to the weaknesses of human nature and the vagaries and ambiguities of the human condition.

The role of sympathetic understanding in prudence has several politically significant implications. Prudent statesmanship calls for political sympathy and fairness, and one of its most effective arms is diplomacy. At the core of diplomatic theory and practice is the idea, so dear to Christian theorists of diplomacy such as Richelieu and Fenelon, of putting oneself in the position of one's adversaries, allies, or trading partners; only then can one assess correctly what their strengths and weaknesses are and what one's policy toward them must be.[15] Diplomacy also entails the capacity for acting fairly toward others. The most successful practitioners of the art are sometimes those states and individual diplomats whose word is reliable and whose reasonableness and fairness are well-known, providing an incentive for negotiation.[16]

Influenced by Aristotle and by centuries of Christian teaching, Edmund Burke remarked that magnanimity is the essence of political wisdom. Burke was referring not so much to the Aristotelian virtue of high-mindedness, which commentators sometimes translate as magnanimity, but to sympathetic understanding that is accompanied by fairness, equity, and a willingness to forgive. Some of the most durable achievements of diplomacy and statecraft—from the Congress of Vienna in 1815, which kept Europe at peace for a century, to the Marshall Plan, which rescued European civilization from the smoldering ruins of World War II—have exhibited this forgiveness amply.

The practical wisdom of politics needs the illumination of a higher wisdom. Much to the delight of later medieval theologians, Aristotle wrote that "without virtue or excellence this eye of the soul (intelligence) does not acquire the characteristic (of practical wisdom)." Unless virtue is its end, prudence is little more than knavery, shallow cleverness. According to Aristotle, "a man fulfills his proper function only by way of practical wisdom and moral excellence or virtue: virtue makes us aim at the right target, and practical wisdom makes us use the right means." In sum, "it is impossible to be good in the full sense of the word without practical wisdom or to be a man of practical wisdom without moral excellence or virtue."[17] For all of its remarkable independence of means, prudence remains secondary to theoretical wisdom. Prudence "has no authority over theoretical wisdom or the better part of our soul (the rational element that grasps necessary and permanent truths)." Prudence "issues commands" to attain theoretical wisdom and makes the provisions "to secure it," but "it does not issue (commands) to wisdom itself. To say the contrary would be like asserting that politics governs the gods, because it issues commands about everything in the state."[18] In Platonic language, prudence is concerned with a contingent, theoretical wisdom with the eternal.

Thus, prudence should be distinguished from value-free pragmatism. The latter has no normative anchor; it is purely a technical process for getting things done. Prudence, on the other hand, is guided by certain values which it weighs and balances, and although its scope is sufficiently comprehensive to include technical or purely political considerations, it goes beyond these to raise the relevant moral and philosophical issues and incorporate them in the decision-making process.

For the Christian, prudence is not an autonomous decision-making process cut off from revelation. The values or "theoretical wisdom" that define the ends of foreign policy receive their ultimate content from broad Christian principles. And the means counseled by prudence are not wholly open-ended. As was suggested earlier, certain means might carry too high a cost in immorality or inhumanity to be fit for practical wisdom. For the Christian, faith and conscience are inseparable walking companions of prudence. In the rough-and-tumble of international politics, faith in a transcendent normative order might be necessary to sustain the prudent statesman and prevent him from collapsing under the weight of despair and the pressures of Machiavellian cynicism and ruthlessness. The thoughtful statesman might also discover that the perplexities of international relations are less likely to drive him into either moral impotence or nihilism if at every step along the road of prudential calculus he lives in that awareness of utter dependence on the Living God that the Bible calls faith. Reinhold Niebuhr had this in mind when he wrote that faith in God's forgiveness makes possible the risk of action. Finally, conscience plays a key role by continually reminding the prudent statesman of the ends he should pursue and of those means which, no matter how tempting they might be, he should avoid.

GENERAL COUNSELS ABOUT THE
CONDUCT OF FOREIGN POLICY

Although it is difficult to derive specific foreign policy prescriptions from Christianity, it is possible to suggest a series of general counsels about the conduct of foreign policy that can be useful to the statesman, not so much as rules but as perspectives to keep in the back of his mind and to integrate into his decision-making process. Some of these counsels are in creative tension with one another.

1. The statesman should never lose sight of the cataclysmic nature of history and of the inherent chaos, unpredictability, and dynamism of many of the forces underlying international politics. A strong defense, military preparedness, and the willingness to use force are the prerequisites for not only survival but also effective negotiation and diplomatic accommodation. This point is, of course, one of the core principles of that tradition known as Christian realism.
2. The statesman also should be aware, however, of the dangers of militarism and the struggle for power becoming ends in themselves rather than remaining what they are supposed to be—limited means to more constructive objectives. Without a higher normative vision to guide and restrain it, power politics degenerates into perpetual militarism, interventionism, the waste of human and national resources, and eventually war and national exhaustion.

3. The best opportunities for constructive moral action in foreign policy arise in situations where moral objectives can be blended with national self-interest. One of the statesman's responsibilities is to look out for such opportunities and to articulate to public opinion the benefits to the national interest of prudently pursuing various moral objectives. As examples of such opportunities for American foreign policy in recent history, one could cite the Marshall Plan, the 1963 Nuclear Test Ban Treaty, and Henry Kissinger's Middle East diplomacy in the aftermath of the Yom Kippur War.

4. Fanaticism or ideological rigidity are less useful instruments of foreign policy than prudence, good sense, and the capacity to exercise political forgiveness under appropriate circumstances (as in our postwar policy toward Germany and Japan).

5. Some limits should be set on the means of foreign policy. Certain acts of outrageous brutality or treachery we should not commit even if the other side does. Otherwise, as in C. S. Lewis's *That Hideous Strength*, we run the risk of becoming like the enemy we seek to defeat. Moreover, it is important for a nation to remind itself in practical ways of those values and that way of life for which it stands.

6. The United States should define its national interest broadly enough to take into account both the long-term consequences of its policies and the realities of an increasingly interdependent world in which America's well-being is enhanced by the stability and prosperity of other societies. Such a broad definition of the national interest might imply the following:

    a. Whenever possible, creative foreign aid and free-trade policies should be put in place to promote economic development and genuine prosperity. These policies need not rest on the view that we have a moral obligation to extend foreign aid because of our alleged past wrongs against the Third World, but on a recognition of the practical benefits to the United States of cultivating mutually profitable relations with other states. Our foreign aid policies should be unsentimental and cognizant of the shortcomings in the foreign aid process, including the blend of corruption and socialist inefficiency which, in countries from Tanzania to the Philippines, has led to massive waste of U.S. resources. Situations might exist, such as that of Ethiopia recently, in which the desire to provide humanitarian aid should be balanced with concerns about whether such aid will be manipulated by the existing regime to strengthen its cruel tyranny.

    b. Together with other countries, the United States should take leadership in addressing the critical problem of the long-term deterioration of the earth's environment. The worldwide extinction of animal species, the destruction of the earth's forests, and the pollution of the oceans and the atmosphere should be of concern to American foreign policy.

c. It is in the long-term national interest of the United States to support human rights within the society in question as long as we have genuine leverage and as long as the alternative to the existing regime is not a more oppressive brand of tyranny. Recent American policies toward Haiti and the Philippines illustrate a prudential concern for human rights at its best. Iran and Nicaragua, on the other hand, remind us of the serious problems posed by a pursuit of human rights without the restraining hand of prudence.

7. The United States should try to understand and empathize with other societies and cultures, even in situations where we ultimately disagree with them on fundamental issues. As Michael Howard warns,

> In dealing with foreign nations, military power is certainly important, and economic strength still more so. But neither can be effective without the third leg of the triad, which I term cultural empathy—an *understanding* not only of the economic interests and military strength of foreign peoples but also of their cultures, their perceptions, what the French call their *mentalité*. Without such an understanding, both economic and military aid are likely to do considerably more harm than good. . . . The twentieth century is replete with disastrous examples of such failures of understanding. . . . But, in the case of the United States, this weakness is all the more tragic, because it frustrates so many tantalizing opportunities opened up for America by its wealth and strength. And it is a weakness for which no amount of military power—certainly not nuclear power—can ever make up.[19]

To take but one example of this problem, the resentment of many Latin Americans toward the United States stems from their accurate perception that, generally, the United States views them not as worthy partners in a common hemisphere, but as inferior. Altering this perception would yield valuable long-term benefits to the United States. Such alteration would require that the United States change to some degree the substance of its policies, but even more important, that it change the *style* of its diplomacy and its overall attitude toward our continental neighbors. Although a change in style would be relatively inexpensive in terms of economic or political costs to the United States, it will not be easy to bring about given the difficulties of achieving transcultural understanding and empathy.

8. At the heart of political wisdom in international relations is moderation in the use of one's power. Louis J. Halle has aptly evoked the medieval Christian ideal of knighthood as a normative paradigm for contemporary American foreign policy.

> The national ideal of a supremely great power like the United States should be that of the gentle knight—exemplified in medieval literature by Lancelot, by Percival, by King Arthur. The gentle knight was

strong, but his strength aroused neither fear nor resentment among the people because they knew it to be under the governance of moral responsibility and in the service of the general welfare. Precisely because he was strong, the gentle knight could afford to be modest, considerate, and courteous. His strength threatened only such outlaws as themselves constituted a threat to society. Consequently, his strength was not only in his arm but in the regard of humankind. Wherever he went, his quiet voice represented legitimacy, speaking with its authority.[20]

The gentle knight must be militarily strong and ever vigilant against actual and potential enemies. But he uses his power carefully, with restraint, believing with Edmund Burke that

among precautions against ambition, it may not be amiss to take one precaution against our *own*. I must fairly say, I dread our *own* power and our *own* ambition; I dread our being too much dreaded.[21]

The gentle knight is on guard against hubris. Aware of his own sinfulness and human malleability, of the tendency "to love deed more than it deserves to be loved," he is on guard against the perpetual expansion of "vital interests" to which all great powers sooner or later seem to succumb. He combines military strength with a willingness to weather the daily storms of international policies patiently, firmly, and without illusions about the self-destructive character of most wars. He plays for time with serenity and quiet confidence.

None of the preceding counsels is exclusively rooted in the Christian tradition. Yet, they form part of a way of thinking, a tradition of statecraft or political wisdom, which Christianity has helped to make part of the broad heritage of Western civilization. Reminding us of that wisdom of statecraft and of its continuing relevance to our perilous times remains one of Christianity's chief political contributions today.

ENDNOTES

1. Nikolai Berdyaev, *Slavery and Freedom* (New York: Scribner's, 1944); Christopher Dawson, *The Judgment of the Nations* (New York: Sheed and Ward, 1942); and Herbert Butterfield, *Christianity and History* (New York: Scribner's, 1949), 68–76.
2. Blaise Pascal, *Pensées*, Brunschwig ed., no. 139; and Fydor Dostoevski, *Notes from the Underground* (New York: Dutton, 1960), 27.
3. Kenneth W. Thompson, *Morality and Foreign Policy* (Baton Rouge: Louisiana State University Press, 1980), 132–33.
4. Jacob Burckhardt, *Reflections on History* (Indianapolis: Liberty Classics, 1979), 332–34.

5. See Bernal Diaz del Castillo, *Historia Verdadera de la Conquista de la Nueva España* (Madrid, 1933).
6. Michael Howard, "Ethics and Power in International Policy," in *Herbert Butterfield: The Ethics of History and Politics*, ed. Kenneth W. Thompson (Washington, D.C.: University Press of America, 1980), 66.
7. Thompson, *Morality and Foreign Policy*, 161.
8. Aristotle, *Nicomachean Ethics*, trans. Martin Oswald (Indianapolis: Bobbs-Merrill, 1962), bk. 6.
9. See Henry Paolucci, ed., *The Political Writings of St. Augustine* (South Bend, Ind.: Regnery/Gateway, 1962), 1–183; and Herbert Deane, *The Political and Social Ideas of St. Augustine* (New York: Columbia University Press, 1963), 62, 83, 116–71. See the discussion of just war in James T. Johnson, *Can Modern War Be Just?* (New Haven: Yale University Press, 1984), 16–29; William V. O'Brien, *The Conduct of Just and Limited War* (New York: Praeger, 1981); and George Weigel, *Tranquillitas Ordinis: The Present Failure and Future Promise of American Catholic Thought on War and Peace* (New York: Oxford University Press, 1987).
10. Thompson, *Morality and Foreign Policy*, 138–39.
11. Aristotle, *Nicomachean Ethics*, bk. 6, 1141b, 15.
12. Ibid., 1142b, 32–35.
13. Ibid., 1143a, 17–33.
14. Ibid., 1137b–38a.
15. Armand-jean du Plessis Richelieu, *The Political Testament*, trans. Henry Bertram Hill (Madison: University of Wisconsin Press, 1961). See Fenelon's essay on the balance of power in Moorhead Wright, ed., *Theory and Practice of the Balance of Power* (London: Dent, 1975).
16. Francois de Callières, *De la manière de negocier avec les souverains* (Paris, 1716); Harold Nicolson, *Diplomacy* (London: Oxford University Press, 1960); and Adam Watson, *Diplomacy: The Dialogue Among States* (New York: McGraw-Hill, 1983).
17. Aristotle, *Nicomachean Ethics*, bk. 6, 1144a, 6–31, 35–37.
18. Ibid., 1144b, 30–33; 1145a, 6–11.
19. Michael Howard, "The Bewildered American Raj," *Harper's* 240, 1618 (March 1985): 55–60.
20. Louis J. Halle, *The Elements of International Strategy: A Primer for the Nuclear Age* (Lanham, Md.: University Press of America, 1894), 120.
21. Edmund Burke, "Remarks on the Policy of the Allies with Respect to France," in *Works*, vol. 4 (Boston: Little, Brown and Co., 1899), 457; cited in Hans J. Morgenthau, *Politics Among Nations*, 5th ed. rev. (New York: Knopf, 1978), 169.